AMERICAN EXCEPTIONALISM AND HUMAN RIGHTS

AMERICAN EXCEPTIONALISM AND HUMAN RIGHTS

Edited by *Michael Ignatieff*

PRINCETON UNIVERSITY PRESS   PRINCETON AND OXFORD

Library of Congress Cataloging-in-Publication Data

American exceptionalism and human rights / edited by
Michael Ignatieff.
p. cm.
Includes bibliographical references and index.
ISBN 0-691-11647-4 (cl : alk. paper)—ISBN 0-691-11648-2
(pb : alk. paper)
1. Human rights—United States—Congresses. 2. United States—
Foreign relations—Congresses. 3. National characteristics, American—Congresses. I. Ignatieff, Michael

JC599.U5A494 2005
323′.0973—dc22   2004060764

British Library Cataloging-in-Publication Data is available

This book has been composed in Sabon

Printed on acid-free paper.∞

www.pupress.princeton.edu

Printed in the United States of America

10 9 8 7 6 5 4 3 2 1

Contents

Chapter 1. Introduction: American Exceptionalism and Human Rights
Michael Ignatieff — 1

PART I. THE VARIETIES OF EXCEPTIONALISM — 27

Chapter 2. The Exceptional First Amendment — 29
Frederick Schauer

Chapter 3. Capital Punishment and American Exceptionalism — 57
Carol S. Steiker

Chapter 4. Why Does the American Constitution Lack Social and Economic Guarantees? — 90
Cass R. Sunstein

Chapter 5. America's Jekyll-and-Hyde Exceptionalism — 111
Harold Hongju Koh

PART II. EXPLAINING EXCEPTIONALISM — 145

Chapter 6. The Paradox of U.S. Human Rights Policy — 147
Andrew Moravcsik

Chapter 7. American Exceptionalism, Popular Sovereignty, and the Rule of Law — 198
Paul W. Kahn

PART III. EVALUATING EXCEPTIONALISM — 223

Chapter 8. American Exceptionalism: The New Version — 225
Stanley Hoffmann

Chapter 9. Integrity-Anxiety? — 241
Frank I. Michelman

Chapter 10. A Brave New Judicial World — 277
Anne-Marie Slaughter

Chapter 11. American Exceptionalism, Exemptionalism,
and Global Governance   304
  John Gerard Ruggie

Contributors   339

Index   341

AMERICAN EXCEPTIONALISM AND HUMAN RIGHTS

Chapter 1 ⸻

Introduction: American Exceptionalism and Human Rights

MICHAEL IGNATIEFF

Defining Exceptionalism

Since 1945 America has displayed exceptional leadership in promoting international human rights. At the same time, however, it has also resisted complying with human rights standards at home or aligning its foreign policy with these standards abroad. Under some administrations, it has promoted human rights as if they were synonymous with American values, while under others, it has emphasized the superiority of American values over international standards. This combination of leadership and resistance is what defines American human rights behavior as exceptional, and it is this complex and ambivalent pattern that the book seeks to explain.

Thanks to Eleanor and Franklin Roosevelt, the United States took a leading role in the creation of the United Nations and the drafting of the Universal Declaration of Human Rights in 1948.[1] Throughout the Cold War and afterward, few nations placed more emphasis in their foreign policy on the promotion of human rights, market freedom, and political democracy. Since the 1970s U.S. legislation has tied foreign aid to progress in human rights; the State Department annually assesses the human rights records of governments around the world. Outside government, the United States can boast some of the most effective and influential human rights organizations in the world. These promote religious freedom, gender equality, democratic rights, and the abolition of slavery; they monitor human rights performance by governments, including—and especially—the U.S. government. U.S. government action, together with global activism by U.S. NGOs, has put Americans in the forefront of attempts to improve women's rights, defend religious liberty, improve access to AIDS drugs, spread democracy and freedom through the Arab and Muslim worlds, and oppose tyrants from Slobodan Milošević to Saddam Hussein.

---

[1] Stephen C. Schlesinger, *Act of Creation: The Founding of the United Nations* (New York: Westview Press, 2003); Mary Ann Glendon, *A World Made New: Eleanor Roosevelt and the Universal Declaration of Human Rights* (New York: Random House, 2001).

The same U.S. government, however, has also supported rights-abusing regimes from Pinochet's Chile to Suharto's Indonesia; sought to scuttle the International Criminal Court, the capstone of an enforceable global human rights regime; maintained practices—like capital punishment—at variance with the human rights standards of other democracies; engaged in unilateral preemptive military actions that other states believe violate the UN Charter; failed to ratify the Convention on the Rights of the Child and the Convention on the Elimination of Discrimination against Women; and ignored UN bodies when they criticized U.S. domestic rights practices. What is exceptional here is not that the United States is inconsistent, hypocritical, or arrogant. Many other nations, including leading democracies, could be accused of the same things. What is exceptional, and worth explaining, is why America has both been guilty of these failings and also been a driving force behind the promotion and enforcement of global human rights. What needs explaining is the paradox of being simultaneously a leader and an outlier.

While the focus of this book will be on human rights, exceptionalism is also a feature of U.S. attitudes toward environmental treaties like the Kyoto Protocol as well as the Geneva Conventions and international humanitarian law. Since the attack of September 11, it has been accused of violating the Conventions as well as the Torture Convention in its handling of prisoners at Guantánamo, Abu Ghraib, and other detention facilities.

This pattern of behavior raises a fundamental question about the very place of the world's most powerful nation inside the network of international laws and conventions that regulate a globalizing world. To what extent does the United States accept constraints on its sovereignty through the international human rights regime, international humanitarian law, and the UN Charter rules on the use of force? To what degree does America play by the rules it itself has helped to create?

In this book, we do not revisit wider historical and sociological debates about why Americans have seen their society as exceptional at least since the Pilgrim Fathers, or why America has been exceptional in its absence of a socialist movement.[2] Nor is this another discussion of American uni-

---

[2] Alexis de Tocqueville, *Democracy in America*, ed. and trans. Harvey C. Mansfield and Delba Winthrop (Chicago: University of Chicago Press, 2001), selections from introduction; vol. 1, pt. 1, chaps. 4–6; vol. 2, Ppt. 1, chaps. 1, 4–6; vol. 2, pt. 2, chaps. 1–4, 19; John Winthrop, "City Upon a Hill" Sermon (1630); Frederick Jackson Turner, *The Frontier in American History* (New York: Henry Holt and Company, 1920), preface and chap. 1, pp. 1–38; Michael Kammen, "The Problem of American Exceptionalism: A Reconsideration," *American Quarterly* 45 (March 1993): 1–43; Richard Wightman Fox and James T. Kloppenberg, eds., "American Exceptionalism," in *A Companion to American Thought* (Cambridge: Blackwell Publishers, 1995), 22–23; Andrew Greeley, "American Exceptionalism:

lateralism in foreign policy, since unilateralism and exceptionalism are
different phenomena, requiring different explanations. Instead the volume is closely focused on U.S. human rights performance in comparative
perspective, since this approach highlights new questions about the relation between U.S. rights traditions and political culture and their influence
on U.S. projection of power, influence, and moral example overseas.

The book is the result of an academic collaboration by the scholars in
this volume, initiated at a seminar series held at the Carr Center for
Human Rights Policy at Harvard's John F. Kennedy School of Government and generously funded by the Winston Foundation. What began as
a scholarly exercise has been given topical urgency by the war in Iraq and
the war on terror. While the volume's contributors engage with both, the
aim of the book is wider: to situate and explain current administration
conduct within a historical account of America's long-standing ambivalence toward the constraining role of international law in general.

In this introduction, I will set out a three-part typology of American
exceptionalism; identify and examine four central explanations offered by
the contributors; and finally raise two questions about policy: What price
does the United States pay for exceptionalism in human rights? What can
be done to exercise human rights leadership in a less exceptional way?

Distinguishing Types of American Exceptionalism

American exceptionalism has at least three separate elements. First, the
United States signs on to international human rights and humanitarian
law conventions and treaties and then exempts itself from their provisions
by explicit reservation, nonratification, or noncompliance. Second, the
United States maintains double standards: judging itself and its friends by
more permissive criteria than it does its enemies. Third, the United States
denies jurisdiction to human rights law within its own domestic law, insisting on the self-contained authority of its own domestic rights tradition.

The Religious Phenomenon," in *Is America Different? A New Look at American Exceptionalism,* ed. Byron Shafer (Oxford: Clarendon Press, 1991); James Chace, "Dreams of Perfect-
ibility: American Exceptionalism and the Search for a Moral Foreign Policy," in *America in
Theory,* ed. Leslie Berlowitz et al. (New York: Oxford University Press, 1988), 249–61;
Joseph Lepgold and Timothy McKeown, "Is American Foreign Policy Exceptional? An Empirical Analysis," *Political Science Quarterly* 110 (Autumn 1995): 369–84; Arthur Schle-
singer, Jr., "Human Rights and the American Tradition," *Foreign Affairs* 57 (1978): 502–
26; Alex Keyssar, *The Right to Vote: The Contested History of Democracy in the United
States* (New York: Basic Books, 2000); Anders Stephanson, *Manifest Destiny: American
Expansion and the Empire of Right* (New York: Hill and Wang, 1995), chaps. 1 and 4;
Seymour Martin Lipset, *American Exceptionalism: A Double-Edged Sword* (New York:
W. W. Norton, 1996).

No other democratic state engages in all three of these practices to the same extent, and none combines these practices with claims to global leadership in the field of human rights.

The first variant of exceptionalism is *exemptionalism*. America supports multilateral agreements and regimes, but only if they permit exemptions for American citizens or U.S. practices. In 1998, the United States took part in the negotiations for the International Criminal Court but secured guarantees that its military, diplomats, and politicians would never come before that court. The Clinton administration signed the treaty before leaving office, only to have the incoming Bush administration unsign it.[3] The Bush administration then went on to negotiate agreements with allied countries requiring them to guarantee that they would not hand over U.S. nationals to the ICC.[4] Over the Land Mines Treaty, America took part in negotiations but sought exemption for American military production and deployment of land mines in the Korean Peninsula.[5]

Exemptionalism, of course, is not confined to the domains of human rights–related treaties. U.S. withdrawal from the Kyoto Protocol on Climate Change fits into the same pattern.[6] Exemptionalism has also been on display in the war on terror in the U.S. insistence that while conditions

---

[3] Sarah Sewall and Carl Kaysen, eds., *The United States and the International Criminal Court: Security and International Law* (Lanham, MD: Rowman and Littlefield, 2000); David J. Scheffer, "The United States and the International Criminal Court," *American Journal of International Law* 93 (January 1999): 12–22; Lee A. Casey and David B. Rivkin, Jr., "The International Criminal Court vs. the American People," in *The Heritage Foundation Backgrounder*, February 5, 1999 (Washington, DC: The Heritage Foundation, 1999); Lawyer's Committee for Human Rights, *The International Criminal Court: The Case for U.S. Support* (New York: Lawyers Committee for Human Rights, 1998); Sean D. Murphy, ed., "U.S. Signing of the Statute of the International Criminal Court," *American Journal of International Law* 95 (April 2001): 397; Marc Grossman, United States Under Secretary for Political Affairs, "Remarks to the Center for Strategic and International Studies," Washington, DC, May 6, 2002, http://www.state.gov/p/9949.htm; John R. Bolton, United States Under Secretary of State for Arms Control and International Security, "Letter to Secretary-General Kofi Annan," May 6, 2002, http://www.state.gov/r/pa/prs/ps/2002/9968.htm.

[4] Colum Lynch, "3 Observers Pulled Out of East Timor: U.S. Move Underscores Vow to Shield Americans from War Crimes Court," *Washington Post*, July 2, 2002; "Explanation of Vote by Ambassador John D. Negroponte, United States Permanent Representative to the United Nations, on the Security Council Resolution on the International Criminal Court," Security Council Chambers, July 12, 2002, http://www.un.int/usa/02_097.htm; Human Rights Watch, "Bilateral Immunity Agreements," June 20, 2003, http://www.hrw.org/campaigns/icc/docs/bilateralagreements.pdf.

[5] Andrew Latham, "Theorizing the Landmine Campaign: Ethics, Global Cultural Scripts, and the Laws of War," in *Ethics and Security in Canadian Foreign Policy*, ed. Rosalind Irwin (Vancouver: University of British Columbia Press, 2002).

[6] "Press Briefing by Ari Fleischer," The White House, March 28, 2001, http://www.whitehouse.gov/news/briefings/20010328.html#KyotoTreaty.

of detention at Guantánamo and elsewhere will comply with Geneva Convention standards, interrogation procedures and determination of status will be determined by executive order of the president.[7]

Exemptionalism is not the same as isolationism. The same administration that will have nothing to do with the ICC is heavily engaged in the defense and promotion of religious freedom abroad, the abolition of slavery, the funding of HIV/AIDS relief, and the protection of victims of ethnic and religious intolerance in Sudan.[8] Nor is exceptionalism a synonym for unilateralism. An administration that will not engage on the ICC is insistently engaged with the UN and other allies on the issue of HIV/AIDS. While some of the U.S. human rights agenda, like the promotion of religious freedom abroad, is exceptional in the sense that other democratic states place less emphasis upon it, much U.S. human rights policy is aligned with those of other European countries and is advanced through multilateral fora like UN Human Rights Committees.

Exemptionalism also involves the practice of negotiating and signing human rights conventions but with reservations. Thus the United States ratified the International Covenant on Civil and Political Rights (ICCPR) in 1991 while exempting itself from the provisions banning the infliction of the death penalty on juveniles.[9] America is not the only country to insist on this type of exemption. Saudi Arabia, for example, insists that international human rights convention language relating to free marriage choice and freedom of belief remain without effect in their domestic law.[10]

---

[7] Alberto Gonzales, White House Counsel to President Bush, "Decision Re Application of the Geneva Convention on Prisoners of War to the Conflict with Al-Qaeda and the Taliban," *Memorandum to the President*, January 25, 2002, available at http://www.msnbc.msn.com/id/4999148/; Jess Bravin, "Pentagon Report Set Framework for Use of Torture," *Wall Street Journal*, June 9, 2004; David Johnston and James Risen, "Aides Say Memo Backed Coercion Already in Use," *New York Times*, June 27, 2004; Suzanne Goldenberg, "Bush Memos Show Stance on Torture," *Guardian*, June 24, 2004.

[8] U.S. State Department Bureau of Democracy, Human Rights and Labor, *International Religious Freedom Report*, December 18, 2003, http://www.state.gov/g/drl/rls/irf/2003/; President George W. Bush, "Remarks by the President during Announcement of Proposal for Global Fund to Fight HIV/AIDS, Malaria and Tuberculosis," The Rose Garden, Washington, DC, May 11, 2001, http://www.whitehouse.gov/news/releases/2001/05/20010511-1.html; President George W. Bush, "State of the Union Address," January 28, 2003, http://www.whitehouse.gov/news/releases/2003/01/20030128-19.html.

[9] See U.S. reservations to the ICCPR in "Reservations, Declarations, Notifications and Objections Relating to the International Covenant on Civil and Political Rights and the Optional Protocols Thereto," CCPR/C/2/Rev. 4, August 24, 1994, http://www.unhchr.ch/html/menu3/b/treaty5_asp.htm.

[10] Harold Koh, "On American Exceptionalism," *Stanford Law Review* 55 (2003); Harold Koh, "Bringing International Law Home" (the 1998 Frankel Lecture), *Houston Law Review* 35 (Fall 1998); Harold Koh, "Is International Law Really State Law?" *Harvard Law Review* 111 (May 1998); Harold Koh, "Why Do Nations Obey International Law?" *Yale Law Journal* 106 (1997).

These exemptions are simply the price that any universal rights regime has to pay for country-by-country ratification. Indeed, it is doubtful that the framework would exist at all if it did not allow latitude for countries to protect the specificity of their legal and national traditions.

While European states also ratify with reservations and exceptions, they question whether a U.S. exemption on the right to life—a core human rights principle—can be justified.[11] Allowing a state to pick and choose how it adheres to such a central principle threatens to empty international conventions of their universal status. Moreover, exemptionalism turns the United States into an outlier. The United States now stands outside an abolitionist consensus vis-à-vis capital punishment that applies to all democratic states and most nondemocratic ones, with the exception of China.[12]

Even when the United States ratifies international rights conventions, it usually does so with a stipulation that the provisions cannot supersede U.S. domestic law. [13] Thus, with a few exceptions, American ratification renders U.S. participation in international human rights symbolic, since adopting treaties does not actually improve the statutory rights protections of U.S. citizens in domestic law.

Exemptionalism also takes the form of signing on to international rights conventions and then failing to abide by their requirements. The U.S. record of treaty compliance is no worse than that of other democracies, but because of the superpower's exceptional political importance, U.S. forms of noncompliance have more impact than those of less powerful states. Examples of noncompliance include failing to inform UN human rights bodies when derogating from treaty standards; failing to cooperate with UN human rights rapporteurs seeking access to U.S. facilities; and refusing to order stays of execution in compliance with the Vienna Treaty on Consular Obligations.[14] Both the Canadian and German governments have sought stays of execution for their nationals in U.S. courts, on the grounds that these nationals were convicted without prior access to their consular officials. Neither Virginia nor Texas paid any at-

---

[11] See objections to U.S. reservations to the ICCPR by Belgium, Denmark, Finland, France, Germany, Italy, the Netherlands, Norway, Portugal, Spain, and Sweden in "Reservations, Declarations, Notifications and Objections Relating to the International Covenant on Civil and Political Rights and the Optional Protocols Thereto."

[12] William Schabas, *The Abolition of the Death Penalty in International Law* (New York: Cambridge University Press, 2002); Austin Sarat, *The Killing State: Capital Punishment in Law, Politics, and Culture* (New York: Oxford University Press, 1999).

[13] See U.S. reservations to the ICCPR.

[14] Oona Hathaway, "Do Human Rights Treaties Make a Difference?" *Yale Law Journal* 111 (June 2002).

tention to these foreign requests, and these states allowed the executions to proceed.[15]

A third element of exemptionalism is the practice of negotiating treaties and then refusing to ratify them altogether or ratifying them only after extended delays. For example, the Senate refused to ratify the Convention on the Rights of the Child, leaving the United States the only nation besides Somalia not to do so. The United States took nearly forty years to ratify the Genocide Convention.[16] Failure to ratify doesn't mean that the United States fails to comply: no one has complained that the United States is currently guilty of genocide. Nor does failure to ratify the Convention on the Rights of the Child mean that standards of child protection in the United States are as poor as those of the other nonratifier, Somalia.[17] Nonratification simply means that U.S. child advocates cannot use international standards in domestic U.S. litigation. Likewise, U.S. refusal to ratify the Convention on Eliminating Discrimination against Women does not leave American women without protections and remedies. Nonratification means that UN instruments and standards have no legal standing in U.S. courts. How serious this is depends on the extent of the gap between current U.S. federal and state standards and international norms. Where this gap is large, Americans may lack rights and remedies available in other democratic states.

The second feature of American exceptionalism is *double standards*. The United States judges itself by standards different from those it uses to judge other countries, and judges its friends by standards different from those it uses for its enemies. This is the feature that Harold Koh identifies as the most costly and problematic aspect of American exceptionalism. The United States criticizes other states for ignoring the reports of UN rights bodies, while refusing to accept criticism of its own domestic rights performance from the same UN bodies. This is especially the case in relation to capital punishment in general and the execution of juveniles in particular, as well as conditions of detention in U.S. prisons.[18] Overseas, the United States condemns abuses by hostile regimes—Iran and North Korea, for example—while excusing abuses by such allies as Israel, Egypt,

---

[15] David Stout, "U.S. Executions Draw Scorn from Abroad," *New York Times*, April 26, 1998; Harold Koh, "Paying 'Decent Respect' to World Opinion on the Death Penalty," *U.C. Davis Law Review* 35 (June 2002); "Agora: *Breard*," *American Journal of International Law* 92 (October 1998).

[16] Samantha Power, *"A Problem from Hell": America and the Age of Genocide* (New York: Perennial/HarperCollins, 2002): 161–69.

[17] Koh, "On American Exceptionalism"; Hathaway, "Do Human Rights Treaties Make a Difference?"

[18] Amnesty International, *United States of America: Rights for All*, September 30, 1998, http://www.rightsforall.amnesty.org/info/report/r01.htm.

Morocco, Jordan, and Uzbekistan. It has been condemned for arming, training, and funding death squads in Latin America in the 1980s, while condemning the guerrillas as terrorists. Hence when the United States called for a global war on all forms of terrorism after September 11, it faced accusations that its own policies toward attacks on civilians had been guilty of double standards. [19]

The third form of exceptionalism—*legal isolationism*—characterizes the attitude of the U.S. courts toward the rights jurisprudence of other liberal democratic countries. The claim here is that American judges are exceptionally resistant to using foreign human rights precedents to guide them in their domestic opinions. As Justice Antonin Scalia remarked, when rejecting a colleague's references to foreign jurisprudence in deciding *Printz v. US*, "We think such comparative analysis inappropriate to the task of interpreting a constitution."[20] This judicial attitude is anchored in a broad popular sentiment that the land of Jefferson and Lincoln has nothing to learn about rights from any other country. As Anne-Marie Slaughter points out in her contribution, this American judicial self-sufficiency is exceptional when compared to other judiciaries, with judges in Israel inspecting Canadian precedents on minority rights cases, and judges in the South African Constitutional Court studying German cases to interpret social and economic rights claims.[21] Historically, the American judiciary has stood apart from the trend toward comparative legal problem solving, although as Slaughter also points out, law is being globalized, like commerce and communications, and in the process American lawyers and judges are being drawn into the global conversation.

The American legal profession in general has not ignored global human rights developments, and American academic experts like Thomas Franck, Louis Henkin, and Thomas Buergenthal have played key roles in international rights institutions.[22] American constitutional scholars as-

[19] Mark Danner, *The Massacre at El Mazote: A Parable of the Cold War* (New York: Vintage Books, 1994); Amnesty International, *Unmatched Power, Unmet Principles: The Human Rights Dimensions of US Training of Foreign Military and Police Forces* (New York: Amnesty International USA Publications, 2002); Raymond Bonner, *Weakness and Deceit: U.S. Policy and El Salvador* (New York: Times Books, 1984); Stephen Schlesinger and Stephen Kinzer, *Bitter Fruit: The Untold Story of the American Coup in Guatemala* (New York: Doubleday, 1982); Sam Dillon, *Commandos: The CIA and Nicaragua's Contra Rebels* (New York: Henry Holt and Company, 1991).

[20] *Printz v. United States*, 521 U.S. 898, 921 n.11 (1997).

[21] Anne-Marie Slaughter, "Judicial Globalization," *Virginia Journal of International Law* 40 (2000); Anne-Marie Slaughter and David Bosco, "Plaintiff's Diplomacy," *Foreign Affairs* 79 (September/October 2000): 102.

[22] Thomas Franck is professor of law at New York University and has provided legal counsel to many governments, including those of Kenya, El Salvador, Guatemala, Greece, and Cyprus. He has also acted as an advocate before the International Court of Justice on

sisted their Eastern European and South African counterparts in drafting constitutions, and U.S. programs of democracy development abroad have an increasingly important rule-of-law component.[23] But the trade in legal understanding continues to be mostly one-way, with the U.S. legal tradition teaching others but not learning much itself. As Frank Michelman points out in his contribution, American judicial interpretation is marked by what he calls "integrity-anxiety," a concern to maintain rules of judicial interpretation that are stable, continuous, and legitimate. These stable canons can appear threatened by indiscriminate or undisciplined recourse to foreign precedents and sources. In addition to concerns about the stability of the interpretive canon, there is the belief of some American judges that foreign judicial attitudes are too liberal—on issues like the death penalty, abortion, sentencing, and so on—and should be resisted as alien to the American mainstream.[24]

---

behalf of Chad and Bosnia and served as a judge ad hoc at the ICJ. Furthermore, Franck has served on the Department of State Advisory Committee on International Law, was president of the American Society of International Law, and served as editor in chief of the *American Journal of International Law*.

Louis Henkin is director of the Columbia University Law School Institute for Human Rights. He serves on the Board of Directors of Human Rights First (formerly the Lawyers Committee for Human Rights) and is a member of the State Department Advisory Committee on International Law. In the past he has served as president of the American Society of International Law, coeditor in chief of the *American Journal of International Law*, and consultant to the United Nations Legal Department. He recently submitted an amici curiae brief on behalf of Jose Padilla in *Donald Rumsfeld v. Jose Padilla and Donna R. Newman* along with Harold Hongju Koh and Michael H. Posner.

Thomas Buergenthal was elected in March 2000 for a nine-year term as the only U.S. judge serving on the International Court of Justice in The Hague. Previously, Buergenthal served as vice chairman of the Claims Resolution Tribunal for Dormant Accounts in Switzerland, on leave from his position as director of the International and Comparative Law Program at the George Washington University School of Law. He also served as chief justice of the Inter-American Court of Human Rights, was a member of the United Nations Truth Commission for El Salvador, and was the first American to serve on the United Nations Human Rights Committee.

[23] Cass R. Sunstein, *Designing Democracy: What Constitutions Do* (Oxford: Oxford University Press, 2001); Stephen Holmes, "Back to the Drawing Board," *East European Constitutional Review* 31 (1993): 21–25; Stephen Holmes, "Conceptions of Democracy in the Draft Constitutions of Post-Communist Countries," in *Markets, States, and Democracy: The Political Economy of Post-Communist Transformation*, ed. Beverly Crawford (Boulder, CO: Westview Press, 1995).

[24] In his dissenting opinion in *Printz*, Justice Breyer argues for the use of comparative constitutional analysis. 521 U.S. at 976–77. Justice Breyer refers to the *Federalist Papers* in arguing for comparative analysis. Ibid. at 977. He states, "Of course, we are interpreting our own Constitution, not those of other nations, and there may be relevant political and structural differences between their systems and our own. But their experience may nonetheless cast an empirical light on the consequences of different solutions to a common legal problem." Ibid.

American mainstream values are more than just the artifact of American conservatism since the 1960s. These values are structured legally by a rights tradition that has always been different from those of other democratic states and increasingly diverges from international human rights norms. As Frederick Schauer shows in his essay, in its free speech and defamation doctrine the United States has always been more protective of speakers' rights than any other liberal democratic state. Canada, France, and Germany permit the punishment of Holocaust deniers. New Zealand criminalizes incitement to racial hatred. UK libel laws provide more remedies against UK newspapers than would be conceivable in the United States.

U.S. law and international human rights standards also diverge markedly. International human rights laws allow more infringements of private liberty, in the name of public order, than do U.S. laws. The International Covenant on Civil and Political Rights mandates specific overrides of free speech if the free speech involves a threat to public order, the defamation of a religious or ethnic group, or the promotion of war propaganda. When the United States ratified the ICCPR, it specifically exempted itself from these provisions, just as it exempted itself from the ICCPR prohibition on juvenile execution.[25] The European Human Rights Convention permits states to suspend political and civil rights in times of national emergency, while the U.S. Constitution has no provision for the declaration of national emergencies and only a single reference to presidential power to suspend habeas corpus.[26]

The U.S. Constitution makes no reference to socioeconomic and welfare rights—entitlements to food, shelter, health care, and unemployment insurance—that are standard features of both international rights regimes and the constitutions of European states. As Cass Sunstein points out in his contribution, U.S. rights, moreover, are defined in negative terms ("Congress shall make no law"), while modern democratic constitutions enunciate rights as positive entitlements to welfare and assistance at the hand of the state. Certain U.S. constitutional rights like the right to bear arms do not feature in other democratic systems.[27] Hence no American ally approaches the problem of regulating the international trade in small arms with this constitutional restraint in mind.

While the West presents an appearance of a common rights identity to the non-Western world, its leader—the United States—increasingly stands

---

[25] Amnesty International, "Killing with Prejudice: Race and the Death Penalty in the USA," May 1999, http://web.amnesty.org/library/pdf/AMR510521999ENGLISH/$File/AMR5105299.pdf.

[26] For an extended discussion of this point, see Michael Ignatieff, *The Lesser Evil: Political Ethics in an Age of Terror* (Princeton: Princeton University Press, 2004), chap. 2.

[27] John R. Bolton, *Statement to the Plenary Session of the UN Conference on the Illicit Trade in Small Arms and Light Weapons*, July 9, 2001, http://www.un.int/usa/01_104.htm.

apart. As international rights conventions proliferate, as newer states like South Africa adopt new rights regimes and older states like Canada constitutionalize rights in new charters of rights and freedoms, the American Bill of Rights stands out in ever sharper relief, as a late eighteenth-century constitution surrounded by twenty-first-century ones, a grandfather clock in a shop window full of digital timepieces.

There is more to the distinctiveness of American rights culture than the fact that the U.S. Constitution is one of the oldest in existence. As various contributions to this book make clear, U.S. rights guarantees have been employed in the service of a political tradition that has been consistently more critical of government, more insistent on individual responsibility, and more concerned to defend individual freedom than the European socialist, social democratic, or Christian democratic traditions.

Changes in European law have widened the legal gulf that now divides the North Atlantic states. The U.S. legal tradition once shared a great deal with British common law. Thanks to the UK's recent incorporation of the European Human Rights Convention into its domestic law, the British rights system now shares more with the Europeans than with the Americans. The British have accepted the jurisdiction of the European Court of Human Rights; whenever that court hands down a ruling requiring legislative or administrative change, Parliament obliges.[28] Such deference to a transnational legal authority would be unthinkable in the United States. All of this helps to reduce the commonality of the common law tradition and to increase the degree to which American rights culture has become an outlier among the other liberal democracies.

Explaining American Exceptionalism

Four types of explanation for American exceptionalism have been offered by the scholars in this volume: a *realist* one, based in America's exceptional power; a *cultural* one, related to an American sense of Providential destiny; an *institutional* one, based in America's specific institutional organization; and finally a *political* one, related to the supposedly distinctive conservatism and individualism of American political culture.

Realism

A *realist* explanation of American exceptionalism would begin with America's exceptional global power since 1945. Exceptionally powerful

---

[28] A. W. Bradley, "The United Kingdom, the European Court of Human Rights and Judicial Review," *Cardozo Law Review* 17 (1995).

countries get away with exemptions in their multilateral commitments simply because they can. Human rights and humanitarian law instruments are weakly enforced in any event. The United States can exempt itself from the ICC—and try to block its operation—because no other country or group of countries has the power to stop it. No other state has the capacity to sanction the United States if it ducks compliance with the Vienna Law of Treaties, ignores the derogation procedures of human rights conventions, and delays ratification of other treaties for decades.

On a realist account, support for international law and willingness to submit to its constraints would be in inverse relation to a state's power. The less powerful a state, the more reason it would have to support international norms that would constrain its more powerful neighbors. The more powerful a state, the more reluctant it would be to submit to multilateral constraint. Support for international law is bound to be strongest among middling powers like France, Germany, and Canada, democratic states that already comply with multilateral rights norms in their own domestic rights regimes, and that want to use international law to constrain the United States. As Joseph Nye, Jr., has put it, "multilateralism can be used as a strategy by smaller states to tie the United States down like Gulliver among the Lilliputians."[29] Thus for middling powers the cost of their own compliance with human rights and humanitarian law instruments is offset by the advantages they believe they will derive from international law regimes that constrain larger powers. For the United States the calculus is reversed. Moreover, as a country with a substantive commitment to the rule of law, not to mention vigilant human rights NGOs, the United States has to take treaty obligations seriously. Faced with strong domestic NGO lobbies seeking actual compliance with human rights treaties, administrations of both parties have rational reasons to endeavor to minimize the sovereignty constraints introduced by international human rights agreements.[30]

Realist explanations of this sort do help to explain why the United States would want to minimize the constraints imposed on it by a multilateral human rights and humanitarian law regime. A realist would argue that the United States seeks to maintain its power in a global order of states at the lowest possible cost to its sovereignty. In this, it behaves just like other states. The problem with realist explanations is that the United

[29] Joseph S. Nye, "Seven Tests: Between Concert and Unilateralism," *The National Interest* (Winter 2001/2002): 9.

[30] Hathaway, "Do Human Rights Treaties Make a Difference?"; see also Oona Hathaway, "Between Power and Principle: A Political Theory of International Law," *University of Chicago Law Review* 71 (May 2005); for a critique of Hathaway, see Ryan Goodman and Derek Jinks, "Measuring the Effects of Human Rights Treaties," *European Journal of International Law* 14 (2003): 171–83.

States has wanted to do much more than this. It has promoted the very system of multilateral engagements—human rights treaties, Geneva Conventions, UN Charter rules on the use of force and the resolution of disputes—that abridge and constrain its sovereignty. Realism alone cannot account for the paradox of American investment in a system that constrains its power. Strident unilateralism or strict isolationism are easier to explain on realist grounds than is the actual pattern of exceptionalist multilateralism.

Culture

What realism fails to explain is why multilateral engagements that do constrain American power have appealed to American leaders as different as Roosevelt and Reagan. It seems impossible to explain this paradox without some analysis of culture—specifically, of the way in which American leaders have understood the relation between American constitutional values and human rights. Across the political spectrum since 1945, American presidents have articulated a strongly messianic vision of the American role in promoting rights abroad. This messianic cultural tradition has a long history, from the vision of the Massachusetts Bay Colony as a "City upon a Hill" in the sermons of the Puritan John Winthrop, through the rhetoric of Manifest Destiny that accompanied westward expansion in the nineteenth century, the Wilsonian vision of U.S. power making the world safe for democracy after World War I, and Roosevelt's crusade for the "four freedoms" in World War II.[31] The global spread of human rights has coincided with the American ascendancy in global politics and has been driven by the missionary conviction that American values have universal significance and application. What is important here is the conflict between national interest and messianic mission. Messianism has propelled America into multilateral engagements that a more realist calculation of interest might have led the nation to avoid. In American domestic politics, this sense of mission has refigured the ideal of a multilateral order of international law, not as a system of constraints on U.S. power, but as a forum in which U.S. leadership can be exercised and American intuitions about freedom and government can be spread across the world.

This desire for moral leadership is something more than the ordinary narcissism and nationalism that all powerful states display. It is rooted in

[31] Walter Russell Mead, *Special Providence: American Foreign Policy and How It Changed the World* (New York: The Century Foundation, 2001): see especially chap. 5: "The Connecticut Yankee in the Court of King Arthur: Wilsonianism and Its Mission"; Stephanson, *Manifest Destiny*, chap. 1.

the particular achievements of a successful history of liberty that U.S. leaders have believed is of universal significance, even the work of Providential design. For most Americans human rights are American values writ large, the export version of its own Bill of Rights.

But if human rights are American values writ large, then, paradoxically, Americans have nothing to learn from international human rights. In the messianic American moral project, America teaches the meaning of liberty to the world; it does not learn from others.[32] Messianism does help to explain the paradox of exceptional multilateralism. Indeed, it suggests that American exceptionalism is not so paradoxical after all: since 1945 the United States has explicitly sought to fulfill its messianic mission at the lowest possible cost to its national interest and with the lowest possible impingement upon its own domestic rights system. U.S. policy, across administrations both Republican and Democratic, has been designed both to promote American values abroad and to safeguard them from foreign interference at home.

As Paul Kahn observes in his chapter, this concern to ward off foreign influence is more than just a powerful state's attempt to make the rules and exempt itself from them. The United States defends these exemptions in terms of the democratic legitimacy of its distinctive rights culture. The rights that Americans accept as binding are the ones written down in their own sacred texts and elaborated by their own courts and legislatures. These rights, authored in the name of "we the people," are anchored in the historical project of the American Revolution: a free people establishing a republic based in popular sovereignty. A realist account would explain exceptionalism as an attempt to defend U.S. sovereignty and power. The messianic account adds to this the idea that the United States is defending a mission, an identity, and a distinctive destiny as a free people.

Despite the fact that ratification of international conventions through the Senate is supposed to vest them with full domestic political authority, international human rights law, Kahn argues, continues to lack the full imprimatur of American democratic legitimacy. Only domestic law, authored in American institutions, meets the test of legitimacy as an authentic expression of national sovereignty. This point can be illustrated by the most controversial issue at stake, discussed by Carol Steiker in her contribution, the death penalty statutes enforced in twenty-eight American states. If the people of the state of Texas conscientiously believe that the death penalty deters crime, eliminates dangerous offenders, and gives public expression to the values that ought to hold Texas society to-

---

[32] Frederick Schauer and Richard H. Pildes, "Electoral Exceptionalism and the First Amendment," *Texas Law Review* 77 (June 1999); Frederick Schauer, *Free Speech: A Philosophical Enquiry* (New York: Cambridge University Press, 1982).

gether—as repeated polls indicate that they do—it is hardly surprising that such majoritarian political preferences should trump international human rights.

The contrast between American and European practice on the death penalty may depend on the institutional power that American voters possess in defining the balance between individual rights and collective moral preferences. Capital punishment has been abolished in most European societies not because electoral majorities support abolition—most polls across Europe indicate continuing support—but because political elites, especially ministers of the interior or home affairs, do not want the moral burden of ordering executions. These moral scruples are in direct contradiction to the expressed preferences of their own citizens.

If this is true, then the European human rights conventions that sustain the abolition of capital punishment are playing an antimajoritarian role in counterbalancing electoral preferences. It seems unlikely that international rights conventions or instruments could ever play such a role in the United States. Rights in America are the rules that a democratic polity constructs to define the scope of public authority. American exceptionalism may be anchored in a fundamental difference with other democratic states about the appropriate relation between rights and majority interests, and in turn the relation between rights and national identity. From an American perspective, rights cannot be separated from the democratic community they serve; they are enforced by that community, and their interpretation must therefore depend solely on the institutions of that community.[33]

America is not the only powerful state that has articulated its identity in terms of its rights and believed in a special mission to export its vision of government. From Napoleon onward, France sought to export its legal culture to neighbors and colonies as part of a civilizing mission.[34] The British Empire was sustained by the conceit that the British had a special talent for government that entitled them to spread the rule of law to Kipling's "lesser breeds."[35] In the twentieth century, the Soviet Union advanced missionary claims about the superiority of Soviet rule, backed by Marxist pseudoscience. Indeed the United States and the Soviet Union each battled for the allegiance of developing nations by advancing messi-

---

[33] Anne-Marie Slaughter's essay contends that my argument neglects the antimajoritarian decisions in American jurisprudence and thus mischaracterizes the contrast between American law and international human rights.

[34] On the "mission civilisatrice" in the French colonies, see Pascal Blanchard and Sandrine Lemaire, *Culture imperiale, 1931–1961: Les colonies au coeur de la Republique* (Paris: Editions Autrement, 2004).

[35] Niall Ferguson, *Empire: The Rise and Demise of the British World Order and the Lessons for Global Power* (London: Basic Books, 2002), chap. 3, "The Mission."

anic claims about the universal validity of their own rights systems. The Soviets sought to convince newly independent countries in Africa and Asia of the superiority of Soviet social and economic guarantees, while the Americans insisted that civil and political rights, guaranteeing property and political participation, were the sine qua non of development. It was not until a faltering Soviet regime signed the Helsinki Final Accord in 1976, allowing the formation of human rights NGOs in the Eastern Bloc, that the Soviets effectively admitted that there were not two human rights cultures in the world but one, in which social and economic rights enjoyed equality of status with civil and political ones.[36]

Viewed against this historical perspective, what is exceptional about American messianism is that it is the last imperial ideology left standing in the world, the sole survivor of imperial claims to universal significance. All the others—the Soviet, the French, and the British—have been consigned to the dustbin of history. This may help to explain why a messianic ideology, which many Americans take to be no more than a sincere desire to share the benefits of their own freedom, should be seen by so many other nations as a hegemonic claim to interference in their internal affairs.

The realist account, when combined with the emphasis on American messianic destiny, helps to explain the power dynamics and the distinctive ideology that shaped American participation in the postwar human rights order. But neither the realist account nor the messianic account is sufficiently fine-grained to account for the fact that American policy has changed in the past and may change in the future. American exceptionalism is not set in stone. Neither national interest nor messianic ideology dictates that it will persist forever.

Institutions

A third explanation would get at these fine-grained and contingent features of American exceptionalism by stressing the distinctiveness of American institutions. Frank Michelman points out that judicial review is more strongly entrenched in the American system of government than in any other liberal democracy. With this entrenchment of judicial power goes a strong institutional imperative to safeguard prerogatives of judicial interpretation and keep them immune to foreign influence. Andrew Moravcsik also focuses on institutional factors, stressing the decisive importance of U.S. federalism and the ratification process for treaties in the U.S. Senate.[37]

---

[36] Daniel C. Thomas, *The Helsinki Effect: International Norms, Human Rights, and the Demise of Communism* (Princeton: Princeton University Press, 2001).

[37] See also Andrew Moravcsik, "Why Is US Human Rights Policy So Unilateralist?" in *The Cost of Acting Alone: Multilateralism and US Foreign Policy*, ed. Shepard Forman and Patrick Stewart (Boulder, CO: Lynne Reiner, 2001).

The U.S. system devolves significant powers to the states, meaning that key dimensions of human rights behavior—like punishment—remain beyond the legislative purview of the central state, as they are in many European countries. Even if it wanted to do so, the United States lacks a central instrument to harmonize U.S. domestic law in the light of international standards. Next, the U.S. Senate requires two-thirds majorities for ratification of international treaties, thus imposing a significantly higher bar to incorporation of international law than do other liberal democracies. These institutional features, created by the founders to protect citizens from big government or from foreign treaties threatening their liberties, impose exceptional institutional barriers to statutory and nationwide compliance with international human rights.

In addition to different institutions, the United States has had a distinctive history of political stability, which increases its sense of political self-sufficiency and reduces incentives to stabilize its own institutions with foreign treaties. Moravcsik argues that the United States has never faced fascism or occupation at home or a credible threat of foreign invasion or subversion. What drove the Western Europeans to create the European Convention on Human Rights was the catastrophe of two world wars, followed by the vulnerability of their postwar democracies. A common human rights framework, enforced by a supranational court, was accepted by sovereign states because it was held to "lock in" the stability of the new democratic regimes in Italy, Germany, and France, against both communist subversion and the resurgence of fascism. Thus sovereign European states reluctantly accepted an enforceable transnational human rights regime limiting their sovereignty because it appeared to protect their democratic experiment. The United States had no such incentive to surrender its sovereign prerogatives as a state and has continued to regard transnational international law regimes as potential violations of its democratic sovereignty.

Politics

Beyond these institutional factors, Moravcsik argues that in comparison to post-1945 Europe, American political culture is significantly more conservative and more influenced by evangelical religious minorities on certain key rights issues relating to abortion, family law, women's rights, and gay marriage. This makes it unlikely that American opinion will ever align with the more liberal international consensus articulated in human rights conventions. The historical strength of American conservatism might qualify as a fourth factor explaining American exceptionalism. It is worth adding, however, that conservatism is not a synonym for isolationism.

Evangelical conservatism has been a driving force behind the cause of religious freedom in China and Sudan. Evangelical conservatism also helped to inspire the intervention in Iraq, configuring it for American domestic consumption as a campaign to bring democracy to the oppressed and unfree.

If America has been more conservative on key human rights issues than Europe, and more inclined toward engagement in issues of religious freedom than more secular Europeans, the next question is whether this conservative orientation is a permanent or a passing difference. Cass Sunstein remarks that the conservative ascendancy in American politics since the late 1960s makes it easy to forget just how strong its ideological competitor—social liberalism and liberal internationalism—used to be. Beginning with Roosevelt's speech to the 1944 Democratic Convention, calling for a second bill of rights, guaranteeing rights to work, food, housing, and medical care, a liberal political consensus in Congress and in the courts drove toward statutory creation of social and economic entitlements, culminating in the social reform legislation of Lyndon Johnson's Great Society and the momentous decisions of the Warren Court.[38] At the high-water mark of American liberalism in the mid-1960s, America would not have looked exceptional. The attitudes of its courts and legislatures toward welfare rights and entitlements would have seemed consistent with the European social democratic consensus of the period. Likewise, in that decade, as Steiker points out, America seemed poised to join the abolitionist consensus emerging in the North Atlantic countries. In the international sphere, at least until the Vietnam debacle, there were relatively few criticisms of American exceptionalism among its allies. The United States exercised global leadership through multilateral alliances and treaties. This period of North Atlantic convergence, however, was brief. Sunstein argues that the social revolution of the 1960s produced a conservative counterreaction, beginning with the Nixon administration and the Burger Court, that endures to this day. In international politics, the conservative ascendancy in American politics has been marked, since Ronald Reagan, by a reassertion of nationalist and exceptionalist rhetoric and policy.

The conservative counterrevolution in American politics does help to explain why America's human rights performance, at home and abroad, has diverged from those of its democratic allies since the 1960s. But there remains a question of whether this is a permanent or a passing phenomenon. If Sunstein is correct, American exceptionalism may wax and wane according to the political fortunes of conservatism and liberalism, evangelicalism and secularism, in American domestic opinion.

---

[38] See also Cass Sunstein, "Social and Economic Rights? Lessons from South Africa," *University of Chicago, Public Law and Legal Theory Working Paper* 12 (May 2001).

Already, one key explanatory factor driving American exceptionalism in human rights—America's particular experience of slavery and racism—may be passing into history. Slavery and segregation made America exceptional among liberal democratic states, and southern politicians led the opposition to American adoption of international rights regimes from the late 1940s to the 1960s.[39] Eisenhower withdrew the United States from participation in the drafting of the International Covenant on Civil and Political Rights in the 1950s largely to appease southern conservative senators. The same politicians who wielded states' rights arguments against the use of federal power to desegregate the South invoked national sovereignty arguments to resist adoption or implementation of international rights regimes. Conservative southern hostility to the use of federal power to promote civil rights at home extended to the use of international human rights to promote racial equality.[40] This dire historical experience may now be over. In the wake of the success of U.S. federal civil rights legislation, U.S. and international human rights norms on racial equality largely coincide. The United States is rarely in the dock of international opinion on matters of domestic race relations, and the rejectionist stance of southern Democrats and Republicans to international human rights standards on race is losing its political influence.

Southern conservatives, however, are still bastions of opposition to international law. Jesse Helms and other southern senators have fought measures like the ICC while they also oppose conventions on the rights of the child and the elimination of discrimination against women because these appear to impose secular and liberal doctrines about family discipline.[41] The United States is thus alone among liberal democracies in hav-

---

[39] Mary L. Dudziak, *Cold War Civil Rights: Race and the Image of American Democracy* (Princeton: Princeton University Press, 2000); Louis Henkin, "U.S. Ratification of Human Rights Conventions: The Ghost of Senator Bricker," *American Journal of International Law* 89 (April 1995).

[40] Gay McDougall, "Competing and Concordant Languages: U.S. Civil Rights and International Human Rights" (presentation given at the American Exceptionalism Seminar Series, Carr Center for Human Rights Policy, John F. Kennedy School of Government, Harvard University, Monday, December 9, 2002).

[41] "Remarks of Senator Phil Gramm (R-Tx) at the Christian Coalition's 'Road to Victory Conference,' " September 8, 1995, *Federal News Service*, available at http://www.lexis-nexis.com/; "Hearing of the Senate Foreign Relations Committee to Consider the Nomination of Madeleine Albright to Be Secretary of State: Afternoon Session," January 8, 1997, *Federal News Service*, available at http://www.lexis-nexis.com/; "Hearing of the Senate Foreign Relations Committee Subject: Nomination of Bill Richardson to Be U.S. Ambassador to the United Nations," January 29, 1997, *Federal News Service*, available at http://www.lexis-nexis.com/; Elisabeth Gusdek-Peterson, "Parental Rights Are Fundamental Human Rights," in *Fifty Years after the Declaration: The United Nations' Record on Human Rights*, ed. Teresa Wagner and Leslie Carbone (Washington, DC: Family Research Council, 2001); William Saunders, "Address to the World Congress of Families" (Washington, DC, October

ing a strong domestic political constituency opposed to international human rights law on issues of family and sexual morality. The same constituency has succeeded in turning the ICC into an issue of patriotism—that is, a question of how to preserve U.S. service personnel from vexatious international prosecutions by anti-American foreign prosecutors.[42] For the moment at least, the domestic conservative forces that have made America exceptional remain in the ascendant.

Evaluating American Exceptionalism

If the previous analysis is correct, then current American exceptionalism, therefore, is fundamentally explained by the weakness of American liberalism. American commitment to international human rights has always depended on the political fortunes of a liberal political constituency, and as these fortunes have waxed and waned, so has American policy toward international law.

The first question in evaluating American exceptionalism is whether it is likely to be an enduring or a passing feature of American involvement in the international order. The contributors to this volume disagree on this matter. Sunstein emphasizes contingency, the unique combination of factors that produced the conservative counterrevolution of the sixties. If exceptionalism in social and economic rights is tied to this alone, then there is good reason to think that the tide of political opinion will turn. Such a view might draw further confirmation from Carol Steiker's essay on the death penalty: she notes that far from always having been in favor of capital punishment, the United States had joined in the abolitionist tide moving through other liberal democracies, like Canada, the UK, Germany, and France, and reversed itself only in the 1970s. This suggests that

---

26–27, 2001), http://www.efamilyaction.org/wcf/William_Saunders.htm; Doug Domenech, "Hands Off Our Children," *National Review Online*, June 11, 2001, http://www .nationalreview.com/comment/comment-domenech061101.shtml; "The New World Order Wants Your Children," *Phyllis Schlafly Report* (Eagle Forum, March 1993), http:// www.eagleforum.org/psr/1993/mar93/psrmar93.html; "Hearing of the House International Relations Committee Subject: International Efforts to End Discrimination against Women," May 3, 2000, *Federal News Service*, available at http://www.lexis-nexis.com/; "Hearing of the Senate Foreign Affairs Committee Subject: Religious Freedom," May 12, 1998, *Federal News Service*, available at http://www.lexis-nexis.com/; National Center for Home Education, "Oppose the United Nations Convention on the Elimination of All Forms of Discrimination against Women," December 13, 1999, http://nche.hslda.org/docs/nche/000000/ 00000024.asp.

[42] In 2000, Tom DeLay (R-TX) and Floyd Spence (R-SC) introduced the American Serviceman's Protection Act. Jesse Helms (R-NC) and John W. Warner (R-VA.) introduced the Senate version of the bill.

death penalty exceptionalism may not be as enduring as America's current outlier position might imply.

Other contributors also think American exceptionalism may be a passing phenomenon, but they do so for different reasons. Anne-Marie Slaughter, John Ruggie, and Frank Michelman focus on the rapid growth of transnational networks that have emerged to address problems that can't be resolved solely within national jurisdictions. These networks—anchored within the UN, the WTO, the European Union, and other international frameworks—are drawing American lawyers, NGOs, and policy makers into an ever tighter web of negotiations and deal making on issues ranging from human rights, to climate change, to corporate social responsibility, international trade, company law, and market regulation. Slaughter argues that the United States cannot remain disengaged from these developments. It will have ever stronger incentives to become less exceptional, to align its laws, markets, trade practices, and even its domestic rights with those of other states. Some of its most urgent national security problems, like terrorism, cannot be solved unilaterally and require ever closer multilateral cooperation with other states. Exceptionalism, in other words, may be out of step with globalization and with the convergence of state interests and practices in an interdependent world.

Other contributors, especially those who stress the historical distinctiveness of American institutions and rights, are skeptical that globalization equals convergence. Frederick Schauer sees no evidence that as America interacts with the free speech doctrines of other democratic states, its First Amendment doctrine will begin to change. Nor does he see any evidence that other nations are converging toward American norms in free speech and defamation law. Andrew Moravcsik, likewise, sees no evidence that the differences of institutional history and political culture between the United States and Europe are diminishing. Increasing integration of economic and security policy across the North Atlantic does not necessarily produce convergence in political vision or rights policy. Finally, Paul Kahn is probably the most intransigent believer in the unchanging nature of American exceptionalism. In his analysis, exceptionalism will endure because it is so deeply tied to the American commitment to sovereignty as an ideal of republican self-rule born of a revolutionary act of national self-creation.

Whether exceptionalism is an enduring or a passing phenomenon, it remains to determine whether it is a good or a bad thing. Here too the contributors divide sharply and so has academic debate.

From the 1950s through the 1970s, the liberal academic consensus held American exceptionalism to be a very bad thing indeed. The liberal international lawyers, like Thomas Franck and Louis Henkin, who believed passionately in America's role as a creator of international law, regarded

American withdrawal from the international human rights drafting table from 1953 onward with unqualified dismay.[43] They believed that international law could not develop without American leadership, and they believed that the international order should reflect American values. Yet this liberal consensus never went unchallenged. It always faced opposition from an influential strand of conservative and nationalist legal thinking, represented in the American Bar Association, some of whose chief members, suspicious of international law and of international organizations, led the opposition to the Genocide Convention and other international agreements.[44] Beginning in the 1980s, a conservative legal counterattack gained ground, taking a strongly Americanist or nationalist view of international law. Academic lawyers like John Bolton, Jeremy Rabkin, and Jack Goldsmith questioned the liberal assumption that American rights conduct needed to measure up to international standards.[45] By 2000, the conservative nationalist consensus had influential support inside the George W. Bush administration, and their influence helped to drive the administration's fierce opposition to the ICC, its withdrawal from Kyoto, and even its insistence that the United States had the right to interpret the Geneva Conventions and the Torture Convention as it pleased. For conservative nationalists, the most powerful state cannot be tied down, like Gulliver, by international human rights norms. Its effectiveness as a world leader depends on being free of such constraints. Besides, its rights performance at home does not stand in need of lessons from abroad. The conservatives did more than defend American national pride and national interest. They raised a key argument of principle: why should a republic, based in the rule of law, be constrained by international agreements that do not have the same element of democratic legitimacy?

In addition to a "nationalist" justification for exceptionalism, conservatives offer a "realist" argument as well. Far from being a problem, excep-

[43] Henkin, "U.S. Ratification of Human Rights Conventions"; Thomas M. Franck, "Dr. Pangloss Meets the Grinch: A Pessimistic Comment on Harold Koh's Optimism," *Houston Law Review* 35 (1998).

[44] See, for example, John Norton Moore, *Treaty Interpretation, the Constitution, and the Rule of Law* (Dobbs Ferry, NY: Oceana Publications, 2001); Phillip R. Trimble, "A Revisionist View of Customary International Law," *UCLA Law Review* 33 (February 1986).

[45] Jack Goldsmith, "International Human Rights Law and the US Double Standard," *Green Bag* 1 (1998); Jack Goldsmith, "Should International Human Rights Law Trump US Domestic Law?" *Chicago Journal of International Law* 1 (2000); Jack Goldsmith and Curtis Bradley, "Treaties, Human Rights, and Conditional Consent," *Pennsylvania Law Review* 149 (2000); John R. Bolton, "Downer Is Right to Tell the UN to Get Lost," *Australian Financial Review*, August 31, 2000; John R. Bolton, "Flaws Undermine Concept," *USA Today*, January 18, 2000; Jeremy Rabkin, *Why Sovereignty Matters* (Washington, DC: AEI Press, 1998).

tionalism might be a solution. By signing on to international human rights, with reservations and exemptions, by refusing to be bound by agreements that would constrain its sovereignty, the United States manages to maintain leadership in global human rights at the lowest possible cost to its own margin of maneuver as the world's sole superpower.[46] Exceptionalism, therefore, achieves a balance: the United States remains within the framework of international human rights law, but on its own terms. Given its preponderant power—and therefore its exceptional influence in the global order—it can dictate these terms. The rest of the world can choose to concede these exceptional terms, or to see the United States stand aside and take either a unilateralist or an isolationist turn. Exceptionalism is the functional compromise, therefore, that enables America to be a multilateral partner in the human rights enterprise.

A liberal internationalist would reply that if America wants to be a human rights leader, it must be consistent. It must obey the rules it seeks to champion. Leadership depends on legitimacy and legitimacy requires consistency. Certainly double standards increase resistance to American leadership, whether the issue is Palestine or Iraq. Double standards also diminish the lure of American example. But the argument that American exceptionalism is a costly mistake cannot be pushed too far. The fact that the United States exempts itself from some international norms does not diminish its capacity to enforce others. U.S. resistance to a permanent criminal court did not preclude its supporting the Hague tribunal or using its influence with Serbia to bring Slobodan Milošević to justice. In Iraq, the United States behaved in an exceptional and unilateralist manner, but the overthrow of the Ba'athist regime was a substantively just outcome. If it had bowed to world opinion on the use of force, a rights-violating regime would still be in power. Multilateralism is a good thing, therefore, only if it produces substantively just results.

Nor has American exceptionalism prevented the development of international human rights and humanitarian law. Other states have taken the lead in developing the ICC statute, and the Land Mines Treaty is in existence despite U.S. opposition. The European Convention on Human Rights did not wait for American inspiration. Of course, there are limits to what other states can achieve when the world's most powerful state opposes or refuses to engage. But equally, American leadership has not proven as crucial, nor its opposition as damaging, to international law as either American internationalists or their European allies are prone to believe.

---

[46] Goldsmith, "International Human Rights and the US Double Standard." See also Jack L. Goldsmith and Eric A. Posner, *The Limits of International Law* (New York: Oxford University Press, 2005), chap. 4.

As John Ruggie points out, American opposition cannot stop multilateral transnational institutions and problem-solving networks from emerging. America may be exceptional in its illusion that it can exempt itself from these processes, but this, Ruggie argues, would be to swim against the tide of increasing international cooperation to master the problems that national governments cannot master on their own. So whether exceptionalism is a good or a bad thing, it may impose increasing costs on the United States in a globalizing world.

Exceptionalism can also directly damage U.S. national security interests. Stanley Hoffmann argues that America's unilateral arrogance in Iraq has alienated friends, made needless enemies, forced the United States to go it alone, and increased the cost of its projection of power overseas. To this might be added the evidence from Abu Ghraib prison. A country that thinks it is too virtuous, too exceptional, to pay respect to the Geneva Conventions and begins to write its own rules about detention, interrogation, and special status can end up violating every value it holds dear. In other words, what Jefferson called "decent respect for the opinions of mankind"—voluntary compliance with international humanitarian law and human rights law—may be essential for the maintenance of American honor and its own values overseas.

Human rights exceptionalism, especially double standards, may also end up endangering U.S. security. America's Iraq policy over the past twenty years demonstrates that when the United States supports authoritarian regimes, ignoring their human rights performance, these authoritarian rulers can metamorphose into a national security threat. Ignoring the rights behavior of Saddam Hussein in the 1980s turned out to be a disaster for U.S. interests in the Gulf region, as did turning a blind eye to the abuses of Sukarno of Indonesia. Pressuring them, before it was too late, to make changes, or quarantining them as a future danger, would have paid better dividends to U.S. security than keeping quiet about their abuses. Reducing double standards requires rethinking the supposed conflict between human rights and security interests. If U.S. policy consistently used human rights standards as a predictor of internal stability and external dangerousness, it would make better national security judgments about whom to trust and whom it can rely on. If it used its security relationships to pressure regimes toward better human rights performance, it would contribute something to stabilizing the regions where U.S. security interests are at stake.

This complementarity between human rights and national security interests is acknowledged, at least at the rhetorical level, in the national security policy of the George W. Bush administration. President Bush's speech in 2003 to the National Endowment for Democracy contends that America's national security interests in the Arab world depend upon the promotion of women's rights, political participation, and market reforms.[47] It is by no means certain that this rhetoric will be transformed into practice, or even whether it can be. What is certain is that turning a blind eye to the human rights abuses rampant in the Arab regimes has eroded U.S. influence by rendering the United States complicit with regimes that have lost the confidence of their people.

Finally, any evaluation of American exceptionalism fundamentally expresses a certain preference for a certain type of America. Those who wish America were less exceptional are actually expressing the desire for it to be a certain kind of good international citizen, one bound, despite its exceptional power, by multilateral definitions of appropriate state responsibility toward its citizens and rules relating to the use of force against other states. The virtue of this multilateral identity is that it would make America more attractive to itself, a benevolent superpower voluntarily restricting its sovereignty for the sake of the greater global good.

The question to ask of this benevolent liberal internationalism is whether it has any sustained electoral appeal among the American public. Under Franklin Roosevelt's leadership, this image was briefly anchored in a constituency of political support. But the fate of this image of American identity has been tied to the fortunes of American liberalism, and these fortunes have not fared well in the past thirty years. For now a liberal multilateralism is more liberal than most Americans would be comfortable to be: against the death penalty, in favor of allowing American citizens to be tried in international courts, and in favor of surrendering some freedom of maneuver to the United Nations. The country that is often called the last fully sovereign nation on earth has yet to be convinced that it stands to gain from this identity.

Conclusion

As a language of moral claims, human rights has gone global by going local, by establishing its universal appeal in local languages of dignity and freedom. As international human rights has developed and come of age, not much attention has been paid to this process of vernacularization. We must ask whether any of us would care much about rights if they were articulated only in universalist documents like the Universal Declaration, and whether, in fact, our attachment to these universals depends critically on our prior attachment to rights that are national, rooted in the tradi-

---

[47] President George W. Bush, "Remarks by the President at the 20th Anniversary of the National Endowment for Democracy" (United States Chamber of Commerce, Washington, DC, November 6, 2003), http://www.whitehouse.gov/news/releases/2003/11/20031106-2.html.

tions of a flag, a constitution, a set of founders, and a set of national narratives, religious and secular, that give point and meaning to rights. We need to think through the relation between national rights traditions and international standards, to see that these are not in the antithetical relation we suppose. American attachment to its own values is the condition and possibility of its attachment to the universal, and it is only as the universal receives a national expression that it catches the heart and the conviction of citizens.

American exceptionalism lays bare the relation between the national and the universal in the rights cultures of all states that have constitutional regimes of liberty. The question is what margin of interpretation should be allowed these nations in their human rights performance, and what margin shades into a permissive surrender of those values that should be universal for all nations. If all nations are, at least to their own citizens, exceptional, we want an international rights culture that welcomes, rather than suppresses, authentic national expressions of universal values. Americans will not believe any truths to be self-evident that have not been authored by their own men and women of greatness, by Jefferson and Lincoln, Martin Luther King, Jr., and Sojourner Truth. The American creed itself—because it speaks so eloquently of the equality of all peoples—enjoins Americans to deliberate, to listen, to engage with other citizens of other cultures. This is what a modern culture of rights entails, even for an exceptional nation: to listen, to deliberate with others, and if persuasive reasons are offered them, to alter and improve their own inheritance in the light of other nations' example. The critical cost that America pays for exceptionalism is that this stance gives the country convincing reasons not to listen and learn. Nations that find reasons not to listen and learn end up losing.

Part I

THE VARIETIES OF EXCEPTIONALISM

Chapter 2

The Exceptional First Amendment

FREDERICK SCHAUER

ALTHOUGH IT WAS not always so, today virtually all liberal democracies protect, in formal legal documents as well as in actual practice, both freedom of speech and freedom of the press. The language used to enshrine the protection varies, with "freedom of expression" the most common contemporary canonical formulation, but in one way or another it is now routine for open societies to guarantee a moderately wide range of communicative freedoms.[1] Moreover, the protection is uniformly of a type that can be characterized as "constitutional," in that the principles of freedom of expression impose entrenched second-order constraints not merely upon pernicious attempts to control communication, and not even merely upon well-intentioned but misguided attempts to control communication, but also, and most important, upon actually well-designed and genuinely efficacious attempts to control speech and the press in the service of important first-order policy preferences. With few exceptions, it is today generally understood worldwide that freedom of expression must be respected even when sound policies would actually be substantially fostered by restrictions on that freedom.[2]

This essay has benefited enormously from the comments of Michael Ignatieff and the other participants in the Carr Center for Human Rights Policy's Exceptionalism Project, and from participant and audience questions when a different version of this essay was delivered at a conference on European and American constitutional law organized by the Venice Commission of the Council of Europe and held in Göttingen, Germany, on May 15–16, 2003. Research support was generously provided by the Joan Shorenstein Center on the Press, Politics and Public Policy.

[1] For purposes of this essay, I will treat "freedom of expression," as in Article 10 of the European Convention on Human Rights, "freedom of communication," as in the May 28, 2003, Declaration on Freedom of Communication on the Internet by the Committee of Ministers of the Council of Europe, and "freedom of speech" and "freedom of the press," as in the First Amendment to the Constitution of the United States, as synonymous, although there are instances in which variations in formulation reflect different substantive understandings and may even make a genuine difference in practice.

[2] On the importance of understanding freedom of expression as just this kind of side constraint, see Frederick Schauer, *Free Speech: A Philosophical Enquiry* (Cambridge: Cambridge University Press, 1982); Thomas Scanlon, "A Theory of Freedom of Expression," *Philosophy and Public Affairs* 1 (1971): 203–21. On second-order constraints on first-order

Yet although a constitutional or quasi-constitutional[3] right to freedom of expression is the international norm, the contours of that right vary widely even among the liberal democracies that understand the value of the right and the importance of enforcing it seriously. And among the most interesting manifestations of that variety among liberal democracies is the way in which the American First Amendment, as authoritatively interpreted, remains a recalcitrant outlier to a growing international understanding of what the freedom of expression entails. In numerous dimensions, the American approach is *exceptional*, and my goal in this essay is first to describe some aspects of American free speech (and free press) exceptionalism, and then to offer as plausible but untested hypotheses various explanations as to why the American protection of freedom of expression is generally stronger than that represented by an emerging multinational consensus—but stronger in ways that may also reflect an exceptional though not necessarily correct understanding of the relationship between freedom of expression and other goals, other interests, and other rights.

Two Types of Exceptionalism

It will be useful at the outset to distinguish between *substantive* and *methodological* exceptionalism. When I speak of the former, I refer to actual outcomes and actual doctrines, but when I speak of the latter, I mean to focus on the methods and approaches, predominantly but not exclusively those of the courts, by which those outcomes and doctrines are produced. Thus, and as I will explain in detail, the American understanding of freedom of expression is substantively exceptional compared to international standards because a range of American outcomes and American resolu-

---

policy preferences as underlying constitutionalism in general, see Frederick Schauer, "Judicial Supremacy and the Modest Constitution," *California Law Review* 92 (2004): 834–57.

   [3] I refer to as "quasi-constitutional" those entrenched protections of rights that exist not as components of written constitutions, but instead within statutes whose modification or repeal is politically or formally more difficult than would be the modification or repeal of so-called ordinary legislation. The phenomenon is most common in countries without formal written constitutions, and thus we see, in the United Kingdom, the Human Rights Act 1998, in New Zealand, the Bill of Rights Act 1990, and, in Israel, the Basic Law: Human Dignity and Liberty (S.H. 1992, No. 1391). For commentary on the constitutional status of each, see Aharon Barak, "The Constitutionalization of the Israeli Legal System as a Result of the Basic Laws and Its Effect on Procedural and Substantive Law," *Israel Law Review* 3 (1997): 3–21; Janet McLean, "Legislative Invalidation, Human Rights Protection and s 4 of the New Zealand Bill of Rights Act," *New Zealand Law Review* [2001]: 421–48; Douglas W. Vick, "The Human Rights Act and the British Constitution," *Texas International Law Journal* 37 (2002): 329–72.

tions of conflicts between freedom of expression and other rights and goals are starkly divergent from the outcomes and resolutions reached in most other liberal democracies. And this is *not* because the First Amendment, 213 years old at this writing and into its ninth decade of serious judicial enforcement,[4] is simply older, with other nations only now just recognizing and catching up to more entrenched American developments. Rather, much of the rest of the developed democratic world has by now carefully considered the American resolution of numerous freedom of expression issues as to which the United States is an outlier, and has after this consideration deliberately chosen a different course.

In contrast to such substantive exceptionalism, methodological exceptionalism reflects a divergence in approach, whether by the courts or by legislative bodies, to resolving freedom of expression controversies. As I shall explain, it is widely believed, in Canada and South Africa and Europe, that the American methodology is marked by a profoundly different understanding of the structure of freedom of expression adjudication, with the American approach characterized by an emphasis on rule-based categorization, in contrast to the more flexible and open-ended balancing approach that generally rides under the banner of "proportionality."[5] Apart from substantive outcome, therefore, it is widely believed in most liberal democracies that the United States is an outlier not only with respect to freedom of expression doctrines and policies, but with respect to freedom of expression methodology as well. Yet although, as I shall argue, the phenomenon of substantive exceptionalism is significant and in need of deeper explanation, methodological exceptionalism, by contrast, may be more ephemeral, explainable largely in terms of a natural course of rights complexification—the way in which simply articulated rights evolve into more complex ones as decision makers confront a larger array of problems, perceive patterns within that array, and develop rules, principles, and presumptions necessary for them to manage that larger array. Insofar as American freedom of expression methodology reflects this process, what look like methodological differences may be little more than

---

[4] The modern First Amendment begins in 1919, with *Schenck v. United States*, 249 U.S. 47 (1919); *United States v. Debs*, 249 U.S. 211 (1919); *Frohwerk v. United States*, 249 U.S. 204 (1919); and *Abrams v. United States*, 250 U.S. 616 (1919), although free speech ideas had haltingly emerged earlier. See David M. Rabban, *The First Amendment in Its Forgotten Years* (Cambridge: Cambridge University Press, 1997); David M. Rabban, "The Emergence of Modern First Amendment Doctrine," *University of Chicago Law Review* 50 (1983): 1205–64.

[5] See Aharon Barak, "Foreword. A Judge on Judging: The Role of a Supreme Court in a Democracy," *Harvard Law Review* 116 (2002): 16–105. See also Richard Moon, *The Constitutional Protection of Freedom of Expression* (Toronto: University of Toronto Press, 2000), 32–75.

the reflection of longer and more extensive American experience with freedom of communication issues. Consequently, as I shall argue, the development over time of a larger experiential base in other regimes might be predicted to produce methods more similar to the American ones. As a result, we are likely to see in the future a degree of methodological convergence even in the face of little change in the current state of substantive divergence.

Substantive Exceptionalism I: The Case of Hate Speech

With the distinction between substantive and methodological exceptionalism having been drawn, it is time to examine each, turning first to the substantive. We will look first, therefore, at the ways in which American freedom of expression policies—in the courts and elsewhere—diverge from those in most other liberal democracies, thus reflecting American substantive choices among competing values that are different from the choices made in much of the balance of the democratic and developed world.

Consider initially the widely debated topic of "hate speech." Although the label "hate speech" tends to be applied capaciously, the phrase can be understood as encompassing four distinct but interrelated freedom of speech issues. First, there is the question of the legitimacy of prohibiting various racial, ethnic, and religious epithets—*nigger, wog, kike, paki, kaffir,* and the like[6]—words whose use, except as ironic self-reference by members of those groups, is invariably intended to harm, to offend, and to marginalize.[7] Second, the question of hate speech sometimes involves the issue of restrictions on circulating certain demonstrably false factual propositions about various racial or religious groups, with prohibitions on Holocaust denial being the most common example.[8] A third hate

---

[6] Similar issues arise in the context of epithets about sexual orientation—*fag, dyke,* etc.— but attempted legal prohibitions are less common.

[7] See Randall Kennedy, *Nigger: The Strange Career of a Troublesome Word* (New York: Pantheon Books, 2002); Richard Delgado, "Words That Wound: A Tort Action for Racial Insults, Epithets, and Name-Calling," *Harvard Civil Rights–Civil Liberties Law Review* 17 (1982): 133–72; Michel Rosenfeld, "Hate Speech in Comparative Perspective: A Comparative Analysis," *Cardozo Law Review* 24 (2003): 1523–67.

[8] The most important judicial discussion of Holocaust denial and freedom of expression is in the Supreme Court of Canada's decision in *R. v. Keegstra* [1990] 3 S.C.R. 697. Noteworthy discussions of *Keegstra* include, inter alia, Kent Greenawalt, *Fighting Words: Individuals, Communities, and Liberties of Speech* (Princeton: Princeton University Press, 1995), 64–70; Roy Leeper, "*Keegstra* and *R.A.V.*: A Comparative Analysis of the Canadian and U.S. Approaches to Hate Speech Legislation," *Communication Law and Policy* 5 (2000): 295–322; L. W. Sumner, "Hate Propaganda and Charter Rights," in *Free Expression: Essays in Law and Philosophy,* ed. W. J. Waluchow (Oxford: Clarendon Press, 1994), 153–74.

speech issue arises with respect to laws prohibiting the advocacy of or incitement to racial or religious intolerance, hatred, or violence, as with explicit calls to race-based violence, explicit appeals for racial exclusion, and explicit calls for repatriation of members of racial or religious minorities to the countries of their ancestry.[9] Finally, hate speech questions are presented, especially in the context of gender, when it is argued that epithets, and occasionally pictures, create a hostile, and therefore marginalizing or excluding, workplace or educational or cultural environment.[10]

On this cluster of interrelated topics, there appears to be a strong international consensus that the principles of freedom of expression are either overridden or irrelevant when what is being expressed is racial, ethnic, or religious hatred. Going back at least as far as the 1965 Race Relations Act in the United Kingdom, Section 4 of the 1965 International Convention on the Elimination of All Forms of Racial Discrimination, and Article 20 of the 1966 International Covenant on Civil and Political Rights,[11] and continuing through numerous other national and international laws, treaties, conventions, covenants, and understandings, the incitement to racial hatred and other verbal manifestations of race-based animosity are

[9] See Eric Barendt, *Freedom of Speech* (Oxford: Clarendon Press, 1985), 163–65; Joseph Magnet, "Hate Propaganda in Canada," in Waluchow, *Free Expression*, 223–50; Mari Matsuda, "Public Response to Racist Speech: Considering the Victim's Story," *Michigan Law Review* 87 (1989): 2320–2404. For an analysis of the difference between hate speech intended to inflict psychic pain on a listener and hate speech intended to incite another hater, see Frederick Schauer, "The Phenomenology of Speech and Harm," *Ethics* 103 (1993): 635–53.

[10] On the relationship between hate speech in the gender context and hate speech in the context of race, see Kathleen Mahoney, "The Canadian Constitutional Approach to Freedom of Expression in Hate Propaganda and Pornography," *Law and Contemporary Problems* 55 (1992): 77–114, and also the various essays in *The Price We Pay: The Case against Racist Speech, Hate Propaganda, and Pornography*, ed. Laura Lederer and Richard Delgado (New York: Hill and Wang, 1995). I will say little more about gender in this essay, in large part because gender issues introduce complexities going well beyond the question of American freedom of expression exceptionalism, and implicating what might be thought to be quite a different form of American exceptionalism. So although it is likely that the emergence of a free speech reaction to speech restrictions generated by concerns about gender discrimination is virtually unique to the United States, the absence in the first instance of such restrictions in most other countries makes the issue more difficult to disentangle. We know that France believes that American hostile environment restrictions are a manifestation of politically correct hypersensitivity—see Abigail C. Saguy, "Employment Discrimination or Sexual Violence? Defining Sexual Harassment in American and French Law," *Law and Society Review* 34 (2000): 1091–1128—but we cannot know for sure what form the opposition would take if, counterfactually, France were to enact such restrictions.

[11] These two conventions are noteworthy, along with Article 13(5) of the 1969 American Convention on Human Rights, in either prohibiting the incitement to racial hatred and other forms of hate speech or requiring their prohibition by signatories. Other conventions expressly or implicitly permit such restrictions by signatory nations, and none appear to prohibit them.

widely accepted as lying outside the boundaries of what a properly conceived freedom of expression encompasses. Consistent with this worldwide consensus and international mandate,[12] the typical non-American domestic regime prohibits various forms of racially hostile speech, with "hate speech" being the common umbrella term for much of the speech that is commonly prohibited for reasons of its contribution to intolerance on the grounds of race, religion, ethnicity, national origin, and, less commonly, gender and sexual orientation.

The precise form of attempting to control hate speech by law varies considerably among the nations of the world. Germany and Israel, among other countries, ban the Nazi Party and its descendants, as well as prohibiting other political parties whose programs include racial hatred, racial separation, and racial superiority.[13] Germany, Israel, and France are among the nations that prohibit the sale and distribution of various Nazi items, including swastikas, Nazi flags, and, on occasion, images of Adolph Hitler and copies of *Mein Kampf*.[14] Canada, Germany, and France, along with others, permit sanctions against those who would deny the existence of the Holocaust.[15] France imposes fines with some frequency on public utterances espousing the racial or religious inferiority of various groups, or advocating the exclusion of people from France on the basis of their race, their religion, their ethnicity, or their national origin. The Netherlands outlaws public insults based on race, religion, or sexual preference.[16] And South Africa, New Zealand, Australia, Canada, the United Kingdom, and all of the Scandinavian countries, among many others, follow the mandates of Article 20(2) of the International Covenant on Civil and Political Rights, and Articles 4(a) and 4(b) of the Convention on the Elimination of all Forms of Racial Discrimination, by making it a crime to engage in the incitement to racial, religious, or ethnic hatred or hostility.

[12] See Wojciech Sadurski, *Freedom of Speech and Its Limits* (Dordrecht, Netherlands: Kluwer Academic Publishers, 1999), chap. 6; David Kretzmer, "Freedom of Speech and Racism," *Cardozo Law Review* 8 (1987): 445–62.

[13] See Friedrich Kübler, "How Much Freedom for Racist Speech? Transnational Aspects of a Conflict of Human Rights," *Hofstra Law Review* 27 (1998): 335–64; Eric Stein, "History against Free Speech: The New German Law against the 'Auschwitz'—and Other—Lies," *Michigan Law Review* 85 (1986): 277–312.

[14] See *Yahoo!, Inc. v. La Ligue Contre le Racisme et L'Antisemitism*, 169 F. Supp. 2d 1181 (N.D. Cal. 2001), denying American enforcement of a French judgment against the Internet service provider Yahoo! for selling Nazi items in an on-line auction. For discussion, see Mark D. Rosen, "Exporting the Constitution," *Emory Law Journal* 53 (2004): 171–232.

[15] *Holocaust Denial Case*, 90 BverfGE 241 (1994); *R. Keegstra* [1990] 3 S.C.R. 697.

[16] See Ineke Boerefijn, "Incitement to National, Racial and Religious Hatred: Legislation and Practice in the Netherlands," in *Striking a Balance: Hate Speech, Freedom of Expression and Non-Discrimination*, ed. Sandra Coliver (London: Article 19, 1992), 202–45.

In contrast to this international consensus that various forms of hate speech need to be prohibited by law and that such prohibition creates no or few free speech issues, the United States remains steadfastly committed to the opposite view.[17] Indeed, the American commitment is so firm that the United States has on First Amendment grounds filed its reservation with respect to Article 4 of the Convention on the Elimination of All Forms of Racial Discrimination, and has, more recently, refused on constitutional grounds, after several years of negotiation, to agree to the "Protocol on the Criminalization of Acts of a Racist or Xenophobic Nature,' which is appended to the 2001 Council of Europe Cybercrime Convention, a convention to which the United States, with the exception of the protocol, is a signatory. These effects on American treaty practice are important in their own right but also reflect a deeper division between the United States and the rest of the world on freedom of expression issues; for as a matter of formal legal doctrine and significantly as a matter of public opinion as well, the American understanding is that principles of freedom of speech do not permit government to distinguish protected from unprotected speech on the basis of the point of view espoused. Specifically, this prohibition on what is technically called "viewpoint discrimination"[18] extends to the point of view that certain races or religions are inferior, to the point of view that hatred of members of minority races and religions is desirable, and to the point of view that violent or otherwise illegal action is justified against people because of their race, their ethnicity, or their religious beliefs.[19] If government may not under the First Amendment distinguish between Republicans and Communists, or prohibit the speeches of the flat-earthers because of the patent falsity of their beliefs, then the government may not,

[17] The statement in the text should possibly be tempered slightly, but only slightly, by reference to *Virginia v. Black*, 123 S. Ct. 1536 (2003), in which the Supreme Court of the United States upheld a Virginia law prohibiting cross burning, concluding that cross burning intended to intimidate constituted the kind of threat unprotected by the First Amendment. What makes the case significant on the issue of hate speech is the Court's conclusion, arguably in some tension with its earlier statements in *R.A.V. v. City of St. Paul*, 505 U.S. 377 (1992), that singling out cross burning for special legal attention did not constitute the kind of content discrimination that the First Amendment cannot countenance. See Frederick Schauer, "Intentions, Conventions, and the First Amendment: The Case of Cross-Burning," *Supreme Court Review 2003* (2004): 197–230.

[18] See *R.A.V. v. City of St. Paul*, 505 U.S. 377 (1992); Geoffrey R. Stone, "Content Regulation and the First Amendment," *William and Mary Law Review* 25 (1983): 189–232; Susan Williams, "Content Discrimination and the First Amendment," *University of Pennsylvania Law Review* 139 (1991): 201–58.

[19] *R.A.V. v. City of St. Paul*, 505 U.S. 377 (1992); Charles Fried, "The New First Amendment Jurisprudence: A Threat to Liberty," *University of Chicago Law Review* 59 (1992): 225–73. See also *American Booksellers Association v. Hudnut*, 771 F.2d 323 (7th Cir. 1985), *affirmed without opinion*, 475 U.S. 1001 (1986).

so American First Amendment doctrine insists, distinguish between espousals of racial equality and espousals of racial hatred,[20] nor may the government prohibit public denials of the factuality of the Holocaust just because of the demonstrable falsity of that proposition and the harm that would ensue from its public articulation.

Some of the American aversion to discriminating against speech because of its point of view, including racist points of view, was spawned when the Supreme Court in 1969[21] established the still-prevailing test distinguishing permitted advocacy from regulable incitement. Advocacy even of illegal conduct, the Court held, was protected by the First Amendment, and only if that advocacy was explicitly directed to urging "imminent" lawless acts in a context in which such imminent lawless acts were "likely"—essentially standing in front of an angry mob and verbally leading them to immediate violence—could the constraints of the First Amendment be overridden. This doctrine applies to the full range of public political or ideological utterances, but for our purposes what is most important is that the doctrine was created in the context of a case in which Clarence Brandenburg, a local leader of the Ku Klux Klan in southern Ohio, had called for acts of "revengance" against African Americans and Jews. But because Brandenburg's advocacy fell short of explicitly urging "imminent" unlawful acts in a context in which those unlawful acts were "likely," his speech was held to be constitutionally immune from criminal (and, almost certainly, civil as well)[22] punishment. In the context of hate speech, therefore, *Brandenburg* stands for the proposition that in the United States restrictions on the incitement of racial hatred can be countenanced under the First Amendment only when they are incitements to *violent* racial hatred, and even then only under the rare circumstances in which the incitements unmistakably call for immediate violent action, and even then only under the more rare still circumstances in which members of the listening audience are in fact likely immediately to act upon the speaker's suggestion. As should be apparent, therefore, the vast majority of non-American laws prohibiting the incitement to racial hatred would be unconstitutional in the United States, as would be the overwhelming proportion of actual legal actions brought under those laws.[23] Jean Le Pen could not be sanctioned in the United States, as he was in France, for accusing Jews of exaggerating the Holocaust,[24] nor could Brigitte Bardot

[20] See *Doe v. University of Michigan*, 721 F. Supp. 852 (E.D. Mich. 1989).

[21] *Brandenburg v. Ohio*, 395 U.S. 444 (1969).

[22] See *Herceg v. Hustler Magazine, Inc.*, 814 F.2d 1017 (5th Cir. 1987); *Olivia N. v. National Broadcasting System Co.*, 178 Cal. Rptr. 888 (Ct. App. 1981).

[23] See Nathan Courtney, "British and U.S. Hate Speech Legislation: A Comparison," *Brooklyn Journal of International Law* 19 (1993): 727–51.

[24] See Debbieann Erickson, "Trampling on Equality—Hate Messages in Public Parades," *Gonzaga Law Review* 35 (2000): 465–513, at 510.

be fined in the United States, as she was in France, for crusading against Islam and urging the deportation of those of Arab ethnicity.[25] Ernst Zundel and James Keegstra can be charged with crimes in Canada for denying the Holocaust, but not in the United States.[26]

The distinction between American practice and that in other liberal democracies exists not only with respect to incitement, but also with respect to racial epithets and insults intended not to rally or motivate the speaker's allies but rather to cause psychic harm and mental distress to those to whom the words are directed. When Frank Collin, then the leader of the American Nazi Party, proposed in 1977 to march with his followers, in full Nazi regalia, in Skokie, Illinois, a community disproportionately populated by survivors of the Holocaust, both the state and federal courts made clear that under the First Amendment there was no plausible cause for prohibiting the march.[27] More recent cases involving racial intimidation,[28] membership in racist groups,[29] and restrictions on racist speech on university campuses[30] have all emphasized that this form of "hate speech" will not be treated differently under the First Amendment (and, as in California, under state statutes and state constitutions that reach nongovernmental entities not strictly subject to the First Amendment) from any other viewpoint or any other form of public offensiveness. If Paul Cohen is protected by the First Amendment when he articulates his objection to military conscription by publicly wearing a jacket emblazoned with the words "Fuck the Draft,"[31] if people who use words like "motherfucker" are protected when they talk back to police officers,[32] and if all forms of vituperation against one's opponents are permitted in

---

[25] See Liza Klaussmann, "Buzz over Bardot Book," *Daily Variety*, May 15, 2003, 14; Maite Seligman, "France's B.B. Gun: Still Shooting from the Lip," *Washington Post*, September 6, 2003, C1.

[26] *R. v. Zundel*, [1992] 2 S.C.R. 731; *R. v. Keegstra*, [1990] 3 S.C.R. 697. See Credence Fogo-Schensul, "More Than a River in Egypt: Holocaust Denial, the Internet, and International Freedom of Expression Norms," *Gonzaga Law Review* 33 (1998): 241–63.

[27] *Collin v. Smith*, 578 F.2d 1197 (7th Cir. 1978); *Village of Skokie v. National Socialist Party of America*, 373 N.E.2d 21 (Ill. 1978). Aryeh Neier, *Defending My Enemy: American Nazis, the Skokie Case, and the Risks of Freedom* (New York: Dutton, 1979); Lee C. Bollinger, *The Tolerant Society: Freedom of Speech and Extremist Speech in America* (New York: Oxford University Press, 1986); Michel Rosenfeld, "Extremist Speech and the Paradox of Tolerance," *Harvard Law Review* 100 (1987): 1457–88.

[28] *R.A.V. v. City of St. Paul*, 505 U.S. 377 (1992). See Elena Kagan, "Regulation of Hate Speech and Pornography after R.A.V.," *University of Chicago Law Review* 60 (1993): 873–914.

[29] *Dawson v. Delaware*, 503 U.S. 159 (1992).

[30] *Doe v. University of Michigan*, 721 F. Supp. 852 (E.D. Mich. 1989); *Corry v. Stanford*, No. 740309 (Cal. Super. Ct. Santa Clara County, February 27, 1995).

[31] *Cohen v. California*, 403 U.S. 15 (1971).

[32] *Gooding v. Wilson*, 405 U.S. 518 (1972); *Lewis v. New Orleans*, 408 U.S. 913 (1972); *Rosenfeld v. New Jersey*, 408 U.S. 901 (1972).

political debate, then the American constitutional prohibition on view-point discrimination prevents treating people who call others "niggers" differently from those who call others "motherfuckers," and prevents treating people who carry Nazi flags differently from people who burn American ones.[33] That even in 1978 the United States Supreme Court deemed the march of the Nazis in Skokie so plainly protected as not even to warrant a full opinion[34] speaks volumes about the First Amendment's unwillingness to treat Nazis differently from Socialists, to treat Klansmen differently from Republicans, or to treat intimidation on grounds of race, religion, or ethnicity differently from any other form of intimidation. In much of the developed world one uses racial epithets at one's legal peril, one displays Nazi regalia and the other trappings of ethnic hatred at significant legal risk, and one urges discrimination against religious minorities under threat of fine or imprisonment, but in the United States all such speech remains constitutionally protected.

Substantive Exceptionalism II: The Case of Defamation

The divergence between American and international approaches to freedom of expression is hardly unique to the issue of hate speech. A similar divergence, for example, exists between American and non-American free speech and free press understandings with respect to defamation law—the law of libel (written) and slander (spoken). Traditionally, the United States shared with the rest of the common law world an English law heritage in which defamation was treated as a strict liability tort. In order to win a lawsuit and recover money damages, a person suing for libel or slander needed only to prove by a bare preponderance of the evidence (the normal burden of proof in civil, as opposed to criminal, cases) that the defendant had uttered (or, more commonly, published) words tending to injure the alleged victim's reputation. The plaintiff/victim was not required to prove that the defendant/publisher was negligent or in any other way at fault, and indeed the plaintiff did not even have to prove that the imputation was false. The defendant could, to be sure, prevent recovery by asserting an affirmative defense and showing that the words were true (although in some countries, it was necessary for the publisher to show not only that the words were true, but also that they had been published for good public purposes), but the fact that the burden of proof was on the publisher to demonstrate truth rather than on the target to demonstrate falsity underscores the way in which the common law of defamation traditionally embodied the view that one published at one's peril. Much

---

[33] *United States v. Eichman*, 496 U.S. 310 (1990); *Texas v. Johnson*, 491 U.S. 397 (1989).
[34] See cases and commentary cited above, n. 29.

of the common law thus reflected an attitude that many associate with the admonition that "if you can't say anything nice, don't say anything at all." Indeed, the fact that the common law required no proof of fault in principally three classes of cases—accidents ensuing from the possession of explosives; injuries that were the consequence of keeping wild animals; and damage to reputation caused by the speaking of defamatory words—offers a juxtaposition of examples that vividly highlights the common law's preference not for speech but for civility and respect.

The United States departed dramatically from this tradition in 1964. In *New York Times Co. v. Sullivan*,[35] the Supreme Court, in the name of the First Amendment, constitutionalized what had previously been the constitutionally untouched[36] common law of defamation, concluding that actions for libel and slander brought by public officials could succeed only upon proof by clear and convincing evidence (and not merely by a preponderance of the evidence, as would be the case in other civil actions) of *intentional* falsity,[37] a burden of proof almost impossible to meet. To the Supreme Court, the traditional common law approach imposed all of the risk of falsity upon the publisher, making publishers wary of publishing even those charges that turned out to be true. This phenomenon, now widely labeled "the chilling effect,"[38] was to the Court inconsistent with a First Amendment part of whose goal was to encourage exposing and thus checking the abuses of those in power.[39] Although requiring intentional falsity to sustain liability would undoubtedly increase the amount of published falsehood, this error, the Court implicitly concluded, was far less grave than the opposite error of inhibiting the publication of political truth. And even if some of what would be published under the new rule turned out to be vituperative and uncivil, this was only to be expected, for the common law ap-

[35] 376 U.S. 264 (1964). For a full description of the factual background, see Anthony Lewis, *Make No Law: The Sullivan Case and the First Amendment* (New York: Vintage Books, 1991).

[36] See *Beauharnais v. Illinois*, 343 U.S. 250 (1952), holding that defamation remedies were not constrained by the First Amendment.

[37] The Supreme Court in *Sullivan* used the term "actual malice," but the Court's understanding of "actual malice" is one that focuses on publication with knowledge of falsity. "Malice" in the common law sense of hostility or ill will has nothing to do with the idea, and in retrospect it is clear that the word has fostered little but confusion. The Supreme Court also said in *Sullivan* that the actual malice standard could be satisfied by publication with "reckless disregard" for the truth but several years later emphasized that reckless disregard for the truth could be sufficient to sustain liability only if it were shown that the publisher published in the face of "actual suspicion" of possible falsity. *St. Amant v. Thompson*, 390 U.S. 727 (1968).

[38] See Frederick Schauer, "Fear, Risk, and the First Amendment: Unraveling the 'Chilling Effect,'" *Boston University Law Review* 58 (1978): 685–723.

[39] See Vincent Blasi, "The Checking Value in First Amendment Theory," *American Bar Foundation Research Journal* (1977): 521–97.

proach was inconsistent with a First Amendment centered on the importance of "uninhibited," "robust," and "wide-open" public debate.

In the ensuing years, the Supreme Court has refused to back away from
the *Sullivan* approach and has indeed substantially extended it. A few
years after *Sullivan* it applied its basic holding to candidates for public
office as well as to office holders,[40] and, more surprisingly and more significantly, to public figures as well as to public officials,[41] even to those
public figures—pop stars, television chefs, and professional athletes, for
example—who have little to no involvement in or effect on public policy
or political debates.[42] The Court then required that even private individuals prove negligence in order to prevail,[43] and thus by 1975 the constitutionalization of American defamation law was complete. Although well-
known libel actions brought in the 1980s by Ariel Sharon against *Time*
magazine and General William Westmoreland against CBS Television
raised American press concerns about the revitalization of American libel
law, both cases were unsuccessful in light of the *Sullivan* rule, and there
have not since been any serious efforts by major public officials or public
figures to employ the law of libel, or any major moves to change the
American approach. For all practical purposes the availability in the
United States of defamation remedies for public officials and public figures, even in cases of provable falsity, has come to an end.

Largely through the efforts of journalists, newspapers, and their lawyers, there has been an active effort to persuade other countries to adopt
the American approach, and to conclude that the harm of unpublished
truth about public officials and public figures is far greater than the harm
of unsanctioned falsity. Yet although these efforts have been successful in
moving most common law countries slightly away from the strictest version of the common law model, and in securing some modifications of
analogous remedies even in civil law countries, the overwhelming reaction
of the rest of the world to the American approach has been negative.[44]
In Australia,[45] New Zealand,[46] Canada,[47] the United Kingdom,[48] and a

---

[40] *Monitor Patriot Co. v. Roy*, 401 U.S. 265 (1971).

[41] *Curtis Publishing Co. v. Butts* and *Associated Press v. Walker*, 388 U.S. 130 (1967).

[42] See Frederick Schauer, "Public Figures," *William and Mary Law Review* 25 (1984):
905–35.

[43] *Gertz v. Robert Welch, Inc.*, 418 U.S. 323 (1974).

[44] See Ian D. Loveland, *Political Libels: A Comparative Study* (Oxford: Hart Publishing, 2000).

[45] *Lange v. Australian Broadcasting Corporation*, (1997) 189 C.L.R. 520 (H.C.); *Theo-
phanous v. Herald & Weekly Times, Ltd.*, (1994) 182 C.L.R. 104 (H.C.). For a full discussion, see Michael Chesterman, *Freedom of Speech in Australian Law* (Aldershot, UK Ash-
gate Publishing, 2000), 79–192.

[46] *Lange v. Atkinson* [1998] 3 NZLR 424 (Ct. App.).

[47] *Hill v. Church of Scientology of Toronto*, [1995] 2 S.C.R. 1130.

[48] *Reynolds v. Times Newspapers Limited*, 4 All E.R. 609 (1999)(H.L.).

number of other countries, the unalloyed American approach has been rejected.[49] Believing that the American model places far too much weight on the freedom of the press side of the balance, and far too little on the reputational side, the rest of even the developed democratic world has been satisfied to leave largely in place defamation remedies and standards that the United States continues to find unacceptable under the First Amendment. And the United States, in turn—and as exemplified by the several cases in which American courts have refused to enforce non-American libel judgments on the grounds of incompatibility with fundamental American free press principles[50]—has been equally satisfied to hew to the *Sullivan* line, refusing to countenance a harmonization with non-American approaches that much of the American free speech and free press culture perceives to be substantially incompatible with a serious commitment to robust public debate.

Although hate speech and defamation provide the most vivid and well-discussed examples, American exceptionalism in fact exists throughout the domain of freedom of expression. In disputes over the persistent and inevitable conflict between freedom of the press to report on criminal prosecutions and the right of the accused to a fair trial uninfluenced by potentially inflammatory pretrial and midtrial publicity, the United States favors the former over the latter to a degree unmatched in the world.[51] In much of the rest of the world, press restrictions, often under the label of sanctions for "contempt," are acceptable as means to preserve the sanctity of the trial process, but in the United States considerable interference with that sanctity is tolerated so that trials, no less than other governmental processes, are open for all that is best and worst about press coverage and public scrutiny. In the same vein, disputes between the interest in privacy of victims of crimes and the interest of the press in reporting on criminal proceedings are typically resolved in favor of the press and against the victim's privacy.[52]

[49] See Ian D. Loveland, ed., *Importing the First Amendment* (Oxford: Hart Publishing, 1998).

[50] *Telnikoff v. Matesuvitch*, 702 A.2d 230 (Md. 1997); *Bachchan v. India Abroad Publications, Inc.*, 585 N.Y.S.2d 661 (Sup. Ct. 1992). Addressing the same issue but remaining inconclusive at this stage of the litigation is *Dow Jones & Co. v. Harrods, Ltd.*, 237 F. Supp. 2d 394 (S.D.N.Y. 2002). On the general issue of American nonenforcement of such foreign judgments, see Mark D. Rosen, "Should Un-American Foreign Judgments Be Enforced?" *Minnesota Law Review* 88 (2004): 783–824.

[51] *Smith v. Daily Mail Pub. Co.*, 443 U.S. 97 (1979); *Nebraska Press Ass'n v. Stuart*, 427 U.S. 539 (1976); *Bridges v. California*, 314 U.S. 252 (1941).

[52] *Florida Star v. B.J.F.*, 491 U.S. 524 (1989); *Cox Broadcasting Corp. v. Cohn*, 420 U.S. 469 (1975).

American freedom of expression exceptionalism extends to still other topics. In protecting the publication of even unlawfully obtained information, First Amendment doctrine goes further than even the most press-protective of liberal democracies.[53] And First Amendment protection of commercial advertising constrains restrictions on tobacco and alcohol advertising that are routine in most developed countries.[54] As a result, for example, American First Amendment objections led both to a significant qualification in the 2003 WHO Framework Convention on Tobacco Control, and also to substantial doubts as to whether even the modified convention, which has been signed by the president, will be ratified by the Senate or upheld by the courts.

In all of these areas, and numerous others as well, interests that are taken to represent legitimate counterweights to freedom of expression in other liberal democracies are understood in the United States to be decidedly subservient to the paramount constitutional concerns with freedom of speech and freedom of the press. Where in the rest of the world freedom of expression appears to be understood as an important value to be considered along with other important values of fairness, equality, dignity, health, privacy, safety, and respect, among others, in the United States the freedom of expression occupies pride of place, prevailing with remarkable consistency in its conflicts with even the most profound of other values and the most important of other interests.

From Description to Explanation

The facts are clear, but they call for explanation. Why does the United States remain such a freedom of expression outlier? In particular areas of free expression law, it might be possible to explain national differences on the basis of historical aspects of certain issues, as for example with the view that the Nazi experience explains German hate speech law (especially with respect to unlawful political parties) in ways that are not replicated in other

---

[53] *Bartnicki v. Vopper*, 121 S. Ct. 1753 (2001); *Landmark Communications, Inc. v. Virginia*, 435 U.S. 829 (1978); *New York Times v. United States* (Pentagon Papers Case), 403 U.S. 713 (1971).

[54] See *44 Liquormart, Inc. v. Rhode Island*, 517 U.S. 484 (1996); *Rubin v. Coors Brewing Co.*, 514 U.S. 476 (1995); Colin Munro, "The Value of Commercial Speech," *Cambridge Law Journal* 62 (2003): 134–59; G. Quinn, "Extending the Coverage of Freedom of Expression to Commercial Speech: A Comparative Perspective," in *Human Rights: A Comparative Perspective*, ed. L. Heffernan (Dublin: Trinity College Press, 1994); Kathleen M. Sullivan, "Cheap Spirits, Cheap Cigarettes, and Free Speech: The Implications of 44 Liquormart," *Supreme Court Review* (1996): 123–61.

countries. Similarly, the American reluctance to ban political parties[55] or accept government assertions about threats to national security[56] might be explained as a reaction to American anti-Communist and antisocialist excesses during the Red Scare of 1919 and the McCarthy era of the late 1940s and early 1950s. But when we look not at particular topics but at the full range of freedom of expression issues, it is apparent that it is not just hate speech, and not just defamation, and not just anything else in which the United States stands alone. Rather, it is throughout virtually the entire range of freedom of speech and freedom of the press topics that the United States is an outlier, and thus if we are seeking to explain this broad-scale divergence, the historical and contextual dimensions of particular doctrines are unlikely to provide much assistance.

Thirty years ago it might have been plausible to explain the broad-scale disparity merely as a matter of differential experience, for thirty years ago the United States had a well-developed body of cases and doctrine on freedom of speech and the press, while almost all other nations, even almost all other open democracies, were just beginning to explore the issue. Now, however, such an explanation is no longer plausible. The same issues that arise before the American courts have been presented to numerous national courts and supranational tribunals. Moreover, given the nature of litigation incentives, it frequently happens that one party in a case involving freedom of expression issues will have an interest in urging the American approach. And with considerable interest in most developed countries (other than the United States)[57] in drawing on comparative approaches in making constitutional decisions, the American approach will not only often be promoted by one of the parties, but the virtues of the American model will also be argued to a court or other decision-making body likely to be open-minded about foreign law. Yet in the face of all of this, American doctrines and understandings about freedom of expression have typically been rejected as extreme, imbalanced, and hardly worthy of emulation. The American version of freedom of expression has undoubtedly been influential in the development of the law worldwide, but the limits of that influence are far more noteworthy than its effects. At the beginning of the twenty-first century, the exceptionalism of the First Amendment remains even more entrenched, and in need of explanation. And in the search for that explanation, a series of hypotheses present themselves for further and more systematic testing.

---

[55] *Healy v. James*, 408 U.S. 169 (1972); *Keyishian v. Board of Regents*, 385 U.S. 589 (1967); *Noto v. United States*, 367 U.S. 290 (1961).

[56] See, for example, *New York Times v. United States*, 403 U.S. 713 (1971), the case of the Pentagon Papers.

[57] This is a large topic in its own right and is well developed by Professor Michelman in this volume.

An Imbalanced Text

A noteworthy feature of the First Amendment is the seeming absoluteness of the text and the broad scope within which that absoluteness appears to apply. Although "Congress [and now the states][58] shall make no law . . . abridging the freedom of speech, or of the press" is well understood not to extend to every use of language,[59] to be subject to override in cases of compelling interest,[60] and to be surrounded by numerous caveats, qualifications, exceptions, tests, doctrines, principles, and maxims, it is potentially important that the language itself remains so stark. Unlike its counterpart provisions in the European Convention on Human Rights, in the Canadian Charter of Rights and Freedoms, and in the Constitution of South Africa, for example, the First Amendment itself makes no provision for overrides, whether "necessary in a democratic society" or otherwise. And in contrast again to Article 10 of the European Convention on Human Rights, for example, which explicitly lists a number of circumstances in which freedom of expression might permissibly be curtailed, the First Amendment lists none. Moreover, with the significant exceptions of the equality protected by the Fourteenth Amendment and the right of the accused to a fair trial protected by the Sixth Amendment, most of the interests that are typically taken as justifying constraints on freedom of expression worldwide do not in the United States Constitution, unlike in many of its counterparts internationally, have explicit constitutional recognition. There may be a moral or political right to reputation, for example, but in the Constitution of the United States, unlike in the German Basic Law, it is not a right that the constitutional text explicitly recognizes. So too with human dignity, explicitly mentioned in many constitutions and even enshrined as preeminent against other rights in Article 1 of the German Basic Law. And the type of privacy interests that again often justify restrictions on freedom of expression are recognized in the United States by statute and by common law, but not in the Constitution. It would be an overstatement to say, as Supreme Court Justices Hugo Black and William O. Douglas were fond of saying, that all of the "balancing" was done prior to the decision as to what would be included in the

---

[58] *Gitlow v. New York*, 268 U.S. 652 (1925).

[59] *Frohwerk v. United States*, 249 U.S. 204 (1919); Kent Greenawalt, *Speech, Crime, and the Uses of Language* (New York: Oxford University Press, 1989); Frederick Schauer, "The Boundaries of the First Amendment," *Harvard Law Review* 117 (2004): 1765–1809.

[60] *New York v. Ferber*, 458 U.S. 747 (1982). The "compelling interest" concept takes numerous forms, of which the "clear and present danger" idea, *Schenck v. United States*, 249 U.S. 47 (1919), is the most famous, but through all of the forms the basic principle is that within the scope of the First Amendment it takes an extremely strong governmental interest to permit restriction.

Constitution and what would be omitted,[61] and it would be an overstatement to take the First Amendment to be as textually absolute as its most enthusiastic celebrants believe, but it is certainly plausible to suppose that the one-sided nature of the First Amendment's text has played at least some role in the development of a constitutional environment in which the rights to freedom of speech and freedom of the press are taken as especially important.

A Preference for Liberty

Many of the controversies about freedom of speech present conflicts between liberty and equality, with the issues regarding hate speech and many forms of pornography among the most noteworthy. Moreover, these controversies between liberty and equality, as well as other conflicts between liberty and what might broadly be called "civility," also highlight a difference between, loosely and roughly, an individualist or libertarian view of the world, and, again loosely and roughly, a collective or communitarian view of the world. And to the extent that such contrasts reflect real differences, it would not be implausible to understand American free speech exceptionalism as a manifestation of the strong libertarian and individualistic aspects of American society itself.[62] Seen from this vantage point, the United States stands apart from much of the rest of the democratic developed world, not just with respect to freedom of expression, but also, for example, with respect to its lower highest marginal tax rate, its willingness to entrust to individual decision and private enterprise matters of health care and retirement income that in more collective societies are taken as community and not individual responsibilities, its protection of private property against regulations common in the developed world, and its lack for more than thirty years of any form of national service. On a large number of other issues in which the preferences of individuals may be in tension with the needs of the collective, the United States, increasingly alone, stands as a symbol for a certain kind of preference for liberty even when it conflicts with values of equality and even when it conflicts with important community values. To some this preference stems from the almost complete absence in the United States of socialist or social democratic traditions, and to others the absence of these traditions themselves is a symptom of a deeper libertarian strain in the American political

[61] See Laurent Frantz, "The First Amendment in the Balance," *Yale Law Journal* 71 (1962): 1424–63.

[62] See Roy Leeper, "*Keegstra* and *R.A.V.*: A Comparative Analysis of the Canadian and U.S. Approaches to Hate Speech Legislation," *Communication Law and Policy* 5 (2000): 295–322.

and cultural tradition. But whether the preference for liberty is a cause or an effect, it is nonetheless real, and the libertarian cast of American political and social thought may help in explaining why freedom of expression is thought preeminent in that host of instances in which limitations on expression might reasonably be thought to advance values of community, values of equality, and values of civility.

A Culture of Distrust

Relatedly, it is well documented that for many years the degree of citizen distrust of government in the United States has been greater than that in a vast number of other developed and developing nations, including some number of countries whose citizens have considerably more reason to distrust their governments than Americans have to distrust their own.[63] Again, it is unclear whether this culture of distrust contributes to American libertarianism, or whether American libertarianism is itself the deeper cause, with distrust of government being merely one of the consequences. Yet regardless of the causes of that distrust, it seems apparent that American distrust of government is a contributing factor to a strongly libertarian approach to constitutional rights. The Constitution of the United States is a strongly negative constitution, and viewing a constitution as the vehicle for ensuring social rights, community rights, or positive citizen entitlements of any kind is, for better or for worse, highly disfavored. Moreover, although it is of course the case that drawing distinctions is an inevitable part of the legislative, regulatory, and judicial enterprises, there remains a pervasive American suspicion of official valuation of ideas and enterprises. And while the libertarian culture that such attitudes of distrust engender is hardly restricted to freedom of communication, this skepticism about the ability of any governmental institution reliably to distinguish the good from the bad, the true from the false, and the sound from the unsound finds its most comfortable home in the First Amendment. It is for neither the government nor the courts, for example, to decide that Nazi ideas are dangerous or that the views of the Ku Klux Klan are as wrong as they are pernicious. So when the Supreme Court proclaimed in a prominent defamation case that "under the First Amendment there is no such thing as a false idea,"[64] it reflected the way in which

---

[63] See Ronald Inglehart, *Modernization and Postmodernization* (Princeton: Princeton University Press, 1997); Pippa Norris, ed., *Critical Citizens: Global Support for Democratic Governance* (Oxford: Oxford University Press, 1999); Joseph S. Nye, Jr., Philip D. Zelikow, and David C. King, *Why People Don't Trust Government* (Cambridge: Harvard University Press, 1997).

[64] *Gertz v. Robert Welch, Inc.*, 418 U.S. 323 (1974).

a radically nonjudgmental First Amendment is the natural repository for a culture in which libertarianism, laissez-faire, and distrust of government remain the hallmarks of a distinctive American ideology.

The Political Culture of the First Amendment

It is a familiar American political adage that one "should never argue with the fellow who buys ink by the barrel." And however true it is that the power of the press should not be taken lightly, this truth is especially vivid with respect to the power of the press when its own prerogatives are concerned. Politicians, bureaucrats, and even judges (who despite their life tenure in the federal system and in some states are not immune from the pressures of promotion and reputation)[65] who cross the press about press rights are especially likely to be excoriated publicly,[66] and the interests of the press in press freedom particularly and freedom of communication generally are different in kind from the interests of the press in any other subject. Moreover, the self-interest of the institutional press in communicative freedoms intersects with the agendas of an array of influential interest groups—the American Civil Liberties Union, People for the American Way, the American Booksellers Association, the American Library Association, PEN, and an assemblage of less institutionally organized representatives of the arts, higher education, and various other individuals and collectivities together constituting a powerful pressure group for the preservation of the maximum amount of freedom of communication.

Yet although such interests together might explain part of why communicative freedoms have become more important than other individual rights (the obvious comparison is with the rights of those accused of crimes, most of whom have little political power and most of whom are guilty of the crimes with which they are charged), it is not clear why the United States should be different from other countries in this regard. After all, the institutional press outside the United States presumably has as much interest in its own freedoms as does the press in the United States. Yet despite this, there appears to be a divergence between the United States and other countries in terms of press interest in press freedom issues, and part of the explanation for the difference might be that in the United States a tradition of private rather than state broadcasting gives

---

[65] I explore this topic at length in Frederick Schauer, "Incentives, Reputation, and the Inglorious Determinants of Judicial Behavior," *University of Cincinnati Law Review* 68 (2000),: 615–36. See also Richard A. Posner, "What Do Judges Maximize? (The Same Thing Everybody Else Does)," *Supreme Court Economic Review* 3 (1994): 1–24.

[66] An especially famous example is William Safire, "Free Speech v. Scalia," *New York Times*, April 29, 1985, A17.

private press interests a stronger and more pervasive voice than exists elsewhere.[67] Moreover, in the United States, unlike in many other countries, the interest in freedom of expression and the interest groups supporting it emerged prior to rather than simultaneously with much of the interest in equality, and prior to the strengthening of many of the most important equality-focused interest groups.[68] A particular manifestation of this history is the way in which an especially strong interest group presence with respect to freedom of expression issues arose in the 1950s, 1960s, and 1970s out of anti-McCarthyism, the civil rights movement, and the Vietnam antiwar movement,[69] social movements in which freedom of expression played a major role. As a result of this history, a history that explains almost all of the substance of American freedom of expression exceptionalism,[70] freedom of expression has long been treated in the United States as a central part of the political program of the political Left in ways that are not replicated in other countries. Reasons of historical provenance and consequent path-dependence thus contribute to an environment in the United States in which freedom of expression interests have a degree of political power and social influence not replicated in countries in which the emergence of freedom of expression interests has a different history.

Finally, the political importance of the First Amendment has been reinforced by a recent shift in, or possibly just an expansion of, the political valence of freedom of expression. On issues such as campaign finance reform, tobacco and other commercial advertising, the ability to exclude picketers from private business property, protests at abortion clinics, and so-called political correctness, among others, the proponents of the strong free speech position have been, in large part, political conserva-

[67] Relatedly, it may not be irrelevant that most of the wealthiest, oldest, and most prestigious universities in the United States are nongovernmental.

[68] Indeed, the most prominent interest groups with an equality focus—the National Association for the Advancement of Colored People, the National Organization for Women, the Human Rights Campaign, and the Anti-Defamation League, for example—tend to have a concern for a particular group, while most of the freedom of expression interest groups have a substantially broader focus.

[69] It is noteworthy that almost all of the law that makes the American approach to freedom of speech and freedom of the press exceptional emerged in a series of Supreme Court cases commencing with *New York Times v. Sullivan*, 376 U.S. 254 (1964) and culminating perhaps as early as *New York Times v. United States* (Pentagon Papers Case), 403 U.S. 713 (1971), and certainly no later than the commercial advertising breakthrough in *Virginia State Board of Pharmacy v. Virginia Citizens Consumer Council, Inc.*, 425 U.S. 748 (1976).

[70] Almost all of the judicial developments that make the United States unique in the world on freedom of expression issues owe their origins to Supreme Court cases starting in the mid-1960s and going through the mid-1970s, and almost all of those cases have something to do with either the civil rights movement, anti-McCarthyism, or protests against the war in Vietnam.

tives. The salience of these issues has produced a shift in the politics of the First Amendment, such that strong protection of freedom of speech and freedom of the press is now seen as an instrument of entrenched political and economic forces as much as it is seen as the instrument of those who would oppose them.[71] This has further reinforced the special political importance of the First Amendment in American political culture, and it has produced an environment in which the American free speech culture has a power and resonance not equaled by anticensorship forces—Article XIX and the Index on Censorship, for example—in other parts of the world.

The Substantive Consequences of Judicial Review

Each of the hypotheses set out in the previous section likely does some work in explaining American freedom of expression exceptionalism, but those hypotheses must be supplemented by another hypothesis that is partly substantive and partly methodological. And so we turn to the way in which a key to understanding freedom of expression lies in understanding that most contemporary democratic proposals for restricting freedom of expression are based on empirically plausible assessments that a particular restriction on communication will efficaciously serve a valuable social goal. Of course even the history of modern liberal democracies is replete with examples of ideas' being suppressed simply because people disagree with them, but it is a mistake to believe that this phenomenon explains the central principles of freedom of speech and freedom of the press. If we are to understand those principles, we must appreciate that freedom of expression protects the expression of information and ideas not because such expression is typically inconsequential or harmless, but despite the harm and the consequences that expression may produce. For reasons that would take us too far afield in this context, restrictions on freedom of expression are best understood not as always bad first-order policies, but as often good first-order policies with frequently good short-term consequences.

To observe that suppression is often good short-term policy does not mean that suppression is desirable in the long term or all things considered. Whether the second-order constraints be rule-consequentialist or anticonsequentialist ones, it is still the case that explaining the idea of

---

[71] See J. M. Balkin, "Some Realism about Pluralism: Legal Realist Approaches to the First Amendment," *Duke Law Journal* (1990): 375–414; Frederick Schauer, "The Political Incidence of the Free Speech Principle," *University of Colorado Law Review* 64 (1993): 935–56.

freedom of speech in any moderately strong way entails explaining the idea of important second-order constraints on well-meaning and often efficacious first-order policy preferences.

If this understanding of the "bite" of freedom of expression is sound, then it should come as no surprise to discover that freedom of communication was stronger, ceteris paribus, in those societies in which institutions existed to check even well-meaning and instrumentally efficacious policy choices. And although there are in theory a variety of such institutions, in practice the most common is strong judicial review coupled with considerable deference to judicial decisions by other political actors and institutions.[72] When free speech ideas, however sound they may be, are in the hands of institutions—legislatures, administrative officials, and the electorate, most obviously—whose primary portfolio is the reflection of first-order policy interests, the ability to subjugate those interests to second-order values will be smallest. So although a considerable degree of freedom of expression undoubtedly flourishes in Great Britain, New Zealand, Israel, Switzerland, the Netherlands, and other countries in which the protection of individual rights in general and freedom of expression in particular has historically been largely in the hands of a legislature or other politically accountable body, it should come as little surprise that the protection is likely to be stronger, controlling for all other variables, in those countries in which the traditions of judicial review and judicial supremacy are longer and stronger. Indeed, given that many strong free speech positions on issues such as defamation, child pornography, hate speech, and sedition are issues as to which popular support for the speaker is lacking and legislative support for the principle is fragile, the relationship between judicial review and the outer reaches of free speech protection is likely to be a close one. The American tradition of strong judicial review is thus not at all unrelated to American free speech exceptionalism, especially with respect to unpopular speakers and unpopular ideas. It is of course true that strong judicial review, although likely a necessary condition for free speech protection as strong as that in the United States, is hardly a sufficient condition. The modern traditions of judicial authority in Canada and South Africa, for example, have not produced an American-style approach to freedom of expression. But if we are nevertheless trying to explain the American approach to freedom of expression, the American approach to judicial authority likely plays at least a significant role.

[72] See Schauer, "Judicial Supremacy and the Modest Constitution." See also Larry Alexander and Frederick Schauer, "On Extrajudicial Constitutional Interpretation," *Harvard Law Review* 110 (1997): 1359–87.

The International Politics of Transnational Legal Influence

I have until now treated American exceptionalism as if it were an entirely American domestic phenomenon, as if the divergence between American and non-American approaches to freedom of expression were entirely a function of American domestic law and the American domestic social, political, cultural, economic, and ideological environment. But treating American exceptionalism in this way is misleading in two ways, and it will be worthwhile pausing to consider them.

First, American free speech exceptionalism is, at least in part, a function of a larger American exceptionalism in which American legal and constitutional doctrine remains somewhere between resistant and hostile to non-American models and guidance. Unlike the constitutionally enshrined obligation to consult foreign law that exists in South Africa, and unlike the less formal willingness to look abroad that is characteristic of an emerging multinational constitutional culture, American courts, American lawyers, and the American constitutional culture have been stubbornly anti-international, far too often treating foreign influence as a one-way process, in which Americans influenced others but were little influenced in return.[73] On numerous questions surrounding freedom of expression, therefore, there is good reason to believe that arguments for adopting non-American models about hate speech, defamation, or numerous other topics would be greeted with great skepticism not only because of the free expression–specific factors discussed above, but also because freedom of expression exceptionalism is, at least in part, a component of and influenced by a larger and more encompassing constitutional and cultural exceptionalism.

But it also takes two to diverge, and American freedom of expression exceptionalism is a function not only of American unwillingness to consult and at times even attempt to harmonize with non-American approaches, but also of an increasing non-American unwillingness to be guided and influenced by American models. Especially with respect to issues of freedom of expression, the United States has historically been highly influential, as even the briefest examination of non-American judicial opinions and legal literature will quickly show. Yet partly because of the rise of Europe, partly because of Iraq and related issues generating hostility to American ideas and models, and partly because of the very phenomenon of American exceptionalism that this volume addresses, the

---

[73] The openness of American constitutional law to non-American ideas, models, and influences has recently become a subject of increasing judicial and nonjudicial debate, as exemplified in, for example, the various opinions in *Lawrence v. Texas*, 539 U.S. 558 (2003).

willingness outside of the United States to look to American free speech
ideas has appeared recently to decline. If American ideas about freedom
of expression were as internationally influential now as they were fifty or
even twenty years ago, the very phenomenon of American free speech
exceptionalism would be much less, not because of American harmonization with non-American approaches, but rather just the opposite.

It can be well documented that patterns of cross-national constitutional
and legal influence are often based on nonoptimizing political, cultural,
and economic forces.[74] Countries try to harmonize their legal traditions
with those of countries whose influence and favor they desire, so it should
come as no surprise, for example, that the Baltic countries adopted legal
models far more with an eye to joining the European Union than from
any other motive. And countries often have complex relationships with
the countries that formerly colonized and occupied them, with multinational organizations such as the World Bank and the International Monetary Fund, with countries whose trade they wish to attract, and with countries whose associations they find uncomfortable. Sometimes these
relationships are positive, as with the relationships between many Commonwealth countries and the United Kingdom, and sometimes they are
negative, as with the relationship between Ireland and Great Britain and
between Vietnam and France, but it would be hard to ignore the way in
which patterns of legal influence follow the complex and often unexplain-
able patterns of international influence generally.

If all of this has more than a grain of truth, then understanding the
spread and nonspread of American free speech ideas cannot be separated
from the complex international politics of American influence. When
American ideas are seen as valuable just because they are American, the
spread of those ideas is likely to be greatest, even controlling for the intrin-
sic merit of the ideas themselves. And when American ideas are seen as
tainted just because they are American, hardly an unusual phenomenon
these days, the opposite effect is likely to occur. If we are to explain the
contemporary reception or nonreception of temporally prior American
free speech and free press ideas, we need to understand the numerous
political, social, economic, cultural, and historical forces that would lead
countries or communities to look to or to look away from the United
States in a larger sense. Indeed, although much of the flavor of discussions
of American exceptionalism, including the discussions in this volume, at-
tributes American exceptionalism to various forms of American recalci-
trance and a range of other American attitudes, we ought not to ignore

---

[74] See Frederick Schauer, "The Politics and Incentives of Legal Transplantation," in *Governance in a Globalizing World*, ed. Joseph S. Nye, Jr., and John Donahue (Washington,
DC: Brookings, 2000), 253–68.

the political and cultural dynamics on the other side of the divide. In seeking to explain American exceptionalism, we need to look not only at why the United States often seems to resist the virtues of international cooperation and harmonization, but also at why, on occasion, even arguably sound American views are resisted just because they are American. International cooperation and harmonization are inextricably linked with larger questions of foreign policy and cross-national influence, and American free speech exceptionalism is likely, at least in part, a function both of American resistance to non-American ideas and of non-American resistance to American ones, resistances that themselves are often caused by concerns far larger and more pervasive than free speech issues themselves.

The Open Question of Methodological Exceptionalism

As I noted earlier in this essay, nations vary not only in the nature and extent of their substantive commitments to various rights, but also in their methodological approach to deciding rights controversies. Following this distinction, it is widely believed that the United States diverges from prevailing international democratic practice not only in the substance of its understandings about freedom of expression, but also in the manner in which it adjudicates freedom of expression claims, a divergence in approach that is thought to make the United States just as methodologically exceptional as it is substantively exceptional.[75] More particularly, it is often said that American free speech adjudication is methodologically distinctive in employing a formal and sharply demarcated two-step process, the first step being a category-based decision about whether some act is or is not encompassed by the First Amendment. Then, if the act is one that is within the First Amendment's purview, the question turns to which of numerous First Amendment rules should be applied. By contrast, it is said,[76] in other constitutional democracies virtually all acts of expression are understood as being encompassed by the scope of the right,[77] and the

---

[75] See, for example, Greenawalt, *Fighting Words*, chap. 2; Paul Horwitz, "Law's Expression: The Promise and Perils of Judicial Opinion Writing in Canadian Constitutional Law," *Osgoode Hall Law Journal* 38 (2000): 101–27; Vicki C. Jackson, "Ambivalent Resistance and Comparative Constitutionalism: Opening Up the Conversation on 'Proportionality,' Rights and Federalism," *University of Pennsylvania Journal of Constitutional Law* 1 (1999): 583–612.

[76] See Adrienne Stone, "The Limits of Constitutional Text and Structure: Standards of Review and Freedom of Political Communication," *Melbourne University Law Review* 23 (1999): 668–97; Lorraine C. Weinrib, "The Supreme Court of Canada and Section One of the Charter," *Supreme Court Law Review* 10 (1988): 469–502.

[77] The view is expressed crisply by the Supreme Court of Canada in *Irwin Toy Ltd. v. Quebec* [1989] 1 S.C.R. 927, at 969.

serious inquiry is devoted to the less formal and more open-ended question of whether a restriction is reasonable, necessary in a democratic society, or, most commonly, proportional in light of the importance of the restriction and the extent of the free expression interest that is restricted.[78] By maintaining a rigid and slightly disingenuous approach to freedom of expression issues, the claim goes, the United States is, and not to its credit, as exceptional about freedom of expression methodology as it is about freedom of expression substance.

The contrast between the two adjudicatory styles does reflect a genuine difference. There *is* a distinction worth marking between a right that is defined narrowly and has enormous stringency within its narrow scope, on the one hand, and a right defined more broadly but with less stringency and more flexibility within that broad scope, on the other.[79] In this respect, it is indeed possible that current differences between the American categorial style and the non-American proportionality style embodied by Canadian,[80] South African, and European decision making reflect genuine differences in judicial style, genuine differences in an understanding of the way in which rights operate, genuine differences about the role of the judiciary, and genuine differences in understandings of the ideas of freedom of expression. Yet although such deeper and thus more permanent differences are possible, it may be too soon to tell whether these differences will be enduring, or instead whether what now appear to be real differences reflect little more than different stages in the development of freedom of expression decision-making structures.

In those legal cultures in which adjudication of freedom of communication ideas is comparatively new, and this would include important dimensions of all of the non-American regimes at issue here, there may not be very much of an accepted understanding of which subjects are encompassed by the right and which are not. So although Canada, for example, may nominally purport to be less concerned (or obsessed, say the critics) than the United States with whether an act of "expression" or "speech" is inside or outside the protection of the Charter[81] or the Constitution, the willingness to find virtually all freedom of expression claims plausible at the first stage, which has been the Canadian practice, may be contingent

---

[78] See, for example, D. J. Harris, M. O'Boyle, and C. Warbrick, *Law of the European Convention on Human Rights* (London: Butterworths, 1995), 396.

[79] For my reflections on these issues, see Frederick Schauer, "Codifying the First Amendment: *New York v. Ferber*," *Supreme Court Review* (1982): 285–314; Frederick Schauer, "Categories and the First Amendment: A Play in Three Acts," *Vanderbilt Law Review* 34 (1981): 265–301; Frederick Schauer, "Can Rights Be Abused?" *Philosophical Quarterly* 29 (1981): 225–31.

[80] See *R. v. Oakes* [1986] 1 S.C.R. 103.

[81] See *Ford v. A.G. Quebec*, [1988] 2 S.C.R. 712, 54 D.L.R. (4th) 577.

upon less of an opportunity to confront cases in which the claim of right is frivolous. In Canada, unlike in the United States, there have not been visible instances of claims that the regulation of securities sales, the regulation of ordinary commercial fraud, and the regulation of price fixing and other unfair trade practices, for example, present freedom of expression issues, although all of these and countless other examples involve expression (or speech, or communication, if you will). As more such cases arise, it may well turn out that what is now an unspoken demarcation in Canada between acts covered and acts not covered by Article 2 (and much the same structure exists in South Africa, Germany, and an increasing number of other jurisdictions) will need to be made more explicit. Will the Supreme Court of Canada spend as much time and care, and exercise as much judicial scrutiny, over such arguably inconsequential free speech as the above-mentioned claims as it does in the case of more serious ones involving, for example, hate speech, defamation, and pornography? If not, and that seems a highly plausible prediction, then it may well be that what looks at the moment like a large difference in style will grow smaller as courts outside the United States find it increasingly necessary to demarcate the claims that will be rejected summarily from the claims that require serious judicial scrutiny. Thus one might speculate that the future will see non-American jurisdictions needing to find some way of sorting at the first step of the analysis, and sorting in light of underlying views about what freedom of expression is all about, which is what American courts have been doing for years under the rubric of defining the scope of the "freedom of speech" that neither the federal government nor the states are permitted to abridge.

In addition to the way in which an open-ended proportionality inquiry may turn out to be unsuited, at least without a fair amount of rule-based supplementation, for a larger number of questionable freedom of expression claims, it may also be ill-suited to simply a larger volume of freedom of expression cases in general. There are of course differences among countries in the degree of discretion that courts will have in adjudicating freedom of expression issues, but time and again, regardless of the subject, we have seen some convergence of rule-based and non-rule-based approaches to legal questions.[82] Just as rule-based approaches often see the edges of the rules rounded off when difficult cases are presented, so too do more open-ended and discretionary approaches (which is what the "proportionality" inquiry amounts to) evolve, for reasons of limits on the human or judicial capacity to deal simultaneously with too many unorganized options, into approaches more reliant on rules. Unless we can con-

[82] Frederick Schauer, "The Convergence of Rules and Standards," *New Zealand Law Review* (2003): 303–28.

trol for case quantity, case variety, and the length of the experience with dealing with these questions—and at the moment we cannot come close to doing that—it may be impossible to tell whether there is genuine methodological exceptionalism in the American approach to freedom of expression, or whether instead the current differences simply show the effect of the difference between a tradition of free speech adjudication that goes back almost a century, and traditions that are largely less than two decades old and have yet to develop the encrustations of doctrines, rules, caveats, qualifications, maxims, principles, exceptions, and presumptions that any mature set of legal or constitutional rights will over time develop. In this respect, the contemporary differences between American and non-American methodological approaches are worth noting, and worth watching over time, but it may still be far too soon to reject with any confidence the hypothesis that what we are seeing is nothing deeper than differences reflecting different stages in the development of legal doctrine, and thus different stages in the development of the legal and constitutional right to freedom of communication.

Conclusion

These last questions of methodological exceptionalism are important, but it is substantive exceptionalism that presents the largest and most difficult issues. And in terms of substantive exceptionalism, it is plain that American approaches to freedom of expression diverge dramatically from those accepted in most of the remainder of the open and democratic world. Many commentators in the United States and in the rest of the world will be (and are) all too willing to offer their opinions on whether American exceptionalism is for good or for ill, and whether American substantive approaches to subjects like defamation, hate speech, and commercial advertising of dangerous products are better or worse than those found elsewhere. In this essay, however, I deliberately avoid such evaluation. In the spirit of genuine comparativism, I seek to identify and to try to begin to explain differences, leaving normative evaluation of those differences to other people or other times.

Chapter 3

Capital Punishment and American Exceptionalism

CAROL S. STEIKER

IN 1931, THE YEAR before his appointment to the U.S. Supreme Court, Benjamin Cardozo predicted that "perhaps the whole business of the retention of the death penalty will seem to the next generation, as it seems to many even now, an anachronism too discordant to be suffered, mocking with grim reproach all our clamorous professions of the sanctity of life."[1] The operative word here has turned out to be "perhaps," given that here we are in the United States almost three-quarters of a century later with capital punishment still a robust institution. But, ironically, Cardozo's prediction proved more or less true for the rest of the Western industrialized world. Soon after World War II and the spate of executions of wartime collaborators that ensued, the use of the death penalty began to decline in Western Europe, and capital punishment for ordinary crimes has at this point been abolished, either de jure or de facto, in every single Western industrialized nation except the United States.

At the same time, the countries that most vigorously employ the death penalty are generally ones that the United States has the least in common with politically, economically, or socially, and ones that the United States is wont to define itself against, as they are among the least democratic and the worst human rights abusers in the world. In recent years, the top four employers of capital punishment were China, Iran, Saudi Arabia—and the United States.[2] Moreover, in the past twelve years, only seven countries in the world are known to have executed prisoners who were

I am grateful to participants in the University of Oregon's conference "The Law and Politics of the Death Penalty: Abolition, Moratorium, or Reform?" to participants in workshops at Harvard Law School, the University of Texas School of Law, and Suffolk University Law School, to discussants from among the Harvard Neiman Fellows of 2000–2001, to participants in Michael Ignatieff's seminar on American exceptionalism at the John F. Kennedy School of Government at Harvard University in the fall of 2002, and to Jordan Steiker for helpful comments. A version of this essay was first published in the *Oregon Law Review* at 81 Or. L. Rev. 97 (2002).

[1] Benjamin N. Cardozo, *Law and Literature* 93–94 (1931).

[2] Amnesty Int'l, *Death Penalty around the World, Facts and Figures on the Death Penalty* (Sept. 2002), at http://www.amnesty-usa.org/abolish/world.html.

under the age of eighteen at the time of their crimes: the Democratic Republic of Congo, Iran, Nigeria, Pakistan, Saudi Arabia, Yemen—and the United States.[3] Stephen Bright, capital defense lawyer and abolitionist activist, mordantly quips, "If people were asked thirty years ago which one of the following three countries—Russia, South Africa, and the United States—would be most likely to have the death penalty at the turn of the century, few people would have answered the United States."[4] Yet it is true that even South Africa and Russia (and many other states of the former Soviet Union) have abandoned the death penalty, while the United States has retained it. And we have not retained it merely formally or even modestly. At the very same time that the pace of abolition quickened in Europe, the pace of executions quickened here in the United States. The rate of executions has risen precipitously since the Supreme Court reinstated the death penalty in 1976 in *Gregg v. Georgia* and its quartet of accompanying cases,[5] and we executed more people in each of the years 1997–2003 than in any other year since 1955.[6]

What accounts for this gross discrepancy in the use of capital punishment between the United States and the rest of the countries that we consider to be our "peers" in so many other respects? The answer to this question must be found primarily in the events of the last three decades or so, for it is only during this time period that America's use of capital punishment has diverged widely from that of Western Europe. Indeed, in the nineteenth century, to the extent that American criminal justice policy diverged from that of Europe, it was in the other direction. In his famous observations in *Democracy in America*, published in 1840, Alexis de Tocqueville commented on the "mildness" of criminal justice administration in America, noting that "whereas the English seem to want to preserve carefully the bloody traces of the Middle Ages in their penal legislation, the Americans have almost made the death penalty disappear from their codes."[7] Tocqueville was not alone; historian Stuart Banner writes that mid-nineteenth-century movements to abolish the death penalty in

---

[3] *Id.*

[4] Stephen B. Bright, *Will the Death Penalty Remain Alive in the Twenty-First Century? International Norms, Discrimination, Arbitrariness, and the Risk of Executing the Innocent*, 2001 Wis. L. Rev. 1, 2.

[5] *See Gregg v. Georgia*, 428 U.S. 153 (1976); *Roberts v. Louisiana*, 428 U.S. 325 (1976); *Woodson v. North Carolina*, 428 U.S. 280 (1976); *Jurek v. Texas*, 428 U.S. 262 (1976); *Proffitt v. Florida*, 428 U.S. 242 (1976).

[6] *See The Death Penalty in America: Current Controversies* 11 tbl.1–3 (Hugo Adam Bedau ed., 1997) (executions from 1950 to 1995); Amnesty Int'l, *The Death Penalty in the U.S., U.S. Executions by Year since 1976* (last modified December 17, 2003), at http://www.amnesty-usa.org/abolish/execsince76/html.

[7] Alexis de Tocqueville, *Democracy in America* 538 (Harvey C. Mansfield & Delba Winthrop eds. & trans., Univ. of Chicago Press 2000) (1840).

the United States positively "astonished" other European visitors to America.[8] These abolitionist movements did not turn out to be permanently successful except in a small minority of states, primarily in the Midwest and Northeast. Hence the United States as a nation did not end up in the abolitionist vanguard, like the Scandinavian countries that led Europe in abolishing capital punishment for ordinary crimes in the first few decades of the twentieth century. But neither did the United States diverge in the other direction from the rest of Western Europe until the 1970s. As recently as the mid-1960s, the status of capital punishment in America would not have been a very promising exemplar of "American exceptionalism." At that time, the United States looked like most of the rest of Europe (and Canada, and most of Australia) with regard to the use of capital punishment: while most states and the federal government had the death penalty on the books, it was rarely used; during the 1960s, the average number of executions nationwide dropped to fewer than a handful each year.[9]

Yet in the decades that followed the 1960s, all of the other Western democracies abandoned the death penalty for ordinary crimes either de jure or de facto, and many countries that had already abandoned it for ordinary crimes abandoned it for all crimes, including terrorism, treason, and military offenses. For example, England provisionally abolished the death penalty for murder in 1965 and then made the abolition permanent in 1969;[10] Canada abolished it for murder in 1976; Spain in 1978; Luxembourg 1979; France in 1981; Australia in 1984; Ireland in 1990; and Greece in 1993.[11] In addition, many European countries that had already abolished the death penalty for murder before the 1960s moved to abolish it for all crimes in the 1970s, 1980s, and 1990s: Sweden and Finland in 1972; Portugal in 1976; Denmark in 1978; Norway in 1979; the Netherlands in 1982; Switzerland in 1992; and Italy in 1994.[12]

This pattern—of European abolition contrasted with American enthusiasm for the death penalty—is widely remarked, especially by abolitionists, both here and abroad, who seek to shame the United States by the dual strategy of highlighting the unsavory character of the rest of the "death penalty club" while at the same time noting that Europe (and Canada, Australia, New Zealand, Mexico, and many other countries)

---

[8] Stuart Banner, *The Death Penalty: An American History* 113 (2002).

[9] *See The Death Penalty in America: Current Controversies, supra* note 6, at 11 tbl.1–3.

[10] *See Murder (Abolition of Death Penalty) Act*, 1965, c. 71 (Eng.) (This act was made permanent by virtue of affirmative resolutions of both Houses of Parliament on December 16 and 18, 1969).

[11] Amnesty Int'l, *The Death Penalty Worldwide, Abolitionist and Retentionist Countries* (Sept. 2002), at http://www.amnesty-usa.org/abolish/abret.html.

[12] *Id.*

seem to manage well enough without resorting to executions.[13] Yet there is surprisingly little sustained commentary, scholarly or popular, about why it is that the United States differs so much from its European counterparts on the issue of capital punishment.[14] The reason for the relative silence on this topic, it seems, is that people think they know why, and their (rather diverse) explanatory theories are often mentioned in passing, without support or elaboration, as if they were perfectly obvious. My object here is to take a sustained look at possible explanations for American exceptionalism with regard to capital punishment, with an eye to questioning and complicating what has been presented, when it has been discussed at all, as obvious or simple. It turns out that the number of possible theories is large, and the provenance of such theories is broad: they range from the sociological, to the political, to the historical, to the cultural, to the legal. Of course, none of these categories is wholly separate from any of the others, and both the boundaries between them and

---

[13] The following quotations from two different French human rights activists are typical of abolitionist sentiment inside as well as outside the United States: "No advanced country does this [uses capital punishment]. America is doing it along with countries like China and Russia and other countries that have terrible human rights records." Suzanne Daley, *Europeans Deplore Executions in the U.S.*, N.Y. Times, Feb. 26, 2000, at A8 (quoting Henry Leclerc, the president of the Human Rights League in Paris). "We are in an age of globalization, and sometimes our American friends have a lesson to teach us, and maybe sometimes we have a lesson to teach them." *Id.* (quoting Patrick Baudouin, the president of the International League of Human Rights).

[14] Scholarly writing on American exceptionalism with regard to capital punishment is sparse and heavily tilted toward student-written law review notes. *See, e.g.*, Cheryl Aviva Amitay, *Note, Justice or "Just Us": The Anomalous Retention of the Death Penalty in the United States*, 7 Md. J. Contemp. Legal Issues 543 (1996); Laurence A. Grayer, *Comment, A Paradox: Death Penalty Flourishes in U.S. While Declining Worldwide*, 23 Denv. J. Int'l L. & Pol'y 555 (1995); Kristi Tumminello Prinzo, *Note, The United States—"Capital" of the World: An Analysis of Why the United States Practices Capital Punishment While the International Trend Is towards Its Abolition*, 24 Brook. J. Int'l L. 855 (1999). Scholarly treatments by nonstudent authors of the reasons for American exceptionalism have tended to be brief and elliptical, if they exist at all, in works otherwise devoted to more empirical, historical, or sociological aspects of capital punishment. *See, e.g., The Death Penalty in America: Current Controversies, supra* note 6 (collection of essays on controversies regarding capital punishment in America); Banner, *supra* note 8 (history of capital punishment in America); Roger Hood, *The Death Penalty: A World-Wide Perspective* (1996) (survey of abolition around the world); Raymond Paternoster, *Capital Punishment in America* (1991) (largely empirical treatment of use of capital punishment in America); William A. Schabas, *The Abolition of the Death Penalty in International Law* (1993) (history of development of international human rights norms dealing with capital punishment); Austin Sarat, *When the State Kills: Capital Punishment and the American Condition* (2001) (cultural analysis of capital punishment in America); Franklin E. Zimring & Gordon Hawkins, *Capital Punishment and the American Agenda* (1986) (comparative assessment of America's movement toward abolition of capital punishment).

the relationship among them are highly contestable. Nonetheless, it is possible to articulate a large number of distinguishable hypotheses, in order to explore their strengths and weaknesses in some depth.

I by no means wish to suggest that I believe there is a single theory out there which can be proven to be "the" reason for the complex phenomenon at issue. Why the United States is currently different from its European friends and allies in its use of capital punishment is no doubt multiply determined in much the same way that the weather is. Meteorologists can identify many of the factors that produce the phenomenon of "weather," like wind speed, barometric pressure, and cloud formation (among many others, no doubt), but they cannot always say what is cause and what is effect, nor can they reliably predict what will happen as the factors change, as we all know! To say that a phenomenon is multiply determined is different from saying that it is overdetermined—that is, inevitably the product of multiple forces, each of which alone or in smaller combinations would produce the same result. Not only do I wish to resist reductionist simplicity, I also wish to embrace the contingency that attends most complex phenomena.

What follows is consideration of ten theories of American exceptionalism. As you will see, many of these theories are interconnected, but the disaggregation is helpful in the evaluation of each theory's strengths and weaknesses. I will close not by declaring a winner among the contending theories, but rather by suggesting that American exceptionalism in the area of capital punishment is better understood as a contingent product of a particular moment in American history than as the ineluctable "fate" that the very abundance of theories of American exceptionalism might seem to suggest.

Homicide Rates

The most common theory one encounters in writing and conversation on this issue is the fairly straightforward, sociological observation that the United States has a much higher homicide rate than do any of our Western European (or other peer) counterparts. Notably, during the 1960s and 1970s—the period when U.S. capital punishment policy first began to diverge markedly from that of Western Europe—the American homicide rate rose dramatically to a level much higher than that of most other Western industrialized nations. Although the rate dropped modestly in the early 1980s, it spiked again later in the decade; as of 1990, the American homicide rate was four and a half times that of Canada, nine times that of France or Germany, and thirteen times that of the United Kingdom.[15] Although the rate fell substantially in the 1990s, as of 1998 the U.S. homicide rate was still "two to four times higher than those of most Western countries."[16]

Often, though not always, this "homicide rates" theory of American exceptionalism regarding capital punishment is proffered with a defensive spin, the underlying implication being, "If you had our problems, you'd have our solutions, too." Of course, there is no way to test this counterfactual, short of seeing Western European homicide rates climb to American levels, and maybe not even then. However, recent studies of comparative noncapital penal policies seriously challenge the general claim that crime policy is determined primarily by crime rates. In his introductory essay to a diverse and impressive collection, *Sentencing and Sanctions in Western Countries*,[17] Michael Tonry unequivocally states his conclusion: "The evidence is clear; national differences in imprisonment rates and patterns result not from differences in crime but from differences in policy."[18] As part of his analysis, Tonry compares violent crime rates from the 1960s to the early 1990s in three countries—the United States, Germany, and Finland—and finds very similar rates of change in violent crime (all three curves go steeply upward) but utterly dissimilar penal policy responses. The United States continuously ups the ante, sending more and more offenders to prison; Finland reacts in the opposite manner, imprisoning many fewer people; and Germany reacts inconsistently, first lowering, then raising, and then again lowering its imprisonment rates, even as violent crime continues its steep rise throughout the period. Tonry concludes that crime rates cannot be viewed as the primary determinant of punitiveness in penal policy (at least as measured by rates of imprisonment); rather, he argues that other factors altogether—such as American moralism, history, and politics—are really at work in the divergence of American penal policy from that of Finland and Germany (and, by implication, other Western European nations).[19]

Tonry's work has obvious implications for the question of the roots of American exceptionalism regarding capital punishment: it would be odd indeed if there were a substantial correlation between homicide rates and rates of capital punishment when there is so little correlation between violent crime rates and rates of imprisonment. One might argue that homicide, especially murder, is a crime of particular horror, and that therefore homicide rates might drive capital punishment policy even if other

[15] Banner, *supra* note 8, at 300–301.

[16] Michael Tonry, *Punishment Policies and Patterns in Western Countries*, in *Sentencing and Sanctions in Western Countries* 13 (Michael Tonry & Richard S. Frase eds., 2001).

[17] *Id.*

[18] *Id.* at 7.

[19] *Id.* at 18.

crime rates do not drive other penal policy, because high murder rates will generate the political will to add a stronger deterrent or the desire for some appropriate public display of revulsion and repudiation. Or one might argue that, even if capital punishment policy does not rise and fall with any great sensitivity to murder rates, once murder rates reach a certain level, or "tipping point" (such as has been reached in the United States but not elsewhere in the industrialized West), the death penalty becomes more thinkable, or desirable, or necessary. In short, one would need some sort of "death is different" argument as to why homicide rates drive capital punishment policy in a way that violent crime rates apparently do not drive ordinary, noncapital penal policy. Any such argument, however, loses some plausibility when one considers the politics of penal policy writ large in the United States, for it is easily apparent that the very same political coalitions generally support either both capital punishment for murder and severe noncapital punishment for other crimes or (in considerably smaller numbers) abolition of capital punishment and less severe noncapital punishment for other crimes. In light of this strong and obvious convergence, it is hard to believe that the wellsprings of political attitudes and action regarding capital punishment derive from a source different from that of the wellsprings of political attitudes and action regarding penal policy generally.

In addition, the "homicide rates" hypothesis for American exceptionalism regarding capital punishment is beset by a further difficulty: examined more closely, homicide rates and execution rates dramatically diverge at important points in the past thirty years; indeed, they diverge much more than they converge.[20] From the mid-1960s to the mid-1970s, homicide rates roughly doubled, while execution rates fell to zero for several years preceding the Supreme Court's temporary invalidation of the death penalty in *Furman v. Georgia* in 1972[21] (though this might have been due, at least in part, to the "moratorium" strategy of the abolitionist litigators leading up to *Furman*).[22] Even more significantly, homicide rates fell precipitously throughout most of the 1990s, while execution rates soared, reaching levels not seen since the 1950s. Moreover, there were some substantial fluctuations in homicide rates even during the 1970s and 1980s,

---

[20] *Compare* Fed. Bureau of Investigation, U.S. Dep't of Justice, *Crime in the United States 1960–2001* (reporting rates for murder and nonnegligent homicide from 1960 through 2001), *with The Death Penalty in America's Current Controversies, supra* note 6, at 11 tbl.1–3 (giving execution rates from 1930 through 1995), and Amnesty Int'l, *U.S. Executions by Year since 1976*, at http://www.amnestyusa.org/abolish/eversince76.html (giving execution rates from 1976 through 2003).

[21] 408 U.S. 238 (1972).

[22] *See* Michael Meltsner, *Cruel and Unusual: The Supreme Court and Capital Punishment* 106–25 (1973).

which are not mirrored at all by fluctuations in execution rates. The strongest response to the disjunction between homicide rates and execution rates must be one of significant "lag time"—that is, that executions took a while to catch up to the rising homicide rates of the 1960s and 1970s, and that they have not yet been deflated by the falling homicide rates of the 1990s. As for the discrepancies between homicide rates and execution rates in the late 1970s and early 1980s, Supreme Court litigation working out the details of post-*Furman* constitutional requirements for capital punishment would necessarily have warped execution rates during that period so as to render comparison with homicide rates meaningless. However, these responses to the disjunction between homicide rates and execution rates founder when one considers death sentencing rates during the same thirty-year period, because one would not expect to see the same degree of "lag time" in this measure. Yet one sees a pattern on death row similar to the one in the death chamber: death row grew much more slowly in the late 1960s, when homicide rates were soaring, than it did in the 1990s, when homicide rates were plummeting.[23] These disjunctions between death sentencing rates and execution rates, on the one hand, and homicide rates on the other, certainly raise some serious problems for the "homicide rates" explanatory thesis.

These problems become only more apparent when one looks at the state and local level. On the state level, the "homicide rates" thesis gets some modest support from the generally higher homicide rates in the southern and border states, which also form the "death belt" primarily responsible for the nation's executions.[24] But the thesis suffers some embarrassment as well, in light of the fact that Texas, Virginia, Oklahoma, Missouri, and Florida—the five leading states in executions in the modern era, accounting together for more than two-thirds of the nation's executions since *Furman v. Georgia*[25]—have five of the lowest homicide rates in the "death belt."[26] Even if homicide rates somehow play a role in the

[23] *See* Death Penalty Info. Ctr., *Size of Death Row by Year* (2003), at http://www.deathpenaltyinfo.org/DRowInfo.html#year.

[24] *See* Death Penalty Info. Ctr., *Facts about Deterrence and the Death Penalty, Murder Rates by State 1995–2002* (last visited December 17, 2003), at http://www.deathpenaltyinfo.org/deter.html [hereinafter Death Penalty Info. Ctr.].

[25] NAACP Legal Defense and Educ. Fund, Inc., *Death Row U.S.A.*, Summer 2003, at http://www.deathpenaltyinfo.org/DEATHROWUSArecent.pdf.

[26] Death Penalty Info. Ctr., *supra* note 24. Of course, proponents of the "homicide rates" thesis and/or the death penalty itself would no doubt argue that the relatively low homicide rates in these five states is the result of their high use of the death penalty. This claim is implausible on many levels, the most obvious being that no state, even the really big users of the death penalty, uses capital punishment with any kind of frequency or reliability at all, so even the staunchest believer in deterrence theory would not expect to see a significant deterrent effect. This commonsense judgment is borne out by recent studies of two of the five

formal retention of the death penalty at the state level,[27] something else is accounting for the use of the death penalty, as reflected in execution rates, within states. The role of "something else" becomes even more clear when one examines intrastate variations in death penalty practices. Within individual states, there is staggeringly large variation among individual counties in death sentencing rates that are clearly attributable to something other than homicide rates. For example, in Texas, which leads the country in executions in absolute numerical terms, Dallas County (Dallas) and Harris County (Houston), two counties with strikingly similar demographics and crime rates, have very different death sentencing rates, with Dallas County returning eleven death verdicts per thousand homicides, while Harris County returns nineteen death verdicts per thousand homicides. One sees a similar disjunction in Pennsylvania between Allegheny County (Pittsburgh) and Philadelphia County (Philadelphia), which have death verdict rates of twelve and twenty-seven per thousand homicides, respectively. In Georgia, another significant death penalty state, the death sentencing rate ranges from four death verdicts per thousand homicides in Fulton County (Atlanta) to thirty-three death verdicts per thousand homicides in rural Muscogee County—a difference of more than 700 percent! One sees similarly large variations within many other states that are completely uncorrelated with differences in either homicide rates or crime rates more generally.[28]

Moreover, if one widens the lens to the larger world, one finds further evidence challenging the persuasiveness of the "homicide rates" thesis. It cannot explain why a large number of countries with extremely high murder rates—such as South Africa, Mexico, and Brazil—have abolished the death penalty, while Japan, with a comparatively low homicide rate, continues to retain it. Obviously, each country has its own peculiar death penalty "story," as testified to by the unique experience of South

---

leading death penalty states. *See* Jon Sorensen et al., *Capital Punishment and Deterrence: Examining the Effect of Executions on Murder in Texas*, 45 Crime & Delinq. 481 (1999) (finding no correlation between execution rates and either murder rates or felony rates in the period studied, 1984–97); William C. Bailey, *Deterrence, Brutalization, and the Death Penalty: Another Examination of Oklahoma's Return to Capital Punishment*, 36 Criminology 711 (1998) (finding no evidence of a deterrent effect on total killings or on any subtype of killing during the period studied, 1989–91, but finding evidence of a "brutalization" effect in the rise of certain subtypes of killings after Oklahoma's return to the use of capital punishment after a twenty-five-year hiatus).

[27] Even this thesis has some trouble accounting for Alaska and Michigan, staunchly abolitionist states, each with a homicide rate higher, by recent count, than that of any of the five leading death penalty states. *See* Death Penalty Info. Ctr., *supra* note 24.

[28] *See* James S. Liebman et al., *A Broken System, Part II: Why There Is So Much Error in Capital Cases, and What Can Be Done About It* (2002).

Africa.[29] But this recognition of the complex singularity of national experiences with capital punishment should only further undermine the simplistic "homicide rates" thesis as fundamentally inadequate or, at the very least, incomplete.

The foregoing demonstrates, at a minimum, that high homicide rates are neither necessary nor sufficient for the formal retention or vigorous use of capital punishment, and that low homicide rates are neither necessary nor sufficient for its abolition or more modest use. This is not at all to suggest that homicide rates play no role at all in America's anomalous retention and use of the death penalty; rather, it is clear that other forces must be at work as well. Hence on to other explanatory theories of American exceptionalism.

Public Opinion

Related to the "homicide rates" theory is the theory that the United States has capital punishment because of strong public support for it; presumably, public support for the death penalty is bolstered, at least in part, by the fear and disgust generated by high homicide rates. There is no dearth of polling data demonstrating American public opinion in support of capital punishment. Particularly helpful in providing a long view are the Gallup polls that were conducted for much of the twentieth century charting answers to the basic question "Do you favor the death penalty for those convicted of murder?"[30] Like most European nations, the United States experienced a decline in popular support for the death penalty during the 1960s. The low point in the United States was 1966, when the Gallup poll of that year revealed—for the first and only time in the century—that more respondents opposed than supported capital punishment (47 percent to 42 percent).[31] That trend, however, has dramatically reversed in the past three decades, with American public support for capital punishment rising precipitously, peaking in 1994 at 80 percent and declining only during recent years to 65 percent in May 2001, and 68 percent in October 2001—substantially lower, but nowhere near the levels of the 1960s.

---

[29] *See* Carol S. Steiker, *Pretoria, Not Peoria: S v. Makwanyane and Another*, 1995 (3) SA 391, 74 Tex. L. Rev. 1285 (1996) (describing decision of the South African Constitutional Court abolishing the death penalty in postapartheid South Africa).

[30] *See* Robert M. Bohm, *American Death Penalty Opinion, 1936–1986: A Critical Examination of the Gallup Polls*, in *The Death Penalty in America: Current Research* 113 (Robert M. Bohm ed., 1991).

[31] *Id.* at 116.

One could argue that the "public opinion" thesis buttresses the "homicide rates" thesis in that the fluctuations in public support for capital punishment in the three decades since the 1960s are much more consonant with fluctuations in homicide rates during that period than are fluctuations in either execution rates or death-sentencing rates. Public opinion in support of capital punishment grew in the late 1960s and early 1970s along with the homicide rate, whereas the execution rate fell to zero and the growth of the death row population slowed. Moreover, public opinion in support of capital punishment fell, albeit modestly, in the last few years of the 1990s, shortly after the homicide rate dropped substantially, whereas the execution rate has remained extraordinarily high, along with the growth in the size of the death row population. The fit is not perfect, primarily because homicide rates rose earlier and faster in the 1960s than did public support for capital punishment, and homicide rates fell earlier and faster in the 1990s than did public support for capital punishment (and there are some other, more modest, divergences along the way), but the case for at least loose correlation has some surface plausibility. Thus one might reasonably argue that high American homicide rates led to strong public support for capital punishment, which promoted formal retention of the death penalty, even if other forces are at play in producing actual death verdicts and executions within individual states.

The problem with this argument is that there are better explanations for the most significant fluctuations in public attitudes about capital punishment during this time period that have nothing to do with homicide rates. While the Gallup polls reveal a modest increase in support for capital punishment between 1966 and 1972,[32] public opinion made a substantial leap immediately after, and apparently in response to, the Supreme Court's decision in *Furman*. Two Gallup polls taken in 1972—one before and one after *Furman*—reveal a 7 percent increase in support for the death penalty immediately after *Furman*, as compared with an 8 percent increase in the six-year period between 1966 and 1972. Moreover, the same two polls reveal a 9 percent decrease in opposition to the death penalty immediately after *Furman*, as compared with a mere 6 percent decrease between 1966 and 1972.[33] Thus it seems likely that the Supreme Court's decision in *Furman* itself played a bigger role in bolstering public support for capital punishment, at least as reflected in polling data, than did rising homicide rates. Similarly, while it is true that homicide rates fell substantially in the 1990s, followed by a significant (but not as large) dip

---

[32] In 1966, 42 percent favored the death penalty; 47 percent opposed. In 1972, 50 percent favored the death penalty; 42 percent opposed. *Id.*

[33] The 1972 polls showed 50 percent in favor of the death penalty and 41 percent opposed pre-*Furman*, and 57 percent in favor and 32 percent opposed post-*Furman*. *Id.*

in public support for the death penalty, this dip in public support is better accounted for by highly disturbing accounts of innocent people exonerated from death row. From Illinois's moratorium on executions as a result of the exoneration of thirteen death row inmates from that state alone,[34] to the proliferation of DNA exonerations in capital and noncapital cases alike,[35] to studies documenting extremely high reversal rates in capital cases in the post-*Furman* era,[36] concerns about the unreliability of the capital process and the possible execution of the innocent are much more likely to be the driving force behind the recent drops in support for capital punishment than is the declining homicide rate. Indeed, respondents overwhelmingly cite this concern when polled about the fairness of the death penalty.[37] Thus the simple story that high homicide rates drive strong public support for capital punishment which in turn drives retention of capital punishment clearly needs some further nuance.

The "public opinion" thesis runs into bigger problems, however, than its failure to buttress the "crime rates" thesis. The most problematic and little-remarked problem for the "public opinion" thesis as an explanation for American exceptionalism with regard to capital punishment is that similar levels of public support for capital punishment existed in Western European countries at the time of abolition. Majorities of roughly two-thirds opposed abolition in Great Britain in the 1960s, Canada in the 1970s, France in the 1980s, and the Federal Republic of Germany in the late 1940s (when capital punishment was abolished in Germany's post–World War II constitution). "Indeed, there are no examples of abolition occurring at a time when public opinion supported the measure."[38] It is true that support for capital punishment has tended to fall in Europe over the last three decades—but only after abolition had already occurred, and thus more likely as a product of abolition (or the forces that produced abolition) than as its cause.[39] Moreover, in countries where support for capital punishment remains high, like Great Britain, efforts to reinstate the death penalty continue to fail, often by wide margins.[40] Perhaps the question to be addressed is not "Why does the United States retain the

---

[34] *See* Ken Armstrong & Steve Mills, *Ryan: 'Until I Can Be Sure'; Illinois Is First State to Suspend Death Penalty*, Chi. Trib., Feb. 1, 2000, at A1.

[35] *See* Barry Scheck et al., *Actual Innocence: When Justice Goes Wrong and How to Make It Right* (2001).

[36] *See* Liebman et al., *supra* note 28.

[37] *See* Ann Coulter, *We're Not Executing the Innocent*, USA Today, May 8, 2001, at A13 (citing Washington Post/ABC News poll in which 68 percent agreed that the death penalty was unfair "because sometimes an innocent person is executed").

[38] Zimring & Hawkins, *supra* note 14, at 22.

[39] *Id.*

[40] Roger Hood, *The Death Penalty: The USA in World Perspective*, 6 J. Transnat'l L. & Pol'y 517, 526 (1997) (noting that "the British Parliament has debated the issue more than

death penalty when Europe has abandoned it?" but rather "Why did European democracies abandon the death penalty despite substantial popular support for it?" The possibility of "European exceptionalism" is discussed further below.[41]

To be fair to the "public opinion" thesis, the polling data that show similar levels of support for capital punishment in the United States and most European countries at the time of abolition almost never purport to measure the comparative intensity of respondents' support for capital punishment. Yet it is plausible, indeed even likely, that Americans care more about capital punishment than their European and other Western counterparts do (or did at the time of abolition), even when raw numbers of those who "support" or "oppose" capital punishment appear similar. There is some modest empirical support for this claim to be found in a consistent pattern of American polling data: a 1974 study found that 79 percent of respondents who supported the death penalty reported a sense of personal outrage when a convicted murderer was sentenced to a penalty less than death;[42] a 1986 opinion poll indicated that 65 percent of all American adult respondents identified the death penalty as an issue they "feel very strongly about";[43] a 1988 presidential election exit poll revealed that more voters identified the death penalty as an issue that was "very important" to them than identified social security, health care, education, or the candidates' political party;[44] and a 1994 New York gubernatorial exit poll found that one in five voters cited capital punishment as the "most important" issue in the race.[45] While there are no comparable "intensity" data from Europe, the tepid popular response in Europe to abolition and the failure of movements for reinstatement to garner widespread support suggest that European voters simply do not share Americans' fervor on this issue. Perhaps the strongest support for the "intensity" spin on the "public opinion" thesis comes from the salience of crime generally,

---

a dozen times in recent years, but on the last occasion, the majority against reinstatement [of capital punishment] was the largest ever").

[41] *See* discussions below, "Populism" and "European Exceptionalism."

[42] Phoebe C. Ellsworth & Lee Ross, *Public Opinion and Capital Punishment: A Close Examination of the Views of Abolitionists and Retentionists*, 29 Crime & Delinq. 116, 155 (1983).

[43] Phoebe C. Ellsworth & Samuel R. Gross, *Hardening of the Attitudes: Americans' Views on the Death Penalty*, J. Soc. Issues, Summer 1994, at 19, 23 (citing Associated Press/Media General poll of the nationwide adult population in November 1986).

[44] *Id.* (citing ABC News exit poll of 23,000 voters in the 1988 presidential election, in which George Bush overwhelmingly defeated Michael Dukakis).

[45] *See* Todd S. Purdum, *Voters Cry: Enough, Mr. Cuomo!* N.Y. Times, Nov. 9, 1994, at B11 (citing exit polls in the 1994 gubernatorial election, in which George Pataki defeated incumbent Mario Cuomo, paving the way for the reinstatement of the death penalty in the state of New York).

and capital punishment particularly, as a political issue in the United States—another obviously intertwined theory of American exceptionalism to which I now turn.

Salience of Crime as a Political Issue

The most persuasive reason to believe that Americans care more intensely about capital punishment is the simple fact that crime and punishment have risen to and remained at the indisputable top of the American political agenda at all levels of government. Since 1968, when Richard Nixon ran for president on a largely "law and order" platform, crime policy has been a hugely salient issue in local, state, and national elections, to a degree not rivaled in any of our peer Western nations. It would not be hyperbolic to conclude that crime has been the central theme in the rhetoric of American electoral politics and in the strategies of elected officials in the decades since 1968.[46]

The death penalty has often come to serve as a focal point in electoral politics already organized around law and order. Particularly frightening and repulsive murders grab the public imagination, while the drama of the death penalty provides an easily accessible symbol of righteousness and order to aspiring politicians. One need not look far at all to find numerous examples of electoral races at all levels of government that were dominated by the death penalty cast as an issue of crime control, and, indeed, election results that were likely determined by the death penalty positions of the candidates.

Starting at the top, it is more than a little odd that we know so much about the positions of presidential candidates on capital punishment, given that 99 percent of executions take place at the state level. Not only do we know about presidential positions on the issue, we really seem to care. Who can forget the pivotal moment during the 1988 presidential debates when Michael Dukakis gave an emotionless response to a question about whether his views on the death penalty would change if his

---

[46] *See* David Garland, *The Culture of Control: Crime and Social Order in Contemporary Society* 152–53 (2001) (proposing that "the increased salience of crime" in the decades following the 1960s was due in large part to the fact that the "social distance between the middle classes and crime was greatly diminished, with consequences for point of view and perspective"). *See generally* Jonathan Simon, *Megan's Law: Crime and Democracy in Late Modern America*, 25 Law & Soc. Inquiry 1111 (2000) (surveying political science, criminology, and sociology literature to support the conclusion that crime was the primary motivating political force in the post-1960s decades).

wife were raped and murdered?[47] No doubt learning from Dukakis's disastrous example, then-governor Bill Clinton flew back to Arkansas from the presidential campaign trail in 1992 to validate the execution of a severely mentally disabled murderer who had survived a suicide attempt during which he had fired a shotgun into his own head.[48] The presidential election of 2000 is notable for the fact that every single one of the initial eleven candidates for president, despite other ideological differences, made clear his support for the death penalty.

The centrality of the death penalty as a political issue gets only more dramatic when one looks at state and local elections. In three major gubernatorial races in 1990 alone, the death penalty played a prominent, even central, role. In California, John K. Van de Kamp ran a television advertisement with a gas chamber in the background, highlighting the number of murderers that he put or kept on death row in his roles as district attorney and attorney general.[49] In Texas, Jim Mattox ran against Ann Richards in the Democratic primary with ads taking credit for thirty-two executions in his role as attorney general.[50] In Florida, incumbent governor Bob Martinez ran ads boasting of the ninety-plus death warrants he had signed while in office.[51]

The governors are not alone in their political resort to the power of the death penalty in electoral politics: the issue has figured prominently in the election and political strategy of legislators, judges, and prosecutors as well, in situations too numerous to count. Some illustrative examples: In 1993, Senate Republicans pledged opposition to judicial nominees they considered "insufficiently committed to the death penalty."[52] This threat was not merely a reflection of the peaking of national death penalty support in 1994; as recently as 1999, Missouri state judge Ronnie White was denied a federal judgeship by Senate Republicans, led by then-senator, subsequently attorney general, John Ashcroft, who declared Judge White "pro-criminal," in part because he opposed the death penalty.[53] California Supreme Court Chief Justice Rose Bird and two of

---

[47] *See* Bill Sammon, *Liberals See Death Penalty as Issue; But Gore Avoids Faceoff with Bush*, Wash. Times, June 14, 2000, at A1.

[48] Marshall Frady, *Death in Arkansas*, New Yorker, Feb. 22, 1993, at 105.

[49] John Balzar, *Van de Kamp TV Ads Focus on Death Row, Will Air Today*, L.A. Times, Mar. 21, 1990, at A3.

[50] Robert Guskind, *Hitting the Hot Button*, Nat'l J., Aug. 4, 1990, at 1887.

[51] Richard Cohen, *Playing Politics with the Death Penalty*, Wash. Post, Mar. 20, 1990, at A19.

[52] Neal A. Lewis, *GOP to Challenge Judicial Nominees Who Oppose Death Penalty*, N.Y. Times, Oct. 15, 1993, at A26.

[53] Stuart Taylor, Jr., *The Shame of the Ronnie White Vote*, Nat'l J., Oct. 16, 1999, at 2949.

her colleagues famously lost their seats because of their votes overturning death sentences, and many other elected state judges have been attacked, and frequently defeated, because of their unpopular votes overturning death verdicts.[54] Prosecutors, who are overwhelmingly elected officials in the United States, face the same political pressures on the issue of capital punishment.[55]

In the United States, two things are indisputably true, and "exceptional," at least as a matter of degree, in comparison to the rest of the industrialized West. First, crime has a political salience that is extraordinarily high, almost impossible to overstate. As a result, themes of "law and order" tend to dominate electoral battles at all levels of government, and the designation "soft on crime" tends to be a political liability of enormous and generally untenable consequence for political actors at all levels of government. Second, the death penalty has become a potent symbol in the politics of "law and order," despite its relative insignificance as a matter of crime control policy. Political actors clearly believe, apparently correctly, that their support for capital punishment translates directly in voters' minds as support for "tough" crime control generally. This strong linkage of the death penalty to the politics of law and order renders more plausible the claim that Americans support capital punishment with a greater intensity, if not in greater numbers, than do Europeans, now or in the recent past.

Populism

Often proffered more as an alternative than as a complement to the "intensity of preference" theory of American exceptionalism is the theory that populism in American politics, as compared to elitism in European politics, best accounts for differences in death penalty policy. As some Americans like to respond to our European detractors, it is not that Americans have different attitudes about capital punishment, it is that our political institutions are more responsive to the public will. In this vein, a provocative and much cited article in the *New Republic* sweepingly claimed, "Basically, then, Europe doesn't have the death penalty because its political systems are less democratic, or at least more insulated from

---

[54] *See generally* Stephen B. Bright & Patrick J. Keenan, *Judges and the Politics of Death: Deciding between the Bill of Rights and the Next Election in Capital Cases*, 75 B.U. L. Rev. 759 (1995) (canvassing the political impact of the death penalty on elected judges).

[55] *See generally* Catherine Ferguson-Gilbert, *It Is Not Whether You Win or Lose, It Is How You Play the Game: Is the Win-Loss Scorekeeping Mentality Doing Justice for Prosecutors?*, 38 Cal. W. L. Rev. 283 (2001).

populist impulses."[56] This theory conveniently purports to explain both why the death penalty continues to flourish in the United States and how Western European nations managed to achieve universal abolition despite widespread popular support for capital punishment.

The "American populism" theory has two dimensions to it, one institutional and one that might better be termed cultural. The institutional dimension emphasizes the populist features of the structures of American political organization, especially as compared to European democracies. Obviously, not all American political structures tend toward the populist, as the presidential election of 2000 amply demonstrated. The Electoral College and the bicameral structure of Congress have often been noted as antipopulist, at least in the sense of antimajoritarian. Nonetheless, there are certain features of American electoral politics that can fairly be described as distinctively populist in comparison to most European parliamentary democracies. The use of the "primary" system to select party candidates in both federal and state elections in the United States is one of the best examples of American political exceptionalism; in other Western democracies, political parties put up candidates for election without throwing the question open to popular intervention—a system much more likely to exclude mavericks and to insulate candidates from hot-button single issues like the death penalty.[57] Similarly, the widespread availability (and somewhat more modest use) of direct democracy tools, such as referenda and initiatives, is another exceptional feature of American politics that, like the "primary" system, tends to increase the power of single-issue voters and to promote populist tendencies in political debates and platforms.[58] In contrast, many European parliamentary systems imitate that of Britain, "in which the ruling political party is tightly disci-

[56] Joshua Micah Marshall, *Death in Venice: Europe's Death-Penalty Elitism*, New Republic, July 13, 2000, at 14.

[57] Note that many of the political contests in which the death penalty was a particularly hot-button issue were primary races. *See supra.*

[58] Nearly half of the states permit direct democracy tools, although only a handful of states have averaged more than one initiative per election cycle. *See generally Citizens as Legislators: Direct Democracy in the United States* (Shawn Bowler et al. eds., 1998); *Referendums around the World: The Growing Use of Direct-Democracy* (David Butler & Austin Ranney eds., 1994); Philip L. Dubois & Floyd Feeney, *Lawmaking by Initiative: Issues, Options and Comparisons* (1998). Successful initiatives on criminal justice issues, not surprisingly, have been almost exclusively of the "tough-on-crime" variety, such as California's famous "three-strikes-you're-out" legislation, mandating life sentences for certain repeat offenders. As one student of initiatives has observed: "Those accused and convicted of crimes, especially violent crimes, are a highly unpopular minority group. In recent decades, large segments of the public have viewed legislatures and courts as being too soft on criminals. Thus, conditions have been ripe for initiatives that restrict the rights of the accused and increase the penalties for those convicted. When 'tough-on-crime' measures appear on the ballot, they almost always win, and often by large margins." Kenneth P. Miller,

plined and in firm control of governmental policy and its implementation until the next election," and thus less susceptible to populist influences.[59]

While these differences in democratic organization certainly do exist, differences in political culture between the United States and the rest of the West appear even more striking. In the United States, politicians are conspicuously antielitist in their rhetoric and folksy in their self-presentation. Plainspoken personal anecdotes tend to displace complex policy analysis, and rolled-up shirtsleeves and cowboy hats are more the sartorial norm than the exception. Even though successful political candidates are frequently consummate political insiders, "it is almost obligatory for American politicians of both the right and the left to profess mistrust of government."[60] Gary Wills, in his recent history of Americans' long-standing distrust of government, argues that Americans have always tended toward a conception of government as appropriately "provincial, amateur, authentic, spontaneous, candid, homogeneous, traditional, popular, organic, rights-oriented, religious, voluntary, participatory, and rotational," as opposed to "cosmopolitan, expert, authoritative, efficient, confidential, articulated in its parts, progressive, elite, mechanical, duties-oriented, secular, regulatory, and delegative."[61] This political culture creates a strong tendency to defer to clear majority sentiment, not merely as a matter of political expediency, but also as a reflection of the role-conception of elected officials.

If one accepts Wills's two lists of opposing values in government, the second more accurately depicts the political culture of most other Western democracies. Unlike the United States, most European countries have a culture of political elitism and careerism, whereby political leaders are produced in large part through education and graduated ascension through professional bureaucracies. The United States simply has no equivalent to France's Ecole Nationale d'Administration (ENA) or Britain's civil service. These institutions both reflect and reinforce a political culture in which political leaders are viewed and view themselves as educated elites who have a duty to make decisions in light of their expertise and thus, more often than in the United States, to lead the public rather than to follow it. In such cultures it is imaginable for a minister of justice to respond to polling revealing substantial popular support for the death

---

Courts as Watchdogs of the Washington State Initiative Process, 24 Seattle U. L. Rev. 1053, 1068 (2001).

[59] Robert A. Kagan, *Adversarial Legalism: The American Way of Law* 69 (2001).

[60] Seymour Martin Lipset, *American Exceptionalism: A Double-Edged Sword* 23 (1996) (quoting Mary Ann Glendon, *Rights in Twentieth Century Constitutions*, in *The Bill of Rights in the Modern State* 521 (Geoffrey R. Stone et al. eds., 1992)).

[61] Gary Wills, *A Necessary Evil: A History of American Distrust of Government* 17–18 (1999).

penalty with the comment, "They don't really want the death penalty; they are objecting to the increasing violence."[62] This anecdote captures a conception of political responsibility that permits, indeed requires, the mediating of popular desires through expertise to a degree that would result in suspicion if not outrage in the United States.

The foregoing is not meant to celebrate the United States as "authentically" democratic in comparison to European bureaucratic elitism; nor, on the other hand, is it meant to exalt European abolition of capital punishment as progressive and "civilized" in comparison to American retention as crude and atavistic. Wills himself denies that either list of contrasting political values is clearly superior or even that they are mutually exclusive; "Ideally," he says, "government should combine all these values in a tempered way, since the one set does not necessarily preclude the other."[63] Rather, to Wills, the two clusters of values reflect poles on a continuum that have historically been perceived to be in tension.[64] Although Wills uses these two poles to reflect competing sets of political values within the United States throughout its history, I suggest that his contrasting poles in fact correspond rather well to contrasting current political realities in the United States and the rest of the West, which in turn, make it correspondingly easier or harder for public opinion to translate directly into policy.

While the most common argument from populism is the one I have sketched above—that populist political structures and political culture in the United States allow popular support for capital punishment to translate more directly into public policy than it can in Europe—there is an alternative argument from populism that treats America's populist political culture more as a motivation for retaining capital punishment than as a mechanism by which retention occurs. This alternative argument proposes that the inherent fragility and insecurity of the more populist versions of democracy create a demand for compelling symbols of strength and sovereignty, of which the death penalty is a potent example. Austin Sarat has made the best case for this claim:

> It may be that our attachment to state killing is paradoxically a result of our deep attachment to popular sovereignty. Where sovereignty is most fragile, as it always is where its locus is in "the People," dramatic symbols of its presence, like capital punishment, may be most important. The maintenance of capital punishment is, one might argue, essential to the demonstration that sovereignty could reside in the people. If the sovereignty of the people is to be genuine, it

---

[62] Marshall, *supra* note 56, at 15 (quoting the Swedish minister of justice in response to a 1997 poll showing that 49 percent of Swedes wanted the death penalty reinstated).

[63] Wills, *supra* note 61, at 18.

[64] *Id.*

has to mimic the sovereign power and prerogatives of the monarchical forms it displaced and about whose sovereignty there could be few doubts.[65]

This argument is a modern echo of one of the founding mythologizers of American populist democracy, Thomas Paine, who wrote in 1776 that

> in America the law is king. For as in absolute governments the King is law, so in free countries the law ought to be King [and ceremoniously crowned as such]; . . . but lest any ill use should afterwards arise, let the crown at the conclusion of the ceremony be demolished, and scattered among the people whose right it is.[66]

There is no more vivid way for the law to be ceremoniously crowned as king than by the use of capital punishment duly authorized and channeled through the legal system.

Unlike the more familiar argument from populism, this latter argument has a harder time establishing that American populist democracy is exceptional, as compared to other Western democracies, in its need for dramatic enactments of popular sovereignty. After all, the entire rest of the Western democratic world also moved, some nations quite dramatically, from monarchical to democratic systems of government. What reasons are there for believing that their democratic structures are any more fragile or insecure than our own? Why would their democracies—all of them newer than our own—not crave the same sort of enactments of popular sovereignty in imitation of former monarchical prerogatives? The basis for American exceptionalism here is harder to clearly identify than it is in the context of political institutions and culture.

Criminal Justice Populism

The argument for the "populism" theory of American exceptionalism with regard to capital punishment gains strength when one recognizes that it is not merely that politics is more populist in the United States, but also that criminal justice is thought to be a particularly appropriate subject for populist influence and control within the political arena. One of the most clearly "exceptional" aspects of the structure of American government is the much greater degree of both lay participation in the crimi-

---

[65] Austin Sarat, *The Law and Politics Book Review*, Mar. 1998, at 114–16 (reviewing *America's Experiment with Capital Punishment: Reflections on the Past, Present, and Future of the Ultimate Penal Sanction* (James Acker et al. eds., 1998)).

[66] Thomas Paine, *Common Sense* (1776), reprinted in *Thomas Paine: Rights of Man, Common Sense, and Other Political Writings* 34 (Mark Philip ed., Oxford Univ. Press 1995).

nal justice system and direct political accountability of institutional actors within the criminal justice system. While many other countries use lay fact finders to a certain extent in criminal trials, no other country authorizes such a large role for criminal trial juries as does the United States.[67] Moreover, the extensive use of lay grand juries in the charging process in the United States is even more truly anomalous.[68] Equally anomalous is the fact that the vast majority of American prosecutors are elected rather than appointed.[69] Judges, too, are directly elected or otherwise politically accountable in a large number of states.[70] This current state of affairs is the result of a uniquely American turn during the nineteenth century toward increasing and entrenching democratic control over state and local governments through state constitutionalism.[71]

These clearly "exceptional" institutional arrangements, like populism in electoral politics, provide a mechanism through which popular support for the use of capital punishment can influence institutional decision making. In this context, however, the influence is not on legislative decision making but rather on prosecutorial charging decisions, judicial conducting of criminal trials, and lay rendering of verdicts and sentences—especially in highly publicized capital, or potentially capital, cases. Elected officials who campaigned on a death penalty platform, or reelected officials who were vigorous advocates for the use of available capital sanctions while in office, no doubt perceive a mandate to use the death penalty in a way that European judges and prosecutors, more isolated products of an elite bureaucracy, could not possibly. There is thus something of a "feedback" loop between voters and elected officials that tends to reinforce and intensify tendencies toward the use of capital punishment. This loop helps to explain some of the extreme intrastate variation noted above[72] in the use of the death penalty: some of the most "active" counties

[67] See *Criminal Procedure: A Worldwide Study* (Craig M. Bradley ed., 1999).

[68] *Id.*

[69] While federal prosecutors are appointed by the president, more than 95 percent of county and municipal prosecutors are selected by popular election. Robert L. Misner, *Recasting Prosecutorial Discretion*, 86 J. Crim. L. & Criminology 717, 734 (1996).

[70] Twenty-three states have popular elections for nearly all levels of the state judiciary, while an additional ten states combine a system of popular election with executive or legislative appointment of judges. 33 Council of State Governments, *Book of the States, 2000/2001*, at 137–39 (2002).

[71] The rise of Jacksonian democracy in the 1820s provided an impetus toward extending the franchise and providing for the popular election of many state and local officials, including judges, prosecutors, and sheriffs. To a large extent, these movements toward republicanism were accomplished by state constitution drafting or revision. See Abraham S. Goldstein, *Prosecution: History of the Public Prosecutor*, in *Encyclopedia of Crime and Justice* 1242, 1243 (Joshua Dressler et al. eds., 2d ed. 2002); G. Alan Tarr, *Models and Fashions in State Constitutionalism*, 1998 Wis. L. Rev. 729, 736–37.

[72] See *supra* pp. 105–06.

have been those with a district attorney highly and vocally committed to the use of capital punishment, such as Johnny Holmes, Jr., in Houston, known as "the Texas Terminator,"[73] and Lynne Abraham in Philadelphia, dubbed "the deadliest D.A."[74]

While the "criminal justice populism" theory offers a plausible account for the role of populism in producing capital charges, verdicts, sentences, and executions, it has less direct relevance to the issue of abolition or retention per se. The election of many state court judges does help to explain why judicial abolition, in the rare instances in which it has been attempted—as it was briefly in federal court and with more lasting influence in the state of Massachusetts—has occurred in jurisdictions where judges are appointed and thus buffered from political influence.[75] But the relevance of criminal justice populism to legislative abolition—where almost all the action has been in the rest of the Western world—is less clear. Perhaps one could argue that the greater use of existing capital statutes in states with greater criminal justice populism makes abolition that much more unthinkable; but one could also argue that greater use of capital punishment is more likely to produce either controversial cases, like the recent capital prosecution of Andrea Yates in Texas,[76] or serious legal error that might undermine confidence in the system of capital justice.[77] However, if declining use of the death penalty or de facto abolition (defined as ten years without an execution) or outright moratorium is a necessary step on the road to abolition, as the experience of many European countries might suggest,[78] then American criminal justice populism may indeed present a serious impediment to American abolition.

[73] James Langton, *The Texas Terminator Keeps Death Row Busy*, London Sunday Tel., July 18, 1999, at 29.

[74] Tina Rosenberg, *The Deadliest D.A.*, N.Y. Times, July 16, 1995 (Magazine), at 21.

[75] *See, e.g., Furman v. Georgia*, 408 U.S. 238 (1972) (invalidating the capital statutes of virtually every American jurisdiction under the Eighth Amendment); *Commonwealth v. Colon-Cruz*, 470 N.E.2d 116 (Mass. 1984) (striking down new death penalty legislation under the Massachusetts Declaration of Rights, even after the passage of a state constitutional amendment authorizing capital punishment); *D.A. for the Suffolk Dist. v. Watson*, 411 N.E.2d 1274 (Mass. 1980) (striking down new death penalty legislation under Massachusetts Declaration of Rights); *Commonwealth v. O'Neal*, 339 N.E.2d 676 (Mass. 1975) (striking down Massachusetts death penalty under the Massachusetts Declaration of Rights).

[76] *See* Paul Duggan, *NOW Rallies to Mother's Defense: Group Says Woman Needs Help, Not Prison, in Drowning of 5 Children*, Wash. Post, Sept. 3, 2001, at A3.

[77] *See* James S. Liebman et al., *supra* note 28, at 164–66 (greater use of the death penalty is correlated with higher error rates).

[78] *See* Amnesty Int'l, *The Death Penalty around the World, Abolitionist and Retentionist Countries* (Sept. 2002), at http://www.amnesty-usa.org/abolish/world. html (revealing the existence of a significant time lag between the last recorded execution and the date of de jure abolition in the vast majority of abolitionist countries).

Federalism

Another "exceptional" feature of American political organization is American federalism. A number of other Western democracies, such as Germany, Switzerland, and Canada, are structured on a federal model, with discrete governmental units allocated some autonomous spheres of authority within the larger federal nation-state. However, the United States is the only country that gives full criminal lawmaking power to individual federal units. This grant cannot be superseded by Congress, as the federal constitution is structured to ensure state dominance over criminal law.[79] As a result, criminal lawmaking and law enforcement are understood and experienced in the United States as primarily a state and local concern, with federal lawmaking and enforcement as a limited, specialized adjunct.[80] This arrangement, unique in Western democracies, necessarily permits local or regional enthusiasts to keep the death penalty going within the United States, even when attitudes and trends are moving in the opposite direction in other parts of the country. Nationwide abolition can thus be achieved, as a legislative matter, only through persuasion of the legislatures of fifty different states and the federal legislature as well.

Coordination is the most obvious challenge for a successful nationwide abolitionist movement in such a system. This coordination problem is exacerbated by the radical decentralization of criminal law enforcement authority within states. Local district attorneys control the use of the death penalty on a countywide basis; thus even achieving statewide abolition is difficult without the cooperation and support of local law enforcement officials whose individual political views and agendas must be accommodated. In addition to the problems of coordination posed by federalism and localism, the continued existence and use of the death penalty in some states (and in some counties within states) makes it more difficult to urge abolition in the larger context and even promotes the attempts of proponents to urge reinstatement in abolitionist jurisdictions. State and local political actors with national political aspirations have

---

[79] See Sara Sun Beale, *Federal Criminal Jurisdiction*, in *Encyclopedia of Crime and Justice*, *supra* note 71, at 775 ("General police powers and the bulk of criminal jurisdiction were not granted to the federal government, and accordingly were uniformly recognized to be reserved to the states").

[80] See Daniel C. Richman, *Federal Criminal Law Enforcement*, in *Encyclopedia of Crime and Justice*, *supra* note 71, at 779 (noting that what is most surprising about the federal enforcement apparatus is its small size, at least when compared to the network of state and local enforcement agencies, which have primary responsibility for patrolling the streets and pursue most of the crimes that happen on or off them).

reasons to oppose abolition (or even to actively promote capital punishment) in their own bailiwicks if their political fortunes depend on other jurisdictions in which support for the death penalty is strong.

Southern Exceptionalism

The natural and intended consequence of American federalism is substantial state and regional variation, which is clearly observable in the context of capital punishment. The vast majority of executions within the United States, at least in the "modern era" of capital punishment since *Furman v. Georgia*, have been carried out by a handful of states located in the American South and Southwest.[81] Hence one theory of American exceptionalism regarding capital punishment is the thesis that the country as a whole is not exceptional; rather the South (if one expands the concept to include the southwestern states) is exceptional within America. This theory, of course, then requires an account of what makes the South exceptional, if it is to provide an explanation for American exceptionalism. Such an account could and should receive more attention than I can offer here,[82] but I will provide a brief sketch of four interrelated theories of American southern exceptionalism.

First, perhaps the most obvious aspect of southern exceptionalism is race. The American South has a distinctive legacy of racial inequality stemming from the practice of chattel slavery and continues to have disproportionately large (though still minority) black populations. From colonial times, the capital punishment policies of the American South were deeply marked by the institution of slavery. The eighteenth century saw the widespread enactment of capital penal policies targeted solely at crimes by slaves.[83] In the first half of the nineteenth century, the movements to abolish capital punishment in the Northeast and Midwest had no southern analogue, in part because of their connection to the movement to abolish slavery[84] and in part because slave owners perceived capital punishment to be a necessary deterrent to serious crimes by slaves.[85]

[81] *See* Death Penalty Info. Ctr., *supra* note 24.

[82] *See, e.g.,* Jordan M. Steiker, *The Empty Death Chamber: The Death Penalty as Symbol versus Practice in Retentionist Jurisdictions in the United States* (draft on file with the author) (offering a detailed account of southern exceptionalism with regard to capital punishment).

[83] *See* Banner, *supra* note 8, at 8. Most of these race-dependent capital crimes, unsurprisingly, were created in the southern colonies. Slaves made up more than half the population of South Carolina by 1720 and nearly half that of Virginia by 1750. To manage these captive workforces, the southern colonies resorted to ever-increasing lists of capital statutes.

[84] *Id.* at 142–43.

[85] *Id.* at 142.

As a result, reports historian Stuart Banner, "By the time of the Civil War ... slavery had produced a wide cultural gap between the northern and southern states in attitudes toward capital punishment."[86] This cultural gap did not close with the abolition of slavery after the Civil War; rather, what followed was a long era of lynchings in which mob executions of black men were common[87] and an even longer era of "legal lynchings" in the South—"executions sanctioned by the forms of judicial process absent the substance of judicial fairness."[88] This long-standing and close association of capital punishment with the formal and informal social control of blacks in the South may contribute to southern unwillingness to part with the death penalty, particularly in an era, as noted above, in which the death penalty plays such a strong symbolic role in the politics of crime control.[89] Indeed, recent empirical studies show that racial prejudice is significantly linked to support both for the death penalty and for tougher crime control policies,[90] and that such prejudice remains stronger among native white southerners than among whites who were born and live elsewhere.[91]

A different facet of American southern exceptionalism is the South's distinctive embrace of Protestant fundamentalism. Indeed, the term "the death belt" is a play on "the Bible belt," with both terms designating the American South. Numerous sociological studies find a correlation between southern fundamentalism and support for the death penalty.[92] How

---

[86] *Id.* at 143.

[87] *See* Randall Kennedy, *Race, Crime, and the Law* 41–47 (1997) (describing and documenting lynchings of black victims in the post–Civil War era, the vast majority of which occurred in the South).

[88] *Id.* at 88.

[89] *See supra.*

[90] *See* Steven E. Barkan & Steven F. Cohn, *Racial Prejudice and Support for the Death Penalty by Whites*, 31 J. Res. Crime & Delinq. 202 (1994) (reporting empirical study in which researchers significantly linked two indexes of racial prejudice to greater support for the death penalty among whites, even after controlling for relevant demographic and attitudinal variables); Robert L. Young, *Race, Conceptions of Crime and Justice, and Support for the Death Penalty*, 54 Soc. Psychol. Q. 67 (1991) (empirical analysis finding that racial prejudice significantly predicts both support for the death penalty and tougher crime control policies).

[91] *See* Christopher G. Ellison, *Southern Culture and Firearms Ownership*, 72 Soc. Sci. Q. 267 (1991) (reporting a significant relationship between racial antipathy and firearms ownership among native southerners).

[92] *See, e.g.,* Marian J. Borg, *The Southern Subculture of Punitiveness? Regional Variation in Support for Capital Punishment*, 34 J. Res. Crime & Delinq. 25 (1997) (reporting empirical study showing that fundamentalist church membership is significantly related to southerners' attitudes toward capital punishment); Chester L. Britt, *Race, Religion, and Support for the Death Penalty: A Research Note*, 15 Just. Q. 175 (1998) (reporting empirical study in which white fundamentalists showed higher levels of support for the death penalty than either black fundamentalists or white and black nonfundamentalists); Harold G. Gras-

exactly the dynamic works connecting southern fundamentalism and attitudes about capital punishment is an interesting and unsettled question,
about which sociologists and theologians will continue to debate. Nonetheless, whether it is fundamentalist doctrine or leadership or something
else that forges the connection, it is hard to gainsay that southern fundamentalist Protestantism plays some role in generating or reinforcing support for capital punishment in the South.

Third, there is substantial support for the view that the American South
has a distinctive subculture of violence, whether it is measured in homicide rates,[93] gun ownership rates,[94] or attitudes toward defensive and retaliatory interpersonal violence.[95] The roots of the greater violence in the
South are hypothesized to stem from a southern "honor culture" in which
dueling, among other forms of interpersonal violence, was a more accepted practice than it was elsewhere.[96] The connection between the relatively more violent southern culture and the use of capital punishment is
speculative, but the southern emphasis on defensive and retaliatory violence on the interpersonal level has some obvious connection to support
for capital punishment, and it would not be surprising, more generally, if
a more violent culture made more violent penalties seem both more necessary and less shocking.

Fourth and finally, the American South is exceptional in the strength
and depth of its resistance to the civil rights movement of the 1950s and
1960s, to which the movement for the abolition of capital punishment
has had strong connections. In the 1960s, death penalty abolition was
promoted by the very same institutional actors who had promoted the
end of racial segregation in the South, and through the very same means—
federal constitutional imposition through litigation. It was the NAACP
Legal Defense and Education Fund that litigated both the major desegre-

---

mick & John K. Cochran, *Religion, Punitive Justice, and Support for the Death Penalty*,
10 Just. Q. 289 (1993) (reporting empirical study finding that evangelical/fundamentalist
Protestantism was correlated with punitiveness in criminal justice policy, including the death
penalty for both adults and juveniles); Harold G. Grasmick et al., *Protestant Fundamentalism and the Retributive Doctrine of Punishment*, 30 Criminology 21 (1992) (reporting empirical study in which individuals affiliated with fundamentalist Protestant denominations
were reported to have the highest punitiveness and biblical literalism measures, of which
only the latter was correlated with greater death penalty support).

[93] *See supra.*

[94] *See* James D. Wright & Linda L. Marston, *The Ownership of the Means of Destruction: Weapons in the United States*, 23 Soc. Probs. 93 (1975).

[95] *See* Christopher G. Ellison, *An Eye for an Eye? A Note on the Southern Subculture of
Violence Thesis*, 69 Soc. Forces 1223 (1991) (finding that older southerners express strong
normative support for defensive and retaliatory interpersonal violence).

[96] *See generally* Richard E. Nisbett & Dov Cohen, *Culture of Honor: The Psychology of
Violence in the South* (1996).

gation cases and the death penalty cases. Some part of southern enthusiasm for capital punishment in the modern, post-*Furman* era may well be a reaction to this connection and to the attempt of the federal government to impose "national" values on southern culture.

It is a fair question whether any or all of these aspects of southern exceptionalism fully account for the disproportionate use of the death penalty in the American South. But the biggest qualification of the "southern exceptionalism" thesis for American exceptionalism with regard to capital punishment comes from the recognition, more fully fleshed out by Jordan Steiker,[97] that states outside the South still make significant use of their capital statutes in the production of death sentences, even though their execution rates are far lower than those of the South. While the South may dominate the country in executions, that is not the only measure of "use" of capital punishment. The United States cannot explain away its national exceptionalism as wholly a product of regionalism.

European Exceptionalism

This theory turns the tables and asks whether there is something distinctive about European politics, culture, or history that would lead to wholesale abolition of the death penalty in the space of only a few short decades. A version of this theory has already been explored above as a contrast to American political populism: bureaucratic elitism in European politics has allowed European political leaders to abolish the death penalty despite substantial popular support for capital punishment at the time of abolition. But this theory does not explain what has led European political leaders to conclude that the death penalty must be abandoned at this precise point in time.

The answer to this question may lie in Europe's distinctive historical experiences during the twentieth century. Europeans and others who have recently and vividly experienced terrible abuses of state power may see more reason to remove the death penalty from the state's arsenal of sanctions. Within the last century, Europe experienced two horrific world wars fought on its soil and witnessed the bloody rules of Mussolini, Hitler, and Stalin. These experiences may have helped to create a climate in which dramatic demonstrations of state-approved violence are disfavored. Moreover, Europe has suffered numerous violent ethnic conflicts throughout the last century, and it may fear that the use of the death penalty could play a role in exacerbating such conflicts. Thus it is not surprising that fears that Irishmen might be wrongly convicted and

---

[97] *See* Jordan Steiker, *supra* note 82.

executed for terrorism have changed the minds of some British supporters of capital punishment,[98] or that capital punishment is not on the table
as an available sanction for the former Yugoslavia war crimes tribunal.
It is worth noting, too, that while methods of execution have been sani-
tized in the United States, at the time of abolition in Britain and France,
the sole mode of execution was the gallows and the guillotine, respectively, each of which carries some significant historical baggage. With
associations to the hanging fairs at Tyburn and the bloody Terror during
the French Revolution, the gallows and the guillotine themselves embodied reasons for British and French political leaders to distance themselves
from capital punishment.

The world wars and ethnic conflicts in Europe no doubt contributed to
Europe's being far more willing than United States to generate and support international norms, especially those related to human rights. The
casting of abolition of the death penalty as an issue of international
human rights (as opposed to a prerogative of purely domestic concern)
has been well documented;[99] the most dramatic and powerful example of
this trend is Protocol No. 6 to the European Convention on Human
Rights, abolishing the use of the death penalty in peacetime, which was
adopted in 1983—many years ahead of the corresponding provisions
adopted by the United Nations or inter-American human rights law.[100]
Membership in the Council of Europe, which is required for admission
to the European Union, now requires adherence to Protocol No. 6, a requirement that ensures both that Eastern Europe will follow the abolitionist trend begun in the West and that there will be no backsliding on the
issue of capital punishment in already abolitionist states. In contrast, the
United States has managed to maintain some version of isolationism
throughout much of the same twentieth century, and a version of such
"anti-internationalism" still runs fairly deep today, in what one commentator calls "the new sovereigntist" vision, which holds that "the United
States can pick and choose the international conventions and laws that
serve its purpose and reject those that do not."[101] One aspect of international law that the United States has steadfastly rejected is the abolition
of capital punishment for adults or even for juveniles.

---

[98] See Hood, *supra* note 40, at 526 (noting that "the revelation of several miscarriages of
justice in cases where the persons—mostly Irish convicted of terrorist murder—would have
been executed has convinced many former advocates that a return to capital punishment
could not be safely administered").

[99] See Schabas, *supra* note 14.

[100] *Id.* at 219–20.

[101] Peter J. Spiro, *The New Sovereigntists: American Exceptionalism and Its False Prophets*, Foreign Aff., Nov.–Dec. 2000, at 9.

American Cultural Exceptionalism

This theory is in some ways the inverse of the "European exceptionalism" thesis and in some ways an extension of the "southern exceptionalism" thesis. Admittedly more popular in Europe than in the United States, this theory posits that the United States (rather than merely the American South) manifests a "subculture of violence" in the larger Western culture. Perhaps because of its relatively recent experience as a "frontier" society, the theory holds, America is simply more violent and crude than the rest of the Western industrialized world. Proponents of this theory note that America is also an outlier on the issue of gun control, regulating firearms to a much lesser degree than do our Western counterparts, and that American popular culture glorifies violence, usually by gun-toting macho men. From GI Joe, to cop shows on TV, to the American western film, American popular culture celebrates violence by soldiers, law enforcers, and righteous men outside the law—promoting exactly the values one might expect to lead to an embrace of capital punishment. Even American intellectual elites occasionally seem to enjoy sending up American society in this way. When French minister of justice Robert Badinter visited the United States in 1983, fresh from leading the successful abolitionist charge in France, the *Washington Post* ran an op-ed reporting, almost gleefully, Badinter's comment that on the day the death penalty was abolished in France, he received a telegram from a Texas millionaire who wanted to buy an outlawed guillotine for his game room.[102]

It is hard to prove or disprove this theory, but there are a number of reasons to be at least somewhat skeptical of it. One reason is that public opinion polls, discussed above,[103] show that Europeans, too, support capital punishment in substantial numbers, despite any "cultural" differences that might exist. Another is that Europeans are huge consumers of exactly the media products that are noted as support for the "American violence" thesis; indeed, as many or more of the top-grossing films in Europe, as compared to the United States, are American films that are R-rated for violence.[104] A third is that there is surprisingly little empirical support for a strong, generalized connection between media violence and violent attitudes or behavior, despite many attempts to forge such a link. And a fourth is that the higher homicide rates in the United States are partly, though not completely, a result of laxer gun control laws and thus not as strong an independent indicator of violence as the foregoing might sug-

---

[102] Colman McCarthy, *Messenger of Life*, Wash. Post, Feb. 12, 1983, at A15.

[103] *See supra.*

[104] *See Movie Ratings—Box Office Charts*, at http://charts.boom.ru/eng/MOVIES/index.htm (last visited June 12, 2002).

gest. These qualifications are not meant to refute the claim that the United States might have a more "violent" culture than the rest of the West, or that this violence might play a role in the retention of capital punishment in the United States, but rather to suggest that such a claim is a good deal hazier and more conjectural than is often acknowledged.

Historical Contingency

This last theory is like the proverbial thirteenth chime of the clock that casts doubt on all that has come before. Perhaps because it fits so poorly with all the other theories, it has been surprisingly neglected. The "historical contingency" thesis holds that the failure of the United States to abolish the death penalty was something of a historical accident—a near miss, if you will. The U.S. Supreme Court did, in fact, abolish capital punishment in 1972 with its decision in *Furman v. Georgia*. Then it reconsidered and reinstated capital punishment in 1976, albeit with some limiting conditions, with its decision in *Gregg v. Georgia* and its four accompanying cases from Florida, Louisiana, North Carolina, and Texas. In 1972, at the time of the *Furman* decision, many believed that the abolition of capital punishment was permanent. If it had turned out to be so, there would be no question of American exceptionalism with regard to capital punishment today: our abolition would have fit perfectly with that of the rest of the industrialized West. If the Supreme Court had managed to speak more clearly, emphatically, and unanimously on the issue in the original *Furman* decision, or if the Court's membership had changed differently between 1972 and 1976, abolition might well have been permanent. But the Court's legitimacy was weakened by its decisions promoting integration, regulating the police, and legalizing abortion, and by 1976, it was willing to retrench on the issue of capital punishment in response to the outpouring of rage that *Furman* had generated.

This theory in some ways dovetails with Cass Sunstein's thesis that the failure of the Supreme Court to recognize social and economic rights in the Constitution was largely a result of the "crucial development" of the presidential election of 1968, which profoundly shaped the Court's membership and moved it as an institution away from its nascent flirtation with promoting affirmative social and economic constitutional rights. What I share with Sunstein is his emphasis on the contingency of the Court's path; in the area of capital punishment, as in the development of social and economic rights, the Court's decisions could well have turned out profoundly differently—and almost did. Where my analysis diverges from Sunstein's is on what, precisely, the contingent events were. Sunstein emphasizes Richard Nixon's presidential victory in 1968 and the change it engendered in the composition of the Supreme Court. This emphasis is too restrictive in the death penalty context, however, because the Court's change of course between *Furman* in 1972 and *Gregg* in 1976 was not solely the product of the Court's change of membership; rather, two of the original *Furman* majority were willing to accept reform rather than wholesale abolition of capital punishment. The contingent events that I would emphasize are the contingencies that helped Nixon to prevail rather than the political fact of his victory; these contingencies also put pressure on the Court to moderate its position. The precipitously rising violent crime rate, the strong and measurable shift in popular attitudes toward capital punishment, the close association of the campaign against capital punishment with the controversial civil rights movement and the powerful southern backlash that this association engendered, and the dwindling legitimacy generally of the Supreme Court as an agent of anti-majoritarian social change all augured against the long-term survival of *Furman*'s effective abolition of capital punishment. Yet if the Court had taken up capital punishment earlier in the 1960s—before the big crime bump, before the shift in public opinion, before its other costly criminal justice innovations such as *Miranda* and social innovations such as abortion rights—*Furman*'s abolition of capital punishment might well have survived and become as much a part of the constitutional landscape now as *Miranda* or *Roe*—contested, battered, but still standing. Thus I embrace many—even all—of the other nine theories of America's exceptionalism with regard to the death penalty as contingencies that came to bear at a particular time in relative proportions that we will probably never know, rather than as single, powerful determinants of the issue.

The 1976 decision of the Court to mend rather than end the practice of capital punishment may itself have played a role in preventing abolition from occurring in the political arenas. From 1976 onward, the Court chose constitutional regulation of capital punishment as its mode of retrenchment. As I have argued at greater length elsewhere, this choice helped to legitimize and stabilize the practice of capital punishment in the United States.[105] The Court's complex capital jurisprudence that grew steadily each year after 1976 created a strong, but unfortunately false, impression that the imposition of the death penalty was both capable of being rationalized by rules and actually subject to careful judicial scrutiny at both the state and federal levels. This impression no doubt contributed in some measure to a degree of comfort with the practice of capital punishment both by institutional actors within the criminal jus-

---

[105] *See* Carol S. Steiker & Jordan M. Steiker, *Sober Second Thoughts: Reflections on Two Decades of Constitutional Regulation of Capital Punishment*, 109 Harv. L. Rev. 355, 426–38 (1995).

tice system and by the public at large, blunting and marginalizing arguments for total abolition.

Moreover, the Court's validation of the continuing use of the death penalty as a matter of constitutional law may have hindered movement toward abolition by creating an impediment to American acceptance of capital punishment as a violation of international human rights law, so prevalent in Europe and elsewhere. Abolition by European countries, especially in the 1980s and 1990s, was almost always couched in the discourse of international human rights. This discourse is much less prominent in, if not absent entirely from, American debates about abolition versus retention, no doubt because it is hard for American political leaders to articulate, or for members of the American public to accept, that there could be a fundamental and universal human right not recognized by our much vaunted Constitution. By noting this impediment, I do not mean to lay primary responsibility for the failure of abolition in the United States at the feet of our "distinctive rights culture," in the words of Michael Ignatieff. Both Ignatieff and Andrew Moravcsik make strong arguments against relying too heavily on this distinctiveness as a complete explanation for American exceptionalism with regard to international human rights generally, and I embrace their caution. Sweeping arguments about our distinctive culture—whether it be about the understanding of rights or about the role of violence—have far too undifferentiated and deterministic a cast. It is always worth asking, as Moravcsik does, *which* rights? and how does any cultural distinctiveness play out in that particular context?

In the context of capital punishment, the Court's early forays played against human rights discourse in the political realm because the very grounds on which some of the *Furman* majority based its later-repudiated abolition sounded in the language of fundamental and universal rights. The Supreme Court's implicit repudiation in *Gregg* of both Justice Douglas's appeal to equality and Justice Brennan's appeal to human dignity in their opinions in *Furman* lent ammunition and credibility to retentionist forces in the political arena. The role of the Supreme Court's rejection of constitutional claims against capital punishment in preventing abolition, however, is dwarfed by the other political and institutional impediments to legislative abolition. This essay is in many ways a list of the political forces and institutional structures that stand in the way of legislative abolition in the United States, and they are daunting indeed. No one could seriously entertain the view that nationwide legislative abolition of capital punishment is even remotely likely in the next generation or two. In the context of abolition of capital punishment, however, the Supreme Court has played and will continue to play a much more salient role than the political branches. In the United States, the Supreme Court is the institution most similarly situated to the abolitionist legislatures that led the rest of the Western industrialized world to abolition. Only the Court has the power in this context to effect change throughout the United States; only the Court is sufficiently insulated from political will that it can, on occasion, lead rather than follow public opinion. Moreover, there is some suggestion that the Court might be moving in the direction of abolishing or seriously limiting the use of capital punishment in the United States for the first time since its decision in *Furman*. The Court's recent declarations in *Roper v. Simmons*, 125 S. Ct. 1183 (2005), that capital punishment is no longer constitutional for juvenile offenders, and in *Atkins v. Virginia*, 122 S. Ct. 2242 (2002), that capital punishment is no longer constitutional for offenders with mental retardation, signal a potential shift toward a radically different constitutional stance, one more open to consideration of international practice and norms in developing death penalty jurisprudence. What we ought to learn from the theories of American exceptionalism with regard to capital punishment that I have canvassed in this essay is that the Supreme Court is the only realistic hope of nationwide abolition in this country, and that the likelihood of this hope's being realized changes from generation to generation—often turning on a dime.

Conclusion

A quick perusal of this essay, taking in simply the sheer number of headings and theories, conveys a sense that powerful forces, unique to the United States, have compelled the result that we see today—anomalous American retention of capital punishment in the Western industrialized world. In fact, a careful reading should promote a much more nuanced view. Some of the most popular and easy theories of American exceptionalism with regard to capital punishment have less to recommend them than meets the eye. Thoughtful reflection impels the conclusion that there was nothing necessary, inevitable, or deeply fated about the retention of capital punishment in the United States. This is not to say that there are not reasons for it—there are plenty of those. But many of those reasons have to do with chance, with timing, and with the functioning of particular institutions and particular people in a particular context. It could easily have turned out otherwise and almost did. We should thus most emphatically not assume that we are destined—owing to sociological facts about our murder rate or to political forces that currently predominate, or to anthropological observations about our culture—to continue to embrace capital punishment. Rather, a sobering recognition of the many contingencies that have attended America's recent "death penalty story" (and all of history) should temper a bleak acceptance of historical "fate."

Chapter 4

Why Does the American Constitution Lack Social and Economic Guarantees?

CASS R. SUNSTEIN

> The alms given to a naked man in the street do not fulfill the obligations of the state, which owes to every citizen a certain subsistence, a proper nourishment, convenient clothing, and a kind of life not incompatible with health.
> —Montesquieu

> This Republic had its beginning, and grew to its present strength, under the protection of certain inalienable rights—among them the right of free speech, free press, free worship, trial by jury, freedom from unreasonable searches. They were our rights to life and liberty.
> As our economy has grown in size and stature, however—as our industrial economy expanded—these political rights proved inadequate to assure us equality in the pursuit of happiness. . . . We have accepted, so to speak, a second Bill of Rights under which a new basis of security and prosperity can be established for all—regardless of station, race, or creed,
> The right to a useful and remunerative job in the industries or shops or farms or mines of the Nation;
> The right to earn enough to provide adequate food and clothing and recreation;
> The right of every farmer to raise and sell his products at a return which will give him and his family a decent living;
> The right of every businessman, large and small, to trade in an atmosphere of freedom from unfair competition and domination by monopolies at home or abroad;
> The right of every family to a decent home;
> The right to adequate medical care and the opportunity to achieve and enjoy good health;
> The right to adequate protection from the economic fears of old age, sickness, accident, and unemployment;
> The right to a good education.
> I ask Congress to explore the means for implementing this economic bill of rights—for it is definitely the responsibility of the Congress to do so.
> —Franklin Delano Roosevelt

Introduction

The Universal Declaration of Human Rights protects a wide range of social and economic rights. It proclaims, for example, that "[e]veryone has a right to work, to free choice of employment, to just and favourable conditions of work and to protection against unemployment." It also provides a "right to equal pay for equal work," a right "to form and to join trade unions for protection," and a right to "just and favourable remuneration ensuring for himself and his family an existence worthy of human dignity, and supplemented, if necessary, by other means of social protection." More broadly still, the Declaration gives "everyone" a "right to a standard of living adequate for the health and well-being of himself and his family, including food, clothing, housing and medical care and necessary social services, and the right to security in the event of unemployment, sickness, disability, widowhood, old age or other lack of livelihood in circumstances beyond his control." The Declaration also provides a "right to education" and to "social security."

The International Covenant on Social, Economic, and Cultural Rights follows the Declaration in creating social and economic rights. So do many constitutions, which guarantee citizens a wide range of social entitlements. Of course this was true for the Soviet Constitution. But many noncommunist and postcommunist constitutions contain these rights as well. The Constitution of Norway imposes on the state the responsibility "to create conditions enabling every person capable of work to earn a living by his work." The Romanian Constitution includes the right to leisure, the right to work, the right to equal pay for equal work, and measures for the protection and safety of workers. The Constitution of Peru announces, "The worker is entitled to a fair and adequate remuneration enabling him to provide for himself and his family material and spiritual well-being." The Syrian Constitution proclaims that the "state undertakes to provide work for all citizens." The Bulgarian Constitution offers the right to a holiday, the right to work, the right to labor safety, the right to social security, and the right to free medical care. The Hungarian Constitution proclaims, "People living within the territory of the Republic of Hungary have the right to the highest possible level of physical health." It also provides that "[e]veryone who works has the right to emolument that corresponds to the amount and quality of the work performed."

I am grateful to many people for valuable comments and discussions, including Jack Goldsmith, Michael Ignatieff, Martha Nussbaum, Eric Posner, and Richard Posner, and participants in workshops at the John F. Kennedy School of Government and at the University of Chicago Law School.

Not every modern constitution creates rights of this sort; such rights are entirely absent from a number of contemporary constitutions. Indeed some nations recognize such rights, but in a way that seems to make them goals and not rights at all. The Constitution of Switzerland, for example, says that "the Confederation and the cantons seek to ensure" certain rights, involving social security, necessary health care, and more. The Constitution of India offers a range of civil and political rights, and also offers "directive principles of state policy," saying that the state shall "direct its policy towards securing" certain rights, including, among others, an adequate means of livelihood and equal pay for equal work for men and women. This strategy is taken as well in Ireland, Nigeria, and Papua New Guinea. The South African Constitution recognizes a wide range of social and economic rights, but also acknowledges resource constraints, typically obliging the state to "take reasonable legislative and other measures, within its available resources, to achieve the progressive realisation of" the relevant right. Provisions of this kind are ambiguous, but they have been held to be justiciable, obliging the government not to default in its basic obligations.[1]

I am concerned here with a particular puzzle. The constitutions of most nations create social and economic rights, whether or not they are enforceable. But the American Constitution does nothing of the kind. Why is this? What makes the American Constitution so distinctive in this regard?

I will explore four possible answers here.[2] In the process I hope to cast some light on the effects of constitutions, cultural differences, and social and economic guarantees in general. The first explanation is chronological; it points simply to the age of the American Constitution, which is the oldest in force in the world. The second, institutional in nature, emphasizes that social and economic right cannot easily coexist with judicial review, a preoccupation of the American legal culture. The third points to "American exceptionalism" as it is standardly understood: the absence of a significant socialist movement in the United States. The fourth, rooted in legal realism, stresses developments within the U.S. Supreme Court in the 1960s and 1970s. In the end my major suggestion will be that the fourth explanation is the most interesting and in an important sense correct. The Constitution means what the Supreme Court says it means; with a modest shift in personnel, the Constitution would have been understood to create social and economic rights of the sort recognized in many modern constitutions, and indeed in the constitutions of some of the American states.

---

[1] See Government of the Republic of South Africa v. Grootboom, 11 BCLR 1169 (CC) (2000).

[2] The issues explored in this chapter are discussed in more detail in Cass R. Sunstein, The Second Bill of Rights (New York: Basic Books, 2004).

An additional word before we proceed: To evaluate the four explanations, we should distinguish between necessary and sufficient conditions
for the recognition of social and economic rights. Judicial interpretation
of an ambiguous constitutional provision is a sufficient condition, though
not a necessary one. Ratification of an explicit provision is a sufficient
condition, though not a necessary one. I am concerned here to explore
both the failure of a serious ratification effort and the absence of a judicial
interpretation that would recognize social and economic rights.

This chapter is organized as follows. First, I offer some conceptual pre-
liminaries. My goal here is to challenge the claim of a sharp dichotomy
between traditional constitutional rights and social and economic rights,
by showing that both of these depend on an active government and indeed
on the expenditure of taxpayer funds. The next section explores the chronological explanation. I then briefly discuss the amendment process and
also the New Deal period, in which social and economic guarantees received prominent public attention. There follows an examination of institutional considerations. The next section investigates the cultural explanation. Thereafter I explore developments in the 1960s and 1970s, suggesting
that the Court came close to understanding the Constitution to create social
and economic rights, and that with slight differences in personnel, the
Court would have done exactly that. The final section is a brief conclusion.

Conceptual Preliminaries

What is distinctive about social and economic rights? What makes them
unusual? The conventional answer is that while ordinary rights create
"negative" checks on government, preserving a sphere of private immunity, social and economic rights impose "positive" obligations on government, creating a set of private entitlements to government assistance. On
this view, negative guarantees are both time-honored and consistent with
the (classical) liberal tradition. Positive rights are novel, a creation of the
New Deal, or social democracy, or perhaps socialism, assimilating to the
category of "rights" what would otherwise be seen as pleas for public
assistance. In a standard formulation, Roosevelt's proposed Second Bill
of Rights, set out above, is distinctive "in linking together the negative
liberty from government achieved in the old Bill of Rights to the positive
liberty through government to be achieved in the new Bill of Rights."[3]

This is indeed a conventional way to see matters, and it has some historical support. Social and economic guarantees, often described as "second-
generation" rights, did receive recognition long after the traditional "negative" rights. But the conventional view is a bad way of understanding

---

[3] Doris Kearns Goodwin, *No Ordinary Time* 485 (New York: Simon & Schuster, 1994).

the relevant categories. Most of the so-called negative rights require government assistance, not governmental abstinence. Those rights cannot exist without public assistance. Consider, for example, the right to private property. As Bentham wrote, "property and law are born together and die together. Before the laws there was no property; take away the laws, all property ceases."[4] In the state of nature, private property cannot exist, at least not in the way that it exists in a free society. In the state of nature, any property "rights" must be protected either through self-help—useful to the strong, not to the weak—or through social norms. This form of protection is far too fragile to support a market economy or indeed the basic independence of citizens. As we know and live it, private property is both created and protected by law; it requires extensive governmental assistance.

The same point holds for the other foundation of a market economy, the close sibling of private property: freedom of contract. For that freedom to exist, it is extremely important to have reliable enforcement mechanisms in the form of civil courts. The creation of such mechanisms requires action, not abstinence. Nor is the point—the dependence of rights on public assistance—limited to the foundations of a market economy. The Fifth, Sixth, Seventh, and Eighth Amendments—a significant part of the original Bill of Rights—regulate the systems of criminal and civil justice. They require jury trials, fair hearings, rules of evidence, and bail. By doing this, and more, they require taxpayers to devote a great deal of money to the administration of justice. Consider the suggestion that it "is only because we are born into this mechanism as we are born into our homes that we take it for granted and fail to realize . . . what an immensity of daily effort on the part of government is required to keep it running. In terms of mechanism and trained personnel, a system of social security is child's play in comparison with the system that gives effect to due process of law."[5]

Or take the right to be free from torture and police abuse, perhaps the defining "negative" freedom. Of course it is possible to say this right is a "negative" safeguard against public intrusion into the private domain, and in a way that statement is true. But as a practical matter, the right to be free from torture and abuse requires a state apparatus willing to ferret out and to punish the relevant rights violations. If the right includes protection against private depredations, it cannot exist simply with government abstinence. If the right is limited to protection against public abuse of power, it can be satisfied by abstinence; but in practice, abstinence from torture and abuse must be guaranteed by a public apparatus that will deter and punish

---

[4] *Principles of the Civil Code*, in *The Works of Jeremy Bentham* (Edinburgh: Simpkin, Marshall, 1843), 507–8.

[5] John R. Ellingston, *The Right to Work*, 243 Annals of the American Academy 27, 33 (1946).

misconduct. Some rights require government to protect against its own rights violations. If we go down the list of conventional private rights, we will see this same point at every turn.

There is a larger implication, with direct relevance to the question of social and economic rights. All constitutional rights have budgetary implications; all constitutional rights cost money.[6] If the government plans to protect private property, it will have to expend resources to ensure against both private and public intrusions. If the government wants to protect people against unreasonable searches and seizures, it will have to expend resources to train, monitor, and discipline the police. If the government wants to protect freedom of speech, it must, at a minimum, take steps to constrain its own agents; and these steps will be costly. It follows that insofar as they are costly, social and economic rights are not unique.

Now it is possible that such rights are unusually costly—that to ensure (for example) that everyone has housing, we will have to spend more than must be spent to ensure (for example) that everyone is free from unreasonable searches and seizures. But any such comparisons are empirical and contingent; they cannot be made on an a priori basis. We could imagine a society in which it costs a great deal to protect private property, but not so much to ensure basic subsistence. Of course most societies are not like that. In most societies, the management of a social welfare system is more expensive than the management of a system to protect property rights. This kind of distinction—quantitative rather than qualitative in nature—is probably the central one.

Chronology

The First Generation of Framers and the First Generation of Rights

If we want to explain the absence from the American Constitution of social and economic guarantees, the most natural point is chronological. The simple claim is that the American Constitution, the oldest existing constitution in the world, was ratified during the late eighteenth century— a time when constitutions were simply not thought to include social and economic guarantees.[7] The American framers were building on rights as understood in the British tradition. No one then suggested, or even thought to suggest, that the Bill of Rights should contain a guarantee of this kind. When it was drawn up, the American approach was entirely

---

[6] This is the theme of Stephen Holmes and Cass R. Sunstein, *The Cost of Rights* (New York: Norton, 1999).

[7] Of course this point itself remains to be explained. But any such explanation would not involve American exceptionalism of any sort, which is my concern here.

standard, and hence the absence of social and economic rights is simply a matter of timing. On this view, there was no American exceptionalism, and there is really no puzzle to be solved. When modern constitutions were drawn up, the international understanding was altogether different, and hence it is entirely to be expected that social and economic rights will be found in the constitutions of (for example) Bulgaria, South Africa, Norway, and Russia. We can predict whether a constitution contains second-generation rights pretty well just by looking at the year of its ratification. With respect to such rights at the constitutional level, American exceptionalism is a myth and an illusion.

The Second Generation in the First: Principle

To highlight the chronological point is emphatically not to suggest that the American framers did not care about poor people. On the contrary, some of their writing suggested a strong commitment to protection for those at the bottom, though not at the constitutional level. James Madison, probably the most influential voice in the founding period, offered the following means of combating "the evil of parties": "1. By establishing a political equality among all. 2. By withholding unnecessary opportunities from a few, to increase the inequality of property, by an immoderate, and especially an unmerited, accumulation of riches. 3. By the silent operation of laws, which, without violating the rights of property, reduce extreme wealth to a state of mediocrity, and *raise extreme indigence toward a state of comfort*."[8] Jefferson, not a framer but a strong influence during the founding period, wrote,

> I am conscious that an equal division of property is impracticable. But the consequences of this enormous inequality producing so much misery to the bulk of mankind, legislatures cannot invest too many devices for subdividing property, only taking care to let their subdivisions go hand in hand with the natural affections of the human mind. . . . Another means of silently lessening the inequality of property is to exempt all from taxation below a certain point, and to tax the higher portions of property in geometrical progression as they rise. Whenever there is in any country, uncultivated lands and unemployed poor, it is clear that the laws of property have been so far extended as to violate natural right. The earth is given as a common stock for man to labor and live on.[9]

It is relevant here that many of the classical liberal thinkers, far from rejecting social and economic rights, explicitly endorsed them. Recall

---

[8] James Madison, 14 *The Papers of James Madison* 197–98 (Charlottesville: University of Virginia Press, 1975) (emphasis added).

[9] Thomas Jefferson, 8 *The Papers of Thomas Jefferson* 681–83 (Princeton: Princeton University Press, 1953).

Montesquieu's claim, quoted above: "The alms given to a naked man in the street do not fulfill the obligations of the state, which owes to every citizen a certain subsistence, a proper nourishment, convenient clothing, and a kind of life not incompatible with health."[10] John Locke was of course a large influence on American political thought, and he wrote in similar terms: "As Justice gives every Man a Title to the product of his honest Industry, and the fair Acquisitions of his Ancestors descended to him, so Charity gives every man a Title to so much of another's plenty, as will keep him from extream want, where he has no means to subsist otherwise."[11]

The chronological account, in short, emphasizes that some of the Constitution's framers believed in protection against acute deprivation, but adds that they did not believe in placing those rights in a constitution, for the simple reason that constitutionalization of such rights was a most foreign concept at the time. Of course it would remain necessary to explain the reason for the rise of second-generation rights—why they were absent when they were absent, and why they arose when they did—but this would not be a question about American exceptionalism in particular. It would be a question about changing conceptions of constitutional rights over time.

A Problem

Undoubtedly the chronological account has considerable truth. But as a complete explanation, it faces a serious problem: The meaning of the Constitution changes over time. In numerous ways, the American Constitution has gone far beyond the original understanding of its authors and ratifiers. Constitutional change is in part a function of explicit constitutional amendments, and this is the place to begin. After the Civil War, the Constitution was of course significantly altered, and here too we find no serious interest in amending the Constitution to include social and economic rights.[12] Why not? Perhaps the same chronological account works here as well: In the late nineteenth century, social and economic rights were generally unfamiliar. But in the New Deal period (on which more shortly), the Constitution was not amended at all; there was no interest in adding such rights to the Constitution. Why not? In the midst of President Johnson's Great Society, and during widespread late twentieth-century interest in reducing poverty through housing rights, welfare rights, health care rights, and the like, America saw no serious debate about constitu-

---

[10] Baron de Montesquieu, *The Spirit of the Laws*, book 23, section 29, p. 25 (Thomas Nugent trans.) (New York: Hafner Press, 1949).

[11] John Locke, *Two Treatises on Government*, book 1, chapter 4.

[12] This statement overlooks some complexities. *See* Sunstein, *supra* note 2, for general discussion.

tional amendments. There was no significant discussion of adding social and economic rights to the American Constitution. The chronological account cannot explain this fact.

There is another problem. Constitutional change is often a product not of constitutional amendment but of interpretation, leading to new understandings of old provisions.[13] Even if the eighteenth-century constitution did not contain social and economic rights, the American Constitution might well have been interpreted to do so. Consider the question whether there is a problem of "American exceptionalism" in the absence of a ban on sex discrimination in the American Constitution. Many contemporary constitutions explicitly ban sex discrimination; why is the American Constitution so different? A chronological account offers part of an answer, but it is ludicrously incomplete. The equal rights amendment (ERA) might have been ratified. It wasn't; why not? Part of the answer points not to American exceptionalism in the context of sex equality but to the change in judicial interpretation of the equal protection clause over time. The American Constitution is now understood to have something very much like a constitutional ban on sex discrimination, not because of the original understanding of its text but because of new judicial interpretations. If this has happened in the context of sex equality, why hasn't it happened for social and economic rights as well? The chronological account offers no answer. And the example could easily be multiplied. In many ways, the American Constitution has come to be interpreted in ways that depart from its original meaning. Why haven't social and economic rights been part of new constitutional understandings?

Detour: Amendments and the New Deal

Procedural Difficulties

The chronological account can be strengthened by reference to a simple fact: It is not easy to amend the American Constitution, even if there is wide support for the amendment. The Constitution moves some way toward locking out changes—not by making them impossible but by making them extremely difficult. The American public broadly supported the ERA, but it nonetheless failed to pass. Because the Constitution creates real obstacles to amendment, immense popular support was not enough to ensure ratification of the ERA. Even if social and economic rights commanded widespread popular support, they might not find their way into the Constitution.

[13] *See* David Strauss, *Common Law Constitutional Interpretation*, 63 U Chi L Rev 877 (1996).

By itself this point appears to be a weak explanation of the failure to create social and economic rights, because no serious amendment effort was made. In these circumstances, it might seem that the difficulty of amending the Constitution cannot explain the situation. But the absence of a serious amendment effort should not be misinterpreted. The very difficulty of amending the Constitution has a strong deterrent effect on efforts to do so, and perhaps such an effort would have been made with a different constitutional structure. Because it is difficult to speculate about counterfactual history, the possibility cannot be ruled out. But there is every reason to think that even with a much easier amendment process, the Constitution would not have been altered to provide social and economic guarantees. The very absence of a significant attempt to alter the Constitution supports this speculation.

Second-Generation Rights in the New Deal

The point can be clarified by reference to the New Deal era. This was the period in which elites in the United States thought most seriously about social and economic guarantees—not with an eye toward constitutional amendments, but nonetheless in a serious and self-conscious manner. Indeed, the New Deal saw a large-scale renovation of the American constitutional structure, amounting to a kind of second American Revolution.[14] The renovation involved the three cornerstones of that structure: federalism; checks and balances; and individual rights.[15] As is well known, the powers of the national government significantly increased, and a great deal of authority was concentrated in the presidency. What is less well known is the nature of the New Deal's renovation of preexisting understandings of legal rights. Before the New Deal, the American legal culture defined "rights" largely in terms of the eighteenth-century catalog of the common law, and hence freedom of contract and private property were prominent illustrations of rights protected from governmental incursion.

The New Dealers believed that the common law catalog included too much and too little. A large part of their argument was an effort to denaturalize the common law. In their view, rights of freedom of contract and private property depended for their existence on a legal apparatus; they were hardly natural but resulted from a form of governmental intervention into private affairs. Thus Roosevelt urged, "We must lay hold of the fact that the laws of economics are not made by nature. They are made

---

[14] Or perhaps third if we include the Civil War Amendments.

[15] For more detail, see Sunstein, supra note 2.

by human beings."[16] This claim did not mean that freedom of contract and private property were bad ideas. But it did mean that they should be evaluated pragmatically and in terms of what they did for or to the human beings subject to them. And on this count, the New Dealers supported many readjustments of common law interests. Rights to governmental protection within the employment market, for example, were insufficiently protected by the common law, as were the interests of the poor, consumers of dangerous food and drugs, the elderly, traders on securities markets, and victims of unfair trade practices.

This basic theme, the central ingredient of New Deal constitutionalism, was prominent throughout Roosevelt's presidency. In his speech accepting the Democratic nomination for the presidency in 1936, for example, Roosevelt argued that although the constitutional framers were concerned only with political rights, new circumstances required the recognition of economic rights as well, because "freedom is no half-and-half affair."[17] The most dramatic statement of this revised notion of entitlement came in President Roosevelt's State of the Union address of 1944, which set forth the "Second Bill of Rights" quoted as an epigraph to this essay.[18]

In coming to terms with Roosevelt's proposal, we might offer three points. The first is the sheer amplitude of the relevant rights, including most of what can be found in the Universal Declaration and in contemporary constitutions. The second is Roosevelt's insistence that the relevant rights had already been "accepted," post–New Deal—that they reflected the nation's official creed in 1944 and hence represent no innovation. The third is that Roosevelt proposed no constitutional amendment, and no judicial role, but instead an effort by Congress to "explore the means for implementing this economic bill of rights." It should be noted in this regard that at the state level, constitutional amendments were indeed ratified, endorsing aspects of the Second Bill of Rights as a matter of state constitutional law. Indeed, a number of states now offer some social and economic rights. The New York Constitution is exemplary: "The aid, care, and support of the needy are public concerns and shall be provided by the state and by such of its subdivisions, and in such manner, and by such means, as the legislature may from time to time determine." The claim of large-scale American exceptionalism as a *cultural* matter is complicated not only by Roosevelt's plea for a Second Bill of Rights but also

---

[16] *Speech before the 1932 Democratic National Convention*, in *The Essential Franklin Delano Roosevelt* 17 (New York: Gramercy Books, 1995).

[17] *5 Public Papers and Addresses of Franklin Delano Roosevelt* 230 (New York: Random House, 1938).

[18] *The Public Papers & Addresses of Franklin D. Roosevelt* (Samuel Rosenman, ed.), vol. 13 (New York: Harper, 1950), 40–42.

by the existence of considerable constitutional innovation at the state level—activity that has not, by the way, made much difference in terms of actual lives of poor people.

But for present purposes, the crucial point is that the New Dealers did not pursue constitutional reform. Their approach on this count is fully consistent with their general strategy, which was to avoid official amendments entirely, and to use political processes and constitutional interpretation to move in the directions that they sought. Part of the reason for this strategy was the sheer difficulty of producing constitutional amendments. Part of it was great suspicion of the conservative judiciary. For those interested in creating a Second Bill of Rights, constitutional amendment did not seem an attractive option in light of the inevitable fact that any such amendment would increase the authority of judges. The point is directly related to the second explanation, to which I now turn.

Constitutions as Pragmatic Instruments

The institutional explanation claims that in the American culture, constitutions are seen as pragmatic instruments—suited for, and not inextricable from, judicial enforcement. And indeed it is useful, even crucial, to distinguish between the *pragmatic* and the *aspirational* conception of constitutions. When presented with a proposed constitutional provision, many Americans tend to ask, "What will this provision do, in fact? How will courts interpret this provision, in fact?"

These questions played a major role in debates over the equal rights amendment—helping to raise qualms about that amendment even for those committed to sex equality. But other people, especially but not only in Europe, tend to think of constitutions as literally declarative—as expressive of a nation's deepest hopes and highest aspirations. They like to ask, "What values does this provision affirm, in principle?" They see a constitution as a kind of declaration, probably not meant for judicial enforcement, and possibly not meant for compliance in the real world.

As analogies, consider the Declaration of Independence or even the Universal Declaration of Human Rights, debated and signed with little attention to the question of judicial enforcement, which was of course not contemplated. And while the United States ratified the International Covenant on Civil and Political Rights, growing out of the Universal Declaration, it was quite unusual, among modern nations, in refusing to ratify the International Covenant on Social, Economic, and Cultural Rights, perhaps because of a belief that the rights contained in the latter are not enforceable. It is important to emphasize here that many of the constitutions containing social and economic rights simply borrowed from the

Universal Declaration. It is also important to note that there is real doubt about whether the many constitutions containing social and economic rights have made any difference at all "on the ground"—that is, there is real doubt about whether such rights have actually led to more money, food, or shelter for poor people.

If we take the pragmatic approach, we will be likely to ask whether social and economic rights would be a sensible part of an enforceable constitution containing the important institution of judicial review. Should a constitution create a "right to just and favourable remuneration"? To "a standard of living adequate for the health and well-being of" one's family, "including food, clothing, housing and medical care and necessary social services"? To "rest and leisure"? What would these provisions mean, concretely? What would they mean in a poor nation with high levels of unemployment and inadequate medical care and housing? What would they mean, concretely, in a wealthy nation like the United States or France? If a nation failed to protect the relevant rights, would courts be authorized to intervene—as they usually are when rights are violated?

If these questions appear difficult to answer, we might explain American exceptionalism in institutional terms, as a response to the conception of constitutional rights as pragmatic instruments. And we might explain the contemporary practice of including such rights, all over the world, as a product of an understanding that they need not mean much, if anything, in practice. Such rights are meant as *signals*, domestically and internationally, but they are not legally enforceable instruments. On this view, Americans should not be thought skeptical of social and economic guarantees in principle; even Ronald Reagan was committed to a social safety net. The real source of skepticism is an account of what kind of document a constitution really is, and of what kinds of rights belong in a document of that sort.

There is considerable truth in this explanation. American courts have been reluctant to recognize social and economic rights in part because of a belief that enforcement and protection of such rights would strain judicial capacities. Political actors, even those interested in helping poor people, have been skeptical about the likely effectiveness of constitutional provisions that might be ignored in practice. Outside of the United States, some nations, including India and South Africa, have been alert to the underlying difficulties and have sharply limited the constitutional status of such rights by reducing judicial authority. And as I have noted, social and economic rights have served as aspirations, with apparently no real-world effects, in many nations in which they are recognized. It is hard to show that when nations are relatively more likely to help poor people, it is because they have constitutional provisions calling for such help.

But the institutional account cannot be all of the picture. For one thing, it is a bit fussy and bookish. It may be possible to *justify* the refusal to constitutionalize social and economic rights by pointing to problems in judicial enforcement; but can we really *explain* that refusal, in the United States, by pointing to those problems? In any case those who want constitutions to be pragmatic instruments need not reject the idea of social and economic rights. In the United States itself, state constitutions protect those rights, and some courts are willing to enforce them, at least to some degree.[19] In South Africa, initial steps have been taken, not toward careful judicial oversight of the welfare system, and not toward ensuring that everyone has decent shelter and food, but toward ensuring that the government at least creates "programs" that ensure minimal attention to basic needs.[20]

It is surely right to say that social and economic rights could strain judicial capacities. Certainly no court, in poor or rich nations, is going to be able to ensure that everyone has decent food, clothing, medical care, and housing.[21] But those who are committed to such rights, in principle, might well urge that courts could take steps to ensure that basic needs receive a degree of legislative priority, and that conspicuous neglect would be corrected. As a result, the institutional explanation has a serious defect.

The Cultural Explanation

I now turn to what may well be the most tempting explanation, one that points to American exceptionalism in general. Socialism has never been a powerful force within the United States. America is said to be exceptional because "it didn't happen here":[22] There was never a strong effort to move the United States in the direction of socialism or social democracy. On this view, the absence of social and economic rights has an explanation in terms of American politics or even culture. No group that might have been interested in such rights was ever powerful enough to obtain them. In the debate over the Universal Declaration, socialist and communist nations were most enthusiastic about social and economic guarantees, whereas capitalist nations were comparatively skeptical. Perhaps this, in a nutshell, is the best explanation for the American Constitution's failure to include such guarantees. The Constitution's content is a political artifact, and American politics is simply distinctive. Recall in this connection

---

[19] *See Tucker v. Toia*, 43 NY2d 1, 371 NE2d 449 (1977).

[20] *Government of the Republic of South Africa v. Grootboom*, 11 BCLR 1169 (CC) (2000).

[21] Compare first-generation rights, which are not very different on this count. The Fourth Amendment, for example, is violated every day.

[22] *See* Seymour Martin Lipset and Gary Marks, *It Didn't Happen Here* (New York: Norton, 1990).

the American skepticism about the International Covenant on Social, Economic, and Cultural Rights.

There is of course an extensive literature on American exceptionalism in general, with many competing views. Some people suggest that American workers have had, or have thought that they have, a high degree of upward mobility, muting dissatisfaction with any particular status quo. Others have suggested that feudalism is a necessary precursor to socialism, and that because America lacks a feudal past, socialism was inevitably going to fail. Others suggest that the American electoral system, with two dominant parties and elaborate checks and balances, dampened socialist efforts in the period in which they succeeded elsewhere. Still others suggest that powerful private groups were quick to suppress socialist movements whenever they threatened to be effective. For present purposes, it is unnecessary to choose among these competing explanations. What matters is the underlying weakness of socialism in the United States.

There is this much truth in the cultural explanation: The existence of social and economic rights, within a nation's constitution, is correlated with the strength of socialist or left-wing elements within that nation. In America, a strong socialist movement might well have sought a constitutional amendment or instead led to political changes that would have produced novel interpretations. As we shall see, a more left-wing political order would have produced a more left-wing Supreme Court, and such a court would likely have interpreted the Constitution to recognize social and economic rights. For this reason it is right to claim that if we are to understand the absence of such rights from American constitutional law, it is helpful to consider the absence of a significant socialist movement in the United States.

But as a full account of the situation, the cultural explanation is plainly inadequate. The reason is that a strong socialist movement is neither a necessary nor a sufficient condition for social and economic rights. It is easy to imagine a nation in which such a movement exists, but that does not think it useful to insist on constitutional provisions of this kind. Consider Canada, Israel, and England, three nations with strong socialist movements but without social and economic rights. It is also easy to imagine a nation without a strong socialist movement but with considerable enthusiasm for social and economic rights. In 1991, a sample of America's citizens was asked whether certain goods were "a privilege that a person should have to earn," or instead "a right to which he is entitled as a citizen."[23] By strong majorities, the respondents answered that a college education, a telephone, and an annual salary increase are privileges, not rights. But by equally strong majorities, they said that the following were

---

[23] *See* Sunstein, *supra* note 2.

rights: adequate housing, a reasonable amount of leisure time, adequate provision for retirement years, an adequate standard of living, and adequate medical care. Strong majorities, in short, endorsed many of the items on the Second Bill. In 1990, Americans were asked whether the government "should provide a job for anyone who wants one." Of those who expressed an opinion, an overwhelming 86 percent agreed. In 1998, 64 percent of Texans agreed that the "government should see to it that everybody who wants to work can find a job."

Franklin Delano Roosevelt was no socialist—indeed he strongly believed in capitalist institutions and free enterprise—but he was committed to "freedom from want," and as we have seen, he sought congressional protection of that form of freedom. It is easy to imagine a somewhat different FDR, one who had the same set of substantive beliefs, but who also believed that the constitutional route was the correct one to take. Why was that FDR not America's FDR? The reason does not lie in the absence of a strong socialist movement in the United States. If an American president could be committed to Roosevelt's Second Bill of Rights for legislative enactment, he could also be committed to a Second Bill of Rights at the constitutional level. The absence of significant American interest in constitutionalizing social and economic rights cannot be explained by reference to culture alone.

The Realist Explanation

I have emphasized that the meaning of the American Constitution changes because of new interpretations. If the Constitution meant, in all respects, what it originally meant, American constitutional rights would be thin indeed. Most of the key rights-protecting provisions now mean far more than they originally meant. For example, no provision of the Constitution forbids the national government to discriminate on the basis of race; but the Fifth Amendment, preventing denials of liberty without due process of law, is now taken to prohibit race discrimination at the national level. The best reading of history is that the First Amendment allowed Congress to regulate a great deal of speech; judicial interpretation, especially in the late twentieth century, has led to a robust free speech principle, far beyond anything envisaged by the First Amendment's authors and ratifiers. I have mentioned that the Fourteenth Amendment, when originally ratified, did not prohibit sex discrimination at all. But the American Constitution is now understood to ban most forms of sex discrimination, and indeed to contain a far more effective ban than can be found under most of the world's constitutions that contain *explicit* bans on sex discrimination.

If the American Constitution meant what it originally meant, the nation would have a lot of explaining to do—and the absence of social and economic rights would be one of the least conspicuous forms of American exceptionalism at the constitutional level. Here is a hypothesis: An interpretation of the Fourteenth Amendment that called for social and economic rights would not, in fact, be much more of a stretch of the document than many interpretations that are now taken for granted in American constitutional law. I cannot defend the hypothesis here; to do so, I would have to say a great deal about what constitutional interpretation entails. But I believe that I am building on conventional understandings.

All this is relatively abstract. Let us identify a more concrete explanation for American practice, one that stresses the contingency of the Constitution's meaning. I shall call this the *realist explanation* because of its connection with the legal realist movement of the 1930s, which emphasized that judicial interpretation of the law, including the Constitution, has a great deal to do with the political commitments of the judges. The realist explanation stresses that American constitutional law is, to a considerable degree, a form of common law, based on analogical reasoning. It suggests that American constitutional law could easily have come to recognize social and economic rights. It urges that the crucial development was the election of President Nixon in 1968, which produced four Supreme Court appointments, which led in turn to a critical mass of justices willing to reject the claim that social and economic rights were part of the Constitution. So described, the realist explanation seems to me entirely correct.

To understand the point, we should notice that there was a serious and partially successful effort, in the 1960s and 1970s, to interpret the existing Constitution to create social and economic guarantees. In some of the cases, the Court went so far as to hold that the government must subsidize poor people in certain domains. In *Griffin v. Illinois*,[24] for example, the Court held that the equal protection clause requires states to provide trial transcripts or their equivalent to poor people appealing their criminal convictions. In *Douglas v. California*,[25] the Court extended this ruling, concluding that poor people must be provided with counsel on their first appeal of a criminal conviction. When the Court struck down the poll tax,[26] it effectively ruled that states must provide the vote free of charge— even though it is expensive to run an election.

These decisions emphatically recognize social and economic rights; they say that the government must provide financial assistance to poor people in certain domains. For this reason it is too simple to say that the Ameri-

---

[24] 351 U.S. 12 (1956).

[25] 372 U.S. 353 (1963).

[26] *Harper v. Virginia Bd. of Elections*, 383 U.S. 663 (1966).

can Constitution is not understood to create social and economic rights. But the reach of these decisions is limited to contexts in which poverty interacts with interests that seem part and parcel of citizenship (the rights to vote and to contest a criminal conviction). In other cases, however, the Court went further. In *Shapiro v. Thompson*,[27] the Court held that the state of California could not, consistently with the Constitution, impose a six-month waiting period before new arrivals to the state could receive welfare benefits. The Court relied on the constitutional right to travel, but it also spoke of people's special needs, contending that California denies "welfare aid upon which may depend the ability of the families to obtain the very means to subsist—food, shelter, and other necessities of life." If the right to travel were all that was involved, this suggestion would seem purposeless.

Indeed, the Court came to give procedural protection to welfare benefits, in the important sense that under the due process clause, the government is not permitted to remove those benefits without giving people a hearing.[28] Hence welfare benefits can count as "property" within the meaning of the due process clause. In its initial decision, the Court emphasized the particular nature of welfare benefits: "Welfare, by meeting the basic demands of subsistence, can help bring within the reach of the poor the same opportunities that are available to others to participate meaningfully in the life of the community. [Public] assistance, then, is not mere charity, but a means to 'promote the general Welfare, and secure the Blessings of Liberty to ourselves and our Posterity.' " With its striking reference to the Constitution itself, the Court seemed to signal its willingness to consider the possibility that some constitutional provision would grant a right to subsistence for those in need. In fact prominent academic writing suggested that the Court was moving in that direction.[29]

By 1970, it was not at all clear that the Court would not eventually recognize a set of social and economic rights. In retrospect, the crucial event was the election of President Nixon in 1968, and his four appointments to the Court: Warren Burger in 1969, Harry Blackmun in 1970, and Lewis Powell and William Rehnquist in 1972. These appointees proved decisive to a series of extraordinary decisions, issued in rapid succession, limiting the reach of Warren Court decisions and eventually making clear that social and economic rights do not have constitutional status outside of certain restricted domains. During the period from 1970 to 1973, the Court cut off the emerging development. Here is a brief outline.

---

[27] 394 U.S. 618 (1969).

[28] *Goldberg v. Kelly*, 397 U.S. 254 (1997).

[29] *See* Frank I. Michelman, *Foreword: On Protecting the Poor through the Fourteenth Amendment*, 83 Harv. L. Rev. 7 (1969).

In *Dandridge v. Williams*,[30] the Court rejected a constitutional challenge to a state law that imposed an upper limit on the size of grants under its welfare program, regardless of the size of the family. The Court recognized that pressing necessities were involved, but found that fact constitutionally irrelevant and said so explicitly. In *Lindsay v. Normet*,[31] the Court upheld a state's summary eviction procedure. The plaintiff contended that the "need for decent shelter" and the "right to retain peaceful possession of one's home" were fundamental interests under the Constitution, subject to intrusion only after a powerful showing of countervailing government justification. The Court rejected the argument, saying that the "Constitution does not provide judicial remedies for every social and economic ill. We are unable to perceive in that document any constitutional guarantee of access to dwellings of a particular quality." Justice Powell wrote the key decision for a 5–4 majority in *San Antonio School District v. Rodriguez*,[32] which upheld a constitutional challenge to local financing of public schools—even though local financing produces large intrastate disparities in per-pupil expenditures. Justice Powell's lengthy opinion understood the Court's previous cases in an exceedingly narrow way, as involving absolute deprivations of constitutionally protected interests. *Rodriguez* was effectively the death knell for social and economic rights in the United States.[33]

This overview should be sufficient to show that the brief period from 1970 through 1973 played a crucial and underappreciated role in American jurisprudence. The Nixon nominees rejected what appeared to be an emerging trend in the direction of recognizing a robust set of social and economic rights. There can be no serious doubt that Humphrey nominees would have seen things very differently. Of course we cannot know what the Court would ultimately have said, nor can we know whether a Humphrey Court would have improved the lives of poor people. But it does not seem to me too speculative to suggest that if Humphrey had been elected, social and economic rights, American-style, would have become a part of American constitutional understandings. The Court was rapidly heading in this direction. The election of Richard M. Nixon stemmed the tide.

Now it would be possible to respond that that very election attests to the strength of the cultural explanation—that Nixon's election was a product of America's distinctive culture, one that is hostile to social and economic rights. And to be sure, Nixon won partly because of cultural forces; his victory had everything to do with the events of the time. I

---

[30] 397 US 471 (1970).

[31] 405 US 56 (1972).

[32] 411 US 1 (1973).

[33] For more detail about the period, *see* Sunstein, *supra* note 2.

cannot explore those events in detail here. But the Civil Rights Act of 1964 helped to convince southern voters to support Republican candidates; and the social unrest of the period, including riots in the cities, protests over the Vietnam War, and the assassinations of the Kennedys and of Martin Luther King, Jr., led numerous citizens to vote for Nixon, with his strong "law and order" platform. In fact Nixon's election might well be seen as signaling the end of a period of liberal ascendancy in American politics, one that reached its peak in the domestic policies of President Lyndon Baines Johnson. Nixon's victory was contingent, but it was hardly an accident; it reflected large-scale social forces. Perhaps those forces included antipathy to social and economic guarantees; perhaps Nixon won precisely because he could be expected to support an understanding of rights that did not include them. Perhaps Nixon was the anti-Roosevelt, and elected partly for that reason.

On the other hand, the 1968 election was exceptionally close, one of the closest in the nation's history, and it would be fantastic to suggest that the outcome was foreordained by a kind of national antipathy to social and economic rights. It is far more plausible to think that such rights were a casualty of an election that was fought out on other grounds. But what of the period since Nixon's election? In the last decades, the Court has shown little interest in reviving the trends that preceded that election. A central reason, of course, is that American presidents have not sought to appoint justices who want to move the Constitution in that direction. Even President Clinton chose two distinguished moderates, Ruth Bader Ginsburg and Stephen Breyer, who seem uninterested in aggressive judicial protection of social and economic guarantees. (I am not saying that they are wrong; in my view, Roosevelt was right to say that decent opportunity and minimal security should be provided politically rather than judicially, but my focus here is on the reasons for American exceptionalism, not on appropriate constitutional design.)

It is undoubtedly true that America's political culture has helped to produce a federal judiciary that no longer focuses on social and economic guarantees. Of course America's constitutional understandings have a great deal to do with its cultural understandings. What I am emphasizing here is that if not for a close and contingent electoral outcome, one that was far from inevitable, the American Constitution would almost certainly recognize some kinds of social and economic rights.

Conclusion

Why does the American Constitution lack social and economic rights? The chronological explanation contains some truth; in the late eighteenth century, such rights simply were not on the viewscreen for constitution makers. But the chronological explanation fails for the simple reason that constitutional meaning changes over time, and chronology alone does not explain the fact that the countless changes in modern constitutional understandings do not include recognition of social and economic rights.

The institutional explanation properly draws attention to the fact that many authors of international documents and constitutions do not think much about the question of enforcement and attempt instead to set out goals or aspirations. American constitutionalism has generally avoided this strategy. Constitutional design, emphatically including constitutional interpretation, has been undertaken with close reference to the possibility of judicial enforcement. The problem with the institutional explanation is that social and economic rights can, in fact, coexist with judicial enforcement. There are difficulties here, but they are not insuperable.

It is tempting to think that the constitutional status of social and economic rights will be very much a function of the power, in the relevant nation, of movements for socialism or for social democracy. To some extent this is certainly true, almost a truism. But it is far from impossible to believe, enthusiastically, in a market economy, and to believe at the same time in the obligation to ensure decent conditions for everyone. The framers of the American Constitution were hardly socialists, but Madison, the most important framer of all, emphasized the need for laws that would "raise extreme indigence toward a state of comfort." The New Dealers were hardly socialists, but Franklin Delano Roosevelt supported a Second Bill of Rights, one that amounts to a match for the most expansive of social and economic rights in international documents and the modern constitutions. Many American conservatives, enthusiastic about free markets, have endorsed the idea of a social safety net for all. For these reasons, it is too crude to invoke American exceptionalism as the explanation of the absence of social and economic rights in the American Constitution.

The realist explanation places a spotlight on the underappreciated fact that the U.S. Supreme Court came very close, in the 1960s and 1970s, to recognizing social and economic rights under the Constitution. A step of this kind would not have been fundamentally different from much of what the Court actually did in the twentieth century. Why did the Court refuse to recognize the relevant rights? A large part of the answer lies in the presidential election of 1968 and in particular in President Nixon's four critical appointments: Chief Justice Warren Burger and Justices Blackmun, Powell, and Rehnquist. In a very brief period in the early 1970s, the Court, led by these nominees, cut the ground out from under an emerging movement. This, I suggest, is a real source of "American exceptionalism" in the domain of social and economic rights.

Chapter 5

America's Jekyll-and-Hyde Exceptionalism

HAROLD HONGJU KOH

SINCE SEPTEMBER 11, "American exceptionalism" has emerged as a dominant leitmotif in the daily headlines. But the very phrase raises three questions: First, precisely what we do mean by American exceptionalism? Second, how do we distinguish among the negative and overlooked positive faces of what I call "America's Jekyll-and-Hyde exceptionalism"? And third, how should we, as Americans, respond to the most negative aspects of American exceptionalism after September 11?

During the last fifteen years, I have had a special opportunity to look at American exceptionalism from both sides now: not just from the perspective of the academy and the human rights world, but from two distinct vantage points *within* the human rights arena: from one angle, as a human rights scholar and nongovernmental advocate; from another, as a U.S. government official.[1] From these twin perspectives, I now see, the term "American exceptionalism" has been used far too loosely and without meaningful nuance. When we talk about American exceptionalism, what, precisely, do we mean?

The Faces of American Exceptionalism

Over the centuries, the very concept of "American exceptionalism" has sparked fierce debate in both the academic and political realms. The term,

A version of this chapter previously appeared as *On American Exceptionalism* in the *Stanford Law Review* at 55 Stan. L. Rev. 1479 (2003). When possible and appropriate, please cite to that version. The chapter echoes ideas expressed in Harold Hongju Koh, *The Law under Stress after September 11*, Yale L. Rep. (2003), and was originally presented in April 2002 to Michael Ignatieff's American Exceptionalism Seminar at the Carr Center for Human Rights Policy at Harvard's Kennedy School of Government.

[1] While in government, I served in the Reagan administration as a Justice Department lawyer and in the Clinton administration as assistant secretary of state for democracy, human rights, and labor. In those positions, I acted, in effect, as America's plaintiff's lawyer in cases where the United States holds a human rights grievance, as well as its defense lawyer when the United States has been charged with human rights abuse. Both before and after my government service, I spent considerable time suing the U.S. government, with regard to its refugee policy, foreign affairs decision making, use of force abroad, and human rights practices. *See, e.g.*, Harold Hongju Koh, *America's Offshore Refugee Camps*, 29 U. Rich. L. Rev. 139 (1994) (Allen Chair issue) (reviewing litigation).

usually attributed to Alexis de Tocqueville, has historically referred to the perception that the United States differs qualitatively from other developed nations, because of its unique origins, national credo, historical evolution, and distinctive political and religious institutions.[2] The phrase sometimes also connotes the idea that America's canonical commitments to liberty, equality, individualism, populism, and laissez-faire exempt it from the historical forces that have led to the corruption of other societies. In American political life, the concept flows through the rhetoric of nearly every American president, from Washington's Farewell Address, to Lincoln's Gettysburg Address, to Reagan's image of a "shining city on the hill," to nearly every post–September 11 speech of George W. Bush.

In the academic realm, the phrase has been variously used to explain America's distinctive cultural traditions, the evolution of the American labor movement, America's differences from Europe, America's peculiar approach to social welfare policy, and America's "frontier anxiety."[3] In foreign policy, the notion of American exceptionalism generally "holds that Americans deprecate power politics and old-fashioned diplomacy, mistrust powerful standing armies and entangling peacetime commitments, make moralistic judgments about other people's domestic systems, and believe that liberal values transfer readily to foreign affairs."[4]

In his introduction to this volume, Michael Ignatieff has approached the matter more systematically. He catalogs various kinds of American exceptionalism, in the process distinguishing at least three different faces of American engagement with the world.[5] The first face Ignatieff calls

---

[2] See generally Is America Different? A New Look at American Exceptionalism (Byron E. Shafer ed., 1991); John W. Kingdon, America the Unusual (1999); Seymour M. Lipset, American Exceptionalism: A Double-Edged Sword (1996); 2 Alexis de Tocqueville, Democracy in America 36–37 (Phillips Bradley ed., Henry Reeve trans., A. A. Knopf 1948) (1835).

[3] See, e.g., Deborah L. Madsen, American Exceptionalism (1998) (cultural traditions); Jonathan A. Glickstein, American Exceptionalism, American Anxiety: Wages, Competition, and Degraded Labor in the Antebellum United States (2002); but see Sean Wilentz, Against Exceptionalism: Class Consciousness and the American Labor Movement, 1790–1820, 26 Int'l Lab. & Working Class Hist. 1 (1984) (labor movement); Robert Kagan, Of Paradise and Power: America vs. Europe in the New World Order (2003) (America's differences from Europe); Seymour M. Lipset & Gary Marks, It Didn't Happen Here: Why Socialism Failed in the United States (2001) (failure of socialism in America); Jacob S. Hacker, The Divided Welfare State: The Battle over Public and Private Social Benefits in the United States 5–28 (2002) (America's approach to social welfare policy); David M. Wrobel, The End of American Exceptionalism: Frontier Anxiety from the Old West to the New Deal (1996); Frederick Jackson Turner, The Significance of the Frontier in American History, in Does the Frontier Experience Make America Exceptional? 18 (Richard W. Etulain ed., 1999) (America's frontier anxiety).

[4] Joseph Lepgold & Timothy McKeown, Is American Foreign Policy Exceptional? An Empirical Analysis, 110 Pol. Sci. Q. 369, 369 (1995).

[5] Michael Ignatieff, American Exceptionalism and Human Rights, chapter 1.

"American exemptionalism"—ways in which the United States actually *exempts itself* from certain international law rules and agreements, even ones that it may have played a critical role in framing, through such techniques as noncompliance; nonratification;[6] ratification with reservations, understandings, and declarations; the non-self-executing treaty doctrine; or the latest U.S. gambit, unsigning the Rome Statute of the International Criminal Court (ICC).[7] Second, he notes America's *legal self-sufficiency*, typified by Justice Scalia's statement in *Stanford v. Kentucky* that the practices of foreign countries are irrelevant to U.S. constitutional interpretation, because, in the construing of open-ended provisions of the Bill of Rights, "it is *American* conceptions of decency that are dispositive."[8] Third, he points to *double standards*, whereby the United States judges itself by different standards from those it uses to judge other states, and judges its friends and its enemies by different standards.

This helpful trichotomy nevertheless lumps together certain forms of exceptionalism and misses others. I prefer to distinguish among four somewhat different faces of American exceptionalism, which I call, in order of ascending opprobrium: distinctive rights, different labels, the "flying buttress" mentality, and double standards. In my view, it is the fourth face—double standards—that presents the most dangerous and destructive form of American exceptionalism.

America undoubtedly has a *distinctive rights culture*, growing out of its peculiar social, political, and economic history. Because of that history, some human rights, such as the norm of nondiscrimination based on race or First Amendment protections for speech and religion, have received far greater emphasis and judicial protection in America than in Europe or Asia. So, for example, the U.S. First Amendment is far more protective than other countries' laws of hate speech,[9] libel,[10] commercial speech,[11] and publication of national security information.[12] But is this distinctive rights culture, rooted in our American tradition, really inconsistent with universal human rights values? On examination, I do not find this distinctiveness too deeply unsettling to world order. The judicial doctrine of "margin of appreciation," familiar in European Union law, permits suffi-

---

[6] Ignatieff treats noncompliance and nonratification as separate categories of American exceptionalism, but for present purposes, I also group these phenomena under the "exemptionalism" heading. *See* Ignatieff, *supra* note 5.

[7] *See* Edward T. Swaine, *Unsigning*, 55 Stan. L. Rev. 2061 (2003).

[8] 492 U.S. 361, 369 n.1 (1989) (emphasis in original).

[9] *Brandenburg v. Ohio*, 395 U.S. 444, 447 (1969).

[10] *New York Times v. Sullivan*, 376 U.S. 254, 269 (1964).

[11] *Landmark Communications, Inc. v. Virginia*, 435 U.S. 829 (1978).

[12] *N.Y. Times Co. v. United States*, 403 U.S. 713 (1971).

cient national variance in protection of the same rights as to promote
some tolerance of this kind of rights distinctiveness.[13]

Similarly, America's tendency to use *different labels* to describe synonymous concepts turns out to be more of an annoyance than a philosophical
attack upon the rest of the world. When I appeared before the Committee
Against Torture in Geneva to defend the first American report on U.S.
compliance with the Torture Convention, I was asked a reasonable question: why the United States does not "maintain a single, comprehensive
collation of statistics regarding incidents of torture and cruel, inhuman
or degrading treatment or punishment," a universally understood concept.[14] My answer, in effect, was that the myriad bureaucracies of the
federal government, the fifty states, and the territories *did* gather statistics
regarding torture and cruel, inhuman, or degrading treatment, but we
called that practice by different labels, including "cruel and unusual punishment," "police brutality," "section 1983 actions," applications of the
exclusionary rule, violations of civil rights under color of state law, and
the like. Refusing to accept the internationally accepted human rights
standard as the American legal term thus reflects a quirky, nonintegration-
ist feature of our cultural distinctiveness (akin to our continuing use of
feet and inches, rather than the metric system). But different labels don't
necessarily mean different rules. Except for some troubling post–September
11 backsliding, which the Bush administration has now renounced,
the United States generally accepts the prohibition against torture, even
if it calls that prohibition by a different name.[15]

---

[13] *See generally* Louis Henkin, Gerald L. Neuman, Diane F. Orentlicher & David W.
Leebron, *Human Rights* 564 (1999). Admittedly, in a globalizing world, our exceptional
free speech tradition can cause problems abroad, as may, for example, occur when hate
speech is disseminated over the Internet. In my view, however, our Supreme Court can moderate these conflicts by applying more consistently the transnationalist approach to judicial
interpretation discussed below.

[14] *See* Harold Hongju Koh, U.S. Assistant Secretary of State, Democracy, Human
Rights & Labor, & William R. Yeomans, Chief of Staff, Civil Rights Division, U.S. Dep't
of Justice, *Reply to Questions from the U.N. Committee Against Torture* 3 (May 11, 2000)
(on file with author).

[15] The most prominent of these, of course, is the outrageous treatment of Iraqi prisoners
at Abu Ghraib prison, but in the wake of that disaster, President Bush has reiterated the
categorical U.S. position against torture as an instrument of state policy. See *President's
Statement on the U.N. International Day in Support of Victims of Torture*, June 26, 2004,
available at http://www.whitehouse.gov/news/releases/2004/06/20040626-19.html ("the
United States reaffirms its commitment to the worldwide elimination of torture. . . . Freedom from torture is an inalienable human right, and we are committed to building a world
where human rights are respected and protected by the rule of law. To help fulfill this commitment, the United States has joined 135 other nations in ratifying the Convention Against
Torture and Other Cruel, Inhuman or Degrading Treatment or Punishment. America stands
against and will not tolerate torture. We will investigate and prosecute all acts of torture

Third, I believe that lumping all of America's exclusionary treaty practices—e.g., nonratification, ratification with reservations, and the non-self-executing treaty doctrine—under the general heading of "American exemptionalism" misses an important point: that not all the ways in which the United States exempts itself from global treaty obligations are equally problematic. For example, although the United States has a notoriously embarrassing record for the late ratification, nonratification, or "Swiss cheese ratification"[16] of various human rights treaties, as my colleague Oona Hathaway has empirically demonstrated, the relevant question is not nonratification but *noncompliance* with the underlying norms, a problem from which the rest of the world tends to suffer more than does the United States.[17] Many countries adopt a strategy of ratification without compliance; in contrast, the United States has adopted the perverse practice of human rights *compliance without ratification.* So, for example, during the thirty-seven years after the United States signed, but before it ratified, the Genocide Convention,[18] no one plausibly claimed that U.S. officials were committing genocide. This was simply another glaring example of American compliance without ratification.

This third face of American exceptionalism Louis Henkin long ago dubbed "America's *flying buttress* mentality." Why is it, he asked, that in the cathedral of international human rights, the United States is so often seen as a flying buttress, rather than a pillar, willing to stand outside the structure supporting it, but unwilling to subject itself to the critical examination and rules of that structure? The short answer is that compliance without ratification gives a false sense of freedom. By supporting and following the rules of the international realm most of the time, but always out of a sense of political prudence rather than legal obligation, the United States enjoys the appearance of compliance, while maintaining the illusion of unfettered sovereignty.[19]

---

and undertake to prevent other cruel and unusual punishment in all territory under our jurisdiction. American personnel are required to comply with all U.S. laws, including the United States Constitution, Federal statutes, including statutes prohibiting torture, and our treaty obligations with respect to the treatment of all detainees").

[16] By "Swiss cheese ratification," I mean U.S. ratification of multilateral treaties with so many reservations, understandings, and declarations that these conditions substantially limit the U.S. acceptance of these treaties.

[17] Oona A. Hathaway, *Do Human Rights Treaties Make a Difference?*, 111 Yale L.J. 1935, 1977, 1980 (2002).

[18] Convention on the Prevention and Punishment of the Crime of Genocide, Dec. 9, 1948, 78 U.N.T.S. 277 (approved by Senate on Feb. 19, 1986).

[19] It is a bit like the driver who regularly breaks the speed limit but rarely gets a ticket, because he uses radar detectors, cruise control, CB radios, and similar tricks to stay just this side of the law. He complies but does not obey, because to obey visibly would mean surrendering his freedom and admitting to constraints, while appearing "free" better serves his

Like "distinctive rights" and "different labels," the flying buttress mentality is ultimately more America's problem than the world's. For example, it is a huge embarrassment that only two nations in the world—the United States and Somalia, which until recently did not have an organized government—have not ratified the Convention on the Rights of the Child. Nevertheless, this ultimately is more America's loss than that of the world. Why? Because the United States rarely gets enough credit for the large-scale moral and financial support that it actually gives to children's rights around the world, in no small part because of its promiscuous failure to ratify a convention with which it actually complies in most respects.[20] But once one weighs in the currently unfavorable alignment of proratification votes in the Republican-controlled Senate, and considers the amount of political capital that U.S. activists would expend to obtain the sixty-seven votes needed for ratification any time soon, one soon concludes that children's rights advocates are probably better off directing their limited energies not toward ratification, but rather toward real strategies to reduce the exploitation of child labor on the ground or to expand the prohibitions in the child-soldiers protocol.

This brings me to the fourth and most problematic face of American exceptionalism: when the United States actually uses its exceptional power and wealth to promote a *double standard*. The most problematic exceptionalism is not distinctive American rights culture, a taste for different labels, or a flying buttress mentality, but rather instances when the United States proposes that a different rule should apply to itself and its allies from the one that should apply to the rest of the world. Recent well-known examples include such diverse issues as the International Criminal Court,[21] the Kyoto Protocol on Climate Change,[22] executing juvenile of-

---

self-image than the more sedate label of being law-abiding. *See* Harold Hongju Koh, *The 1998 Frankel Lecture: Bringing International Law Home*, 35 Hous. L. Rev. 623, 626–32 (1998) (describing difference between compliance and obedience).

[20] The glaring exception, of course, is article 37(a) of the Children's Rights Convention, which says that "capital punishment . . . shall [not] be imposed for offences committed by persons below eighteen years of age." Convention on the Rights of the Child, G.A. Res. 44/25, annex, U.N. GAOR, 44th Sess., Supp. No. 49, art. 37(a), U.N. Doc. A/44/49 (1989) (entered into force Sept. 2, 1990). *See Roper v. Simmons*, 125 S. Ct. 1183 (2005) (holding, by a five-to-four vote, that the Eighth Amendment prohibits execution of juvenile offenders who committed their offenses while under the age of eighteen).

[21] Although the United States initially refused to accede to the Rome Statute of the International Criminal Court, President Clinton signed the treaty on December 31, 2000, without submitting it to the Senate. *See Clinton's Words: "The Right Action,"* N.Y. Times, Jan. 1, 2001, at A6. In May 2002, however, the Bush administration purported to unsign the treaty and notified the United Nations that it did not intend to become a party to the Rome Statute. *See* Letter from John R. Bolton, Under Secretary of State for Arms Control and International Security, to Kofi Annan, U.N. Secretary General (May 6, 2002), *available at* http://www.state.gov/r/pa/prs/ps/2002/9968.htm.

[22] *See Kyoto Protocol to the Framework Convention on Climate Change*, U.N. FCCC, 3d Sess., U.N. Doc. FCCC/CP/1997/7/Add.2 (1997), *reprinted in* 37 I.L.M. 22 (1998).

fenders or persons with mental disabilities,[23] declining to implement orders of the International Court of Justice with regard to the death penalty,[24] or claiming a Second Amendment exclusion from a proposed global ban on the illicit transfer of small arms and light weapons.[25] In the post-9/11 environment, further examples have proliferated: particularly, America's attitudes toward the global justice system, and holding Taliban detainees on Guantánamo without Geneva Convention hearings, about which I will say more later.

[23] *See Atkins v. Virginia*, 536 U.S. 304 (2002) (persons with mental retardation); *In re Stanford*, 123 S. Ct. 472 (2002) (Stevens, J., dissenting) (juvenile offenders). At the time that the Supreme Court voted to ban the execution of persons with mental retardation, the United States was the only nation in the world engaging in this practice, and the United States had criticized other nations for harsh treatment of those with retardation. *See generally* Harold Hongju Koh, *Paying "Decent Respect" to World Opinion on the Death Penalty,* 35 U.C. Davis L. Rev. 1085 (2002) (arguing for internalization of international standards regarding the execution of persons with mental disabilities). Until 2005, of all the established democracies in the world, only the United States was known to execute individuals who were younger than eighteen when the crime was committed, and three states—Texas, Virginia and Oklahoma—account for 81 percent of the 22 executions of children since 1972. Curiously, in 1979, representatives of the U.S. State Department had represented to Congress that juvenile execution was no longer a practice engaged in by the United States. See Harold Hongju Koh, *International Law as Part of Our Law*, 98 Am. J. Int'l L. 43, 51 (2004). In *Roper v. Simmons*, 125 S. Ct. 1183 (2005), The Supreme Court finally declared that practice unconsitutional.

[24] In the LaGrand Case (*F.R.G. v. U.S.*), 2001 I.C.J. 104 (June 27), Germany sued the United States in the World Court for threatening to execute two German nationals without according them rights pursuant to the Vienna Convention on Consular Relations. Although the ICJ issued provisional measures enjoining the execution of Karl LaGrand, American officials ignored the orders, the United States Supreme Court declined to intervene, and LaGrand was executed. The World Court finally found that the United States had violated the Vienna Convention, but, subsequently, American courts have treated the ICJ's ruling as having no legal effect within the United States. *See generally Symposium, Reflections on the ICJ's LaGrand Decision: Foreword*, 27 Yale J. Int'l L. 423, 424 (2002); Harold Hongju Koh, *Paying Decent Respect to International Tribunal Rulings*, 2002 Proc. Am. Soc'y of Int'l L. 45 (discussing post-LaGrand U.S. cases).

Recently, in *Avena v. Other Mexican Nationals (Mexico v. United States)*, March 31, 2004, *available at* http://www.icj-cij.org/icjwww/idocket/imus/imusframe.htm, the International Court of Justice ruled that the United States had breached its obligations to Mexico and to fifty-one Mexican nationals by the failure of state officials to inform the detained foreign nationals of their right to contact consular officials for assistance under the Vienna Convention before sentencing them to death. The ICJ directed the United States to review and reconsider the convictions and sentences of the Mexican nationals in light of the treaty violation. In March 2005, President Bush finally ordered the Texas state courts, as a matter of comity, to grant the review and reconsideration required by the ICJ's judgment.

[25] *See* John R. Bolton, *Statement to the Plenary Session of the U.N. Conference on the Illicit Trade in Small Arms and Light Weapons in all Its Aspects* (July 9, 2001), *available at* http://www.un.int/usa/01_104.htm ("The United States will not join consensus on a final document that contains measures abrogating the Constitutional right to bear arms"). For a critique of this argument, see Harold Hongju Koh, *A World Drowning in Guns*, 71 Fordham L. Rev. 2333 (2003).

For now, we should recognize at least four problems with double standards. The first is that when the United States promotes double standards, it invariably ends up not on the higher rung, but on the lower rung with horrid bedfellows—for example, with such countries as Iran, Nigeria, and Saudi Arabia, the only other countries that have not in practice either abolished or declared a moratorium upon the imposition of the death penalty on juvenile offenders.[26] This appearance of hypocrisy undercuts America's ability to pursue an affirmative human rights agenda. Worse yet, by espousing the double standard, the United States often finds itself co-opted into either condoning or defending other countries' human rights abuses, even when it previously criticized them (as has happened, for example, with the U.S. critique of military tribunals in Peru, Russia's war on Chechen "terrorists," or China's crackdown on Uighur Muslims).[27]

Third, the perception that the United States applies one standard to the world and another to itself sharply weakens America's claim to lead globally through moral authority. This diminishes U.S. power to persuade through principle, a critical element of American "soft power." Fourth, and perhaps most important, by opposing the global rules with the aim of modifying them to suit America's purposes, the United States can end up undermining the legitimacy of the rules themselves. The irony, of course, is that, by doing so, the United States disempowers itself from invoking those rules, at precisely the moment when it needs those rules to serve its own national purposes.

America's Overlooked Exceptionalism

Having focused until now on the four negative faces of American exceptionalism, I must address a fifth, much-overlooked dimension in which the United States is genuinely exceptional in international affairs. Looking only at the half-empty part of the glass, I would argue, obscures the most important respect in which the United States has been genuinely

[26] According to Amnesty International, the United States has executed 70 percent of the juvenile offenders executed worldwide since 1998, and, in 2002, the state of Texas (with three executions) was the only known jurisdiction in the world to execute a juvenile offender. *See* Amnesty Int'l, *Indecent and Internationally Illegal: The Death Penalty against Child Offenders* (abridged ed. 2002), *available at* http://www.amnestyusa.org/abolish/reports/amr51_144_2002.pdf.

[27] *See, e.g.,* Tom Malinowski, *Overlooking Chechen Terror,* Wash. Post, Mar. 1, 2003, at A19 (noting that the United States has added three Chechen organizations to the State Department list of terrorist groups, apparently to avoid Moscow's veto of the Iraq resolution before the UN Security Council).

exceptional, with regard to international affairs, international law, and promotion of human rights: namely, in its *exceptional global leadership* and activism. To this day, the United States remains the only superpower capable, and at times willing, to commit real resources and make real sacrifices to build, sustain, and drive an international system committed to international law, democracy, and the promotion of human rights. Experience teaches that when the United States leads on human rights, from Nuremberg to Kosovo, other countries follow. When the United States does not lead, often nothing happens, or worse yet, as in Rwanda and Bosnia, disasters occur because the United States does not get involved.[28]

Let me illustrate with two anecdotes from my own experience. The first comes from my time as assistant secretary of state. A young British diplomat I knew came from the British Foreign and Commonwealth Office to work "on detail" at the State Department's Bureau of European Affairs. As he was returning to the British Embassy, I asked him, "So what was the major difference between your two jobs?" His immediate answer: "When something happens in the world, the Americans ask, 'What should we do?' The British ask, 'What will the Americans do?' "

This explains in part the Bush administration's cynicism about the French. Can you remember the last major human rights campaign led by the French? If you cannot remember, it is because in fact they have led very few, even while notoriously fraternizing with abusive regimes in such countries as China, Iraq, and Burma.

My second, bittersweet anecdote comes from my childhood. My late father, Dr. Kwang Lim Koh, served as minister to the United States for the first democratically elected government in South Korea. In 1961, a military coup overthrew the democratic government of Prime Minister Chang Myon, who was placed under house arrest amid rumors that he would shortly be executed. To plead for Chang's life, my parents brought Chang's teenage son to see Walt W. Rostow, then the deputy national security adviser to the president. Rostow turned to the boy and said simply, "We know where your father is. Let me assure you, he will not be harmed." Rostow's words stunned my father, who simply could not believe that any country could have such global power, reach, and interest. The story so impressed my father that he repeated it on countless occasions as I grew up, as proof of the exceptional goodness of American power.

---

[28] For compelling discussions of how the United States failed to intervene in time in Bosnia and Rwanda, *see* Richard C. Holbrooke, *To End a War* (1998); Samantha Power, *A Problem from Hell: America and the Age of Genocide* (2002).

But after I entered the State Department, I came to realize that what I had understood to be exceptional behavior is in fact America's diplomatic rule: every day in virtually every embassy and consulate around the world, American diplomats make similar interventions for and inquiries about political prisoners, opposition politicians, and labor leaders, even in countries that most Americans could not locate on any map. Without question, no other country takes a comparable interest or has comparable influence worldwide. Both America's global interest and its global influence are genuinely exceptional.

Ironically, as I grew older, I came to realize that this canonical story was inherently double-edged. On the one hand, it showed that America both has and exercises exceptional power, every day and in every country on the planet. But the real problem in the Korean case was not that the United States did too much, but that it probably did too little.[29] The United States was ready to intervene to save Prime Minister Chang's life, but not to take the additional steps necessary to restore democracy in South Korea. Instead of doing more to effectuate its human rights commitment, for several decades during the Cold War, the United States instead supported a military government committed to authoritarian rule and economic growth.

What this taught me is that human rights problems as often arise when the United States does not exercise its exceptional leadership in human rights as when it does. If critics of American exceptionalism too often repeat, "America is the problem, America is the problem," they will overlook the occasions where America is not the problem but the solution, and if America is not the solution, there will simply be no solution.

To illustrate, let me cite three timely examples: Afghanistan, the Middle East, and North Korea. In Afghanistan, the United States led an extraordinarily swift and successful military campaign in early 2002 to oust the Taliban and restore democracy.[30] In Bosnia, the United States famously "went in heavy" after the Dayton Accords, committing 60,000 NATO peacekeepers, including some 20,000 Americans.[31] But in Afghanistan, the United States initially committed fewer than 500 of fewer than 6,000 NATO peacekeepers to a significantly larger geographic area. The predictable result: while Hamid Karzai nominally acts as president of Afghani-

[29] For historical accounts of this period in South Korean political life, see Sungjoo Han, *The Failure of Democracy in South Korea* (1974); Gregory Henderson, *Korea: The Politics of the Vortex* 177–91 (1968).

[30] For a probing analysis, see Stephen Biddle, *Afghanistan and the Future of Warfare*, Foreign Aff., Mar.–Apr. 2003, at 31.

[31] See Ann Devroy & Dana Priest, *Clinton Aides Debate Size of U.S. Peacekeeping Force for Bosnia*, Wash. Post., Sept. 21, 1995, at A24.

stan, outside of Kabul much of the country remains under the de facto control of warlords and druglords. Human rights abuses continue, but under the name of some Northern Alliance leaders whom the United States supported during the war.[32] Yet instead of making the additional financial commitments necessary to secure Afghanistan and promote serious nation building, the Bush administration initially allocated *zero* dollars in its 2004 budget for Afghan reconstruction, until embarrassed congressional staffers finally wrote in a paltry line item of $300 million to cover the oversight.[33] So the problem in Afghanistan has not been what the United States has done, but what it has not done. The United States won the Afghan war but did not make the necessary commitments to secure the peace, even as it has moved on to a far more ambitious war and nation-building exercise in Iraq.

A parallel story can be told about the Middle East peace process, which accentuates the contrast between America's military exceptionalism and its relative diplomatic impotence. The Afghan and Iraqi wars remind us that no one fights modern wars the way Americans can. Yet the magnitude of American hard power in Iraq contrasts with a remarkable decline in diplomatic initiative by the United States in the Middle East. From 1973 on, administrations of both political stripes played an activist, mediating role in the Middle East peace process, most notably at the Clinton and Carter Camp David summits, and at the Madrid peace process of the first Bush administration. The working assumption was that the United States was the only country with the power and position to play the role of honest broker in the regional process. The diplomatic mechanism was a special envoy system for the Middle East that engaged in moment-to-moment shuttle diplomacy, ensuring that the highest-ranking officials would work on the Middle East peace process virtually every day.[34] Yet

[32] *See* Dexter Filkins, *The Anxiety of Postwar Afghans*, N.Y. Times, Mar. 31, 2002, at D5; Carlotta Gall, *Afghan Leader Swears In 5 Deputies with an Eye to Balance*, N.Y. Times, June 28, 2002, at A6 (explaining Hamid Karzai's attempts to negotiate a political alliance with powerful regional-ethnic warlords and Rashid Dostum's ongoing resistance to a centralized Afghan state); Press Release, Human Rights Watch, *Anti-Pashtun Violence Widespread in Afghanistan*, Human Rights News (Mar. 3, 2002), *available at* http://www.hrw.org/press/2002/03/afghanistan0303.htm. For an account of competing hegemonic influences in postwar Afghanistan, see Michael Ignatieff, *Nation-Building Lite*, N.Y. Times, July 28, 2002, at F26.

[33] Paul Krugman, *The Martial Plan*, N.Y. Times, Feb. 21, 2003, at A27.

[34] In the Clinton administration, that group included President Clinton; Vice President Gore; Secretary of State Madeleine Albright; National Security Adviser Sandy Berger; U.S. Ambassador to the United Nations Richard Holbrooke; Assistant Secretary for Near Eastern Affairs Martin Indyk; and Dennis Ross, who served as Special Middle East Envoy for both Republican and Democratic administrations.

after January 2001, the United States abruptly withdrew from this activist role, discontinued the special envoy system, and disengaged from diplomatic mediation, with consequences akin to removing adult supervision from a playground populated by warring switchblade gangs.

Since then, the situation has dramatically deteriorated. Left in the hands of Ariel Sharon, the late Yasir Arafat, and parties beyond either of their control, the peace process has stumbled. New, repeated spasms of violence have broken out that have greatly multiplied the challenges of mediation in the Middle East. The Bush administration finally reengaged diplomatically and committed itself to a new "road map" for negotiations, which at this writing remain uncertain. Thus, even as the United States directs exceptional energy toward Iraq, the greater danger is that that effort will undermine our capacity to do enough elsewhere in the Middle East, in which the United States is undeniably the indispensable player.

My third example is North Korea. When I went to Pyongyang, North Korea, in November 2000 with then–secretary of state Madeleine Albright, the United States had chosen an activist option toward North Korea: creating in 1994 an Agreed Framework for multilateral diplomatic engagement and negotiation as its preferred mechanism for alleviating long-term tensions on the peninsula.[35] North Korea plainly violated that agreement in part. But still, the Agreed Framework yielded clear benefits.[36] Most important, North Korea engaged in bilateral dialogue with South Korea, under South Korean president Kim Dae Jung's "Sunshine Policy," which brought Kim Dae Jung to Pyongyang for a historic June 2000 North-South summit meeting with North Korean president Kim

---

[35] Under the Agreed Framework, the United States, South Korea, and Japan would all engage diplomatically with North Korea around a coordinated message and negotiating strategy. The Agreed Framework sought to freeze North Korea's plutonium program, including operations at the Yongbyon nuclear reactor. In exchange, the West promised light-water reactors and oil shipments to replace Yongbyon's energy output, and the longer-term goals of U.S. disavowal of hostile intent toward North Korea, help in dismantling North Korean weapons facilities, and eventual expansion of South Korean and Japanese social, cultural, and economic links.

[36] In addition to the freeze at Yongbyon, over the next decade, North Korea reduced its nuclear missile production, placed a moratorium on tests of long-range missiles, admitted that it had kidnapped Japanese citizens in the 1970s and 1980s, and allowed U.S. inspections of a mountain suspected as a site of further nuclear-weapons work. As Deputy Secretary of State Richard Armitage acknowledged recently, in testimony before the Senate Foreign Relations Committee, "I think it's quite clear that from 1994 to now, Yongbyon itself did not produce more plutonium, which could be turned into nuclear weapons. And so, there are dozens of nuclear weapons that North Korea doesn't have because of the framework agreement, and we have to acknowledge that, I believe." *Testimony of Deputy Secretary of State Richard Armitage before the Senate Foreign Relations Committee on North Korea*, Fed. News Service, Feb. 4, 2003.

Jong Il.[37] Bolstered by having won the Nobel Peace Prize, in late 2000 Kim Dae Jung talked of ways to expand the North-South dialogue, even considering holding the semifinal of the 2002 World Cup Soccer Championships in Pyongyang.[38]

The Clinton administration left an agreement to stop certain kinds of missile development and proliferation just short of completion. But when U.S. administrations changed, the new administration broke off talks and withdrew from direct engagement with North Korea, over the objections of President Kim Dae Jung and even of former president George H. W. Bush and his key Asia advisers. By his January 2002 State of the Union Address, the younger President Bush had famously labeled North Korea part of the "Axis of Evil," along with Iraq and Iran. North Korean president Kim Jong Il was faced with the question of how to get U.S. attention back on his own terms.[39] His chosen solution: building more bargaining chips by lifting the freeze at Yongbyon, beginning to enrich plutonium to make nuclear weapons, ousting weapons inspectors, openly cheating on other international agreements, and in January 2003 announcing North Korean withdrawal from the Nuclear Nonproliferation Treaty.

America's "hard power" alternative—disarming North Korea militarily—raises such a threat to the people of South Korea and the nearly forty thousand U.S. troops stationed there as to be effectively unusable. Yet the passive alternative initially chosen by the Bush administration would have let North Korea go nuclear, while seeking to isolate and contain it in hopes of bringing about the eventual collapse of the North Korean regime. Under intense pressure from Seoul and Tokyo, the administration finally shifted back to a diplomatic alternative: to reinitiate multilateral talks (which have only recently begun) and to reengage diplo-

---

[37] See James T. Laney & Jason T. Shaplen, *How to Deal with North Korea*, Foreign Aff., Mar.–Apr. 2003, at 16. "Whether by desire or by necessity, the North finally appeared to be responding to the long-standing concerns of the United States, South Korea, and Japan. Equally important, Pyongyang seemed to have abandoned its policy of playing Washington, Seoul, and Tokyo off one another by addressing the concerns of one while ignoring those of the other two. For the first time, the North was actively (even aggressively) engaging all three capitals simultaneously." *Id.*

[38] Remarkably, the actual semifinal match pitted South Korea against a reunited Germany before a wildly exuberant Korean audience. Had that match been played in Pyongyang, with global media attention, and South Korean and North Korean fans cheering together for the South, it would have had a cultural impact upon North Korea's isolation many times greater that of than U.S.-Chinese "ping-pong diplomacy" of the 1970s.

[39] My personal observation of Kim Jong Il convinces me that however strange, isolated, and maladjusted he may be, he is neither uninformed nor unintelligent. When President Bush suddenly announced in January 2002 that North Korea is part of an "Axis of Evil" with Iraq, when nothing had really changed on the ground, Kim surely concluded that he needed to shift his own policy to counter the new American hostility. See Paul Krugman, *Games Nations Play*, N.Y. Times, Jan. 3, 2003, at A21.

matically, with soft power, but only after having lost both critical time and valuable ground.

In each of these cases, my historical account and policy prescription may be controversial, but my broader point should not be. American exceptionalism has both good and bad faces. On the Korean Peninsula, in Afghanistan, and in the Middle East, the United States cannot disengage, and the world simply cannot afford to let the United States disengage. Rather, the United States must reengage in each of these areas, not with hard power—which has limited resolving effect in these delicate diplomatic situations—but with "soft" diplomatic power backed by carrots and sticks. In each of these cases, American passivity has demonstrably made matters worse. By constantly stressing the ways in which America is the problem, single-minded critics of American exceptionalism may perversely encourage dangerous passivity in places where the United States presents the only viable solution to a festering global problem.

As important, in all three cases, the best face of American exceptionalism proves to be the face that promotes the rule of law. In each case, the broader goal of American power should be not the blunt use of force but the creation of new, constraining and facilitating legal orders—a democratic constitutional government in Afghanistan; a new domestic and international order among Israel and the Palestinians; and a new set of international legal norms to govern North Korea's behavior. In the end, American exceptionalism succeeds best when it seeks not simply to coerce but, rather, to promote sustainable solutions through the generation of legal process and internalizable legal rules.

Entrenching Exceptionalism

The second Gulf War with Iraq in March 2003 brought with it the inescapable sense that the phenomenon of American exceptionalism and the debate over it had reached a new watershed.[40] Under the Bush administration, an exceptionalist strategy seems to have become America's dominant response to the horrendous terrorist attacks of September 11.

Looking back, we can now see that September 11 created a cleft in the age of globalization that began with the fall of the Berlin Wall. In hindsight, the immediate post–Cold War era now looms as a time of "global optimism," when too many commentators were exuberantly optimistic about the constructive possibilities posed by the globalization of transport, commerce, finance, and communications. But then we learned that the same coin has a dark side: that terrorists can exploit that same inter-

[40] See, e.g., Fareed Zakaria, *The Arrogant Empire*, Newsweek, Mar. 24, 2003, at 18.

connectedness to turn airplanes into missiles, to use the global financial system to move money across borders, to turn ordinary mail into a delivery system for biological weapons, and to plant viruses in email as a tool for cyberterrorism. Since September 11, we have almost literally left the light and entered the shadows of a new age of global pessimism, in which we have realized with alarm that all of the interdependent dimensions of the age of globalization could be equally turned against us.

The Bush administration's response to this startling challenge has been not interstitial but architectural. The emerging Bush Doctrine now has five identifiable elements:

- First, *Achilles and his heel*. September 11 brought upon the United States, like Achilles, a schizophrenic sense of its exceptional power coupled with its exceptional vulnerability. Never has a superpower seemed so powerful and vulnerable at the same time. Given that we have already suffered some three thousand civilian casualties in the war against terrorism, the question fundamentally posed by the Bush Doctrine is how best to use our superpower resources to protect our vulnerability.

- The answer given has been *Homeland Security*, in both the defensive and preemptive senses of that term. In the name of preserving American power and forestalling future attack, the United States government has instituted sweeping strategies of domestic security, law enforcement, immigration control, security detention, governmental secrecy, and information awareness at home,[41] even while asserting a novel right under international law to forced disarmament of any country that poses a gathering threat, through strategies of preemptive self-defense if necessary.[42]

- Third, the administration has justified this claimed sovereign right under international law by a shift in emphasis in human rights. In 1941, when Franklin Delano Roosevelt summoned the Allies to arms against an earlier "Axis of Evil," he did not simply call America to war. Instead, he painted a positive vision of the world we were trying to make: a postwar world of four fundamental freedoms: freedom of speech, freedom of religion, freedom from want, freedom from fear.[43] Since 1941, U.S. human rights policy

[41] *See generally* Lawyers Comm. for Human Rights, *Imbalance of Powers: How Changes to U.S. Law and Security since 9/11 Erode Human Rights and Civil Liberties* (2003), *available at* http://www.lchr.org/us_law/loss/imbalance/powers.pdf; Lawyers Committee for Human Rights, *A Year of Loss: Reexamining Civil Liberties since September 11* (2002), *available at* http://www.lchr.org/pubs/descriptions/loss_report.pdf.

[42] *See* President of the United States, *The National Security Strategy of the United States of America* 34 (2002), *available at* http://www.whitehouse.gov/nsc/nss.pdf; Bill Keller, *The I-Can't-Believe-I'm-a-Hawk Club*, N.Y. Times, Feb. 8, 2003, at A17 (noting claim of right of forced disarmament).

[43] Franklin Delano Roosevelt, *Eighth Annual Message to Congress* (Jan. 6, 1941), in 3 *The State of the Union Messages of the Presidents, 1790–1966*, at 2855 (Fred L. Israel ed., 1966).

in both Democratic and Republican administrations has followed the broad contours of the "Four Freedoms" speech. This framework foreshadowed a postwar human rights construct—eventually embedded in Eleanor Roosevelt's Universal Declaration of Human Rights[44] and subsequent international covenants—that would emphasize comprehensive protection of civil and political rights (freedom of speech and religion), economic, social, and cultural rights (freedom from want), and freedom from gross violations and persecution (e.g., the Refugee Convention, the Genocide Convention, and the Torture Convention). But after September 11, administration officials have reprioritized *"freedom from fear"* as the number one freedom the American people need to preserve. Instead of declaring a state of emergency, however, or announcing broadscale changes in the rules by which the United States had previously accepted and internalized international human rights standards, the administration has opted instead for a two-pronged strategy of creating *extralegal zones*, most prominently the U.S. naval base at Guantánamo Bay, Cuba, where scores of security detainees are held without legal recourse, and *extralegal persons*—particularly those detainees labeled "enemy combatants," who, even if American citizens on American soil, are effectively accorded no recognized legal avenue to assert either substantive or procedural rights.

• Fourth, beginning with Afghanistan and now continuing with Iraq, the administration has asserted a new strategy toward democracy promotion. From Ronald Reagan's famous 1982 Westminster speech until September 11, successive administrations had supported the promotion of democracy as a fundamental goal of U.S. foreign policy.[45] President Reagan's address to the Houses of Parliament called for a broad public-private effort "to foster the infrastructure of democracy—the system of a free press, unions, political parties, universities—which allows a people to choose their own way, their own culture, to reconcile their own differences through peaceful means."[46] During the Bush-Clinton years, the democracy-promotion strat-

---

[44] *See generally* Mary Ann Glendon, *A World Made New: Eleanor Roosevelt and the Universal Declaration of Human Rights* (2001).

[45] For history, see Thomas Carothers, *Aiding Democracy Abroad: The Learning Curve* 30–32 (1999); Tony Smith, *America's Mission: The United States and the Worldwide Struggle for Democracy in the Twentieth Century* (1994); Harold Hongju Koh, *A United States Human Rights Policy for the 21st Century*, 46 St. Louis U. L.J. 293 (2002).

[46] President Ronald Reagan, *Promoting Democracy and Peace* (June 8, 1982), *available at* http://www.iri.org/reaganspeech.asp. At that time, Congress approved the National Endowment for Democracy—a government-financed, private nonprofit fund that has continued to this day to make significant grants to business and labor—and effectively gave birth to the two political party institutes that now give support for the development of political parties and electoral processes overseas—the National Democratic Institute, of which former Secretary of State Madeleine Albright is now the chair, and the International Republican Institute, of which Senator John McCain is now the chair.

egy developed into a broader aspiration, captured by President George H. W. Bush's January 29, 1991, State of the Union message, for "a new world order—where diverse nations are drawn together in common cause, to achieve the universal aspirations of mankind: peace and security, freedom and the rule of law."[47] But the consistent theme during these years was "democracy promotion from the bottom up," not imposed from the top down. Since the U.S. invasion of Afghanistan, democracy-promotion efforts have shifted toward *militarily imposed democracy*, characterized by U.S.-led military attack, prolonged occupation, restored opposition leaders, and the creation of resource-needy postconflict protectorates.[48] At this writing, a new, four-pronged strategy seems to be emerging: "hard," militarily imposed democracy promotion in Iraq and Afghanistan; "soft," diplomatic democracy promotion in Palestine; optimistic predictions of "domino democratization" elsewhere in the Middle East; and reduced democracy-promotion efforts elsewhere. But if extended globally, as was done during the Cold War, such a U.S. strategy of making "the world safe through imposed democracy" could soon transform into an unsustainable strategy requiring near-unilateral military interventionism, extended support for client governments, and imperial overstretch.[49]

- Fifth and finally, as Strobe Talbott has observed, to implement the various elements of this emerging doctrine, the Bush administration has opted for "*strategic unilateralism and tactical multilateralism.*" By its nature, such a strategy resists enforced obedience to international treaties and institutions as dangerously constraining on U.S. national sovereignty.[50] But as with the "flying buttress" mentality described above, to win the illusion of unfettered sovereignty, the United States surrenders its reputation for being law-abiding.

---

[47] In his successful campaign for president, Bill Clinton criticized George H. W. Bush by arguing that "[o]ur nation has a higher purpose than to coddle dictators and stand aside from the global movement toward democracies. . . . President Bush seems too often to prefer a foreign policy that embraces stability at the expense of freedom." Harold Hongju Koh, *The "Haiti Paradigm" in United States Human Rights Policy*, 103 Yale L.J. 2391, 2427 n.206 (quoting Governor Bill Clinton, Remarks to the University of Wisconsin Institute of World Affairs (Oct. 1, 1992)).

[48] *See* Chibli Mallat, *Focus on Human Rights Offers Hope of Reconciliation*, Times (London), Mar. 29, 2003, at A13. "Welcome to the post-modern war. Even before it started, this war appeared surreal, not least for the idea that the United States and Britain were 'liberating Iraq' while refusing to involve any Iraqi in the process of change. . . . Even [hawkish Iraqis] are uneasy about American plans to rule Iraq 'directly,' echoing a universal rejection in the Arab world of American or British occupation." *Id.*

[49] Even the successful impositions of top-down democracy in Germany and Japan were accomplished after a single conflict, not pursuant to the laborious and expensive "seriatim strategy" that Afghanistan and Iraq may now portend.

[50] Talbott argues that, by contrast, the Clinton administration, in which he served as deputy secretary of state, pursued a foreign policy based on strategic multilateralism and tactical unilateralism.

This loss of rectitude diminishes America's moral authority and reduces the soft power American needs to mobilize multilateral responses in a post–September 11 world.

If these are the elements of the emerging Bush Doctrine, why is it so troubling? *Because such a doctrine makes double standards—the most virulent strain of American exceptionalism—not just the exception but the rule.* Each element of the emerging Bush Doctrine places the United States in the position of promoting genuine double standards, one for itself and another for the rest of the world. The exclusive focus on American vulnerability ignores the far greater vulnerability of such countries as, for example, Israel and Turkey (which, being a neighbor of Iraq, surely had more to fear from Saddam Hussein than did the United States, yet still denied American soldiers the right to stage ground operations from Turkish bases). Even while asserting its own right of preemptive self-defense, the United States has properly hesitated to recognize any other country's claim to engage in forced disarmament or preemptive self-defense in the name of homeland security.[51] The technique of creating extralegal "rights-free" zones and individuals under U.S. jurisdiction necessarily erects a double standard *within* American jurisprudence, by separating those places and people to whom America must accord rights from those it may treat effectively as human beings without human rights.

Similarly, the oxymoronic concept of "imposed democracy" authorizes top-down regime change in the name of democracy. Yet the United States has always argued that genuine democracy must flow from the will of the people, not from military occupation.[52] Finally, a policy of strategic unilateralism seems unsustainable in an interdependent world. Because the United States is party to a global network of closely interconnected treaties enmeshed in multiple frameworks of international institutions, unilateral administration decisions to break or bend one treaty

---

[51] *See* Mary-Ellen O'Connell, *The Myth of Preemptive Self-Defense* 3 (2002) (stating "the United States as a government has consistently supported the prohibition on such preemptive use of force"), *at* http://www.asil.org/taskforce/oconnell.pdf. Indeed, had such a doctrine existed at the time of the Cuban Missile Crisis, one wonders whether Castro would have invoked it to engage in preemptive self-defense against the United States.

[52] *See* U.S.-Sponsored Resolutions on the "Right to Democracy," C.H.R. Res. 1999/57, U.N. CHR, 55th Sess., U.N. Doc. E/CN.4/RES/1999/57 (1999) (51–0, with two abstentions); C.H.R. Res. 2000/62, U.N. CHR, 56th Sess., U.N. Doc. E/CN.4/RES/2000/62 (2000) (30–17, with six abstentions). In so arguing, the United States explicitly invoked legal scholarship asserting the existence of a right to democratic governance under international law. *See, e.g., Democratic Governance and International Law* (Gregory H. Fox & Brad R. Roth eds., 2000); Gregory H. Fox, *The Right to Political Participation in International Law*, 17 Yale J. Int'l L. 539 (1992); Thomas M. Franck, *The Emerging Right to Democratic Governance*, 86 Am. J. Int'l L. 46 (1992); Henry J. Steiner, *Political Participation as a Human Right*, 1 Harv. Hum. Rts. Y.B. 77 (1988).

commitment usually trigger vicious cycles of treaty violation. In an interdependent world, the United States simply cannot afford to ignore its treaty obligations while at the same time expecting its treaty partners to help it solve the myriad global problems that extend far beyond any one nation's control: the global AIDS and SARS crises, climate change, international debt, drug smuggling, trade imbalances, currency coordination, and trafficking in human beings, to name just a few. Strategic unilateralism undermines American soft power at the exact moment when the United States is trying to use that soft power to mobilize those same partners to help it solve problems it simply cannot solve alone: most obviously, the war against global terrorism, but also the postwar reconstruction of Iraq, the Middle East crisis, and the renewed nuclear militarization of North Korea.

If the emerging Bush Doctrine takes hold, the United States may well emerge from the post-9/11 era still powerful, but deeply committed to double standards as a means of preserving U.S. hegemony. Promoting standards that apply to others but not to us represents the very antithesis of America's claim, since the end of World War II, to apply *universal* legal and human rights standards. The real danger of the Bush Doctrine is thus that it will turn the United States, which since 1945 has been the major architect and buttress of the global system of international law and human rights, into its major outlier, weakening that system and reducing its capacity to promote universal values and protect American interests.

Responding to American Exceptionalism

Given this analysis, how should we respond to American exceptionalism? In recent months, four distinct approaches have emerged: triumphalism; criticizing the critics; blaming American culture; and my preferred solution, triggering transnational legal process. What does each entail?

First, triumphalism, or "getting used to it." A speechwriter for a prominent conservative senator once said to me, "American exceptionalism is a reality. The rest of the world should get used to it. The world should accept it and the U.S. should trumpet it. In a one-superpower world, American exceptionalism is not just inevitable, it is good." To me, such a blindered response ignores the dark side of American exceptionalism. Triumphalism alone does nothing to address the most negative aspects of American exceptionalism, particularly the growing problem of promoting double standards.

A second counterproductive course is to criticize the critics of American overreaching, and to lay the blame on "the human rights discourse."[53]

---

[53] Those who have recently asserted some version of this view include Michael Ignatieff, David Rieff, and Christopher Hitchens. See also David Kennedy, *The Dark Sides of Virtue: Reassessing International Humanitarianism* (2004).

Under this view, the human rights era is ending, but human rights advocates fail to recognize that the way they talk about human rights is dated. The solution, these critics suggest, is to change our rhetoric.[54] Yet I see no need to change America's human rights rhetoric, which has been remarkably consistent from Wilson to Bush; rather we must change the way we *act upon* our rhetoric. Over the decades, America's rhetoric has consistently been human rights–oriented and progressive; what has varied is its willingness to act on this rhetoric in a consistent way that promotes universal values without sacrificing American national interests.[55]

A third possible response, often expressed by European critics, is to locate the causes of American exceptionalism within a deeply rooted American culture of unilateralism and parochialism.[56] But the problem with this response is that it does not acknowledge that every American is not equally well positioned to provoke an incident of American exceptionalism. It should be self-evident that some people are better placed than others. For example, in recent years, secretary of defense Donald Rumsfeld, former chair of the Senate Foreign Relations Committee Jesse Helms, and Supreme Court justice Antonin Scalia have each, in his own way, prevailed over other participants within their respective institutional environments who were pressing for less exceptionalist outcomes. But the American discourse of opposition to the International Criminal Court has arisen less from broadly entrenched American cultural beliefs than from the skill and maneuvering of particular well-positioned individuals, who, by serving as key institutional choke points, have successfully promoted particular well-publicized acts of American exceptionalism.[57]

That brings me to a fourth possible response: trigger transnational legal process. Under my argument, the real cost of American exceptionalism comes when U.S. insistence upon double standards (in crude terms, "bad exceptionalism") diminishes or inhibits its capacity to display exceptional leadership in a post–Cold War world ("good exceptionalism"). To reduce that cost, we, as American lawyers, scholars, and activists, should make better use of transnational legal process to press our own government to avoid the most negative and damaging features of American exceptionalism.

---

[54] Michael Ignatieff, *Is the Human Rights Era Ending?*, N.Y. Times, Feb. 5, 2002, at A25.

[55] For detailed illustration, see Jonathan D. Greenberg, *Does Power Trump Law?*, 55 Stan. L. Rev. 1789 (2003).

[56] For a powerful statement of this position, see Jed Rubenfeld, *Unilateralism and Constitutionalism* (unpublished manuscript, on file with author). *Cf. Bowling for Columbine* (Dog Eat Dog Films 2002) (seeking cultural explanation for American devotion to guns).

[57] Mariano-Florentino Cuéllar, *The International Criminal Court and the Political Economy of Antitreaty Discourse*, 55 Stan. L. Rev. 1597 (2003).

What is transnational legal process? While most legal scholars agree that most nations obey most rules of international law most of the time, they disagree dramatically as to why they do so. As I have explained elsewhere, I believe that nations obey international law for a variety of reasons: power, self-interest, liberal theories, communitarian theories, and what I call "legal process" theories.[58] While all of these approaches contribute to compliance with international law, the most overlooked determinant of compliance is what I call "vertical process": when international law norms are internalized into domestic legal systems through a variety of legal, political, and social channels and obeyed as domestic law. In the international realm, as in the domestic realm, most compliance with law comes from *obedience*, or norm internalization, the process by which domestic legal systems incorporate international rules into domestic law or norms.

Under this view, the key to understanding whether nations will obey international law, I have argued, is *transnational legal process*: the process by which public and private actors—namely, nation-states, corporations, international organizations, and nongovernmental organizations—interact in a variety of fora to make, interpret, enforce, and ultimately internalize rules of international law.[59] The key elements of this approach are interaction, interpretation, and internalization. Those seeking to create and embed certain human rights principles into international and domestic law should trigger transnational *interactions* that generate legal *interpretations*, and that can in turn be *internalized* into the domestic law of even resistant nation-states.

In my view, "transnational legal process" is not simply an academic explanation as to why nations do or do not comply with international law; it is, more fundamentally, a bridging exercise between the worlds of international legal theory and practice. My time in government confirmed what I had suspected as a professor—that too often, in the world of policy making, those with ideas have no influence, while those with influence have no ideas. Decision makers promote policy without theory; activists implement tactics without strategy; and scholars generate ideas without influence. If transnational legal process is to bridge this triangle, how can

[58] For elaboration of this point, see Harold Hongju Koh, *Why Do Nations Obey International Law?*, 106 Yale L.J. 2599 (1997).

[59] This argument is presented more fully in Harold Hongju Koh, *Why Nations Obey: A Theory of Compliance with International Law* (forthcoming). The pieces of the argument may be found in Koh, *supra* note 58; Koh, *supra* note 25; Koh, *supra* note 19; Koh, *supra* note 47; Harold Hongju Koh, *How Is International Human Rights Law Enforced?*, 74 Ind. L. J. 1397 (1999); Harold Hongju Koh, *Transnational Legal Process*, 75 Neb. L. Rev. 181 (1996); Harold Hongju Koh, *Transnational Public Law Litigation*, 100 Yale L. J. 2347, 2358–75 (1991).

we use that concept to press our government to preserve its capacity for positive exceptionalism by avoiding the most negative features of American exceptionalism?

Let me illustrate in two contexts: first, America and the global justice system; second, the rights of 9/11 detainees.

The Global Justice System

First, consider the global justice system. In retrospect, the early post–Cold War years revived and rejuvenated the Nuremberg concept of adjudication of international crimes. That rejuvenation found particular expression during this period of global optimism I have described, from 1989 to 2001. The revival could be seen in the International Criminal Tribunals for the former Yugoslavia and Rwanda, the Lockerbie trial, the move to create mixed international-domestic tribunals in Cambodia and Sierra Leone, the Pinochet prosecution in Spain and Chile, and the civil adjudication of international human rights violations in U.S. courts under the Alien Tort Claims Act. From the U.S. perspective, the symbolic high-water mark came on December 31, 2000, when President Clinton signed the International Criminal Court Treaty during his last days in office, a treaty that entered into force in July 2002.[60]

But in the wake of September 11, every one of these hallmarks of the age of optimism about global justice has been placed under stress. With the trial of Slobodan Milošević, the Yugoslav tribunal faces its make-or-break case. The Rwanda tribunal has been singularly unsuccessful,[61] and the Lockerbie result disappointed many Western governments. For a time, the United Nations pulled out of the Cambodia tribunal,[62] and the Sierra Leone tribunal has yet to decide any case. Pinochet was never tried, and a follow-on effort to try Chadian dictator Hissene Habre in Senegal stalled. Academic commentators and some judges have started to challenge the rise of human rights litigation in U.S. courts.

With the global justice system teetering, enter the Bush administration. The new administration faced four options: first, supporting the growth and development of the global justice system; second, constructive engagement with that system, to try selectively to encourage it to develop in a manner that served long-term American accountability interests; third, benign neglect—to leave the system alone to evolve its own way; or fourth,

---

[60] See supra note 21.

[61] Victor Peskin, Rwandan Ghosts, Legal Aff., Sept.–Oct. 2002, at 20.

[62] As of March 2003, however, the United Nations and Cambodia reached a new agreement on the establishment of a hybrid "domestic international" tribunal. See Seth Mydans, U.N. and Cambodia Reach an Accord for Khmer Rouge Trial, N.Y. Times, Mar. 18, 2003, at A5.

declaring hostility to that system and placing the United States outside of it, in effect adopting a double standard toward global adjudication.

Although Colin Powell initially signaled his preference for benign neglect,[63] the Bush administration has now opted, with four decisive measures, to pursue a hostile course. First, the United States announced that it would cease funding the Yugoslav and Rwanda tribunals by 2008, but it failed to specify clearly that this defunding would be conditioned upon participating countries' cooperating fully with those tribunals, thus potentially encouraging defendants to pursue foot-dragging measures that would wait out the tribunals.[64] In effect, this decision gave every defendant currently before the tribunal an incentive to stall until 2008 to avoid getting tried. Second, at a time when a logical strategy for a country seeking allied support for a war on terror was to treat President Clinton's December 2000 signature of the International Criminal Court Treaty with benign neglect, in May 2002 the Bush administration took the surprising step of sending UN secretary-general Kofi Annan a letter seeking to undo that signature, effectively declaring war on the ICC.[65] Third, the administration initially vetoed extension of the UN law enforcement assistance mission in Bosnia. The United States objected because the Security Council would not grant an indefinite and universal exemption from ICC jurisdiction for all U.S. officials engaged in peacekeeping operations, but it ultimately consented to continuation of the mission in exchange for a one-year exemption (the maximum the Security Council could provide under the Rome Statute). Fourth, the much-criticized U.S. proposal to try certain foreign terrorist suspects for war crimes before ad hoc domestic military commissions has signaled a symbolic decoupling from international criminal adjudication.[66] For the military commission proposal de facto "unsigns" our commitment to a global adjudication system by declaring that claims involving international crimes of terrorism should henceforth be heard not in international court, or even in U.S. civilian or military courts, but rather in ad hoc military commissions under the control of the U.S. military, and set up at the U.S. naval base in Guantánamo Bay, Cuba.

---

[63] See Statement and Testimony of Secretary of State-Designate Colin L. Powell before the U.S. Senate Committee on Foreign Relations, Jan. 17, 2001. "Take note of the fact, though, that once America signs a treaty such as this, we are in some ways expected not to defeat its purpose, intended purpose. And the expectation is that we would ultimately ratify it. But in this case I don't think it likely you'll see this administration send it up for ratification." Id.

[64] Paul Richter, U.S. Calls International Court a Waste, Chi. Trib., Mar. 1, 2002, at 6.

[65] See Bolton, supra note 21. Less than a week after President Clinton first signed the ICC Treaty, Bolton urged its "unsignature." See John R. Bolton, Unsign That Treaty, Wash. Post, Jan. 4, 2001, at A21.

[66] Harold Hongju Koh, The Case against Military Commissions, 96 Am. J. Int'l L. 337 (2002).

Each of these decisions ignores two realities. First, for more than half a century, the United States has promoted international criminal adjudication as being in our long-run national interest. This policy has stemmed from a sensible prediction that, on balance, the United States is far more likely to act as a plaintiff than as a defendant before these tribunals and thus has much more to gain than to lose from their effective functioning. Bosnia, for example, taught that indictment alone can be a valuable political tool. Although two of the leading architects of ethnic cleansing in Bosnia, Radovan Karadžić and Ratko Mladić, have not yet been brought to trial, their indictment before the International Criminal Tribunal for the former Yugoslavia (ICTY) has effectively removed them from political life, creating space for more moderate political forces to emerge.

Second, in many cases, supporting global adjudication has served U.S. national interests by sparing us from far more costly military interventions. Our support for global criminal adjudication before the Yugoslav tribunal helped relieve the United States from the tough decision whether to send troops to Belgrade to seize and oust Slobodan Milošević. The ICTY both helped create the conditions that allowed Milošević's ouster and served as a tool for his removal from political life. Without the tribunal's indictment, the Clinton administration would have faced difficulty isolating Milošević internationally, and his domestic opposition would have had trouble persuading Serbian voters that Milošević was weak enough to be worth challenging. Nor is it likely that the Bush administration, openly disdainful of U.S. involvement in the Balkans, would have maintained pressure on Belgrade but for the clear, independent signal from the tribunal. Absent that pressure, Milošević might have regained power or retained his freedom, remaining a divisive force threatening Kosovo, Europe's newest democracy. Instead, his removal was accomplished in a way that advanced democracy, spilled no blood, and reinforced U.S. support for a people working to rid itself of a violent regime.

The second Gulf War has already underscored America's shortsightedness in rejecting a permanent standing international criminal court. As the war began, both President Bush and Secretary of Defense Rumsfeld announced that high-ranking Iraqi war criminals, including Saddam Hussein, would be prosecuted. Yet their announcement only raised the obvious question: "Where?"[67] Neither the United States nor Iraq has ratified

---

[67] See Press Release, The White House, *President Says Saddam Hussein Must Leave Iraq within 48 Hours* (Mar. 17, 2003), *available at* http://www.whitehouse.gov/news/releases/2003/03/20030317-7.html ("[A]ll Iraqi military and civilian personnel should listen carefully to this warning. In any conflict, your fate will depend on your action. . . . War crimes will be prosecuted. War criminals will be punished. And it will be no defense to say, 'I was just following orders' "); Secretary Rumsfeld & General Myers, *Department of Defense*

the ICC, eliminating that as a possible venue. Nor, given the intense misgivings that Security Council permanent members France and Russia expressed about the war, can the United States now easily persuade the Security Council to create an ad hoc tribunal under chapter VII of the UN Charter, as it did in spearheading the movements to create international tribunals to try war criminals from the former Yugoslavia and Rwanda.[68] Unlike ad hoc courts, a permanent criminal court cannot be so easily dismissed as dispensing "victor's justice." Moreover, states reluctant to extradite their citizens to national courts will find it far easier to hand suspects over to an ICC that is perceived as politically balanced and not inclined to tailor its procedures for particular defendants. Once again, the United States failed to see that accountability flows best not from American military power but from the use of global accountability mechanisms as a modulated instrument of American soft power.

In these circumstances, how could transnational legal process help? In three ways. First, those who support eventual U.S. participation in the ICC can seek to internalize recognition of the legitimacy and usefulness of that court within the relevant community of U.S. officials, legislators, and opinion elites.[69] Supporters should provoke interactions between the U.S. government and the ICC with an eye toward persuading U.S. officials that the ICC actually serves American interests. Although the United States was neither a member of the League of Nations nor a party to the statute of the Permanent Court of International Justice (PCIJ), an eminent American participated in the drafting of the Permanent Court's statute, Americans regularly nominated candidates to be judges, and four Americans were successively elected as PCIJ judges.[70] Over time, growing familiarity gradually demystified the court's processes and helped to facilitate

---

News Briefing (Mar. 20, 2003), *available at* http://www.dod.gov/news/Mar2003/ 3202003_t0320sd.html. "If Saddam Hussein or his generals issue orders to use weapons of mass destruction, . . . [t]hose who follow orders to commit such crimes will be found and they will be punished. War crimes will be prosecuted, and it will be no excuse to say, 'I was just following orders.' Any official involved in such crimes will forfeit hope of amnesty or leniency with respect to past actions." *Id.*

[68] Even if the United Nations were to create a tribunal, no UN court would be authorized to sentence a war criminal to death, which would likely bring it into conflict with the United States, for reasons discussed below.

[69] This is what I elsewhere call "political internalization." *See* Koh, *supra* note 19, at 642.

[70] *See* Manley O. Hudson, *International Tribunals: Past and Future* 155–56 (1994); Henry J. Steiner, Detlev F. Vagts & Harold Hongju Koh, *Transnational Legal Problems* 173 (4th ed. 1994).

the United States' eventual participation in the PCIJ's successor tribunal, the International Court of Justice.

The Rome Treaty has now entered into force, eighty-nine countries have ratified it, and an impressive initial complement of eighteen judges has been elected. Given that the ICC is now a fait accompli, America's wisest course would be to return to the strategy of constructive engagement: to work with this tribunal to make its functioning more fair. The United States should seek to ensure the selection of able and unbiased prosecutors, to provide their office with resources, and to encourage the court as a whole to develop a balanced, respectable jurisprudence of war crimes and crimes against humanity.[71] By snubbing the ICC, the United States has perversely enhanced the chances that it will take on an anti-American focus, thus turning the administration's hostility toward the court into a self-fulfilling prophecy.

Second, human rights groups should recognize that the ICC is far more likely to survive if the United States sees it as helpful, rather than hostile, to its foreign policy interests. ICC supporters should therefore seek to identify cases that the new prosecutor, Luis Moreno Ocampo, could bring before the International Criminal Court as a way of illustrating both the court's responsibility and its political usefulness. Moreno got off to a promising start, for example, by choosing as his first case prosecution of those who recruit child soldiers in Uganda. Similarly, as U.S. involvement in Iraq proceeds, nongovernmental advocates should identify issues upon which Saddam Hussein or his leading subordinates could be tried before the Iraqi tribunal that has now been set up to try Iraqi war crimes. As Allison Danner has suggested, by identifying appropriate cases, human rights groups would in effect be suggesting the contours of prosecutorial guidelines that the prosecutor's office could internalize to preserve independence, enhance public credibility, and constrain discretionary decisions.[72] By winning convictions and obtaining domestic compliance, the prosecutor would also begin the process of internalizing ICC decisions into the domestic law of various target nations, in the same way as European Court of Human Rights rulings have now become deeply internalized into the law of member states.

---

[71] For a description of how the United States and other states have the power to influence the work of the International Criminal Court's prosecutor, see Allison Marston Danner, *Navigating Law and Politics: The Prosecutor of the International Criminal Court and the Independent Counsel*, 55 Stan. L. Rev 1633 (2003); Allison Marston Danner, *Enhancing the Legitimacy and Accountability of Prosecutorial Discretion at the International Criminal Court*, 97 Am. J. Int'l. L. (forthcoming 2003) [hereinafter Danner, *Enhancing Legitimacy and Accountability*].

[72] *See* Danner, *Enhancing Legitimacy and Accountability, supra* note 71.

Third, transnational legal process could be used to erode the force of the novel U.S. tactic of unsigning the Rome Treaty.[73] Under international law, it is unclear what the precise legal force of "unsigning" a previously signed treaty should be. At present, the U.S. letter of unsigning is simply lodged with the UN depositary of treaties, along with a notation of President Clinton's prior signature.[74] Nor is the matter automatically controlled by the administration's stated desire to reject the ICC. In 1994, for example, the United States attempted to modify its acceptance of the compulsory jurisdiction of the International Court of Justice to avoid a suit by Nicaragua, but the court itself eventually rejected that attempt as legally ineffective and proceeded to judgment against the United States.[75]

As a policy matter, it is by no means clear that governments should be allowed to enter and exit their human rights obligations with equal ease. If that were so, other countries could invoke the U.S. "unsigning" precedent to justify backing out of other international commitments of importance to the United States.[76] In each case, the goal should be not to give these nations an easy way out of their commitments but to enmesh them within the global treaty system to encourage them to internalize those norms over time. Nor can the United States so forthrightly protest North Korea's acknowledged violation of the 1994 Agreed Framework, when the United States itself is unsigning solemn commitments it previously made.

[73] For background, see Swaine, *supra* note 7.

[74] Under the Vienna Convention on the Law of Treaties, art. 18, *opened for signature* May 23, 1969, 1155 U.N.T.S. 331, 8 I.L.M. 679 (1969), "[a] State is obliged to refrain from acts which would defeat the object and purpose of a treaty when . . . it has signed the treaty . . . until it shall have made its intention clear not to become a party to the treaty." The Bolton letter says "that the United States does not intend to become a party to the [International Criminal Court] Treaty. Accordingly, the United States has no legal obligations arising from its signature on December 31, 2000. The United States requests that its intention not to become a party, as expressed in this letter, be reflected in the depositary's status lists relating to this treaty." Bolton, *supra* note 21. The Bolton letter may absolve the United States of responsibility under the Vienna Convention for post-unsigning steps it may take to oppose the operation of the court. But as I argue in the text, nothing in the Bolton letter bars the United States from future cooperation with the court on a case-by-case basis, cooperation that would effectively repudiate the juridical act of "unsignature" through subsequent state practice.

[75] *See* Steiner et al., *supra* note 70, at 182–86. Similarly, many international lawyers and judges have never accepted the legality of the United States's Connolly Reservation to the ICJ's jurisdiction. *See* Interhandel Case (*Switz. v. U.S.*), 1959 I.C.J. 6 (Mar. 21) (separate opinion of Judge Lauterpacht) (Preliminary Objections).

[76] Iraq, for example, has signed but not ratified a convention on hostage taking. China and Turkey have signed but not ratified the International Covenant on Civil and Political Rights. Yugoslavia has signed but not ratified the International Convention for the Suppression of the Financing of Terrorism; and Afghanistan has signed but not ratified the Convention on the Elimination of All Forms of Discrimination Against Women.

Rather than taking America's unsignature at face value, a transnational legal process approach would recognize that the unsigning actually marks the beginning, not the end, of the United States' relationship with an ongoing International Criminal Court. Henceforth, every act of American cooperation with the court will constitute a de facto repudiation of the categorical, but theoretical, act of unsignature. Thus, in a well-chosen case, a state party to the court could request that the United States provide evidence to support an ICC prosecution—as was done, for example, when the United States made classified evidence available to the International Criminal Tribunal for the former Yugoslavia to support the indictment of Slobodan Milošević. Alternatively, another state could seek to extradite to the ICC a suspect located on U.S. soil. If the United States were to cooperate—as it well might in a case that served U.S. interests—the incident could reduce American exceptionalism, undermine the force of the May 2002 unsigning, and help shift the United States toward a new, more pragmatic long-term policy of cooperating with the court on a case-by-case basis.

9/11 Detainees

A similar transnational legal process strategy is currently being applied with regard to post–September 11 detainees. In particular, two issues have driven a wedge between the United States and its allies: first, the U.S. refusal to accord full Geneva Convention rights to Taliban detainees being held on Guantánamo; and second, the U.S. insistence upon labeling suspected terrorists as "enemy combatants," a term that, under international law, does not relieve the United States of its Geneva Convention obligations.

Each issue illustrates a U.S. effort to create a double standard. Although the United States may want its own exceptional "rights-free zone" on Guantánamo, it surely does not want the Russians to create a similar offshore facility for their Chechen terrorists or the Chinese to erect offshore prisons for their Uighur Muslims. Second, even while the United States has been holding Taliban detainees in the exceptional legal category of "enemy combatants" without Geneva Convention hearings, it has been ferociously protesting the denial of Geneva Convention rights to American prisoners of war captured during the Iraq war. So how to use transnational legal process to mitigate American exceptionalism in these areas? Human rights advocates are currently litigating both issues, not just in domestic courts, but simultaneously in foreign and international arenas.

In *Rasul v. Bush*,[77] the U.S. Supreme Court rejected the Bush administration's claims that Australian, British, and Kuwaiti detainees on Guan-

---

[77] 124 S. Ct. 2686 (2004).

tánamo could not pursue a writ of habeas corpus to challenge their American captivity, because they were being held outside the United States on territory over which the United States is not sovereign. In previously rejecting the detainees' claim, the U.S. Court of Appeals for the D.C. Circuit had relied heavily on *Johnson v. Eisentrager,* a musty U.S. Supreme Court decision that had rejected similar rights for German prisoners being held in Germany, after having been taken into custody in China after World War II.[78] Yet what the D.C. Circuit had misunderstood is that Guantánamo's location outside the United States does not automatically extinguish the procedural rights of all foreign detainees being held there. As the U.S. Court of Appeals for the Second Circuit had previously recognized in the Haitian refugee litigation, detainees being held on Guantánamo are subject to *exclusive U.S. jurisdiction and control,* and thus are subject only to U.S. law.[79] It was thus of no moment that the Guantánamo detainees are subject to nominal Cuban *sovereignty,* as they clearly will find no legal relief in Cuban courts. The relevant question was whether the United States could subject them to punishment exclusively under U.S. law yet simultaneously afford them no avenue under that law to object to that punishment, to challenge their nontreatment as prisoners of war, to speak to legal counsel, or even to assert claims of mistaken capture.

To clarify that challenge, human rights lawyers chose to litigate the status of Guantánamo detainees in parallel settings: not just before the U.S. courts, which were least likely to be sympathetic, but also before the Inter-American Human Rights Commission, and before British courts, with regard to a habeas petition brought there by a British citizen

---

[78] 321 F.3d 1134 (D.C. Cir. 2003), citing *Johnson v. Eisentrager,* 339 U.S. 763 (1950).

[79] *Haitian Ctrs. Council v. McNary,* 969 F.2d 1326, 1343 (2d Cir. 1992): "It does not appear to us to be incongruous or overreaching to conclude that the United States Constitution limits the conduct of United States personnel with respect to officially authorized interactions with aliens brought to and detained by such personnel on a land mass exclusively controlled by the United States. . . . We note that, in the present case, applying the fifth amendment would not appear to be either 'impracticable' or 'anomalous' since the United States has exclusive control over Guantánamo Bay, and given the undisputed applicability of federal criminal laws to incidents that occur there and the apparent familiarity of the governmental personnel at the base with the guarantees of due process, fundamental fairness and humane treatment that this country purports to afford to all persons." *Id.* (citation omitted). *See Haitian Ctrs. Council v. Sale,* 823 F. Supp. 1028, 1041 (E.D.N.Y. 1993): "The U.S. Naval Base at Guantánamo Bay, Cuba, is subject to the exclusive jurisdiction and control of the United States where the criminal and civil laws of the United States apply. The courts have protected the fundamental constitutional rights of noncitizens in other territories subject to exclusive U.S. jurisdiction and control, including the former American Sector of Berlin, the Canal Zone, and the Pacific Trust Territories." *Id.* (citations omitted). When the Haitian detainees on Guantánamo were ultimately released into the United States in mid-1993, this litigation was settled, and these decisions vacated by party agreement, leaving the Second Circuit (and other courts) free now to reassert this position on similar facts.

detained on Guantánamo. In generating these legal interactions, these advocates are pursuing a threefold goal: to win in non-U.S. fora different legal interpretations from those being asserted by the Bush administration before U.S. courts; to discourage the administration from bringing new detainees from Iraq and elsewhere to Guantánamo; and, particularly with respect to prisoners whose countries are close American allies in the Iraq war, to generate enough media and political pressure to promote the release of Guantánamo detainees not by court order but through diplomatic means.[80]

The outcome in *Rasul* vindicated this legal strategy. The Inter-American Commission swiftly declared the illegality of the detentions,[81] and the British courts and judges assailed the American governments for holding the detainees in a "legal black hole."[82] The U.S. Supreme Court majority resoundingly rejected the Bush administration's claim, distinguishing *Eisentrager* in part because of the breadth of exclusive U.S. power over Guantánamo. Justice Kennedy's concurrence went so far as to state that "Guantánamo Bay is in every practical respect a United States territory."[83]

A similar pattern is developing with regard to the status of "enemy combatant." The contours and means of proving that status are currently being litigated in two cases: those of Jose Padilla (the so-called dirty bomber)[84] and Yasser Hamdi, a Louisiana-born soldier captured in Afghanistan, brought to Guantánamo, and later detained in a military brig on U.S. soil.[85] Both cases raised not the question of rights-free territory (i.e., Guantánamo) but that of rights-free people (so-called enemy combatants): whether U.S. courts should permit U.S. citizens to be held indefinitely and without counsel on U.S. soil based on ambiguous statutory authority, solely by placing such citizens in the essentially rights-free status of "enemy combatant," as distinct from the statuses of "prisoner of

---

[80] Such political objectives are usually the goal of what I have elsewhere called "transnational public law litigation." *See* Koh, *supra* note 59, at 2368–72. The British and Australian governments have already weighed in to demand that their citizens on Guantánamo not be tried under procedures that might subject them to the death penalty.

[81] Jess Bravin, *Panel Says U.S. Policy on Detainees in Cuba Breaks International Law*, Wall St. J., Mar. 14, 2002, at B2; Inter-Am. Comm'n on Human Rights, *Request for Precautionary Measures, Detainees in Guantánamo Bay, Cuba* (Mar. 12, 2002), *available at* http://www.photius.com/rogue_nations/guantanamo.html.

[82] *See* Regina *ex rel. Abbasi v. Secretary of State for Foreign and Commonwealth Affairs*, [2002] EWCA Civ 1598, ¶ 64 ("in apparent contravention of fundamental principles recognised by both jurisdictions and by international law, Mr Abbasi is at present arbitrarily detained in a 'legal black-hole'."); Lord Johan Steyn, *Guantánamo Bay: The Legal Black Hole*, 53 Intl Comp L Q 1 (2004).

[83] 124 S. Ct. at 2700 (Kennedy, J., concurring in the judgment).

[84] *Rumsfeld v. Padilla*, 124 S. Ct. 2711 (2004).

[85] *Hamdi v. Rumsfeld*, 124 S. Ct. 2633 (2004).

war" or "criminal defendant," both of which carry well-recognized procedural rights.[86]

In both *Hamdi* and *Padilla*, scores of amicus curiae briefs urged the U.S. Supreme Court to reject the government's overbroad claim. In *Padilla*, the Court deflected that claim on a jurisdictional ground;[87] but in *Hamdi*, a majority of the Court squarely rejected the notion that an American citizen labeled an enemy combatant has no procedural rights. Instead, the majority rebuffed the Bush administration by holding that the constitutional concept of "due process demands that a citizen held in the United States as an enemy combatant be given a meaningful opportunity to contest the factual basis for that detention before a neutral decisionmaker."[88]

Following the government's resounding defeat in *Hamdi*, the administration began negotiating to release Yasser Hamdi, in an effort to limit the decision's precedential weight.[89] Thus a transnational legal process approach has already shown its power in winning a form of relief for Hamdi himself.[90] Moreover, in remanding the *Hamdi* case for further action, Justice O'Connor's plurality opinion noted that "[t]he legal category of enemy combatant has not been elaborated upon in great detail. The permissible bounds of the category will be defined by the lower courts as subsequent cases are presented to them."[91]

As these and other cases develop before the lower courts, a transnational legal process approach would suggest that foreign governments and nongovernmental organizations should take the Court's invitation to seek opinions from recognized interpreters of international humanitarian law interested in the global, rather than the parochial, implications of the "enemy combatant" label. Such interpreters could include the International Committee of the Red Cross, the European Court of Human Rights, or foreign courts. In appropriate cases, the issue could even be raised before U.S. courts of military justice, which have deeply internal-

---

[86] Significantly, when Richard Reid, the so-called sneaker bomber, was sentenced, the federal judge took pains to punish him with full recognition of his procedural rights. The judge told Reid, "I will not dignify you by calling you an enemy combatant. You are a terrorist. You are a criminal." Lawyers Comm. for Human Rights, *supra* note 41, at 68.

[87] The Court held, in effect, that Padilla's lawyers had brought their habeas petition on his behalf in the wrong court, but remanded the matter for them to refile in the district courts of South Carolina, near the brig where he was being detained.

[88] 124 S. Ct. at 2635. This conclusion was joined by six justices.

[89] See Thomas E. Ricks & Jerry Markon, *U.S. Nears Deal to Free Enemy Combatant Hamdi: American Citizen Who Was Captured in Afghanistan Has Been Held Since 2001*, Washington Post, August 12, 2004 at A02.

[90] See Koh, *Transnational Public Law Litigation*, *supra* note 59 (arguing that goal of transnational litigation is less to win favorable judgments than to generate political pressure and achieve concrete practical results).

[91] *Id.* at 2642 n. 1 (opinion of O'Connor, J.).

ized the Geneva Conventions as operating rules and display a strong incentive not to promote legal interpretations that would leave American soldiers abroad without legal protections. Indeed, even while suggesting that "[w]hether, or to what degree, the Government is in fact violating the Geneva Convention and is thus acting outside the customary usages of war are not matters I can resolve at this point," Justice Souter's concurring opinion enumerated a set of persuasive arguments as to why under U.S. law, Hamdi should in fact be treated as a prisoner of war for purposes of the Geneva Conventions.[92] In short, if American exceptionalism is to be reduced in this area, as in others, it makes sense for litigants to pursue legal interactions that provoke interpretations promoting internalization of universal, rather than unilateralist, understandings of the Geneva Conventions.

In sum, the fate of 9/11 detainees likely rests in the capacity of advocates to persuade domestic courts to internalize norms of international law and in the capacity of foreign allies to use political process to force the U.S. government to face the negative consequences of American double standards. In both cases, the most promising strategy is to trigger transnational interactions that generate interpretations of human rights principle, and that can in turn be internalized into evolving U.S. law and policy.

Conclusion

In short, the question is not how do we feel about American exceptionalism, but do we have a strategy to encourage the right kinds of exceptionalism, namely, exceptional American leadership, while discouraging double standards? I have argued that there are many faces of American exceptionalism, and that our goal should be to reduce double standards while expanding our capacity for global leadership. My preferred channel to pursue both goals is transnational legal process.

As this war on terror wears on, a transcendent issue in the debate over U.S. foreign policy will be what kind of world order is emerging, and what America's role in it will be. After September 11, the United States does not have the option of isolationism. Like it or not, Americans must be internationalists, but we do have a choice. America's choice is not isolationism versus internationalism; rather, what version of internationalism will we pursue? Will it be power-based internationalism, in which the United States gets its way because of its willingness to exercise power whatever the rules? Or will it be norm-based internationalism, in which American power derives not just from hard power but from per-

---

[92] *Id.* at 2658–59 (opinion of Souter, J.).

ceived fidelity to universal values of democracy, human rights, and the rule of law?

As a nation conceived in liberty and dedicated to certain inalienable rights, the United States has strong primal impulses to respond to crisis not just with power alone, but with power coupled with principle. After September 11, our challenge, as American lawyers, academics, and activists, is not to condone double standards or to declare the human rights era over, but to use process to prod the country we love to follow the better angels of its national nature.

Part II

EXPLAINING EXCEPTIONALISM

Chapter 6

The Paradox of U.S. Human Rights Policy

ANDREW MORAVCSIK

AMERICAN "EXCEPTIONALISM" in international human rights policy—the U.S. aversion to formal acceptance and enforcement of international human rights norms—poses a paradox.[1] The paradox lies in the curious tension between the consistent rejection of the application of international norms, on the one hand, and the venerable U.S. tradition of support for human rights, in the form of judicial enforcement of human rights at home and unilateral action to promote civil and political rights abroad. The United States has, after all, the oldest continuous constitutional tradition of judicial enforcement of a written bill of rights in the world today. Nowhere in the world are civil liberties more robustly debated and defended in public and in court. From support for revolutionary France in the first years of the republic to military intervention in Haiti during the 1990s, moreover, American politicians and citizens recognized the integral link between the spread of civil liberties abroad and the defense of American ideals and interests. U.S. efforts to enforce global human rights standards through rhetorical disapproval, foreign aid, sanctions, military intervention, and even multilateral negotiations are arguably more vigorous than those of any other country.[2] The United States acts even where—

---

[1] I gratefully acknowledge research assistance from Mark Copelovitch, Jonathan Cracraft, Aron Fischer, James Perry, and Christopher Strawn; constructive criticism from Antonia Chayes, Stanley Hoffmann, Michael Ignatieff, Alex Keyssar, Harold Koh, Frank Michelman, Diane Orentlicher, Samantha Power, John Ruggie, Frederick Schauer, Anne-Marie Slaughter, Henry Steiner, two anonymous critics, and participants in colloquia at Harvard's Carr Center for Human Rights, New York University, Princeton University, and Yale Law School. I acknowledge use of an unpublished paper by Hema Magge. I am grateful to the Weatherhead Center for International Affairs and the Human Rights Committee at Harvard University for research support. This paper draws on material introduced in Andrew Moravcsik, "Why Is U.S. Human Rights Policy So Unilateralist?" in *Multilateralism and U.S. Foreign Policy: The Cost of Acting Alone*, ed. Stewart Patrick and Shepard Forman (Boulder, CO: Lynne Rienner, 2001).

[2] For useful overviews of U.S. unilateral policies, see David Forsythe, "The United States, the United Nations, and Human Rights," in *The United States and Multilateral Institutions: Patterns of Changing Instrumentality and Interest*, ed. Margaret Karns and Karen Mingst (Winchester, MA: Unwin Hyman, 1990), 261–88. The United States is so active that some

as in Kosovo—the potential costs are high, and in some cases such leadership has been essential to the success of human rights enforcement.[3] Levels of overall U.S. public support for international human rights policy, like support for multilateral commitments—and even popular views on issues like the death penalty—are not strikingly dissimilar to levels in other advanced industrial democracies.[4] The United States is, finally, the home of the largest and most active community of nongovernmental organizations and foundations devoted to human rights promotion in the world today.

Yet the United States stands nearly alone among Western democracies in that it fails to acknowledge and implement domestically the global system of interlocking multilateral human rights enforcement that has emerged and expanded since 1945. Phenomena referred to as American "exemptionalism," noncompliance, nonratification, and double standards can be seen as different versions of the same essential phenomenon, namely, an American unwillingness to impose on itself general international rules that the U.S. government accepts in principle as just.[5] True, the United States has ratified one of the two UN Covenants, as well as conventions on political rights of women, genocide, slavery, forced labor, racial discrimination, and torture.[6] It stands out, however, for not ratifying international instruments on discrimination against women (CEDAW), rights of the child, socioeconomic rights, and migrant workers, as well as the relevant regional document, the American Convention of Human Rights. This level of rejection is unique. The Convention on the Rights of the Child, for example, has been ratified by every UN member except the United States and nearly stateless Somalia.

In the few cases where the United States does ratify human rights treaties, such as the Genocide Convention, it has done so only after a long delay and with greater substantive and procedural reservations than any other developed democracy.[7] Domestically, the United States stipulates in

---

have interpreted global human rights regimes as the result of American hegemony. E.g., Tony Evans, *U.S. Hegemony and the Project of Universal Human Rights* (London: Macmillan, 1996).

[3] See Harold Hongju Koh, "Foreword: On American Exceptionalism," *Stanford Law Review* 55 (2003): 1479–1527.

[4] For a summary of poll results, see Edward C. Luck, *Mixed Messages: American Politics and International Organization, 1919–1999* (Washington, DC: Brookings Institution Press, 1999), 34–40. On the similarity of U.S. and European views on the death penalty, see Andrew Moravcsik, "The New Abolitionism: Why Does the US Practice the Death Penalty While Europe Does Not?" *European Studies* 31:1 (September 2001).

[5] Michael Ignatieff, introduction to this volume.

[6] Jack Goldsmith makes much, perhaps too much, of this formal adherence. See Jack Goldsmith, "Should International Human Rights Law Trump US Domestic Law?" *Chicago Journal of International Law* 1 (2000): 327–39.

[7] Louis Henkin, "US Ratification of Human Rights Conventions: The Ghost of Senator Bricker," *American Journal of International Law* 89 (1995): 341–49.

every case that human rights treaties are not self-executing. Internationally, the United States flatly refuses to accept the jurisdiction of external enforcement tribunals. In contrast to all other Western democracies, the United States offers its own citizens no opportunity to seek remedies for violations of internationally codified rights before either a domestic or an international tribunal.[8] Moreover, in contrast to nearly all European democracies, the United States has incorporated few regional or international human rights norms into domestic law.[9] Indeed, the mere prospect of acknowledging and enforcing international human rights norms at home triggers virulent partisan opposition—even in cases where the possibility of any change in U.S. policy is remote.

The paradoxical international human rights policy of the United States is widely criticized as embodying a double standard. The Lawyer's Committee on Human Rights has charged outright hypocrisy in the implicit American view that "one set of rules belongs to the U.S. and another to the rest of the world."[10] Human Rights Watch and the American Civil Liberties Union denounced U.S. ratification in 1992 of the UN International Covenant on Civil and Political Rights (ICCPR) on the ground that the reservations restricting domestic enforcement rendered it a "half step" based on "the cynical view of international human rights law as a source of protection only for those outside U.S. borders."[11]

This policy mix is what I refer to here as "the paradox of American exceptionalism," and what I seek to explain. Potential and proposed explanations fall into two broad categories.

In the first category are found those explanations that attribute this form of American exceptionalism to the enduring, broadly based "rights culture" of the United States. Such explanations view American exceptionalism in human rights as the result of widely held, long-standing cultural values about procedural legitimacy that render international norms intrinsically unattractive to Americans. Among the norms that are often cited as explanations for American skepticism about enforcing global human rights are popular sovereignty, local government, constitutional

[8] See Henry J. Steiner and Philip Alston, *International Human Rights in Context: Law, Politics, Morals. Text and Materials*, 2nd ed. (Oxford: Oxford University Press, 2000), 1049–81.

[9] See Goldsmith, "Should International Human Rights Law Trump US Domestic Law?" 335–36. Exceptions include several specifics of the genocide and torture conventions, adopted after some decades.

[10] Letter from the Lawyer's Committee on Human Rights to Senator Claiborne Pell, March 2, 1992, published in *Human Rights Law Journal* 14:3–4 (1992): 129; Evans, *U.S. Hegemony and the Project of Universal Human Rights*, 189.

[11] *Human Rights Violations in the United States: A Report on US Compliance with the International Covenant on Civil and Political Rights* (New York: Human Rights Watch and the American Civil Liberties Union, 1993), 2.

patriotism, nationalism, and libertarianism. Almost all existing literature on the subject employs these explanations.

I shall consider these explanations in detail, but my primary purpose here is to present the arguments underlying, and the evidence supporting, a second category of explanations. These explanations are more rarely discussed, but—I shall seek to demonstrate—more valid empirically. These explanations attribute the exceptional ambivalence and unilateralism of the U.S. human rights policy to the calculation of American politicians about the domestic consequences of adherence to international norms, which in turn reflects the distinctive constellation of perceived interests and political institutions. I argue that *the U.S. government has tended to be skeptical of domestic implementation of international norms because it is geopolitically powerful; it has long been stably democratic; it contains a concentrated, active conservative minority; and it possesses decentralized and fragmented political institutions.* Superpower status means that the United States has more credible unilateral alternatives to full participation in multilateral institutions than, say, the smaller democracies of Western Europe. The stability of its domestic democratic system means that, in contrast to postwar (and post–Cold War) Europe and contemporary Latin America, its domestic actors lack the strongest self-interested motivation for implementing human rights norms, namely, the defense of domestic democratic institutions and the promotion of further democratic rights. Even more important, the existence of a vocal conservative minority in the United States actively opposed to aggressive civil and political rights enforcement through judicial review makes domestic application more controversial than it is elsewhere. Finally, and most important of all, those structural aspects of American political institutions that create veto groups and empower minorities—in particular, supermajoritarian treaty ratification rules in the Senate, the federal system, and the strength of the judiciary—render domestic legal reform via international treaties much more difficult, yet also much more consequential, than it is elsewhere.

Any one of these four general characteristics—external power, democratic stability, conservative minorities, and veto-group politics—would render governments less likely to accept binding multilateral norms. *The United States is the only advanced industrial democracy that possesses all four characteristics—and hence it is predictably the country, among democracies, least likely to fully acknowledge the domestic force of human rights norms.* In social scientific terms, the conception of American "exceptionalism" advanced here is generalizable: the United States is exceptional primarily because it occupies an extreme position in four structural dimensions of human rights politics, from which we would expect extreme behavior on the part of any government. These geopolitical, institutional, and ideological characteristics are more important, I argue, than the precise set of beliefs about legitimate political process embedded in national political cultures.[12] Note that I am *not* arguing that "interests" rather than "cultural beliefs" explain U.S. human rights policy—a claim as simplistic as it is vague. My argument is more specific: U.S. policy is as it is, above all, because of the perceived substantive interests and beliefs of a conservative minority of Americans favored by a biased set of political institutions, not because of any distinctively American political culture that rejects in principle the constitutional procedures employed by international human rights institutions. To the extent that pluralist pressures interact with "rights culture," which of course they do, it is pluralist pressures that have the more powerful effect.[13]

On their face, pluralist and rights cultural explanations both offer plausible explanations for the U.S. failure to enforce international human rights domestically. How then are we to evaluate them? Here we shall proceed by examining the broader political context. Any explanation should account not just for American exceptionalism but for the *paradox* of American exceptionalism with which we started. Why do we observe an unwillingness to implement international norms on the part of a country with centuries of experience with robust judicial enforcement of do-

---

[12] If extended to Asia, for example, such explanations would tend to call into question widespread interpretations based on particular "Asian values." For an argument along these lines, see Andrew Moravcsik and James Perry, "Why No Regional Human Rights Regime? Liberal Theory and Democratic Delegation in East Asia" (paper prepared for conference, "Bringing Politics Back In: Globalization, Pluralism, and Securitization in East Asia," sponsored by the Ford Foundation Project on Non-Traditional Security, Hong Kong, July 9, 2004).

[13] This claim is easily misunderstood, given the simple dichotomies between rationalist/material and cultural/constructivist causes often found in modern international relations theory. I do not argue that culture and values are irrelevant in explaining U.S. human rights policy. The source of conservative political preferences or separation of powers in the United States, to cite as examples two factors that I argue are important, may well, in either an imminent or a long-term historical sense, result from some form of cultural socialization and may continue to be buttressed by such processes. I seek to argue only, more precisely and more modestly, that "rights culture," strictly construed—that is, the existence of an autonomous set of preferences among Americans regarding constitutional forms—does not play a dominant and independent role in explaining U.S. policy in this area. Still, this explanation is more consistent with a historical institutionalist account of American political history than with a political cultural one. For this general interpretation, see Sven Steinmo, Kathleen Thelen, and Frank Longstreth, eds. *Structuring Politics: Historical Institutionalism in Comparative Analysis* (Cambridge: Cambridge University Press, 1992). Cf. Samuel Huntington, *American Politics: The Promise of Disharmony* (Cambridge: Harvard University Press, 1981).

mestic civil rights standards and a strong tradition of unilateral action abroad to enforce human rights? Moreover, any explanation should be consistent with particular details about the domestic political process by which policy is made—the rhetoric and, more important, the domestic coalitions and tactics of supporters and opponents.[14]

In the first section of this essay I evaluate "rights culture" explanations empirically. In the second, I evaluate "pluralist" explanations that rest on instrumental calculation of social and political pressures within existing political institutions. In the final section, I draw some more speculative and skeptical conclusions about the consequences of U.S. noncompliance.

A Distinctive American Rights Culture?

Many attribute U.S. domestic nonimplementation of global human rights norms to a distinctive culture of American "exceptionalism"—that is, a pervasive sense of "cultural relativism," "ethnocentrism," or "national-

---

[14] Specifically, I examine the following: (1) *Scope:* U.S. policy rejects domestic application across a wide range of both political and socioeconomic rights; (2) *Tactical Choices:* The United States consistently contributes to the negotiation of human rights norms, engages in robust unilateral human rights enforcement policies, and has a strong domestic tradition of human rights enforcement, but does not permit domestic enforcement; (3) *Cross-national Comparison:* Other advanced industrial democracies have accepted international enforcement, while the United States has not; (4) *Domestic Cleavages:* Human rights enforcement is a partisan issue, dividing U.S. liberals and conservatives largely along ideological, and thus often partisan, lines; and (5) *Rhetoric:* What specific substantive arguments have opponents of human rights enforcement employed? Each of these empirical indicators of motivation has its dangers, but taken together they provide a mass of evidence enabling us to weigh and evaluate alternative causes. In this regard, I distinguish *thin* and *thick* explanations of the phenomenon. A *thin* explanation of U.S. nonacknowledgment of international norms is one that offers a coherent prima facie motivation for U.S. rejection of international human rights norms. Such explanations are easy to generate—all the cultural and political factors mentioned above easily meet this standard. Moreover, since any serious politician tends to voice multiple, redundant justifications for his or her actions, it is not difficult to find abundant rhetorical evidence of the importance of any number of factors. Such explanations are so easy to generate, they tell us little. A *thick* explanation, by contrast, would not only account for the U.S. rejection of the domestic application of multilateral norms per se but must also be consistent with the more detailed aspects of the process and broader context of the policy: the substantive scope of U.S. rejection, the more positive position of other countries, the domestic political cleavages, the rhetoric of opponents, and so on. For detailed discussions on process tracing, see Andrew Bennett and Alexander L. George, "Process Tracing in Case Study Research" (MacArthur Foundation Workshop on Case Study Methods, October 17–19, 1997), and Alexander L. George and Andrew Bennett, *Case Studies and Theory Development* (Cambridge: MIT Press, forthcoming).

ism."[15] J. D. van der Vyer, for example, maintains that "[t]he American approach to international human rights is as much a manifestation of cultural relativism as any other sectional approach to international human rights founded on national ethnic, cultural or religious particularities. American relativism, furthermore, also serves to obstruct the United Nations' resolve to promote *universal* respect for human rights and fundamental freedoms for all without distinction as to race, sex, language, or religion."[16] Natalie Kaufman, a leading historian of postwar Senate deliberations, characterizes consistent concern among American politicians to protect the sanctity of U.S. political institutions in a diverse world as evidence of "an ethnocentric world view, a perspective suspicious or disdainful of things foreign" dating back at least to the early 1950s.[17] David Forsythe points to "American nationalism . . . intellectual isolationism and unilateralism."[18] Others charge the United States with outright "hypocrisy."[19]

Such rhetoric is often little more than normatively charged criticism of U.S. policy, rather than an explanation for it. In the international legal community, in particular, labeling a policy as an instance of "cultural relativism" rather than adherence to a "universal" norm is a customary rhetorical means of delegitimizing it.[20] Still, some such claims are more thoughtful and are meant, if only implicitly, as causal explanations of U.S. policy. To evaluate them empirically, however, we must distill a more precise understanding of the "national ethnic, cultural and religious particularities," the "cultural relativism," and the "ethnocentrism" that, according to critics like van der Vyer, underlie American exceptionalism.

[15] This relates to another of Ignatieff's arguments about American exceptionalism. As he notes in his introduction, the distinctive rights culture is both an element of exceptionalism and a possible explanation for it.

[16] J. D. van der Vyver, "Universality and Relativity of Human Rights: American Relativism," *Buffalo Human Rights Law Review* 4 (1998): 77.

[17] Natalie Kaufman, *Human Rights Treaties and the Senate: A History of Opposition* (Chapel Hill: University of North Carolina Press, 1990), 45. Kaufman argues, for example, that southern racism and Cold War McCarthyism came together in the early 1950s and set the rhetorical mold for subsequent debates.

[18] Forsythe, "The United States," 269, 282.

[19] Quotation from Moravcsik, "Why Is U.S. Human Rights Policy So Unilateralist?"

[20] For classical international lawyers, a nation either accepts, at least in principle, uniform application of all international human rights norms or it is "culturally relativistic." This critique also assumes, without proof, that commitment to multilateralism is the most efficient means to promote global human rights. In real existing systems of international adjudication, such as the European Convention on Human Rights system, in fact the distinction is far less clear. All but the most essential human rights are interpreted with varying deference to a "margin of appreciation" retained by national governments in determining the precise scope and meaning of the right.

Here I construe these sorts of "political culture" arguments to distinguish those explanations for U.S. "exemptionalism," nonratification, and noncompliance that invoke the tendency of the American public, elite, or leadership to interpret rights differently by virtue of ideological or cultural predispositions in favor of specific procedural forms. I mean thereby to distinguish cultural commitment to *procedure* from commitments, ideological or otherwise, to particular *substantive* policy outcomes, which might then lead domestic groups to interpret rights instrumentally in a distinctive way. The latter I shall treat below under "pluralist" arguments. Thus a causal link between a widespread belief in "states' rights" and U.S. nonratification of international instruments is a "rights cultural" explanation, whereas a predisposition to oppose abortion or to favor the death penalty as a policy, which then translates instrumentally into opposition to international norms (and perhaps also a defense of states' rights domestically) is a pluralist explanation based on the strength of support for conservative policy outcomes per se. The two may be, as an empirical matter, quite difficult to distinguish, but as a theoretical matter, the distinction is fundamental.

When analysts invoke "rights culture" as an explanation rather than simply as a normative criticism, they generally mean one or more of three things: (a) international obligations violate a widespread "reverence" toward the U.S. Constitution and political institutions as "sacred symbols" among U.S. legal elites and citizens; (b) a long-standing American belief in "popular sovereignty" and "local government" predisposes Americans to oppose centralized judicial norms; and (c) a popular American "rights culture" of negative liberties rooted in an individualist worldview is incompatible with international human rights obligations. Let us examine each in turn.

Constitutional Patriotism and Other Forms of Nationalism

Do international obligations violate a general culture of "reverence" among American legal elites toward the U.S. Constitution as a "sacred symbol"? The claim here is that Americans, and particularly the country's legal elites, are unusually attached to their Constitution. It is clearly true, as David Golove has written of human rights law, that

> Americans . . . are accustomed to thinking that our legal system, especially our constitutional commitment to fundamental rights, provides a model that other countries would be well advised to emulate. This confident, perhaps arrogant, self-conception as a moral beacon for the rest of the world has deep roots in U.S. history and seems as strong today as it has ever been. In contrast, many Americans are apt to be far less comfortable with the notion that when it comes

to justice, we may have something to learn from other nations—that we may benefit from the importation, not just the exportation, of rights.[21]

The United States appears unusually committed to the sanctity of its Constitution, as the current spread of "originalist" legal interpretation suggests. It is those who hold this view who are most critical of U.S. application of international human rights norms.[22]

Why should this be so? Perhaps simply because the U.S. Constitution has been around so long.[23] Perhaps because the United States is, as Tocqueville noted, a nation of laws and lawyers, in which "hardly a political question . . . does not sooner or later turn into a judicial one."[24] Perhaps because, lacking a distinct ethnonational identity, Americans identify their nationality with a single liberal-democratic political creed to a greater extent than do the citizens of other modern nations.[25] In *American Politics: The Promise of Disharmony*, Samuel Huntington famously argued about this civic nationalism: "In the United States, as in no other society, ideology and nationality are fused and the disappearance of the former would mean the disappearance of the latter."[26] As a result, Huntington argues, "the relation of its institutions [of] foreign relations to the ideals and values of its foreign policy" and, in particular, "to what extent . . . the United States [should] attempt to make the institutions and policies of other societies conform to American values" become more serious problems for the United States than for most other societies.[27]

One version of this argument sees the constraint on U.S. policy imposed by American "constitutional culture" as taking the form of diffuse views held among the mass public. Polls reveal that Americans possess exceptional national pride in their distinctive political institutions, and that this makes them evaluate those institutions much more favorably than do publics in other advanced industrial democracies.[28]

Yet we encounter a number of related difficulties linking this characteristic of public opinion to human rights policy. First, the public has gener-

---

[21] David Golove, "Human Rights Treaties and the U.S. Constitution," *DePaul Law Review* 52 (Winter 2002): 579.

[22] Jeremy Rabkin, *Why Sovereignty Matters* (Washington, DC: American Enterprise Institute, 1998).

[23] Bruce M. Russett and John R. O'Neal, *Triangulating Peace: Democracy, Interdependence, and International Organizations* (New York: W. W. Norton, 2001).

[24] *Democracy in America*, vol. 1, chap. 16.

[25] See Louis Hartz, *The Liberal Tradition in America: An Interpretation of American Political Thought since the Revolution* (New York: Harcourt, Brace, & World, 1955), and Huntington, *American Politics*.

[26] Huntington, *American Politics*, 25–27.

[27] Ibid., 236.

[28] Seymour Martin Lipset, *American Exceptionalism: A Two-Edged Sword* (New York: Norton, 1996), 50–52.

ally viewed international human rights treaties, like multilateralism in general, considerably more positively than do decision makers, particularly those in the Senate. In the 1950s, to take one prominent example, the Genocide Convention was backed by groups claiming a combined membership of 100 million voters, including organized groups of veterans, racial minorities, religionists, workers, and ethnic Americans, while opponents could call on little more by way of organized groups than the American Bar Association.

Second, the scholarly research on U.S. human rights policy, more broadly, suggests that elite rather than mass opinion guides U.S. human rights policy. Human rights are not salient or high priority issues for either elites or the mass public—and, indeed, their salience has been declining since the end of the Cold War.[29] Such are the sort of issues on which the public is more likely to follow opinion leaders. (Over time, moreover, there is reason to believe that public opinion on issues like the death penalty tracks elite behavior and policy outcomes, rather than the reverse.)[30] Though mass and elite opinions tend to move in parallel and to respond to the same incentives, elite views tend to be more polarized and more coherent—that is, more consistently correlated with partisan considerations, domestic ideology, and positions on other foreign policy issues. In 1986–90, for example, the difference between the level of poll support for human rights between Democrats and Republicans in the population was only 4 percent, whereas the difference between Democratic and Republican elites was 21–38 percent. Elite opinion was generally more tightly linked to belief systems about, and other issues of, domestic and foreign policy.[31] Differences in elite support for specific U.S. international human rights policy are closely correlated both with "a general series of foreign and military issues" and with domestic political ideology.[32] The gap in support for international human rights between liberal and conservative opinion leaders approaches 50 percent (e.g., 73 percent liberal vs. 25 percent conservative elite support for propositions like "too many Iraqis were killed in the [first] Persian Gulf War").

[29] Ole Holsti, "Public Opinion on Human Rights in American Foreign Policy," in *The United States and Human Rights: Looking Inward and Outward*, ed. David Forsythe (Lincoln: University of Nebraska Press, 2000), 142 ff.

[30] Until the mid-1970s, support for the death penalty declined steadily to about 50 percent in both the United States and Europe. European governments abolished it and support remained stable or trended slowly downward, while the United States failed to abolish and a state-level movement gained support over the next few decades. See Moravcsik, "The New Abolitionism."

[31] Holsti, "Public Opinion," 145–47.

[32] David P. Forsythe, *Human Rights and U.S. Foreign Policy: Congress Reconsidered* (Gainesville: University of Florida Press, 1988), 41. This is corroborated by the data in Holsti, "Public Opinion."

This leads us to a second, Tocquevillian variant of the "constitutional culture" explanation. Here the argument is that American elites are disproportionately composed of lawyers, and American lawyers tend to revere the Constitution. At first glance, this explanation seems more promising. During the Bricker amendment controversy of the early 1950s—for some, the defining moment of postwar U.S. human rights policy—we see such an alignment. Legal elites stood consistently at the forefront of opposition to the human rights norms, as against a broad coalition of religious, labor, and civic groups. In this period, the American Bar Association (ABA) led the fight against human rights treaties, which fell short of congressional ratification (in a watered-down form) by one vote. Moreover, the ABA defended its position by advancing arguments about the legitimacy of particular American constitutional elements, such as states' rights.[33]

Yet a broader historical and comparative view calls the Tocquevillian view into question. The 1950s, it appears, were exceptional. In the late 1940s the ABA was in fact strongly internationalist and favorable to human rights policy, pushing for a global bill of rights and a strong international court of justice. Around 1950 it shifted to opposition but then shifted back to support for global norms in the late 1960s and 1970s in response to the civil rights movement. The ABA currently supports ratification of CEDAW, ICC, and the Convention on the Rights of the Child—though the United States does not; it is open-minded with regard to domestic application of global norms.[34] A comparison with Canada is similarly instructive. Like its U.S. counterpart, the Canadian Bar Association strongly opposed international human rights enforcement in the 1950s but shifted in the two following decades. Canada reversed its position on global human rights norms under Prime Minister Pierre Trudeau, and today Canada ratifies treaties and accepts international jurisdiction—except that of the Inter-American Court of Human Rights. U.S. policy, by contrast, moved only symbolically in response to the shift in legal opinion, suggesting that elite legal opinion is not the whole story. In the United States, the political system normally generates outcomes more conservative than those preferred by legal elites.

There is a deeper point here: The detailed history of the ABA's position and the specific constitutional arguments advanced against applying

[33] The ABA is the most influential legal organization in the United States—more than half of American lawyers are members—and it has taken an interest in international jurisprudence since it was founded in 1878.

[34] For complete background information on the ABA's current positions, see http://www.abanet.org/poladv/priorities/intltreaties.html#Background. The ABA also supports financial assistance to promote human rights NGO activities and international rule-of-law initiatives aimed at strengthening independent judiciaries abroad.

global norms (in particular, the defense of states' rights), the nature of the opposition (largely focused among southern senators), and its timing (in the 1950s, with a reversal when the civil rights movement gains ascendancy) suggests further that ideological positions taken by the legal elite, and the defense of the sanctity of the Constitution itself, are not evidence of a unified cultural ethos but a tactic to defend certain domestic political interests, notably segregation and other conservative positions on the rights of minorities. That is, while the position of U.S. legal elites generally is incoherent and inconsistent, there *is* a correlation between domestic positions and international ones. Those who support a vigorous U.S. international human rights policy are also domestic supporters of penal reform, school busing, abolition of the death penalty, and the equal rights amendment.[35] For their part many prominent opponents of international human rights norms are guided by conservative views about the proper role of the judiciary today. This is consistent with the established view that "originalism" in constitutional jurisprudence is driven, at least in part, by substantive commitment to a particular set of conservative policy positions.[36] In domestic courts, the Left would be aided in its efforts by the domestic application of international norms, whereas the Right would generally be impeded. In this sense, the particular forms of legal doctrines—originalism, "sovereigntism," states' rights—are epiphenomenal. The conflict, as we shall see in more detail when we turn to interests and institutions, is really a pluralist one between the Left and the Right to influence judicial institutions—the Left seeking to move the constitutional clock "forward" in accordance with international norms, the Right seeking to turn it "back" to the 1920s.[37] For conservative opponents, what is most trou-

[35] Holsti, "Public Opinion," 150–53.

[36] For example: "Originalism is a political slogan that stands for strong disagreement with a particular subset of modern decisions, not an unqualified commitment to wholesale restoration of the Founders' Constitution." Larry Kramer, "Originalism and Historical Truth: On Finding (and Losing) Our Origins," *Harvard Journal of Law and Public Policy* 26 (Winter 2003): 107. This also dovetails with criticisms of Huntington's interpretation for its exaggeration of the level of consensus in U.S. society. For a critique that stresses underlying conflicts over competing ideals and interests—and, in particular, between liberals committed to equality and conservatives committed to liberty—see Rogers M. Smith, "The 'American Creed' and Constitutional Theory," *Harvard Law Review* 95 (1982): 1691–1702.

[37] Lest this seem hyperbolic, it is important to note that some critics of U.S. application of international norms are quite explicit about their desire to roll back the shift toward federal power that resulted from the New Deal, the Cold War, and the civil rights movement. For an analysis of Jeremy Rabkin and William Cash, originally developed in debate at the American Enterprise Institute, see Andrew Moravcsik, "Conservative Idealism and International Institutions," *Chicago Journal of International Law* 1:2 (Autumn 2000). Against such claims, I argue that selectivity in the defense of "sovereignty" (e.g., the WTO and NATO are fine, but not the ILO or the UN) as a means to defend constitutional retrogression is a constant of conservative discourse in the United States and the United Kingdom.

bling about turning over judgment on human rights matters to international tribunals is not that they are international, but that they are courts.

Popular Sovereignty and Local Government

Contemporary conservative criticisms of the expansion of the scope of international organizations—and, in particular, international tribunals—often appeal to democracy and alarms about an encroaching "democratic deficit."[38] Criticism of international regimes these days rarely misses a chance to contrast unelected bureaucrats in international organizations with the "legitimate" role of constitutionally elected representatives in national polities.[39] The basis of the resulting critique—a critique shared by British Tory Euroskeptics—is generally that there is neither a subjective sense of an international polity (a "*demos*") nor working global representative institutions, and thus there cannot be democratic accountability, either in theory or in practice. It follows that global governance is distant, technocratic, and judicialized decision making that encourages arbitrary rule by moralist or socialist elites.[40] It would seem to follow that Americans would be suspicious of all global human rights norms, and that the rhetoric of opposition to their application in the United States would be, as it is, tinged with patriotism. Could a distinctively American (or Anglo-American) commitment to popular sovereignty be the source of American ambivalence with regard to the application of global human rights norms?

Certainly critics of human rights treaties wrap themselves in the mantle of democracy, but is it in fact the root cause of their concern?[41] It is surely true that in certain respects, the United States is committed to popular sovereignty.[42] Yet in comparative perspective, the perception of the United States as a "populist" country is a curious one. The American Constitution—with its checks and balances, federalism, and, most important for our purposes here, strong judiciary—instantiates anything but the ideal of popular sovereignty. Indeed, in formal terms it is near the opposite extreme. Most polities in Europe—notably the majority based on some notion of sovereignty exercised by a directly elected parliament—have political traditions far closer to that idea and, as a result, intrinsically more

---

[38] For a summary and critique, see ibid.

[39] E.g., see Luck, *Mixed Messages*, 45–46.

[40] Normative appeals to popular sovereignty are often found in policy analysis, political rhetoric, and political philosophy, and occasionally in constitutional law scholarship surrounding rights claims. For critiques of this notion, see Christopher Eisgruber, *Constitutional Self-Government* (Cambridge: Harvard University Press, 2001).

[41] I have discussed this issue in more detail in "Conservative Idealism."

[42] See Edmund S. Morgan, *The Rise of Popular Sovereignty in England and America* (New York: W. W. Norton, 1988).

hostile to checks and balances, judicial lawmaking, and individual litigation to resolve disputes.[43] (The exceptions to this rule are almost all either constitutions rewritten or imposed on previously fascist countries after World War II or a subsequent democratic transition.)[44] For most Western European polities, international human rights systems are the only experience with *ex post* judicial review for human rights purposes they have ever had. If a commitment to "popular sovereignty" has led any region of the world to oppose human rights, it should have been Europe.[45] By contrast, the United States is widely viewed as the classic example of a system in which the legitimacy of courts to overrule the popular will in defense of human rights is widely accepted. While scholars may debate the legitimacy of a "countermajoritarian" institution like the Supreme Court, polls reveal high levels of perceived legitimacy for courts in the United States.[46] Courts are often linked with commitments to individualism and "equality of opportunity." As compared to the citizens of other countries, Americans may retain a "Lockean" suspicion of government coercion in such matters as taxation, government ownership, welfare, and the managed economy, but few question the legitimacy of courts to render decisions on issues of human rights.[47]

To rescue the popular sovereignty explanation, one might argue that Americans hold a principled belief in local, small-scale democracy within a federal system, which predisposes them to reject centralized forms of rights enforcement, particularly at the international level. It is certainly true that Americans report suspicion about "big government" in Washington, and tend to trust state and local officials more.[48] The United States has more elected offices per capita than any country in the world.[49] The practice of electing local judges, viewed with abhorrence in most of the developed world, is widely accepted in

[43] On differential levels of litigiousness, see Lipset, *American Exceptionalism*, 50.

[44] Andrew Moravcsik, "The Origins of International Human Rights Regimes: Democratic Delegation in Postwar Europe," *International Organization* 53:2 (Spring 1999): 267–306.

[45] And, indeed, in Britain, France, and Scandinavia, we see substantial opposition of just this type.

[46] The classic casebook of Louis Henkin et al. is premised on this view—a parallel unthinkable in most constitutional systems in the world. Louis Henkin, Gerald L. Neuman, Diane F. Orentlicher, and David W. Leebron, *Human Rights* (New York: Foundation Press, 1999).

[47] On trust in the court, see http://www.pollingreport.com/institut.htm. On the tension between the egalitarian ideals of American society and the aversion to coercive government action to achieve them, see Seymour Martin Lipset, introduction to *The First New Nation: The United States in Historical and Comparative Perspective* (New York: Norton, 1963, repr. 1979), xxxiii–xxxiv; Seymour Martin Lipset, "The Paradox of American Politics," *The Public Interest* (Fall 1975): 142–65.

[48] http://www.pollingreport.com/institut.htm.

[49] Lipset, *American Exceptionalism*, 43.

the United States. Consistent with this view is the tendency of opponents of centralized judicial power in the United States, many of whom also oppose international human rights enforcement, to stress the importance of "states' rights." Trust in the Supreme Court remains high.

Yet an explanation based on localism runs into some of the same sort of objections as do the arguments from democracy or constitutional patriotism. There are other political systems in the world, such as Italy, Germany, Belgium, Canada, and Spain, with substantial attachment to local government—though such systems are fewer than strong parliamentary systems—and they do not seem to translate these views into virulent opposition to multilateral treaties.[50] In comparative perspective, many who inhabit these decentralized systems have strong commitments to regional identity—perhaps stronger than those of members of the more mobile U.S. population. The relevant difference for global human rights, I submit, is likely to lie not in some distinctive American conception of legitimate procedure but in the fact that certain issues relevant to rights enforcement are uniquely important to certain regional identities in the U.S. context, and, in large part as a result, specific institutional functions (notably various rights questions and modes of federal representation) have been devolved in a way that creates political opportunities—a point to which I shall return.

To distinguish "rights cultural" objections, we must ask whether those who criticize the Supreme Court in the United States, and international tribunals by extension, do so primarily because they hold a particular philosophy of localism or because their substantive preferences in regard to political outcomes are better served by local government. How many principled defenders of "states' rights" exist today? By contrast, how many support states' rights because they favor a weakening of federal policies with regard to race, the death penalty, criminal rights, and welfare? The intensely partisan nature of the disputes—Democrats tend to support federal civilian initiatives more than do Republicans, consistent with their positions on international human rights issues—suggests a concrete underpinning to ideological positions. A full discussion of this issue is beyond the scope of this essay, but below we shall consider some more evidence that substantive issue positions are indeed dominant.[51]

---

[50] We see something similar, perhaps, in the tension between the prerogatives of the German Bundesländer and that country's commitments to the EU. Fritz Scharpf, "The Joint-Decision Trap: Lessons from German Federalism and European Integration," *Public Administration* 66 (Autumn 1988): 239–78.

[51] The same question can be posed in historical perspective. Even if many conservatives oppose international human rights norms out of sincere commitment to certain procedural ideals, were the strength and maintenance of these ideals themselves a function of restricted institutional choices? I side with those who believe they were. See John W. Kingdon, *America the Unusual* (New York: Worth Publishers, 1999).

Libertarianism and the Substance of Rights

A third and final "culturalist" conjecture holds that the U.S. conception of "limited government," understood as a libertarian preference for negative as opposed to positive rights, predisposes Americans to reject application of global human rights norms. This view rests on the most widely accepted understanding of "American exceptionalism" in political science and history. This classic view refers to the absence of a true socialist party and to extensive social welfare institutions present in nearly all other advanced industrial democracies.[52] In this view, the United States rejects global human rights norms because they embody a different philosophical conception of rights—one skewed toward "positive" socioeconomic rights and positive duties rather than "negative" civil and political rights. In sum, Americans stress liberty, whereas others stress equality.

Certainly the divergence between the United States and other advanced industrial democracies on the question of the scope of rights—and, in particular, the inclusion of social and economic rights—has influenced postwar international human rights policy. Recent historiography has revealed the important role of the Soviet bloc and the developing world (not least in Latin America) in promoting positive duties and socioeconomic rights in the UN Universal Declaration.[53] In 1953, at the height of the Bricker amendment controversy, a leading American opponent, president of the American Bar Association Frank Holman, wrote:

> [The UN human rights system] would promote state socialism, if not communism, throughout the world. . . . Internationalists . . . propose to use the United Nations . . . to change the domestic laws and even the Government of the United States and to establish a World Government along socialistic lines. . . . They would give the super-government absolute control of business, industry, prices, wages, and every detail of American social and economic life.

It is unclear to what extent this was, variously, a sincere expression of concern, a tactical effort by southern segregationists (the core of opponents to international human rights in this period) to find allies among business-oriented Republicans, or a manipulative use of McCarthy-era rhetoric—but it is certainly consistent with a libertarian ethos. To this day, the United States has failed to ratify the UN Covenant on Economic and So-

---

[52] For a recent review of this literature, see Seymour Martin Lipset and Gary Marks, *It Didn't Happen Here: Why Socialism Failed in the United States* (New York: W. W. Norton & Co., 2000); Kingdon, *America the Unusual*; Lipset, *American Exceptionalism*, 88–109.

[53] For a systematic archival analysis, see Johannes Morsink, *The Universal Declaration of Human Rights: Origins, Drafting, and Intent* (Philadelphia: University of Pennsylvania Press, 1999). For an overview focusing more on Eleanor Roosevelt, see also Mary Ann Glendon, *A World Made New: Eleanor Roosevelt and the Universal Declaration of Human Rights* (New York: Random House, 2000).

cial Rights, even with reservations, and shuns more specialized treaties on subjects like the rights of migrant workers, as well as nearly the entire (rather large) corpus of the International Labor Organization.

There is, I shall argue, one more nuanced strand or interpretation of this libertarian versus egalitarian argument for which there is substantial evidence. Before coming to it, however, let us set aside three simpler and more extreme interpretations for which there is less evidence.

The first implausible interpretation is that the main reason for U.S. ambivalence lies in a cultural aversion to socioeconomic ("positive") rights in the strong sense of welfare entitlements or labor rights. While the United States and most of the rest of the Western world do differ in this regard, this divergence has little relevance for the matter at hand. With the exception of the Universal Declaration, an unenforceable document, the international human rights system strictly separates civil and political rights from socioeconomic ones. The UN system, for example, distinguishes between the modestly enforceable Covenant on Civil and Political Rights, favored at the time of negotiation by Western governments, and what has remained a symbolic and rhetorical Covenant on Social and Economic Rights. Some Europeans aspire to extend the international enforcement of socioeconomic rights—an act that would be in their commercial interest as well—yet even the European Convention system and the EU do not effectively protect socioeconomic rights, and no serious effort has been made to have them do so. The United States could, therefore, at any time simply ignore socioeconomic documents, while ratifying and implementing civil and political ones—as it has indeed done in the process of negotiation. This is why, beyond intermittent rhetorical excesses exemplified by the quotation from Frank Holman above, almost no attention has been paid to economic rights in U.S. domestic debates. The exceptional level of U.S. opposition is really all about civil and political rights.[54]

The second implausible interpretation rests on the claim that U.S. ambivalence stems from a culture of strict philosophical adherence to libertarian principles. Again this seems questionable on its face.[55] For there is no clear correlation between libertarian philosophical foundations and issues that

[54] For a characteristic example of the rare domestic attention—usually in the form of an exhortatory law review article—see Barbara Stark, "U.S. Ratification of the Other Half of the International Bill of Rights," in *The United States and Human Rights: Looking Inward and Outward*, ed. David Forsythe (Lincoln: University of Nebraska Press, 2000), 75–93. Stark asserts that interest groups avoided the Economic Covenant "with its troubling foreign policy implications," but provides no evidence of any such conscious strategy. Mostly groups simply paid no attention, as is often true domestically. Stark also asserts that the Cold War was the dominant factor pushing economic rights off the agenda in the United States, but again she provides no evidence—and the reverse might equally well have been the case.

[55] I am indebted to Frank Michelman for encouraging me to render this section more precise.

appear to motivate the most salient conservative criticism of international human rights norms—which is not surprising, given that economic rights have been taken off the table.[56] U.S. critics of human rights treaties take an explicitly antilibertarian position—that is, a position advocating government intervention to limit individual freedom vis-à-vis the state on matters of criminal defense, the death penalty, prison conditions, abortion, religious rights, prisoners of war, and, in the 1950s, segregation. Opposition to rights of equal opportunity (antidiscrimination) with regard to women, racial minorities, and gay people, as well as opposition to children's rights, might be interpreted as consistent with a libertarian conception of negative rights, but these cases are ambiguous at best.[57]

The third implausible interpretation holds that the United States rejects international standards because they would undermine the high levels of existing protection afforded to particular individual rights by the more "libertarian" U.S. system. True, in comparative perspective, the American Constitution and jurisprudence do enshrine and interpret expansive conceptions of certain liberties—freedom of speech, freedom to bear arms, and procedural rights of the criminal defendant, to name three. Yet again this is manifestly not the source of domestic opposition. International human rights treaties do not engage some of these issues (e.g., arms). In the case of those they do engage, norms rarely undermine existing protections, in part because they are almost always enforced to set a floor on basic rights, and in part because of the widespread recognition of a "margin of appreciation" for state policy in international human rights jurisprudence.[58] And even if they were to do so, there is little evidence that such concerns are the source of domestic U.S. opposition to international treaties. The American Civil Liberties Union and their liberal allies are not spearheading the anti–human rights crusade! The concern of conservative opponents is not that judicially enforced rights will diminish, but that they will expand.

A final interpretation of "libertarian" rights culture, however, is at least prima facie plausible. It links U.S. ambivalence to a diffuse aversion to big government.[59] Specifically, Americans tend to shy away from state intervention to redress social inequality—now established in most advanced industrial democracies as the primary fiscal task of the state. The aversion

---

[56] Nor is it surprising that U.S. conservatives would not be consistently libertarian, given the influence of various sets of Christian values.

[57] The case by critics against the International Criminal Court (ICC) is also puzzling from a libertarian perspective, as one would expect support for tight judicial control over military action.

[58] See Frederick Schauer's essay in this volume.

[59] Jed Rubinfeld, "The Two World Orders," *Wilson Quarterly* 27 (Autumn 2003): 22–36.

to state intervention is a distinctively American trait as compared to the political cultures of other advanced industrial democracies, which tend to be far more egalitarian, redistributive, and social democratic.[60] This applies directly to human rights. The most salient and enduring concerns of U.S. critics of international human rights treaties all share an explicit opposition to state intervention to promote equality. The apparent motivations of supporters of international human rights standards for criminal defense, the death penalty, segregation, antidiscrimination law, social welfare, and the rights of the child are largely based on an instinctive sense that the state can and should intervene to promote egalitarian social outcomes. What appears to link conservatives across a range of controversial and sensitive issues is a rejection of that premise.

Here we reach the very extremes of a "rights cultural" argument—a place where they become very difficult to disentangle from the material and institutional arguments I term "pluralist." One might debate, and many have, to what extent these conservative policy preferences are truly procedural and to what extent they reflect (or reflect a legacy of) distinctively American conceptions of appropriate desired substantive outcomes—perhaps informed by specific racial, class, or religious values. One might similarly debate the extent to which these policy preferences are autonomous or held in place by exogenous material, institutional, or ideational forces—or the legacy left by such forces in past time. Many scholars have made the case that much of the conservatism underpinning hostility to international human rights norms is the legacy of an antimajoritarian U.S. constitutional and federal structure, two centuries of southern overrepresentation in U.S. politics, the conservative influence of the judiciary, and so on. This is not the place to make a contribution to that venerable debate—although I think the institutionalists have rather the better of the debate at the moment. My point here is that only a "cultural" aversion to particular procedures that is almost indistinguishable from a substantive commitment to particular conservative policy positions offers a plausible account of U.S. policy. This finding directs us toward the pluralist explanations for the paradox of American exceptionalism.[61]

We have learned that simple arguments based on a homogeneous American "political culture"—that is, the cultural or ideological preference of American elites or citizens for specific procedural forms—tend to display fatal weaknesses. Such accounts explain change and cross-national differences poorly.[62] Perhaps their most serious failing, and it is a classic failing

---

[60] This is the classic sense of "American exceptionalism," dating back to Werner Sombart's classic query: "Why No Socialism in America?"

[61] For a balanced assessment, see Kingdon, *America the Unusual.*

[62] The U.S. culture of foreign policy in general, and international human rights policy in particular, have changed greatly over time. Not fifty years ago, the conventional view held

of such theories, lies in the lack of an account for the extreme domestic cleavages over human rights. Rather than tracking broad ideological, professional, or sociological strata—such as legal training—procedural beliefs seem to track preexisting cleavages, often partisan ones, over substantive issues that divide Americans by race, class, and political ideology.[63] In other words, this issue pits liberals against conservatives. This opens up the possibility that a procedural ideology is in fact a tactical choice in partisan competition.[64] Supporters of segregation, for example, employed "states' rights" and other constitutional objections as more politically acceptable justifications for limiting federal jurisdiction in matters of race.[65] All these reasons warrant suspicion of ideological or cultural explanations of U.S. human rights policy.[66] We must seek other explanations that can account for the cleavages over specific rights that have emerged in the American pluralist system, and ways in which concrete institutional mechanisms for articulating those preferences influence the outcome of political conflict.

---

that "Americans deprecate power politics and old-fashioned diplomacy, mistrust powerful standing armies and entangling peacetime commitments, make moralistic judgments about other people's domestic systems, and believe that liberal values transfer readily to foreign affairs." Within a few years, the policy was reversed—and the conventional view is now the opposite. Joseph Lepgold and Timothy McKeown, "Is American Foreign Policy Exceptional? An Empirical Analysis," *Political Science Quarterly* 110:3 (Autumn 1995): 369. For one cleverly (if only partially) cultural explanation, see Jack Snyder, *Myths of Empire: Domestic Politics and International Ambition* (Ithaca: Cornell University Press, 1991).

[63] I am indebted to Alex Keyssar for insights on this point.

[64] All assessments of motivation in politics require a measure of empirical inference, and any empirical indicator or technique for doing so has dangers. The most commonly employed indicator of motivation is public rhetoric—and it is probably the least reliable measure of motivation.

[65] In general, cultural accounts are disproportionately dependent on an interpretation of policy makers' rhetoric—the slipperiest indicator of true motivation. Talk can be cheap, cheaper than other forms of political investment, and there are thus strong incentives for politicians to deploy rhetoric, especially public rhetoric, strategically to simplify, disguise, or diversify their motivations. Self-interest is often presented as principle, extremists target swing voters to build coalitions, and narrow purposes are often made to seem broad. At the very least, cultural explanations (e.g., "Americans are committed to local government") are often simplified shorthand for a more complex process of political choice (e.g., "The United States has a federal constitution with checks and balances that hampers the centralization of policy making"). Very often politicians also diversify public justifications, which leads to long lists of factors that are easy to cite but difficult to weight—some of which may have played little or no role in the ultimate decision. A skillful politician leaves many thinking they "caused" a decision to be taken. Finally, politicians are sometimes outright duplicitous.

[66] They are, in the language adopted above (see n. 14), *thin* rather than *thick* explanations of U.S. policy.

Pluralist Explanations for American Unilateralism

Pluralist views stress, in lieu of political culture and the "logic of appropriateness," the interplay of interests and institutions and a "logic of consequences." Support for and opposition to domestic enforcement of international norms reflect an assessment of costs and benefits in terms of policies favored by alternative political constituents. Such a pluralist calculus reflects institutional structures, substantive policy positions, and the distribution of political power. To restate the central claims of the pluralist view in general (and thus implicitly comparative) terms: Opposition to domestic application of multilateral norms is less likely in countries that possesses strong unilateral bargaining power abroad, stable democratic institutions at home, preferences about substantive rights that diverge from the international consensus, and decentralized political institutions that empower small veto groups. The United States has been a liberal democracy with a history of intense concern about domestic civil rights and a sense of solidarity with other liberal democracies, yet the fact that it occupies an extreme position with regard to every one of these characteristics—power, democratic stability, conservatism, and veto-group politics—provides an empirically more viable explanation of America's exceptional ambivalence toward international human rights norms. Let us consider each of these four characteristics in turn.

The Ambivalence of a Great Power

The first general factor is *the superpower status of the United States in world affairs.* A straightforward "realist" argument links power to unilateralism.[67] The costs of multilateralism for any given state lie in the necessity to sacrifice a measure of unilateral or bilateral policy autonomy in order to impose a uniform policy. All other things being equal, the more powerful (or self-sufficient) a state—that is, the more efficiently it can achieve its objectives by domestic, unilateral, and bilateral means—the greater these "sovereignty costs" are likely to be.[68] Powerful governments

---

[67] "Realist" theories of international relations stress the impact of material power (above all military power) on interstate politics. They predict the recurrence of phenomena such as bids for hegemonic power, balances of power, and coercive bargaining. Such dynamics, realists argue, are particularly prevalent among the great powers. Since the early twentieth century, the United States has been one of the world's great powers in political, military, economic, and even cultural terms; today, many argue, the United States is the only remaining superpower in what some have described as a "unipolar" international system.

[68] For realist views, see James McCall Smith, "The Politics of Dispute Resolution Design: Explaining Legalism in Regional Trade Pacts," *International Organization* 54:1 (Autumn

are therefore more often skeptical of procedural equality in international forums than are their smaller neighbors. This is not to say that, on balance, great powers will always oppose multilateralism, for the benefits of intense cooperation may outweigh the costs—as the United States has decided in the cases of postwar trade agreements and military alliances. Indeed, these benefits may, as hegemonic stability theorists have argued, accrue to a superpower disproportionately.[69] Yet at the same time, the hegemon retains greater bilateral capabilities and bargaining power. There is reason to expect, therefore, that great powers will feel greater ambivalence toward multilateralism than will their less powerful neighbors.[70] Great power ambivalence toward multilateralism seems to pervade many areas of U.S. foreign policy, including trade, monetary, financial, and security policies. The United States, a strong supporter of the GATT, the UN, and the international financial institutions at the beginning of the postwar period, has been a problematic participant, prone to unilateral and even coercive diplomacy thereafter.

The same logic obtains for human rights policy. Almost alone in the world today, the United States enjoys the luxury of making a real choice between viable unilateral and multilateral means of promoting international human rights. For human rights–conscious countries like Denmark, Chile, or South Africa, the choice is between a multilateral policy and none at all. We might, moreover, expect great power ambivalence to be more pronounced in human rights than elsewhere, because the typical model of multilateral human rights enforcement is often judicial rather than legislative. Whereas multilateral organizations like the WTO and UN essentially provide forums for legislation via interstate bargaining over new rules—a mode of interaction in which the powerful generally retain disproportionate influence—human rights norms are typically enforced through formal legal adjudication at the domestic or international level. To participate fully in such arrangements, in contrast to most legislative institutions, powerful countries must generally sacrifice some bargaining power.[71]

2000): 137–80; Robert Gilpin, *War and Change in International Politics* (New York: Cambridge University Press, 1981); Kenneth N. Waltz, *Theory of International Politics* (Reading, MA: Addison-Wesley, 1979), 200.

[69] See Robert O. Keohane, "The Theory of Hegemonic Stability and Changes in International Economic Regimes, 1967–1977," in *Change in the International System*, ed. Ole R. Holsti, Randolph M. Siverson, and Alexander L. George (Boulder, CO: Westview Press, 1980), 131–62. On trade, see Bruce Ackerman and David Golove, "Is NAFTA Constitutional?" *Harvard Law Review* 108 (February 1995): 801–929.

[70] Since more powerful states also have more expansive socioeconomic and political-military interests, moreover, they may also benefit more from international cooperation. We therefore expect them to demand advantageous provisions and special exceptions. See Smith, "Politics of Dispute Resolution."

[71] The threat of unilateral noncompliance or withdrawal remains, but these are precisely the elements that constitute typical great power ambivalence.

Certainly there is evidence that the superpower status of the United States influences its attitude toward international human rights norms. It is generally the case that great powers are warier of international dispute resolution.[72] Great powers—the United States, Russia, the United Kingdom, China, Brazil, Mexico, India—tend to view international human rights enforcement with skepticism.[73] The United States has usually been backed by Britain, France, China, and Russia in opposing efforts by smaller states, backed by international tribunals, to restrict the scope of permissible reservations to such treaties.[74] One might extend the argument by noting that—at least in the Cold War—the American balance-of-power strategy led it to defend nondemocratic leaders of South Vietnam, Pakistan, Iran, the Philippines, Nicaragua, Chile, Taiwan, South Korea, Saudi Arabia, and eventually even the People's Republic of China. Through the realist lens, by which "the enemy of my enemy is my friend," these were viewed as essential "second-best" tactics in the Cold War.[75] In this context, human rights was a propaganda tool. Even the Carter administration, though ideologically sincere in its commitment to human rights enforcement, was famously selective—a policy culminating in the image of its National Security Advisor waving an M-16 at the Khyber Pass. This is consistent with the fact that the United States appears slightly more willing to ratify multilateral human rights treaties after the Cold War than it was amidst it: The Senate ratified no legally binding treaty in the 1950s and one each in the 1960s, 1970s, and 1980s, but four during the early 1990s—though after 9/11 the United States appears to have redoubled its

[72] James McCall Smith, "The Politics of Dispute Resolution Design: Explaining Legalism in Regional Trade Pacts," *International Organization* 54:1 (Autumn 2000): 137–80.

[73] This supposition has commonly been advanced to explain why many great powers opposed strong enforcement within the UN system. See P. G. Lauren, *The Evolution of International Human Rights: Visions Seen* (Philadelphia: University of Pennsylvania Press, 1998); and John P. Humphrey, *On the Edge of Greatness: The Diaries of John Humphrey, First Director of the United Nations Division of Human Rights*, ed. A. J. Hobbins (Montreal: McGill University Library, 1994). This explanation is, in my view, incorrect, for reasons set forth elsewhere. See Moravcsik, "Origins of International Human Rights Regimes."

[74] Reservations are a means to unilaterally clarify or restrict the scope of a treaty. Reservations have legal standing if they do not contravene the explicit scope and purpose of the treaty—a quality itself open to dispute and adjudication. When treaties limit reservations, as with the ICC and land mines, for example, the United States has stayed aloof. Regional powers, notably Brazil and Mexico in the Western Hemisphere, have made particularly extensive use of reservations, further confirming a general tendency for great powers to defend their discretion in the face of multilateral commitments. Ryan Goodman, "Human Rights Treaties, Invalid Reservations, and State Consent," *American Journal of International Law* 96 (2002): 531–60.

[75] Some realists predict that in a bipolar world, two superpowers will each be likely to view third states in zero-sum terms: For each, the enemy of an enemy is a friend. See Waltz, *Theory of International Politics*, for a more subtle and differentiated argument.

traditional ambivalence.[76] When international human rights treaties—the Genocide Convention in the 1950s and 1970s, and the International Criminal Court (ICC) today, for example—raise the possibility, albeit remote, that U.S. soldiers might be prosecuted, the United States consistently stands aloof.[77] Is it just coincidence that the governments of countries with significant foreign military involvement or power projection capabilities—Russia, Israel, France, Great Britain, and China—were among initial skeptics of a strong ICC and continue to demand exceptional treatment now that it has been established?

Whereas the superpower status of the United States may be an important consideration, it does not provide a satisfactory account of U.S. policy overall. If geopolitical flexibility were the only goal of the United States, any American administration could have its cake and eat it too by ratifying multilateral treaties *and* maintaining a parallel unilateral human rights policy, while aggressively employing reservations to cordon off specific areas of heightened concern. Such a combination—essentially that pursued by countries like France, Britain, Russia, and even China with regard to many multilateral commitments—might indeed be viewed as more legitimate around the globe. Moreover, since the controversy over the Bricker amendment, the locus of opposition has lain in the Senate, not with the president, who is traditionally responsible for maintaining geopolitical flexibility.[78] Whether or not a country possesses unilateral options, it can—as the United States often does—participate in an international organization but resist

[76] Some have attributed this upward trend to the backlog of treaties, but with changes in the composition of the Senate, the trend does not continue past the mid-1990s.

[77] The United States finally ratified the Genocide Convention under President Ronald Reagan. By that time, the convention could no longer have any impact on (postsegregationist) race relations in the United States, and the post-Vietnam United States was not involved in major direct military interventions abroad. This ratification is widely perceived as an opportunistic effort to deflect criticism of the Reagan administration's human rights policies. Tamar Jacoby, "The Reagan Turnaround on Human Rights," *Foreign Affairs* 64:5 (Summer 1986).

[78] The most powerful postwar movement in opposition to human rights treaties, the effort in the early 1950s to pass a constitutional amendment (the so-called Bricker amendment) limiting the domestic enforceability of treaties, came within one senatorial vote of passage. On January 20, 1954, Senate debate began on a bundle of proposals generally referred to as the Bricker amendment. The actual amendment proposed by Bricker failed after receiving a vote of only 52–40 in favor. A weaker version proposed by Senator Walter George, a Democrat of Georgia, failed after receiving a vote of 61–30 in favor—one short of the two-thirds required for a constitutional amendment. Hence the received (but misleading) wisdom that the "Bricker amendment" failed by one vote. See Kaufman, *Human Rights*, 34. The Bricker amendment was a response to a real, if modest, trend in U.S. jurisprudence during the 1940s and 1950s toward the enforcement of international standards. The rhetorical, political, and legal focus of that episode lay almost entirely on the implications of human rights treaties for the U.S. legal system, not on the projection of American power abroad. Republicans and Democrats have accepted the desirability of adherence to human rights by other governments.

domestic implementation of its norms. Insofar as such opportunistic policy options remain viable, there is no particular reason why we should assume that a large country is less likely to sign on to a human rights treaty than is a smaller one.[79]

The geopolitical account also fails to explain the virulently ideological and partisan domestic politics that surround international treaty ratification in the United States. Domestic U.S. debates on human rights issues do not simply track the conventional geopolitical concerns of a superpower.[80] For fifty years, domestic debates about adherence to treaties have been concerned almost exclusively with the *domestic* implications of adherence to human rights treaties.[81] If the United States simply possesses a broader set of options, we should expect a measure of apathy or opportunism. The United States overcame strong domestic opposition to enter into far more significant (although not unbounded) treaty commitments, such as NATO and other Cold War military alliances, trade institutions (GATT/WTO), and international financial institutions (the IMF and World Bank). To understand why American legislators are so hesitant to cede sovereignty, we must therefore turn to the domestic determinants of U.S. human rights policy.[82]

The Ambivalence of a Stable Democracy

A second factor contributing to U.S. ambivalence toward multilateral human rights commitments is *the exceptional stability of democratic governance within its borders*. At first glance this assertion may seem puzzling. In the broad sweep of history, human rights are closely linked to liberal democracy. Established, stable democracies have long encouraged,

---

[79] This is so unless we assume that benefits of membership—influence over positions, agendas, or photo ops—will be rationed according to domestic compliance. There is little evidence that this is the case in any international human rights regime, but this may be a concern for some countries in, say, northern Europe.

[80] This extreme hostility persisted, moreover, through the rise and the decline of the Cold War, even in periods when both political parties were generally internationalist and staunchly anti-Communist in foreign policy.

[81] Kaufman, *Human Rights*, passim. See also, for example, U.S. Congress, Senate Committee on Foreign Relations, *International Human Rights Treaties: Hearings before the Committee on Foreign Relations*, 96th Congress, 1st Session on Ex. C, D, E, and F, 95–2—Four Treaties Relating to Human Rights, November 14, 15, 16, and 19, 1979 (1980); United States, Senate Committee on Foreign Relations, *International Covenant on Civil and Political Rights: Hearing before the Committee on Foreign Relations*, 102nd Congress, 1st Session, November 21, 1991 (1992).

[82] This is not to rule out a realist account entirely. Perhaps the practice of unilateralism in other areas "spills over" into human rights, or there is some more subtle link between adherence and membership.

assisted, and even fought bitter wars to uphold democracy abroad, both for idealistic reasons and because they tend to view democracy—correctly so, it now appears—as integrally linked to world peace.[83]

Yet the relationship between stable democratic governance and international human rights regimes is typically (or, at least, was until recently) more ambivalent. While they support human rights in principle, and recognize a link between democracy and security, established democracies are often skeptical of enforceable international human rights norms. This underlying ambivalence, I have argued elsewhere, was particularly evident in the period from 1950 to 1980—the founding period of the major postwar international human rights regimes such as the European Convention on Human Rights, the American Convention on Human Rights, and the UN system. In the founding negotiations of these regimes, the most stable, well-established democracies, in alliance with repressive governments, consistently *opposed* effective enforcement of international norms.[84]

A simple theoretical insight drawn from "republican liberal" theories of international relations—and from well-established theories of domestic delegation to courts and administrative agencies—offers one reason why, namely, that stable democracies gain little (and may lose more) at home from such treaties.[85] Of course no national government likes to see its discretion limited through external constraints imposed by a judicial tribunal—whether international or domestic.[86] Why would a government, democratic or

[83] Most interpretations of international human rights regimes stress the spread of democratic ideas outward from liberal societies through the actions of NGOs and public opinion, as well as the direct exercise of state power by established democracies. Many well-established democracies are the strongest supporters of international human rights enforcement. Margaret Keck and Kathryn Sikkink, *Activists beyond Borders: Transnational Advocacy Networks in International Politics* (Ithaca: Cornell University Press, 1999); Thomas Risse, Kathryn Sikkink, Steven Ropp, eds., *The Power of Human Rights: International Norms and Domestic Change* (Cambridge: Cambridge University Press, 1999); Audie Klotz, *Norms in International Relations: The Struggle against Apartheid* (Ithaca: Cornell University Press, 1995). Tony Smith, *America's Mission: The United States and the Worldwide Struggle for Democracy in the Twentieth Century* (Princeton: Princeton University Press, 1994); Michael W. Doyle, "Kant, Liberal Legacies, and Foreign Affairs," *Philosophy and Public Affairs*, 12:3 and 4 (Summer and Fall 1983): 205–35, 323–53.

[84] Moravcsik, "Origins of International Human Rights Regimes."

[85] On liberal theory generally, see Andrew Moravcsik, "Taking Preferences Seriously: A Liberal Theory of International Politics," *International Organization* 51:4 (Autumn 1997): 513–53.

[86] For generalized game theoretical results arguing that the relationship between political volatility and credible commitment holds for central banks, independent agencies, prosecutors, and even postwar settlements, see Robert Powell, "The Inefficient Use of Power: Costly Conflict with Complete Information" (unpublished Paper, University of California at Berkeley, August 2003). See also Rui de Figueiredo, "Electoral Competition, Political Uncertainty, and Policy Insulation," *American Political Science Review* 96 (June 2002): 321–35.

not, risk the unpleasant possibility that its actions would be challenged or nullified when individual citizens bring complaints before a supranational body? Political scientists argue that the most important rational reason to nonetheless delegate authority to such an external institution—whether a domestic constitutional court, central bank, or administrative agency, or an international counterpart—is to "lock in" particular domestic institutions against short-term or particularistic political pressures ("political uncertainty").[87]

From this perspective, support for enforceable international human rights norms—at least in early phases of the development of a human rights system—can be seen, at least in part, as an act of calculated national self-interest designed to serve an overriding purpose, namely, to stabilize and secure democratic governance at home against threats from the extreme Right and Left. What sort of country benefits most from such an arrangement in the area of international human rights? Certainly not authoritarian or totalitarian regimes, which bear the brunt of unwelcome enforcement efforts. Yet not the most stable democracies either, for to the extent that they are already confident in the stability of democratic governance at home, they gain little additional support from international delegation. So for stable democracies, a strong normative empathy or interest in the stability of neighboring democracies, perhaps derived from potential security threats, is required to overcome this essential lack of self-interest. On self-interested grounds, the strongest supporters are likely, therefore, to be the governments of newly established and transitional democracies concerned about their future stability. They accept international constraints because these serve to stabilize their own democratic political systems, even at the cost of potential short-term inconvenience. At the founding of the European Convention on Human Rights, the most effective system of international human rights enforcement in the world today, for example, the governments of every stably established democracy in Western Europe (Great Britain, the Netherlands, Sweden, Denmark, Norway, Belgium, and Luxembourg) sided with Greece and Turkey

---

[87] In international affairs, the goal of an international commitment is to lock in a certain policy outcome. Each government may seek primarily to lock in policies in *other* countries (the classic prisoner's dilemma) or to lock a certain policy in at home. Since human rights regimes restructure the relationship between a state and its citizens more than they do the relationship between states, we would expect the motivation to "self-bind" to be stronger relative to the motive to bind others. On self-binding, see Judith Goldstein, "International Law and Domestic Institutions: Reconciling North American 'Unfair' Trade Laws," *International Organization* 50:4 (Summer 1996): 541–64; Robert D. Putnam, "Diplomacy and Domestic Politics," *International Organization* 42:3 (Summer 1988): 427–61; Andrew Moravcsik, *Why the European Community Strengthens the State: International Cooperation and Domestic Politics*, Center for European Studies Working Paper Series No. 52 (Cambridge: Harvard University, 1994).

(and implicitly Spain and Portugal) against mandatory enforcement.[88] The supporters were instead those countries with a recent fascist or colonial past and/or a strong domestic communist threat in the present (Italy, Ireland, Iceland, Germany, Austria, France). Similar evidence exists for the UN and Inter-American systems.

The United States has long been a very stable democracy with a robust system of domestic judicial review.[89] In contrast to Europe in the 1950s or 1990s, and Latin America over the past two decades, The United States manifests no overarching sense of the need to protect domestic democratic institutions from right- or left-wing authoritarianism. Domestic observers have noted the consequences of the lack of a compelling domestic self-interest. Democratic congressman Tom Harkin, a leader in the florescence of congressional interest in human rights during the mid-1970s, noted a "disheartening change of attitude" on the issue in Congress beginning in 1978—the year of a strong midterm electoral shift toward the GOP. In particular, Harkin sensed reluctance on the part of his colleagues "to make a closer connection between the promotion of human rights at home and abroad"—an attitude Harkin described as "I've got mine, the hell with you."[90] This lack of self-interest on the part of established democracies may also help explain why the rhetoric of opponents to human rights treaties in the United States tends to be replete with praise of the strong U.S. domestic constitutional tradition, occasional concerns that international treaties might dilute domestic enforcement of individual rights, and skepticism toward the legitimacy and effectiveness of newly created inter-

---

[88] "Mandatory enforcement" in such regimes requires, at a minimum, that the hearing of disputes be formally independent of the control of national executives. In practice, this requires two elements: individual petition and compulsory jurisdiction. (This is only one of a number of conditions required for effective international adjudication. For a fuller treatment, see Moravcsik, "Origins of International Human Rights Regimes." Critical for many new (or reemerging) democracies is the experience—as during the interwar period—of democratically elected extremists slowly undermining democratic institutions by curtailing human rights: something centrist European politicians also feared from the postwar Communist Left. Recent research has uncovered similar patterns in the Inter-American and UN human rights systems, as well as many other international organizations, where transitional democracies, notably in Latin America, have consistently taken the lead. Moravcsik, "Origins of International Human Rights Regimes." (The coding of Belgium has been revised.)

[89] In other Western countries, either governments were concerned about the stability of domestic democracy—as in postwar Germany, Italy, and arguably France, posttransition Spain and Portugal, and post–Cold War Eastern Europe—or they used international instruments to introduce a bill of rights or *ex post* judicial review for the first time, as in Britain, the Netherlands, and Scandinavia. Only in the United States was there *both* a preexisting system of *ex post* judicial rights enforcement *and* no concern about democratic stability.

[90] Sandy Vogelgesang, *American Dream, Global Nightmare: The Dilemma of U.S. Human Rights Policy* (New York: W. W. Norton and Company, 1980), 247. The year 1978 also saw a substantial midterm electoral swing against the Democrats in both houses.

national institutions. Further, this may help to explain why large coalitions of lukewarm supporters of human rights treaties (for example, the Genocide Convention) let themselves be consistently outmobilized and outspent by smaller but more intense groups of opponents.

Finally, the fact that the United States already has—almost alone among advanced industrial democracies—a tradition of *ex post* judicial review that predates World War II[91] creates a different set of incentives for both judges and human rights advocates. For supporters of human rights enforcement, this means that domestic constitutional and legal reform would be a preferred means of achieving their goals and thus would undermine support for international commitments. At the same time, recognition of the legal validity of international standards might have more real impact in areas where *ex post* judicial review is already established—such as constitutional issues involving discrimination and individual rights. Furthermore, some judges may be especially conservative in applying such standards, for fear of undermining their own prerogatives.[92] The overall tendency would be both to polarize domestic politics and to induce more intense opposition to international treaty commitments.

Yet the predictable stability of American democracy does not provide a fully satisfactory explanation for U.S. reluctance to accept multilateral human rights commitments. Two anomalies are most striking.

The first is comparative. The opposition of well-established democracies to binding human rights treaties may have been the norm between the 1950s and the 1970s, but it is no longer. U.S. reluctance was similar to that of many other advanced industrial democracies until recent U.S. opposition to the Convention on the Rights of the Child or the ICC placed America in the company of rogue and failed states. Why has the United States failed to evolve as far in the same direction as have European governments?

The second anomaly concerns domestic politics. U.S. attitudes toward human rights treaties have not been characterized by apathy and ignorance, as one might expect if the problem were simply the lack of concrete benefits (or geopolitical alternatives). Nor is the most intense opposition found among judges. Instead, American domestic debate over human rights has

[91] Mary Ann Glendon, *Rights Talk: The Impoverishment of Political Discourse* (New York: Free Press, 1991); Anne-Marie Slaughter, *A New World Order* (Princeton: Princeton University Press, 2004).

[92] The best research on international tribunals clearly shows that the incentives generated for judges seeking judicial power and autonomy play a decisive role in the domestic acceptance of international norms. See, for example, Karen J. Alter, *Establishing the Supremacy of European Law: The Making of an International Rule of Law in Europe* (Oxford: Oxford University Press, 2001).

been bitterly partisan and intensely ideological, and opposition is led by those who argue that international human rights norms pose a fundamental threat to the integrity of American political institutions.[93] Any explanation of U.S. policy must account, therefore, for the significantly greater intensity of opposition within the United States than within any other advanced industrial democracy—even as the latter become stably democratic. The greater stakes, given the preexistence of judicial review, explain some of the differences, but not their more populist aspects. We must investigate the values and interests underlying the partisan nature of domestic cleavages on this issue.

The Opposition of Conservative Constituents

The third general factor helping to shape U.S. international human rights policy is *the existence of concentrated conservative opposition to an expansion and enforcement of many individual rights*. An "ideational liberal" (or "liberal constructivist") perspective on world politics highlights the preferences of domestic groups concerning the provision of public goods—national identity, political institutions, socioeconomic redistribution—that underlie fundamental policy goals.[94]

From this perspective, tensions among distinctive national conceptions of rights create conflict concerning any effort to promulgate and enforce a common set of international human rights standards. One expects those countries whose views about human rights are supported by a majority in the organization (the "median voter" in the international system, as it were) to be least inconvenienced by the imposition of multilateral norms, and therefore to be most supportive of them. Governments whose views are furthest from the global norm—and, in particular, those countries whose ideal conception of rights stands to be overturned—have

---

[93] Further support for the distinctiveness of human rights comes from studies of U.S. multilateralism, which see U.S. multilateral commitments as generally weakening over the past few decades, whereas in the area of human rights, they appear to have strengthened slightly. See, for example, Margaret Karns and Karen Mingst, "The United States and Multilateral Institutions," in *The United States and Multilateral Institutions: Patterns of Changing Instrumentality and Interest*, ed. Karns and Mingst (Winchester, MA: Unwin Hyman, 1990), 1–24.

[94] Such arguments might be termed "ideational liberal" or "liberal constructivist." Moravcsik, "Taking Preferences Seriously." These sorts of "bottom-up" arguments about preferences have secured more empirical support than have claims about top-down international socialization. See, e.g., Peter Katzenstein, ed., *The Culture of National Security: Norms and Identity in World Politics* (New York: Columbia University Press, 1996). Cross-national studies reveal, for example, that social democratic governments feel a greater obligation to dispense development assistance than do conservative ones. David Halloran Lumsdaine, *Moral Vision in International Politics: The Foreign Aid Regime 1949–1989* (Princeton: Princeton University Press, 1993).

sound reasons to be skeptical of the domestic application of binding international norms.

In comparative perspective, splits over human rights enforcement are generally reflected in partisan cleavages, with center-left parties supporting a more expansive enforcement of individual rights and center-right parties supporting the same or less.[95] There are two substantive reasons for this. First, since the core corpus of international political rights law does not, as a rule, protect either property rights or rights to private education, both of primary concern to the postwar Right, and since the basic right to practice religion is unchallenged in Western societies, there is little for a center-right or right-wing party to gain through such norms—except, as we have just discussed, if they fear for the stability of democracy against the extreme Right or Left. This was the major motivation for postwar Christian Democratic parties in many Western European countries to become open champions of global human rights. Even more aspirational elements in international human rights law—such as socioeconomic rights under the UN Covenant, labor rights under the ILO, and various cultural rights—tend clearly to be favored more by the Left than by the Right. Second, insofar as they remain controversial in stably established democratic societies, the basic corpus of international civil and political rights—the ban on torture, freedom of expression, freedom of religion, freedom of association, due process and criminal defendant's rights, refugee rights, abortion rights, abolition of the death penalty, privacy and gay rights, and antidiscrimination rules regarding women and racial minorities—are often viewed, as we saw in considering libertarian values above, as means to realize egalitarian policy goals generally favored by the Left.[96] This is particularly true of *ex post* constitutional adjudication.[97]

For these reasons, international human rights has proved bitterly controversial in the United States. American conservatives in the 1950s and 1960s viewed international human rights treaties as part of a broader movement to impose liberal federal standards—in particular, provisions banning segregation and other forms of racial discrimination—on the practices of

---

[95] An exception is when both center-right and center-left are threatened by more extreme factions at home or abroad, in which case we find ourselves in the situation of a transitional democracy in the republican liberal theory.

[96] In particular, the abolition of discrimination against racial, gender, and sexual-preference minorities, constraints on the police power of the state, abolition of the death penalty, and immigrants' rights are all areas in which, at least until recently, the body of international human rights law creates an additional tool for the enforcement of the rights of relatively weak individuals vis-à-vis democratic majorities and the state.

[97] It need not be true of all courts. The EU's European Court of Justice was created as, and essentially remains, a commercial court. Its jurisprudence is, thus, broadly acceptable to the Right.

certain states, notably those in the South. Civil rights has remained among the most salient issues in American politics since 1945, generating exceptionally strong domestic opposition and eventually triggering an epochal partisan realignment. Over the years, those who support or oppose aggressive federal enforcement of civil rights have tended, respectively, to support or oppose full adherence to international human rights norms.[98]

At the beginning, the most salient concern—clear even despite the incentives to obscure it with the constitutional language of states' rights and senatorial prerogative—was race.[99] From the 1940s through the 1960s, concerns about race were linked to the fear that other minorities, including but not primarily Communists, would mobilize around the race issue.[100] Already in Senate Foreign Relations Committee hearings on the UN Charter in 1945, Senator Eugene Millikin (R-CO) posed a thinly disguised question to State Department officials to ascertain whether if there were "racial questions on the Southern shores of the Mediterranean that might have very explosive effects under some circumstances . . . this organization [the UN] might concern itself with them." (The answer was af-

---

[98] One might also mention religion. To a greater degree than is found in other advanced industrial democracies, American conservatives are closely allied to a highly organized and influential Protestant religious Right, which plays an important role in U.S. politics. The views of this group—suspicion of a secular state, skepticism of public (or any organized) education, support for the death penalty, powerful anti-Communism, and earlier support for racial segregation—find little parallel in other countries. In many postwar industrial countries, to be sure, right-wing parties have maintained close links to the Catholic Church, but these have also tended to be "catchall" parties with a broad appeal. In cultural matters, as in socioeconomic ones, right-wing parties reached compromises with the secular state, and over the decades Catholic beliefs have become less central to voting and party membership. The right wing of the U.S. political spectrum in the twentieth century is thus nearly unique among advanced industrial democracies in that it contains self-conscious, intensely mobilized, and influential groups representing the conservative Protestant religious groups, often allied with southern conservatives. This raises a complex set of issues concerning the relationship between church and state.

[99] An example is the statement from Harry Berger, who represented the National Economic Council: "The convention goes much further than to punish or prevent mass murder. It aims to regulate . . . the words and writings of individuals. . . . Thus, it is clear that . . . the refusal of employment, or blackballing a person for membership in a union or social club, or the publishing of any comment . . . with respect to any member of a minority, could be deemed by the 'international penal tribunal' . . . to constitute 'mental harm.' . . . The slightest reference to a member of a minority race or religion—such as a newspaper article identifying a man under arrest as a Negro—might be deemed a punishable act." Kaufman, *Human Rights*, 43–44.

[100] One member of the ABA committee stated, "I leave to your imagination as to what would happen in . . . municipal law if subversive elements should teach minorities that the field of civil rights and laws had been removed to the field of international law." Kaufman, *Human Rights*, 46.

firmative.)[101] In discussions of the Genocide Convention in 1949—a series of hearings, one historian has observed, in which "the major arguments enunciated against *all* human rights treaties were first articulated"—one supporter observed: "You have to face that . . . in getting down to realities . . . the practical objection, the thing that is behind a lot of people's minds on this convention is—is it aimed at lynching in the South. You have to face that."[102] Not until the civil rights legislation of the late 1960s, which, along with the Vietnam War, inspired a new generation of congressmen and senators to support civil and human rights, did congressional opinion shift at all.[103] In 1970, Richard Nixon renewed the request for Senate ratification of the Genocide Convention, only to see southern senators shoot it down—some arguing that "the convention would let Black Panthers and other 'extremists' bring charges against the president."[104] The Carter administration refused to push for ratification, preferring to save its political capital for higher priorities, like the Panama Canal Treaty. The Genocide Convention was not ratified until 1988—almost forty years after it was negotiated—and even then only with reservations so extensive that some believed that the United States had not really ratified at all or, if it had, should not have been permitted to do so.[105]

Overt opposition to civil rights may seem anachronistic today, but the underlying cleavages still dominate discussion of human rights. To be sure, once the Supreme Court reinterpreted the Constitution to forbid segregation and once congressional powers via the commerce clause and the Fourteenth Amendment were understood as broad enough to support civil rights legislation, then "the civil rights campaign in the United States became entirely domestic, any thought of effecting change in United States law by treaty was abandoned, [and. . . .] the Bricker Amendment campaign became ancient history."[106]

Why, then, did the Senate remain so recalcitrant? Historians and legal academics have appealed to mystical metaphors: "Senator Bricker's ghost has proved to be alive in the Senate, and successive administrations have become infected with his ideology."[107] It is more plausible to argue that

---

[101] Louis Sohn and Thomas Buergenthal, *International Protection of Human Rights*, cited in Henry Steiner and Philip Alston, *International Human Rights in Context: Law, Politics, Morals* (Oxford: Clarendon Press, 1996), 751–52.

[102] Kaufman, *Human Rights*, 37, 56.

[103] On the shift, see Vogelgesang, *American Dream*, 121–24.

[104] Ibid., 120.

[105] For a balanced review of the issues, see Matthew Lippman, "The Convention on the Prevention and Punishment of the Crime of Genocide: Fifty Years Later," *Arizona Journal of International and Comparative Law* 15 (Spring 1998): 415–514.

[106] Henkin, "US Ratification of Human Rights Conventions," 341.

[107] Ibid. See also Kaufman, *Human Rights*, for a similar account.

the issues underlying the aggressive enforcement of civil rights—or enforcement of norms of criminal law, housing, education, discrimination, privacy, and religion connected to race—remain controversial, albeit in an indirect form. And such controversy calls international human rights treaties into question. In comparative perspective, this distinguishes the United States from Europe.[108] Important cases before the European Court of Human Rights have tended to involve a handful of exceptional and isolated issues such as due process under conditions of martial law (e.g., criminal and police procedure for Britain in occupied Cyprus and Northern Ireland), gay rights, corporal punishment, pornography, and the speed of trials in Italy. In the United States, by contrast, criminal procedure, police brutality, freedom of speech and religion, criminal defense, the death penalty, privacy and gay rights, prison conditions, the behavior of the armed forces abroad, and racial and gender discrimination—even when decided by domestic courts—have been and remain salient partisan issues. There is a substantial body of conservative opinion that rejects the entire rights revolution since the 1920s, driven by the New Deal, the Cold War, and the civil rights movement, and supports its reversal in favor of an "originalist" understanding of the Constitution—a doctrinal tendency less salient elsewhere.[109] The domestic (or international) application of global norms would be a substantial barrier to the realization of this agenda.

Thus the conservative fear of international influences is not paranoid. Human rights advocates are quite explicit about their intention to use international norms to challenge U.S. practices—precisely the emerging threat that triggered Brickerism in the 1950s.[110] In 1993, as a response to U.S. ratification of the ICCPR the previous year, Human Rights Watch and the American Civil Liberties Union jointly issued a report entitled "Human Rights Violations in the United States." The list of violations focused, as it happened,

---

[108] Perhaps this will change, as working-class suspicion of immigrants and minorities increases in Europe, but for the moment, the enforcement of such rights remains relatively uncontroversial in Europe, particularly among elites.

[109] For relevant citations and critiques, see Moravcsik, "Conservative Idealism," 291–314; Christopher L. Eisgruber, *Constitutional Self-Government* (Cambridge: Harvard University Press, 2001); and Kramer, "Originalism and Historical Truth."

[110] See, for example, *Human Rights Violations in the United States: A Report on US Compliance with the International Covenant on Civil and Political Rights* (New York: Human Rights Watch and the American Civil Liberties Union, 1993), 5–8. Religious rights might appear to be a concern of Republicans, but in fact the report calls exclusively for aggressive judicial enforcement of the Religious Freedom Restoration Act, a piece of legislation passed by a Democratic Congress and signed by President Clinton in late 1993. See 165 ff. In addition, the authors of the report mention, but do not analyze in detail, some areas to which they believe the treaty would apply—notably discrimination against gay men and lesbians, as well as against people with disabilities. See 4. The authors also mention policies on public and university education.

almost exclusively on issues championed by the Democratic Party: discrimination against racial minorities, women, linguistic minorities, immigrants, as well as prison conditions, police brutality, the death penalty, freedom of information, and religious liberty. Clearly the domestic application of international standards would favor some ideologies, and thus some political parties, over others.

These structural constraints continue to influence the most recent debates, including that surrounding the Convention on the Rights of the Child (CRC).[111] The CRC was adopted unanimously by the UN General Assembly in 1989. Within three years, it had gained 127 adherents. To date, 191 nations have ratified, including all but two UN member states—the United States and Somalia. In the United States the classic pattern of domestic partisan contestation dating back to the Bricker amendment emerged, with more liberal, mostly Democratic, senators supporting ratification, and more conservative, largely Republican, counterparts opposing. The first President Bush refused to sign or submit the treaty; in 1995, President Clinton signed and submitted the convention despite a Senate resolution sponsored by leading fellow Republicans, who controlled the Senate, urging him not to do so.[112]

Why has the Senate remained so skeptical? The issue has no geopolitical relevance. Nor does the treaty have any institutions for effective enforcement. Hence the United States would sacrifice little of its unilateral bargaining power in the (unlikely) event that it sought to deploy it to promote the rights of children. Advocates argue that ratification would permit the United States to participate in the CRC monitoring committee and would strengthen the U.S. role as a world leader—the closest thing to a major foreign policy argument for ratification.[113] Consistent with the argument of this essay, most domestic debate (particularly domestic criticism) focuses instead on the substantive consequences of the treaty provisions in

[111] This section follows Hema Magge, "Vocal Opposition and Fragmented Support: The US Failure to Ratify the U.N. Convention on the Rights of the Child" (unpublished paper, Harvard University, May 2000).

[112] With a Republican colleague, Senator Richard Lugar, Senator Bill Bradley drafted and secured passage of Senate Resolution 231, which urged the president to forward the CRC to the Senate for its consent. Bradley claimed bipartisan support for ratification, and the Democrats controlled both houses. No response was forthcoming.

[113] The United States, they argue, will lose credibility in the global community, both within the specific issue-area of human rights and more generally, if it refuses to ratify a popular document designed to protect children. Opponents challenge such arguments with their own alternative conception of the "national interest." Ratification, they argue, would simply place the United States under another UN regime dominated by developing nations with radical agendas. This may be a particularly important concern for Senator Helms, a prominent UN skeptic.

the United States.[114] This is paradoxical, since the convention would seem to have relatively few domestic implications for a country where children's rights are already strongly embedded in national law. Still, the issue triggers deep domestic ideological cleavages.

Supporters are led by human rights and child welfare activists, who maintain that governments should do more to combat the abuse and exploitation of children. Prominent advocates of the CRC include Democratic politicians and political liberals, as well as human rights groups like Amnesty International, Human Rights Watch, and the American Bar Association; child welfare groups such as the Children's Defense Fund; general humanitarian groups such as the American Red Cross; and more than three hundred other organizations. Behind Republican senators stand numerous conservative groups, of which the best-organized, best-funded, most vocal, and most influential are linked to religious groups—including the Christian Coalition, Concerned Women for America, Eagle Forum, the Family Research Council, the National Center for Home Education, the John Birch Society, and numerous conservative think tanks. Such groups maintain that the CRC is unnecessary, permits state policy (dictated by an international organization) to usurp the primary role of the family, and thus violates the concept of "parental rights" to make decisions regarding the upbringing of their children. The Family Research Council sets forth more concrete criticisms of the explicit rights promulgated in the CRC—in particular, ironically, the civil and political rights added in response to U.S. pressure—that might allow children to air their grievances against their parents in a legal forum, view "objectionable or immoral materials, often disseminated in schools," forbid parents to send their children to church if they did not want to attend, prohibit parents from preventing their children from associating with harmful company, and legalize abortion without parental consent and homosexual conduct within the home. Supporters respond that the United States is generally already in compliance with the convention, in the sense that it has established social programs addressing the issues raised in the CRC, that the language of the convention would be unenforceable without domestic law detailing more precise terms, and that reservations could handle specific concerns. They add that the CRC establishes standards for national policy to improve the condition of children all over the world but creates few, if any, enforceable rights.

Whatever the substantive merits, the domestic debate over ratification of the CRC has been dominated by its opponents. The CRC has triggered

---

[114] Some opposition appears to reflect traditional conservative hostility toward human rights treaties in general. Moreover, whereas other countries may aim to exploit loopholes, they argue, the United States tends to examine all existing federal and state laws closely in

visceral opposition among religious conservatives mobilized by any hint of a threat to their particular conception of family values. Hema Magge's research and interviews suggest that they appear to be better organized, better funded, and more motivated than supporters. Some Senate staffers report that they receive a hundred opposition letters for every letter supporting the CRC. While the general human rights community remains convinced of the importance of participating in the international promulgation of the rights of the child, the bulk of liberal public and elite opinion remains uninformed and apathetic. One particular reason for the imbalance between supporters and opponents is the lack of a compelling domestic justification for U.S. adherence. Many of the most important child advocacy groups, such as the Children's Defense Fund, perhaps the most prominent such group, focus primarily on the direct provision of services to children, rather than on lobbying for rights—and have therefore been criticized for placing a low priority on ratification of the CRC. According to one leading activist, partisan Democrats simply do not care enough about the issue to move it up on the agenda.[115]

A parallel divergence between the United States and other Western governments lies in the status of socioeconomic rights. In comparative perspective, the United States has a relatively informal and underdeveloped (i.e., nonsolidaristic) conception of economic rights, particularly in the areas of labor and social welfare policy.[116] There has long been opposition, not least in the South and West, to aggressive centralized enforcement of labor and welfare rights.[117]

For a half century, these sorts of issues—racial discrimination and the legacy it has left, labor rights, and various lifestyle-related issues—have placed the United States outside the mainstream of the global consensus on the definition of human rights. The result has been intense partisan conflict. Strong conservative opposition on such issues means that firm

---

order to assure compliance. Conservatives charge that other nations ratified hastily, without reviewing the CRC thoroughly enough to understand its full implications.

[115] Some have argued that the construction of such issues is part of a deliberate effort to mobilize Americans around ideological issues with little chance of concrete action. Either way, it is a political strategy aimed at advancing substantive interests. For an influential discussion, see Thomas Frank, *What's the Matter with Kansas? How Conservatives Won the Heart of America* (New York: Metropolitan Books, 2004).

[116] Since Werner Sombart's classic 1906 book, *Why No Socialism in America?*, commentators have recognized that the United States is the only advanced industrial country without a significant socialist movement or labor party. For an analytical overview of this phenomenon, see Seymour Martin Lipset, "American Exceptionalism Reaffirmed," in *Is America Different? A New Look at American Exceptionalism*, ed. Byron Shafer (Oxford: Clarendon Press, 1991), 1–45.

[117] Some have linked this tendency in the 1950s to McCarthyism, in part sparked by the Truman administration's anti-Communist rhetoric, but opposition to socioeconomic rights has long outlived this era. Cf. Kaufman, *Human Rights*, 12–14.

adherence to international human rights norms does not command support from a broad centrist coalition, as is generally true in Europe, but instead created a deep Left-Right split between liberals and conservatives—one that fell increasingly during the post–World War II period along strict party lines. Partisan opposition in the 1950s was led by southern Democrats opposed to federal civil rights policy; today it is led by Republican senators, owing to their (globally idiosyncratic) stand on socioeconomic and racial rights, and also religious, educational, and cultural issues. In general, support for international human rights treaties comes disproportionately from Democratic presidents and members of Congress, while opposition comes disproportionately from Republican presidents and members of Congress.[118] As David Forsythe's study of legislative behavior concluded, "human rights voting in Congress is largely . . . a partisan and ideological matter."[119]

The decisive importance of partisan cleavages over human rights becomes immediately evident if we examine the record of executive submission and Senate consent concerning the twelve most important human rights treaties over the past fifty years. Strong Democratic control of the Senate appears to be a necessary condition for the ratification of such treaties, even in a watered-down form. Ten of eleven initial submissions to the Senate for advice and consent were made by Democratic presidents, eight of twelve postwar agreements were signed by Democrats, and, most strikingly, *the Senate has never ratified an international human rights treaty (even with reservations) when Democrats held fewer than fifty-five seats*.[120] If we add to this the fact that most southern Democrats were likely to vote against the party majority on this issue, then the passage of legislation, let alone a treaty, was unlikely at all until the 1970s. This suggests that partisan control of the Senate and, secondarily, the presidency, imposes a binding constraint on U.S. policy.

---

[118] In contrast to the way this issue is often presented, this central cleavage does not primarily divide isolationists and internationalists. Major opponents of international enforcement of human rights—from Henry Cabot Lodge, John Bricker, and Henry Kissinger to Jesse Helms—have not been isolationist.

[119] Forsythe, *The United States and Human Rights*, 50.

[120] This record cannot be attributed to background conditions. Democrats commanded a majority of at least 55 votes only 50 percent of the time (14 sessions out of 28). The Senate contained a Democratic majority for 19 sessions and a Republican majority for 9 sessions, while each of the two parties commanded the presidency for roughly equal periods since 1947. Note also that the pattern of submission and ratification does not follow from the (somewhat exogenous) timing of negotiation and signature, since those presidents who submitted the treaties were not typically the same presidents who signed the respective agreements. The Helsinki Treaty, which generated considerable conservative support, did not apply to the United States. On the Torture Convention, the Senate consented in 1990 subject to subsequent passage of implementing legislation, which passed four years later. No U.S. implementing legislation has ever been passed for the UN Covenant on Civil and Political Rights.

TABLE ONE
The United States and Multilateral Human Rights Treaties, 1945–2000: Executive Action and Congressional Consent

	Negotiated (U.S. Vote)	Transmitted to the Senate	Senate Consent (Seats / Majority)
Genocide Convention	Truman (Y)	Truman/ Nixon/ Reagan	1986 (55 Dem)
Convention on the Political Rights of Women	Truman (Y)	Kennedy	1974 (56 Dem)
Supplemental Slavery Convention	*Eisenhower* (Y)	Kennedy	1967 (68 Dem)
ILO Convention on Forced Labor	Eisenhower (Y)	Kennedy	1991 (56 Dem)
Convention on Racial Discrimination	Johnson (Y)	Carter	1994 (57 Dem)
Covenant on Civil and Political Rights	Johnson (Y)	Carter / *Bush*	1992 (56 Dem)
Optional Protocol to the ICCPR	Johnson	NO	NO
Covenant on Economic and Social Rights	Johnson	Carter	NO
American Convention on Human Rights	Carter (Y)	Carter	NO
Convention to Eliminate Discrimination Against Women (CEDAW)	Carter (Y)	Clinton	NO
Torture Convention	*Reagan* (Y)	*Reagan*	1990 and 1994 (55 and 57 Dem)
Convention on the Rights of the Child	*Bush* (Y)	Clinton	NO

Yet in order to explain U.S. human rights policy fully, we need to go beyond the power of a concentrated conservative minority in America. Even taken together with the two other factors discussed above (superpower status and stable democratic institutions), this explanation leaves unanswered critical questions about support for U.S. human rights policy. As we are about to see in more detail, ratification of human rights treaties has at times been supported by a coalition of interest groups claiming to represent more than half the U.S. public, as well as by more than half of incumbent senators. Presidents, even Republican presidents, have been at times relatively supportive.[121] On a number of issues, U.S. and European publics converge. On the death penalty, for example, a plurality on both sides in nearly all Western countries has traditionally supported retention or reestablishment.

Yet these presidents, backed by majorities of legislators, voters, and public opinion in favor of stricter adherence to international human rights norms have failed to gain their objective. If conservatives have rarely commanded a majority of interest groups, voters, or senators, why were they nonetheless able to prevail? And why were fifty-seven or more senators, not just fifty, required to alter U.S. human rights policy? One explanation is simply that, as we have discussed in this section, conservative activists and voters feel more intensely about the issue, and it is more likely to influence their vote. Perhaps. But another explanation, more consistent with the political history, is that they are privileged by biases in the existing U.S. constitutional procedures. To this we now turn.

The Biases in Domestic Political Institutions

The fourth and final determinant of U.S. human rights policy is bias stemming from *the fragmented nature of American political institutions*. It is a clich of comparative politics that the American system of government stands out in comparative perspective for its extreme commitment to the Madisonian schema of "separation of powers" and "checks and balances." All other things equal, the greater the number of "veto players," as political scientists refer to those who can impede or block a particular government action, the more difficult it is for a national government to accept international obligations.[122] The U.S. political system is in most

---

[121] We have also seen that Republican presidents in three cases—Eisenhower with the Supplementary Slavery Convention and the Convention on the Political Rights of Women, and Bush with the Rights of the Child—were unable or unwilling to block the negotiation of international human rights treaties, even though they made no subsequent effort to secure their ratification. Indeed, until the recent treaty establishing the ICC, no American government appears to have voted in an international forum against a human rights treaty that passed—though U.S. negotiators have attempted to water down a number of provisions. This suggests that centrist presidents (and even a conservative like Ronald Reagan) and advocates of human rights treaties alike labor under tight political constraints imposed by decentralized American political institutions.

[122] Putnam, "Diplomacy and Domestic Politics." Cf. Lisa Martin, *Democratic Commitments: Legislatures and International Cooperation* (Princeton: Princeton University Press, 2000).

respects exceptionally decentralized, with the consequence that a large number of domestic political actors must approve major decisions. Three such characteristics of the U.S. political system are of particular importance to an understanding of U.S. human rights policy: supermajoritarian voting rules and the committee structure of the Senate, federalism, and the salient role of the judiciary in adjudicating questions of human rights.

THE SENATE

The most immediate veto group involved with human rights treaties, a one-third minority of recalcitrant senators, is created by the unique U.S. constitutional requirement of a two-thirds "supermajority" vote to advise and consent to an international treaty. This is a threshold higher than that in nearly all other advanced industrial democracies, which generally ratify international treaties by legislative majority.[123] The need to secure the support of the Foreign Relations Committee chairman may render ratification doubly difficult if that position is held, as it generally has been in the postwar period, by a politician with conservative views.[124] Overriding the decision of a committee chairman to block consideration of a treaty on the floor is nearly impossible. It is hardly surprising, therefore, that the primary barrier to the ratification of human rights treaties has been the inability to muster the necessary supermajority in the Senate. The decentralized U.S. electoral system rarely generates a sufficiently decisive partisan majority (in recent decades, Democratic, and before that, a majority sufficient to circumvent southern Democrats and their allies).

The resulting history of senatorial suspicion of liberal multilateralism spans the twentieth century—from the debate over Woodrow Wilson's proposal for a League of Nations in 1919 to the present.[125] Its decisive importance for U.S. human rights policy is illustrated by the failure of the Senate to ratify international agreements in many cases where there existed (simple) majority support in the Senate. This was true of the League of Nations, which was blocked by a Senate minority. We have seen that groups totaling 100 million members supported the Genocide Conven-

[123] Switzerland requires a referendum for certain commitments.

[124] This may help explain why large Democratic majorities, the Watergate generation of legislators, the civil rights movement, and the rise of public interest groups in the late 1960s and early 1970s did not lead to the ratification of many international human rights treaties in the United States. These groups controlled the House of Representatives, where they were able to influence foreign policy through appropriations, but they had far less influence on the Senate. Cf. Norman J. Ornstein and Shirley Edler, *Interest Groups, Lobbying and Policy-Making* (Washington, DC: Congressional Quarterly Press, 1978), 4–7.

[125] For an engaging overview, on the role of conservative southern Democrats, see Robert Caro, *Master of the Senate: Lyndon Johnson*, vol. 3 (New York: Knopf, 2002).

tion, yet what mattered most were the attitudes of the senators themselves, who are disproportionately representative of conservative southern and rural midwestern or western states.[126] More than fifty senators publicly declared their support for the Convention to Eliminate Discrimination against Women (CEDAW), yet this treaty long remained bottled up in committee by Senator Helms and appears to lack the requisite two-thirds support needed to pass on the Senate floor.[127] The unique constitutional role of the Senate helps explain why robust U.S. action to support international human rights norms—whether unilateral or multilateral—tends typically to originate in either the executive branch or the House of Representatives, and often uses budgetary, regulatory, or diplomatic instruments, rather than the process of treaty ratification and domestic legal change.[128]

THE STATES

Constitutional separation of powers also establishes important prerogatives for the states vis-à-vis the federal government, and this in turn permits conservative opponents to resist imposition of federal and global human rights norms. States' rights, as we have seen, has been an important tool for domestic opponents of international human rights treaties, and underlying this apparently principled defense of states' rights was a distinct substantive agenda. The legal structure of federalism is a favorable institutional context in which to oppose the imposition of human rights norms.[129]

Perhaps the most striking example of the decisive importance of federal institutions is the nagging issue of capital punishment. As near as we can tell, the historical fundamentals of public support for the death penalty among Americans are not strikingly different from those of Europeans. Support slowly declined from more than 60 percent to just 45 percent during the 1960s and early 1970s. (Only in the late 1970s, with intense organization around the issue, did U.S. public opinion support rise once again.) This is more or less the pattern in Europe, where sup-

---

[126] Kaufman, *Human Rights*, 37–38.

[127] Cited in Magge, "Vocal Opposition."

[128] Forsythe, "The United States," 271–72; Vogelgesang, *American Dream*. On exceptions, see Ackerman and Golove, "Is NAFTA Constitutional?"

[129] The overt concern with race is one important reason—a reason perhaps more important than commitment of principle—why "the main opposition to the treaty was rooted in states' rights." Kaufman, *Human Rights*, 52–53. Some southerners went further, claiming that "the abrogation of states' rights was the major objective of the genocide treaty." Certainly much of the Senate debate concerned these constitutional issues. Kaufman, *Human Rights*, 44–63.

port for the death penalty has declined, but it nonetheless continues to command plurality support. Even today, after a generation of abolition, a plurality or majority of Canadians (70 percent), Britons (65–70 percent), Austrians and Italians (50 percent), and Swedes and French (49 percent) favor the reinstatement of the death penalty.[130]

The difference between the continents lies in the response of political institutions. In Europe, one ruling party after another abolished the death penalty in the 1970s and 1980s, despite near majorities in favor of its retention—whereupon the issue disappeared as a matter for public contestation. Surely this was possible in part because, as compared to the federal and separation-of-powers system in the United States, European parliamentary systems tend to discourage regional and single-issue politics and to create clearer partisan majorities unhampered in this area (even in federal states) by subnational prerogatives. Regional institutions like the EC and ECHR have further entrenched and extended European abolitionism.

In the United States, by contrast, abolition of capital punishment would require fundamental constitutional change in a system where such change is nearly impossible. Criminal law is largely the province of the individual states, and any effort to standardize state policy must therefore coordinate legislative, electoral (notably referenda), and judicial action in the thirty-eight states that currently impose the death penalty. Any federal legislation to limit capital punishment would face the de facto supermajoritarian rules in the Senate and would in any case be limited to federal crimes. The only centralized political instrument able to achieve abolition would therefore be a declaration that capital punishment is unconstitutional. In the United States during the 1970s, the U.S. Supreme Court came close to doing just that, and the death penalty had in any case fallen into disuse at the federal level. (At last count, only nineteen of more than thirty-seven hundred American death row prisoners are in federal prison, and there were no federal executions between 1963 and the recent executions of Timothy McVeigh and Juan Raul Garza.) Yet the U.S. Court backed down in the face of a state-level movement beginning with the most conservative areas of the country. The only remaining recourse would be a constitutional amendment, which would be impossible without even broader support—three-quarters of the state legislatures or a similar congressional supermajority. State courts, though often more liberal, have been even less willing to act, perhaps because many judges on the state bench are elected and abolitionist actions can trigger successful efforts to defeat or

---

[130] For a more detailed analysis, see Moravcsik, "The New Abolitionism"; "The Death Penalty: Getting beyond Exceptionalism (A Response to Silvia and Sampson)," *European Studies* 1:3 (December 2001).

recall judges. The result: State politicians and publics are empowered to set death penalty policy in accordance with local preferences—which encourages the penalty's perpetuation.[131]

The basic lesson to be drawn from the case of capital punishment is thus the decisive importance of the incentives and opportunities created by political institutions. This suggests two corollaries. The first, contra Cass Sunstein in this volume, is that we should be cautious about attributing too much impact to a single contingent decision by political actors at one point in time—in this case, the Supreme Court's reversal on the death penalty in the 1970s.[132] It is true that a bolder Supreme Court might have abolished the death penalty for good. Yet the deeper lesson of this episode is that most of the time in the U.S. political system, this will not occur, because the conservative position is favored by federal prerogatives and political opportunities, by senatorial stasis, and by the intensity of feeling among a conservative minority. What is striking is not that the Supreme Court did not act, but that the structural window of opportunity was so brief, that similar windows are so rarely seen in other areas of human rights, that the decision was never in the hands of a directly elected chief executive or legislative majority, and that other countries responded to similar opportunities quite differently.

The second corollary to draw from the case of capital punishment is that we should be suspicious of facile claims about the autonomous importance of shared values or public opinion. The evidence suggests both that the death penalty is an issue of little salience, as compared to bread-and-butter issues of taxing and spending, and that public opinion on such issues can be and is often manipulated. Public opinion on the death penalty tends to track national political decisions, political manipulation by politicians, and pressure from small intense interest groups. So in Europe, where the institutions do not facilitate mobilization on the death penalty, the issue has little salience and public opinion is adapting—albeit slowly. In the United States, where institutions permit decentralized action, long-term trends in public support for the death penalty appear to have been buoyed up by pressure from intense conservative minorities.

THE COURTS

The decisive basis of most successful international adjudication and judicial enforcement systems lies with the domestic judiciary.[133] The U.S. sys-

---

[131] This argument follows Moravcsik, "The New Abolitionism."

[132] See Cass Sunstein's essay and Michael Ignatieff's introduction in this volume.

[133] Anne-Marie Burley and Walter Mattli, "Europe before the Court: A Political Theory of Legal Integration," *International Organization* 47 (Winter 1993): 41–76; Robert O. Keo-

tem of *ex post* constitutional review for conformity with individual rights guarantees is distinctive in comparative perspective. Combined with the relative paucity of promising institutional opportunities for mass collective action to promote social policy, it places the courts at the center of domestic redistributive conflicts in a way unmatched in other Western democracies.[134] To a certain extent, then, Americans might be said to be more ambivalent about international human rights enforcement because it is more controversial, and it is more controversial because, given the preferences of the American electorate and the nature of the American judicial system, it matters more. This helps explain why the American judiciary is the subject of political conflict to an extent unmatched among advanced industrial democracies.

The decisive importance of a domestic judiciary became clear in the immediate postwar period, as the federal and state judiciaries began to shift their role from that of a conservative to that of a reformist force in U.S. politics. Accordingly, in the early 1950s numerous senators opposed the application of international human rights norms because of the quite immediate threat of judicial challenges to the policies of the states, notably those having to do with race. Such challenges had already arisen, most notably in the California state court system. Of course such critics voiced fears that a ban on discrimination might be imposed by an international organization ("world government") in which the United States possessed a "distinctly minority vote."[135] Yet this was largely for rhetorical effect. The real fear was that documents like the Genocide Convention and the UN Covenants would be exploited by plaintiffs and the federal judiciary at the expense of specific civil rights policies.[136] In the 1950s, an ABA spokesman made the link to civil rights plain:

---

hane, Andrew Moravcsik, and Anne-Marie Slaughter, "Legalized Dispute Resolution: Interstate and Transnational," *International Organization* 54 (Summer 2000): 457–88.

[134] In recent years, the spread of systems of postauthoritarian or international *ex post* judicial review has generated some similar dynamics in South Africa, Britain, the European Union, and elsewhere.

[135] Kaufman, *Human Rights*, 45.

[136] Ibid., 10–12. As we have seen, many senators—most notably Senator Bricker—were deeply concerned about the tendency of state and federal courts in the late 1940s to cite international treaty commitments in support of domestic human rights claims. His fears were well grounded to the extent that the federal courts, in alliance with the executive branch, were emerging as an important venue for pressing claims of federal power over the states, not least in the area of civil rights. There was a convergence of interest between the judiciary and the executive in favor of expanded federal power that Senator Bricker, an opponent of the emerging "national security state" in the Cold War, feared in foreign affairs. Despite the opposition of the Eisenhower administration, which dropped its support for all international human rights treaties to undermine Bricker's support, the amendment—albeit in a watered-down form—failed by only a single vote in the Senate. For an interesting political history, see Caro, *Master of the Senate*, vol. 3.

Minority groups in this country are not vigorously seeking to have . . . discrimination abolished by Federal legislation. Can there be any reasonable doubt that if Congress fails to enact the civil rights laws now being urged upon it and if this convention is ratified as submitted, members of the affected groups will be in a position to seek legal relief on the ground that this so-called Genocide Convention has superseded all obnoxious state legislation.[137]

In scenarios such as this, the primary fear of conservatives was that individuals would seek legal relief *before U.S. courts.* In recent years, similar rhetoric has been employed to oppose the International Criminal Court—with the specter of a kangaroo court of international technocrats sitting in judgment over GIs—whereas the primary (if often unspoken) fear is actually that U.S. military prosecutors would be forced to prosecute U.S. soldiers under U.S. law to preempt international action. Similar concerns have been voiced about abortion, the death penalty, and other issues.[138]

Does It Matter?

It is natural to ask: What are the consequences of U.S. "exemptionalism" and noncompliance? International lawyers and human rights activists regularly issue dire warnings about the ways in which the apparent hypocrisy of the United States encourages foreign governments to violate human rights, ignore international pressure, and undermine international human rights institutions. In Patricia Derian's oft-cited statement before the Senate in 1979: "Ratification by the United States significantly will enhance the legitimacy and acceptance of these standards. It will encourage other countries to join those which have already accepted the treaties. And, in countries where human rights generally are not respected, it will aid citizens in raising human rights issues."[139] One constantly hears this refrain.

Yet there is little empirical reason to accept it. Human rights norms have in fact spread widely without much attention to U.S. domestic policy. In the wake of the "third wave" democratization in Eastern Europe, East Asia, and Latin America, government after government moved ahead toward more active domestic and international human rights policies without attending to U.S. domestic or international practice.[140] The human

---

[137] George Finch, cited in Kaufman, *Human Rights,* 54.

[138] The failure of the Supreme Court to abolish the death penalty, along with the launching of a state-level movement in certain parts of the country to expand its use, owes much to the opportunities created by state and local government. See Moravcsik, "The New Abolitionism."

[139] Patricia Derian, cited in U.S. Congress, *International Human Rights Treaties,* 33.

[140] Some argue that the democratic waves that swept through Eastern Europe and Latin America in recent decades were facilitated by civil society networks that were, in turn, fostered by international regimes. But this argument has little to do with U.S. domestic practice.

rights movement has firmly embedded itself in public opinion and NGO networks, in the United States as well as elsewhere, despite the dubious legal status of international norms in the United States. One reads occasional quotations from recalcitrant governments citing American non-compliance in their own defense—most recently Israel and Australia—but there is little evidence that this was more than a redundant justification for policies made on other grounds. Other governments adhere or do not adhere to global norms, comply or do not comply with judgments of tribunals, for reasons that seem to have little to do with U.S. multilateral policy. Perversely, anti-Americanism may indeed fuel the solidarity of others behind the promulgation of multilateral human rights norms—as appears to have been the case in the closing days of the ICC negotiations.[141]

The pluralist account defended in this essay suggests instead that the primary winners and losers of U.S. nonadherence to international norms are various groups of *American citizens*.[142] This is so for two reasons. First, adherence to international human rights regimes would signal a significant symbolic shift in—and likely have an eventual practical impact on—the nature of human rights enforcement in the United States, not least by courts.[143] Jack Goldsmith has argued:

A domesticated ICCPR would generate enormous litigation and uncertainty, potentially changing domestic civil rights law in manifold ways. Human rights protections in the United States are not remotely so deficient as to warrant these costs. Although there is much debate around the edges of domestic civil and political rights law, there is broad consensus about the appropriate content and scope of this law . . . built up slowly over the past century. It is the product of years of judicial interpretation of domestic statutory and constitutional law, various democratic practices, lengthy and varied experimentation, and a great deal of practical local experience. Domestic incorporation of the ICCPR would threaten to upset this balance. It would constitute a massive, largely standardless delegation to federal courts to rethink the content and scope of nearly every aspect of domestic human rights law.[144]

Conservative critics like Goldsmith may hold extreme views (in global and domestic perspective), but they are not, given the power of the judi-

---

[141] Lawrence Wechsler, "Exceptional Cases in Rome: The United States and the Struggle for an ICC," in *The United States and the International Criminal Court: National Security and International Law*, ed. Sarah B. Sewall and Carl Kaysen (Lanham, MD: Rowman & Littlefield, 2000).

[142] For a more detailed argument, see Moravcsik, "Why Is U.S. Human Rights Policy So Unilateralist?" 364–70.

[143] For various scenarios, see Goldsmith, "Should International Human Rights Law Trump US Law?" 332–35. For a detailed and definitive treatment of "judicial cross-fertilization," see Slaughter, *A New World Order*.

[144] Goldsmith, "Should International Human Rights Law Trump US Law?" 332.

ciary in the United States, deluded as to the potential practical risks of signing such treaties. It is striking, in this regard, that the United States tends to ratify treaties in an explicitly non-self-executing form.[145] The political conflict that results from this prospect is, I argue, the most important root cause of American exceptionalism.

Second, nonadherence may undermine the ability of the United States to use multilateral human rights institutions to further its own foreign policy goals.[146] In this regard, I am less convinced by the consequences for U.S. human rights policy per se. Human rights advocates consistently maintain—in the words of assistant secretary of state for human rights Patricia Derian twenty years ago—that "failure . . . to ratify has a significant negative impact on the conduct of [U.S.] human rights policy," undermining its "credibility and effectiveness."[147] While there is little evidence to suggest the impact is great, there are some reasons to believe that U.S. influence in particular cases would be greater if it were able to work more credibly internationally. Before ratifying the ICCPR, for example, the United States could neither vote for members of its Human Rights Committee nor have its citizens either serve on the committee or petition it. In May 2001, the United States failed to be reelected to the fifty-three-member UN Human Rights Commission in Geneva—according to Philip Alston "the single most important United Nations organ in the human rights field."[148] The United States had held a seat continuously since the commission was established in 1947. Many human rights activists attributed this rebuff to the poor U.S. voting

---

[145] There is some evidence from judicial decision making from the 1940s through the 1960s to suggest that, absent explicit Senate action, the U.S. judiciary might well have moved toward making international treaties self-executing, as occurred in the investment area, and enforcing human rights.

[146] Moravcsik, "Why Is U.S. Human Rights Policy So Unilateralist?" 366–68. I am indebted to conversations with Harold Koh on this point.

[147] Statement of Patricia Derian, in U.S. Congress, *International Human Rights Treaties*, 33. In the same Senate hearings, Morton H. Sklar, chairman of the U.S. Helsinki Watch Committee, asserted that, absent ratification of formal treaties, "our efforts abroad to achieve human rights and a greater commitment to the principles of freedom and democracy and human dignity will be very severely damaged." This view is echoed by many major legal scholars. Statement of Morton H. Sklar, in U.S. Congress, *International Human Rights Treaties*, 261. See, for example, van der Vyver, "Universality and Relativity," 64–66; Henkin, "US Ratification of Human Rights Conventions"; Peter Malanczuk, "The International Criminal Court and Landmines: What Are the Consequences of Leaving the US Behind?" *European Journal of International Law* 11:1 (March 2000): 77–90; Hurst Hannum and Dana Fischer, eds., *Ratification of the Human Covenants on Human Rights* (Washington, DC: The American Society of International Law, 1993), 285–89.

[148] Philip Alston, "The Commission on Human Rights," in *The United Nations and Human Rights: A Critical Appraisal*, ed. Alston (Oxford: Oxford University Press, 1992), 126.

record on human rights issues.[149] It is not clear that this is truly the case, and it is even less clear that U.S. membership on bodies like the UN Human Rights Commission matters much.[150]

Recent events under the administration of President George W. Bush suggest also that the attainment of overall national security and diplomatic goals of the United States has been undermined by the failure of the United States to be perceived as a country that upholds human rights. This perception results in part from specific actions of the United States both domestically, as with the continued practice of the death penalty, and internationally, as in U.S. support for Israeli tactics in the occupied territories and in the handling of detainees connected with the wars in Afghanistan and Iraq, epitomized by the scandals emerging from Abu Ghraib and Guantánamo. An additional factor of some importance, however, has been the U.S. refusal to acknowledge widely accepted international legal norms with regard to the Geneva Conventions, the International Criminal Court, and various other international conventions. This has undermined the legitimacy of U.S. foreign policy internationally by giving the impression that the United States rejects the application of basic universal human rights norms to itself as a matter of principle. Some argue that this has undermined the war on terrorism by blurring any principled distinction between terrorism and counterterrorism, by exacerbating political and social conditions that breed terrorism, and by undermining international cooperation.[151]

Conclusion

I have argued that rights-cultural explanations for U.S. opposition to the domestic application of global human rights norms—explanations based on diffuse cultural commitments to procedural values like popular sovereignty, democratic localism, constitutional patriotism, national par-

---

[149] "US Thrown Off UN Human Rights Body," *BBC News Online* (Thursday, May 3, 2001) reported that "France, Australia and Sweden were elected to the three seats allocated to Western countries. . . . Joanna Weschler, the UN representative of Human Rights Watch, told Reuters news agency that many countries on the Economic and Social Council, whose members elect the commission, resented the poor US voting record on issues like land mines and the availability of AIDS drugs." Kenneth Roth of Human Rights Watch has mentioned also that the United States cast nearly the only vote against a declaration of the right to food (speech at Harvard Law School, May 4, 2001).

[150] This is an area requiring more focused research, but see Oona Hathaway, "Do Human Rights Treaties Make a Difference?" *Yale Law Journal* 111 (June 2002): 1935.

[151] Kenneth Roth, "Counterterrorism and Human Rights: An Essential Alliance" (paper delivered at conference, "The Nexus of Terrorism and WMDs: Developing a Consensus," Princeton University, December 12–14, 2004).

ticularity, and negative rights—are both vague and empirically unconvincing. Some such explanations fail to provide even a "thin" prima facie explanation for the rhetoric employed by politicians, and none provide a "thick" explanation that can also account for the nature of domestic cleavages, change over time, and the elements that make U.S. behavior paradoxical, namely, the strong domestic tradition of rights enforcement and bold unilateral and sometimes multilateral policies to promote human rights abroad.

Insofar as empirical evidence supports any rights-cultural explanation, it is not those variants that stress broadly held procedural norms of constitutional patriotism or popular sovereignty, but only that variant stressing the existence of an intense minority in the United States committed to a series of conservative positions allied with, but not derived from, skepticism about state power. This is, of course, closely related to the classic and undisputed description of American political exceptionalism, namely, the lack of a socialist movement—and thus a social welfare state—in America. (The close link to such a widely documented aspect of American political life should give us greater confidence in the basic claim.) From 1945 to 1970, the dominant substantive concern motivating such conservative opposition was undoubtedly race, and, like conservative opposition to expansion in the jurisdiction of the federal government, it aimed primarily to defend segregation and racial discrimination. Since then the relevant conservative agenda has broadened to include issues often connected with race, but also lifestyle issues of greatest importance to a religious minority: abortion, the traditional family, religion, capital punishment, and criminal procedure.

It is important to note that this variant of a rights-cultural argument, as opposed to truly procedural variants, is more consistent with what I have termed a "pluralist" explanation based on the substantive interests of powerful minorities as filtered through political institutions. Scholars disagree, moreover, as to whether the persistence and power of conservative views ought to be regarded as an autonomous cultural phenomenon at all, or whether it reflects the combined power and historical legacy of moneyed interests, minorities organized around intense concerns, and political institutions like the Senate and federalism that have long magnified conservative influence. The case of the death penalty suggests that public opinion often reflects, rather than drives, institutional and policy shifts.

For this reason and others, pluralist explanations of American ambivalence with regard to international human rights commitments—U.S. power, democratic stability, conservative extremism on particular issues, and fragmented American political institutions—offer a theoretically more precise and empirically more plausible explanation for the extraordinary status of the United States. No other nation in the modern world is characterized by the same combination of geopolitical power, democratic stability, conservative ideology, and institutional decentralization. Thus it is no surprise that no other country pursues as ambivalent and unilateralist a human rights policy as does the United States.

This is a sobering conclusion, for it suggests that U.S. ambivalence toward international human rights commitments is not a short-term and contingent aspect of specific American policies. It is instead woven into the deep structural reality of American political life.[152] This is so not, for the most part, because international human rights commitments are inconsistent with a particular understanding of democratic ideals like popular sovereignty, local control, or expansive protection of particular rights shared by most Americans. It is true, rather, because a conservative minority favored by enduring domestic political institutions has consistently prevailed in American politics to the point where its values are now embedded in public opinion and constitutional precedent. The institutional odds against any fundamental change in Madison's republic are high. To reverse current trends would require an epochal constitutional rupture—an Ackermanian "constitutional moment"—such as those wrought in the United States by the Great Depression and the resulting Democratic "New Deal" majority; in Germany, France, and Italy by the end of World War II; and in all European countries through a half century of European human rights jurisprudence.[153] Short of that, this particular brand of American ambivalence toward the domestic application of international human rights norms is unlikely to change anytime soon.

---

[152] I am indebted to Michael Ignatieff for posing the question of structure and contingency more sharply.

[153] See Bruce A. Ackerman, *We the People* (Cambridge: Harvard University Press, 1991).

Chapter 7 _____

American Exceptionalism, Popular Sovereignty, and the Rule of Law

PAUL W. KAHN

To UNDERSTAND the power and character of American exceptionalism, we have to look in a direction that political scientists and international-law scholars often fail to notice. We have to examine the intimate relationship among American political identity, the rule of law, and popular sovereignty. When we do so, we find a set of concepts associated with the eighteenth-century project of revolution. These concepts continue to have a surprising contemporary vitality. This vitality is less a matter of political theory than one of political symbolism; it lies in the dimension of rhetoric, not logic.

The critical elements of the American political imagination were put in place very early: the connection of Revolution and Constitution.[1] Revolution is an act by the popular sovereign through which it declares its birth by acting out its freedom. Constitution is the product of the popular sovereign forming itself by imposing an institutional shape upon itself. This produces the absolute bedrock of the American political myth: the rule of law is the rule of the people. Participation in the Constitution and the laws that carry out the constitutional scheme is participation in the popular sovereign. Law had long been thought to express the will of the sovereign. In America, this simple proposition survives entry into modernity, such that law now means constitutionalism and the sovereign means the people. These are the elements of an American civic religion, with which any global regime must contend.

Outside the United States, claims of national uniqueness and of the politics that supports such claims bear a history of dangerous and destructive political experiences. In Europe, this was the language of fascism; in Latin America, the language of authoritarianism. Abroad, the appeal of a global rule of law lies in the promise of protection against the pathologies of internal domestic politics. A transnational rule of law suggests a

_____

[1] See P. Kahn, *The Reign of Law: Marbury v. Madison and the Construction of America* (1997).

kind of internal depoliticalization.[2] The United States, however, has not shared this experience of political pathology. Ours remains a triumphal history. Not a perfect past, but one that is seen as a story of progress leading toward an enduring ideal. Our moments of political failure have become elements of a progressive narrative of self-realization. The consequence of this is that the United States remains the quintessential, modern nation-state in an increasingly postmodern world. Our very modernity makes the transition to the contemporary, international order so difficult. Of course, other nations have made or are making this transition, but they have often done so under the severe shock of external events and internal failure.

I am not suggesting that American self-perceptions are true as a matter of fact. There is plenty to criticize in the American past, as well as in its present—plenty of exclusions, of inequalities, and of plain evil. Facts are not the issue, but rather the imaginative conditions that support a powerful belief in the American myth. My aim is neither to justify the myth nor to explain the historical conditions that made it possible: a combination of Protestantism, exile to the wilderness, Enlightenment thought, and the birth of markets.[3] In this essay, I want only to describe the conceptual architecture—the shape of the belief—of our national political project. Once that description is in place, we will more clearly see the ground of the difficulty of American participation in the contemporary phenomenon of the globalization of the rule of law.

American exceptionalism is rooted in the powerful and totalizing character of the American experience of politics. Politics, here, refers not to a factional politics of preference and policy, but to the deep structure of the imagination when we understand ourselves as participants in a common, transgenerational project of creating and maintaining the state. Politics, in this sense, is not distinct from law; nor is it distinct from war. Indeed, law and war—or at least the possibility of war—are two of our most characteristic forms of the experience of the political.

A Classical View of the Modern Political Imagination

All modern Western states—as well as those that model themselves on the West—have claimed to be democratic: this has been the age of "people's republics." The coming into existence of the modern state required the destruction of a premodern order in which the state was seen as a part of a natural—or divine—order. Authority in the state was an instance of the

---

[2] *See* L. Siedentop, *Democracy in Europe* 30–40 (2001).

[3] I take up this account of origins in P. Kahn, *Putting Liberalism in Its Place* (2005).

same normative order that ruled everywhere and at all times. There were, of course, competing interpretations of natural authority in its political manifestations; there were diverse views of the relationship between the merely natural and the divine.[4] Nevertheless, all behavior, political and otherwise, was subject to the same norms. The task was to decipher that normative order and make it operative in one's behavior.[5] Law—public and private, international and national—should express this order. Real law, accordingly, was "natural law," which set forth a single rule for the individual and the state. Reasoning through the state, one quickly met God, the sovereign; one most certainly did not meet a sovereign people. Just for this reason, the appearance of the people was announced by revolution.[6]

No modern, Western state purports to rest on a divine order, an order of nature, or even a privileged class among the people in general. Governments base their authority on a claim of representation: they represent the people who retain sovereignty. Facing the state, the citizen is to see him- or herself. The state appears as a purely human construction, and the author of that construction is the people. These propositions are descriptive, but they do not describe facts about a political order. Rather, they describe the beliefs about that order characteristic of what we might call the "nonskeptical, modern citizen." They describe a popular political ideology of legitimation. As such, these propositions are also normative— every political order *should* express the will of the popular sovereign. This ideology renders problematic the grounds of international law. What had traditionally been based on natural law, or on the universal order of reason, must now rest on state consent. The ready acceptance of international law in the early national jurisprudence has been progressively displaced by a certain skepticism, the causes of which lie as much in the changing conceptual model by which we view the rule of law as in a policy of American isolationism.

These claims about popular sovereignty describe the basic structures of belief within which modern political argument has gone forward. This popular, political ideology, however, operates at such a level of generality that it can be used by both supporters and opponents of a particular government or a particular policy. It does not tell us where or how the will of the people is expressed. It does not tell us who the people are. To under-

---

[4] Consider, for example, Grotius, who saw no difference between the norms that should govern private and those that should govern public conflict. *See* H. Grotius, *De Jure Belli Ac Pacis Libri Tres* in 2 *Classics of International Law* (J. Scot ed. F. Kelsey trans. 1925).

[5] *See* M. Foucault, *The Order of Things*, chap. 1 (1970).

[6] *See* H. Arendt, *On Revolution* 40 (1965) (Louis XVI's belief that he confronted a revolt was corrected by the Duc de La Rochefoucauld-Liancourt, who announced "c'est une révolution").

stand American exceptionalism, we have to turn to the particular content of these beliefs in the American political tradition. We begin to understand that when we examine the inflection of the term "nation-state" that has operated here.

The modern state of popular sovereignty is the nation-state—a term that has generated considerable confusion. Too often, it is read with the emphasis on the word "nation." On this reading, it refers to the principle that a nation should gain political institutionalization as a state. If so, the nation precedes the state. This Wilsonian reading has gained increased currency in the contemporary period, despite the fact that it continues to generate the same practical conundrums that have always attended it: there are far more nations than there are possible states. The nightmare of a Wilsonian world of nation-states is global chaos as existing states fracture into smaller and smaller geographical units that map national identity.

The Wilsonian conception of the nation-state is actually the opposite of the distinctive, modernist experience of the nation-state. That experience put the emphasis on the second term: "state." The idea was that a nation could be created out of a state, not that the state must track the preexistent nation. The political self-formation of a state would itself create a nation, quite independently of a prepolitical, ethnic nation. Wilson was trying to bring order to the Old World, and to that end he deployed what seemed to him an old-world conception of politics. About America, Wilson had no doubt that nationhood followed statehood.[7] This belief remains central to the American self-conception.[8]

The nation-*state* was an Enlightenment idea, resting on a conception of the free self-formation of a collectivity. Citizens would form a nation by virtue of their common political activity as members of the same state. This idea of the nation-state made possible the belief that a community of diverse immigrants could form a vibrant state. Citizens would find a common identity in and through this political project of state formation. A political conception of the self would form the basis of individual identity. That which one was prior to, or apart from, this political self-formation would be reconceived as "private." Ethnicity, family, and religion become prepolitical phenomena that are subordinate to the public. The private always has about it the taint of physical need and of the irrational.

---

[7] *See* W. Wilson, *Constitutional Government* 23 (1890) ("Every man in a free country is, as it were, put upon his honor to be the kind of man such a polity supposes its citizens to be").

[8] Recently, George Fletcher has argued the contrary position. He believes that the Civil War Amendments constituted a new founding and a new Constitution. In that new republic, nationhood preceded statehood. *See* G. Fletcher, *Our Secret Constitution* (2000).

A multiethnic nation finds a common ground in a public politics of reason. That, at least, is the modern ideal.[9]

The American political order was the first truly modern state because it imagined itself to be founded simultaneously on a revolutionary act by the popular sovereign and on "inalienable truths." When nationhood is imagined to follow political action, a space is opened up for rational argument, for "deliberation and choice," as Alexander Hamilton writes on the first page of the *Federalist Papers*. Political theory becomes an inseparable part of autonomous political construction because truth now derives its power from reason, not from God and not from ethnicity. Truth, however, is not enough. The successful nation-state must affirm those truths through an act of collective will: the product of that act of the popular sovereign is the rule of law.

As the first modern state, America is paradigmatic of the task of politics in the modern period: Every state is to be made, or remade, on the basis of deliberation and choice.[10] This is the revolutionary project of modernity—a project inextricably linked to both popular sovereignty and the rule of law. One way of marking the contemporary moment is to describe it as the end of the age of revolution and the beginning of the age of globalization. A global order of law would break the connection between popular sovereignty and the rule of law. One way of understanding American exceptionalism—ironic as it sounds—is to say that America remains bound to the age of revolution. It is a deeply conservative, revolutionary state. "Conservative" here refers to an attachment to its own tradition, history, and texts; not to the conservative-liberal opposition of contemporary politics.

We can use Aristotle's concept of the "four causes" to gain a better understanding of the connection of law to political identity in the United States. Aristotle explained that every object or event can be understood from four different perspectives. The efficient cause is that course of action that brings an object or event into being. The actions of the craftsman are the efficient cause of that which he produces. The formal cause is the principle of order that gives shape or meaning to an object or event. It is the plan or design that the craftsman attempts to realize in the object of production. The material cause is that out of which the object is made. For the craftsman, it might be wood or stone. And the final cause is the end for which the production is pursued. For the craftsman, it may be

---

[9] This same ideal drives the understanding of decolonization within borders inherited from the colonial experience: prepolitical life is to be privatized, while a politics of constitutional self-formation can sustain itself.

[10] *See* P. Kahn, *Reason and Will in the Origins of the American Constitutionalism*, 98 Yale L.J. 449 (1989).

earning a living; for the artist it may be the experience of the beauty of the object itself.[11]

Applying the Aristotelian schema to the American nation-state, we can ask what process brought it into being, what principle of order it realizes in its institutional arrangements, what material bears this order, and for what end it is maintained. Different answers to these questions will be reached as the position of the inquirer changes. The historian, for example, will investigate different causes from those that appear to the economist. My concern here is not with the variety of scholarly possibilities, but with those answers that are maintained in the citizen's self-conception, that is, in the ordinary person's understanding of himself as a citizen with obligations and responsibilities to the state as well as rights to be protected by the state. The American experience of the autonomy of the political is the belief that the state is its own cause in each of these four dimensions.

No such account could be an exhaustive explanation of the terms of American political self-understanding. At most, one can identify substantial themes and trace the ways in which they relate to each other. This inquiry is successful to the extent that it clarifies why particular arguments take the form they do in our national political project. There is no proof that can be offered, but only a series of interpretive interventions that move back and forth between examples and structural claims. I suspect the terms I offer are likely to be more compelling to the constitutional law scholar than to others. Legal scholars encounter the ideology of popular sovereignty constantly. Not accidentally, American exceptionalism may be most familiar, and least problematic, to those who spend their time making and studying constitutional arguments.[12]

The Efficient Cause of the State: Revolution

The efficient cause of the modern state is located in the idea of revolution: revolution creates the state. The revolutionary subject—the collective entity that carries out the revolution—is the popular sovereign. A revolution is different from a coup just in this claim that it is action by the popular sovereign. Revolution begins with the establishment of a kind of negative freedom. The people must free themselves, before they can form themselves. The revolutionary breach is the paradigmatic political act, successfully creating a new collective identity by naming an enemy. It breaks the bonds of authority under which the polity is subordinate to a political

[11] *See* Aristotle, *Physics* 2.3, 7.
[12] *See, e.g.,* F. Michelman's essay in this collection.

power that is now conceived as external to the people themselves—regardless of whether that power is actually a foreign state. This is really nothing more than a performative utterance: existing authority becomes the enemy when the people declare it to be. Declaring authority to be the enemy, the people constitute themselves as a historical presence.

Revolution is successful when the moment of negative freedom is followed by an expression of positive freedom: the organization of a new constitutional order. Unsuccessful revolution is not revolution at all, just as an unsuccessful effort in any craft or art is not the cause of any product. Actor and act are tightly bound together through the form of an efficient cause: an unsuccessful revolution not only fails to produce a product, it fails to mark an appearance of the popular sovereign. Absent revolution, the people are not present at all. Wherever the people appear, they succeed.

The American nation-state brings itself into being by an act of popular sovereignty. Other events may be the occasion for the popular sovereign to act, but the act itself cannot be reduced to other causes or events. We go wrong, however, if we believe the people to be a subject apart from these acts of negative and positive freedom—as if first there is a subject who then decides to act. Popular sovereignty is only a particular way of viewing the state. It has no other form, place, or time apart from the state itself. The popular sovereign is the state conceived as efficient cause of its own existence. We will not find it anywhere else but in a narrative of efficient causes by which the state first brings itself into existence and then maintains itself as the particular state that it is.[13]

Accordingly, the nation-state is the product of no subject's actions apart from its own self-creation. Those who participated in the creation of the state acted as the sovereign people. Apart from this, they would have had no authority to create a set of political institutions that bind their successors. They could do so because, viewing those past actions, the citizen sees only an expression of the popular sovereign of which he or she remains a part. For this reason, the popular sovereign, even as it is understood to be the efficient cause and thus the "originator" of the state, always has a transtemporal character that resists chronological time. It is timeless because it is nothing more than a form of self-perception within the state.

The popular sovereign is, therefore, the state conceived as the efficient agency of its own construction. Imagining political creation as an act com-

---

[13] In fact, the relationship of the popular sovereign to maintenance of the state is always difficult to conceive because of the absence of the explicit appearance of efficient causes. This leads to theories of "tacit consent" under which the popular sovereign is always acting in its very failure to act.

parable to the divine creation ex nihilo, we imagine a subject capable of having or expressing such an act of will. This popular sovereign shares many characteristics with the divine sovereign of Western monotheism. First, it is omnipotent: all political forms are open to its choice. Second, it wholly fills time and space: it is equally present at every moment of the nation's life and in every location within the nation's borders. Third, we know it only by its product. We do not first become aware of the popular sovereign and then ask what it has accomplished. We know that it must exist, because we perceive the state as an expression of its will. We deduce the fact of the subject from the experience of its created product. Finally, we cannot be aware of this sovereign without experiencing it as a normative claim that presents itself as an assertion of identity. We understand ourselves simultaneously as a part, and as a product, of this sovereign. In it, we see ourselves.[14]

The Formal Cause of the State: Constitution

To move from the efficient to the formal cause is to move from revolution to constitution. The formal cause of the modern state is that order realized in the revolutionary act of popular self-creation. The constitution expresses the principles of order that give the nation-state its positive identity. Without a constitutional moment, the revolutionary act of popular sovereignty can only be the destruction of the old order.

The constitution begins as a document or formal plan, in the same way that a blueprint provides the formal order for the construction of a building. Just as the blueprint provides the unity of the construction, the constitution holds the diverse parts of the state in a single, unified project. A state that operates under the rule of men, not law, has no unity over time; it is as various as the interests of those who come to rule. Conversely, constitutionalism always suggests unity despite apparent diversity. Constitutional inquiry theorizes about the unity of the legal order—that is, it is often a search for the grand principle or principles that explain the whole.[15] This idea of unity in diversity takes concrete form in the constitutional doctrines of separation of powers and federalism.

Alone, the concept of formal cause does not tell us anything about membership in the political community—does it include women or mi-

[14] Because the Constitution provides for the possibility of amendment, the popular sovereign does not quite appear with a claim of omniscience. Nevertheless, there is a substantial inclination to treat the constitutional order as complete, i.e., as fully capable of ordering any event. *See* P. Kahn, *The Reign of Law* 63–64 (on amendment as reform, not revolution).

[15] *See, e.g.,* A. Amar, *Intratextualism* 112 Harv. L. Rev. 747 (1999); J. Ely, *Democracy and Distrust* (1980); L. Tribe, *American Constitutional Law* 1–2 (1988).

norities? Nor does it tell us anything about the content of claims of legal right or even about institutional structure. All of these have changed substantially in the course of American history. Yet already in 1803, Chief Justice Marshall was able to describe the American political order as "a government of laws, and not of men."[16] The limits on the political order imposed by the idea of a formal cause are not a function of the idea of law alone. They are a function of surrounding beliefs, of where and how we are prepared to see that order. Beliefs about the best order of the state will fuel a debate about the appropriate character of law within the state. The modern state has, accordingly, invited a continuing argument in political theory about the appropriate order of law.

This question of the form of legal self-construction inevitably connects the political and the moral orders. Just here, we find the powerful connection between liberalism as a set of moral beliefs founded on the individual's capacity for reason and autonomous choice, and modern constitutionalism. Because liberalism is our reigning moral discourse, our political discourse appeals to it in arguments over the content of the law: "what should the law be?"[17] We care deeply about the content of the law. We want it to express the morally correct order of rights as well as legitimate institutions of representative democracy. We care because it is *our* law, just as we care deeply about the character of our children because they are *ours*. In each case, the truth of the normative content will not explain the character of our attachment. To think otherwise would be like thinking we could explain the passion for a sport by looking at its rules, or that of religious faith by looking at theological doctrine.

Political self-construction in the modern nation-state is a way of being in the world. We do not grasp that way of life in and through politics by examining its rules—although the rules are hardly irrelevant—but only by understanding the personal and communal identity that it sustains. We don't choose our political identity on the basis of the content of the state's law—although in extreme cases, we might disavow our political identity, if we judge the formal order of the state to be a moral travesty. The fundamental relationship is the other way around, we choose—that is, work for—a morally compelling legal order on the basis of our political identity. To understand political identity, we cannot limit the inquiry to formal causes but must consider the citizen's relationship to the state in each of the causal dimensions.

Because our constitutionalism is a matter of political identity rather than the elaboration of an abstract logic of rights, American legal schol-

---

[16] See *Marbury v. Madison*, 5 U.S. (1 Cranch) 137, 163 (1803).

[17] See R. Unger, *What Should Legal Analysis Become?* (1996), and P. Kahn, *The Cultural Study of Law* (1999).

ars—unlike those from virtually everywhere else—are quite comfortable speaking of the political role of the courts. Our law bears a political burden quite uncharacteristic of the function of law elsewhere. Thus one of the most important works of modern constitutional theory bears the subtitle *The Supreme Court at the Bar of Politics*.[18] The legitimacy of the Court is located not in the "science of law" but in politics. Only in America would legal scholars so easily claim to speak in the voice of "We the People"—a remarkably political claim for the elite scholar.[19] Only here does the national political identity focus so clearly and quickly on a legal text. Our deepest politics, that which defines our political self-understanding, merges into our understanding of ourselves as a people under the rule of law. For the Constitution is law as an expression of popular sovereignty. This is the American political myth: through the Constitution we participate in a sovereign act of self-government. In this conception, rights are a product of law, not an external limit on law. Our discourse of rights is one of interpretation of a text, and the authority of that text is fundamentally political: it is the product of the popular sovereign.

Constitution and Revolution are not related to each other as different moments of political experience in the life of the nation; they are not to each other as sleeping is to wakefulness, or private life to public action. Rather, each purports to be the truth of the other; they are reciprocal images of each other. Thus if we ask about the legitimacy of the Constitution, the answer we inevitably hear is that it is the product of the popular sovereign. It is the self-formation of We-the-People. That process of popular self-formation is exactly what we mean by Revolution. But if we ask after the truth of the Revolution—how do we know that this particular set of actions was indeed a revolution?—the only answer we have is the Constitution. We know the People acted by virtue of their product. Had there been no product, we might decide we were looking at a coup or a majority faction in the Madisonian sense. We see the People only through the Constitution; we see the Constitution because we see the People expressing themselves in Revolution.

The citizen understands the self as a part of the popular sovereign not just at moments when issues of constitutional import are open, but also when they are answered. Constitutional authority rests on the citizen's self-conception as a member of the popular sovereign. This is celebrated

[18] A. Bickel, *The Least Dangerous Branch: The Supreme Court at the Bar of Politics* (2d ed. 1986).

[19] *See, e.g.,* B. Ackerman, *We the People: Foundations* (1991); A. Amar, *Philadelphia Revisited: Amending the Constitution outside Article V,* 55 U. Chi. L. Rev. 1043 (1988); J. Rubenfeld, *Freedom and Time: A Theory of Constitutional Self-Government* (2001).

in the constitutional deliberations of the Supreme Court, and it is proclaimed constantly as the fundamental character of our political faith.
Living under the rule of law is not some lesser form of political life,
awaiting the possible rebirth of the national political spirit in a constitutional moment.[20] Rather, it is itself the celebration of a national political
life as a form of popular sovereignty.

For Americans, the Constitution bears our character as a particular
political community. This is what it means to describe the Constitution
as the formal cause. The defining political question we ask about any
particular law or official act is "Is it constitutional?" By this, we ask
whether it is consistent with our national identity embodied in the Constitution. If not, it needs to be excised from the body politic. Such a provision
only appeared to be a law; it was not really a part of us at all. It was an
action only "under color of law."[21] This idea of law that is not law takes
us right back to Rousseau's popular sovereign who never errs. This question of constitutionality is surprisingly close to the surface of our political
life. It is institutionally represented in the Supreme Court. Every citizen
believes that he or she has a right to take issue with a law or action, and
to try to push the challenge to the Supreme Court. Before the Court, the
government has no special claim to speak in the name of the sovereign
people. When the government loses its case, we say that the people
have won.

Of course, most citizens don't understand this process in a legal sense.
They suspect that its technical character might overwhelm them. They
know that the process requires professional guidance and institutional
support. Yet they intuit the possibility as a right of political membership.
They know that the Court has the final word over the political life of the
nation, and that not even the president is above the law. They have a
faith in the Constitution and in the Court. These are there not just in an
emergency—as in *Bush v. Gore*—but as the institutional guarantors of
the whole. Citizens imagine that each of these objects of their faith is there
for them personally as a right. They form the background conditions of
their day-to-day lives as members of the polity.

This tight linkage of popular sovereignty and constitutionalism, medi-
ated through the institution of the Supreme Court that speaks in the voice
of the People, characterizes the American version of the autonomy of
the political. The French, for example, who are equally serious about
popular sovereignty and its expression in law, did not develop a similar
constitutional tradition. The locus of popular sovereignty remains Parliament and its legislative output. Their courts never successfully claimed to

---

[20] Compare Ackerman, *We the People*.
[21] *See Ex Parte Young*, 209 U.S. 123 (1908).

speak in the name of the people. They have no equivalent of *Marbury v. Madison*. The French, as a modern nation, may have been no less interested in their exceptional character, but that exceptionalism did not take a constitutional form.

A formal cause has an ambiguous status: as formal, it may be considered abstractly, but as a cause it has no existence apart from its material embodiment. We cannot search for the formal character of the state in some abstract ideal of justice, some divine plan, or some natural order. Instead, we must look to the way in which the state is organized, the way in which it maintains its own institutions and relationships between rulers and ruled. In this respect, the nation-state is more organic than artificial: we cannot separate the form from that of which it is the form.[22] Members of the state do not seek the plan of the state in some external source; they, too, must study its law. This does not mean that abstract considerations of justice are irrelevant. We appeal to justice to criticize law, and to work toward the reform of law. We also recognize, however, that a claim that a law is not just is not the same as a claim that a proposition is not law. The only measure of whether it is law is within the law itself.

The contrast of perspectives of efficient and formal causes is found behind many of the debates about the nature of law. An account that focuses on efficient causes will tend to present arguments about the legitimacy of law that rely on an account of origins. These are "pedigree" theories of the nature of law. In a democracy, a legal system is legitimate when it is the product of the people's consent. An account focusing on formal causes will offer a justification of the legal order based not on pedigree but on the rationally compelling nature of the law. Even in a democracy, we want law to be not only legitimate but also just. An account of efficient causes alone will not, for example, deal with the problem of majority tyranny. Neither will without reason nor reason without will can account for the normative order of the modern nation-state. Reason and will work together as formal and efficient causes in the state's self-understanding, and as arguments of justification and legitimacy for legal authority.

We bring this double approach—appealing to both efficient and formal causes—not just to the whole of the constitutional order that is the nation-state, but to every particular legal regulation as well. We can always explain why something is law by pointing to the institutions responsible for its production.[23] In the modern state, the efficient causes of legal rules are nothing apart from the state understood as a self-governing set of

---

[22] *See* Justice Holmes for the Court in *Gompers v. United States*, 233 U.S. 604, 610 (1914).

[23] Hart's "rule of recognition" arises out of this general concern with efficient causes. *See* H.L.A. Hart, *The Concept of Law* 92–97 (1961).

institutions. We speak of law as a product of congressional or parliamentary action—or perhaps the action of courts—but not as the product of lobbying by special interest groups. Thus the state creates and maintains its own order. We read in every legal regulation a narrative of the state's self-creation.

Laws, however, are not contracts. Laws are not only legitimated by an account of their origins, they are also justified. Justification is a matter not of historical origins but of reasonableness. Law always appears as an effort to bring reason to an otherwise unreasonable world. To interpret the law, to understand its character and reach, we assume that it expresses a rational policy. Irrationality is ruled out in advance.[24] Accordingly, we imagine every law as the product of an ideal legislative process in which the participants acted on the basis of their best understanding of the demands of reason, which include justice. A particularized history is replaced by universal reason.[25] This is reading the law through its formal cause.

The state continually creates and maintains itself by creating law. Of course, the capacity of these institutions to express the popular will may be questioned. They may be criticized for their representational failures, just as they can be criticized for their failures of rationality. In fact, both criticisms will coincide: a law that advances the interests of only a special interest—a faction—will simultaneously fail the test of reason. Such criticisms, however, simply ask whether our political institutions realize their own internal norms.

Nothing I have said is meant to suggest either that rights don't matter or that an identity-based conception of law somehow eliminates debate and disagreement over the content of our law. To identify the rule of law as the formal cause of the American nation-state is to put legal rights at the very center of national political identity. Calling law a formal cause is a way of expanding the context within which we understand the operation of law and legal rights, not a way of dismissing their importance. The United States does not differ from other Western states in this dimension of formal causes. There are, of course, interpretive disagreements over specific claims of right, but all agree that the order of the state is to be a rule of law that guarantees individual rights and representative institutions. The substantial disagreement is in each of the other dimensions of the causal account. Even where the content of the

---

[24] Thus the minimum rationality test of constitutional law; see Williamson v. Lee Optical 348 U.S. 483 (1955).

[25] See, e.g., J. Thayer, The Origin and Scope of the American Doctrine of Constitutional Law, in Legal Essays (1972) (on the ideal legislature); Unger, What Should Legal Analysis Become? at 72 ("Rightwing Hegelianism is . . . the secret philosophy of history of the rationalizing legal analyst").

law is the same, the close connection of law to political identity—and through that to popular sovereignty—grounds a political practice of American exceptionalism.

The Material Cause of the State: The Citizen's Body

The material cause of the modern nation-state is the citizenry considered as the bearers of popular sovereignty. The popular sovereign has a material existence only in the bodies of the citizens. Modern states do not attach themselves to a natural geography, although all have a geography. Nor do they attach to the prepolitical organizations of family, congregation, or other corporate forms. The unit of membership is the individual. Even in a federal state, the national political order is not simply a coalition of subgroups. If it is, we have a federation, not a single nation-state.

Since the French Revolution, the preferred term of individual identity has been "citizen." To be a citizen is not just to acknowledge a jurisdictional claim of state authority but to affirm an identification with the popular sovereign. The boundaries of the modern nation-state have been constituted by the willingness of individuals to take on this set of political meanings as their own. This idea of materiality has supported both inclusion and exclusion. On the one hand, it made possible the very idea of a "nation of immigrants." The modern state has remained particularly open to immigration. On the other hand, the same idea made the state particularly wary of the possibility of admitting immigrants who were thought not to be capable of taking on this material identity. This produced the American pattern of openness linked to exceptions, the largest of which was the black slave population.[26]

A material cause has no identity apart from its formation; it is pure potential. From the perspective of modern politics, the citizen apart from the state is nothing at all. He or she has no cognizable existence apart from the distinctive shape of the political order. The stateless person lacks something essential to his or her very identity: a political life.[27] One mark of the emergence of a distinctly postmodern conception of an international rule of law is the shift in the characteristic paradigm of the individual: no longer the citizen, but the refugee.

The American nation-state attaches directly to the individual who understands himself as a citizen.[28] This is not the autonomous individual

---

[26] The direct expression of this idea of the political immateriality of the black population was *Dredd Scott v. Sandford*, 60 U.S. 393 (1856).

[27] *See, e.g., Trop v. Dulles*, 356 U.S. 86 (1958) (revocation of citizenship would be cruel and unusual punishment).

[28] In U.S. history, this is the message of *McColloch v. Maryland*, 17 U.S. 316 (1819), and of numerous federalism cases. It is why it is easier for the federal government to regulate

who chooses to be a member of the polity, already having a substantive individual identity. It is, rather, the individual who has no character prior to his membership in the polity. Thus the Fourteenth Amendment establishes that citizenship attaches at birth. This, however, is only a figurative representation of a deeper point: citizenship is not one role among others but constitutive of identity. A citizen has a private life; the private person does not become the citizen.

While in liberal theory the idea of the private precedes the public, in the modern state the private is always a function of the public. Citizens may have rights to privacy, but they have them as a function of law. Claims to a private self beyond or apart from the law are simply noncognizable from within the polity. In every direction we look, law is already there. A liberal state restrains its exercise of power in order to leave room for the private. It nevertheless reserves the power wholly to absorb the private: property can be appropriated, as can life itself when the political circumstances require it.

The constitutive character of citizenship is not fully captured by either the idea of consent or that of birth. The totalizing character of citizenship is fully revealed only in the willingness to sacrifice for the state. The modern nation-state makes a potential claim on the life of every citizen. All understand that political identity can be a matter of life or death. The legitimacy of the nation-state turns in substantial part on whether citizens see this claim as an authoritarian imposition or as a moment of self-sacrifice.

The nation-state is the sole source of its own existence, and it exists only as a meaning borne by citizens willing to invest their bodies in its continued existence as an order of law. The power of the state rests on the willingness of individuals to understand themselves as citizens, to take up as their own self-identity the identity of the state. Seeing themselves as citizens, individuals have shown themselves willing to devote themselves completely to the continued existence of the state. Indeed, there was a glorification of war throughout the nineteenth and twentieth centuries as the moment at which the ordinary person could overcome the limits of his own particularity. We have, for the most part, abandoned the glorification, yet we have hardly abandoned the idea of self-transcendence through sacrifice.

The modern nation-state has shown itself to be an extremely effective instrument of sacrifice. It has been able to mobilize its population to make sacrifices in order to sustain its own historical existence. Modernity has been an age of political faith even more destructive than the age of reli-

---

directly the behavior of individuals than to try to regulate that behavior through directions to the state governments. *See Printz v. United States*, 521 U.S. 898 (1997).

gious faith that preceded it. The extravagant character of American consumerism may have misled many into thinking that ours is no longer a sacrificial political culture. The reactions to September 11, however, suggest that this is not so. September 11 itself stands for the risk to life that attaches directly to political identity. The victims suffered for no reason particular to themselves, but only for their political character.[29]

The modern American understands that he may be called upon to sacrifice himself for the Constitution. That does not mean that he is enthusiastic about the prospect or that he would blindly follow the government whenever it decided to use force. It means only that he understands that circumstances may arise in which he can legitimately be called to sacrifice, and that he will have no political or legal argument to ground his refusal. He understands modern war as a test of whether a state "dedicated to a proposition" can survive. Modern war has quite literally been a test of national wills. We know that will only as it takes a formal shape—the rule of law—and achieves a material embodiment in the citizen. Thus war is a test fought out in the very real bodies of its citizens. War has been the act of sacrifice for law and a means by which law continues its historical existence.

A nation-state comes into existence only when there is a popular sovereign that expresses itself by imposing a formal order on itself, which means that there is no popular sovereign until it achieves a material existence through individual citizens. Unless conceived as a material first principle, the popular sovereign is always caught in logical paradoxes of inclusion and exclusion. There is no reasoning to the boundary between those within and without the state; there is only the fact of the existence of the popular sovereign as borne in the bodies of individuals who conceive of themselves as citizens.[30] Believing in the Constitution as that which can demand our sacrifice, we affirm an identity with all who came before and will come after. We know who we are as subjects of a political community that exists in an imaginative space beyond the universalism of reason and the particularity of desire.

If citizens refuse to see themselves as the material bearers of the popular sovereign, then the nation-state quickly becomes a mere abstraction. Formally, it may continue, but its political life ceases for its population. We saw this happen in the collapse of the Soviet Union and its satellite states. Without individuals willing to invest themselves in the existing state, those states simply had no power to sustain themselves. Citizens came to

[29] The victims did include many non-Americans. In part, this was collateral damage—the targets were symbolic of American power. In part, however, it was also a matter of targeting the political identity of the West more generally.

[30] *See* L. Brilmayer, *Justifying International Acts* (1989).

understand themselves as members of new popular sovereigns, in some instances hollowed out from within the existing states. In the modern nation-state, geography follows popular sovereignty. The material reality of the state is not its geographic distribution but the bodies of its citizens.

The Final Cause of the State: Constitutionalism without End

The final cause of the modern nation-state is nothing more than the perpetuation of the state's own existence. The state is not trying to achieve any end apart from the continued realization of itself. In it, means and ends collapse into each other. It is a means to no other end than its own existence. Thus the American nation-state understands itself as a temporal project without limit.[31]

Every modern state claims to realize a just order. Nevertheless, this justice is not something that exists apart from the state itself. The state is not a transitional moment in a move toward something else, whether a vision of universal justice or economic well-being. The modern nation-state could not subordinate itself to another state it believed to be more just, nor to one it believed to promise greater wealth. If contemporary states look to participation in a global order for both justice and well-being, there has been a fundamental transformation of the nature of the state, of the meaning of the political, and of the character of citizenship. This would be a distinctly postmodern politics.

The modern nation-state has understood itself as a temporal project without limits. Constitutions do not contain sunset provisions; they are simply to continue without end. Of course, states do end, but not on their own terms. They do not "use themselves up"; they are a limitless resource. The termination of the state is not simply defeat by external forces—a state can exist in a privative mode, if it continues to inform citizen self-identity. We know what it means to be an "occupied state." Nation-states end when the idea of the state fails in the imagination of the citizen.

Self-defense is a necessary element of the nation-state, because there is no value higher than its own continued existence. This is the point at which war and constitutions intersect in the modern period. War is the defense of the rule of law because law is the state understood as an order of meaning—as formal cause. The inverse form of this proposition is that even during war the Court continues to have a role of speaking law to

---

[31] These words sound, perhaps disturbingly, a good deal like Richard Dawkins's description of the final cause of all life: to perpetuate the information encoded in DNA and embodied, at any moment, in particular organisms. *See* R. Dawkins, *River Out of Eden* (1996). The nation-state may be more literally organic than I, at least, care to imagine.

power: final and formal causes must coincide. The Court's recent decision in *Hamdi v. Rumsfeld* concerning executive detention of an American citizen alleged to be an enemy combatant emphasized just this point: "It is during our most challenging and uncertain moments that our Nation's commitment to due process is most severely tested; and it is in those times that we must preserve our commitment at home to the principles for which we fight abroad."[32]

In war, the state expresses the necessity of its own existence. This is not a necessity external to the state but the very principle of political autonomy characteristic of the modern nation-state. The nation-state knows only itself; it knows that it must continue without end. This does not mean that the life of the nation is at issue in every deployment of force. Any government policy, including a military action, can be seen as merely a mistake. For many, the American action in Vietnam came to be seen as a mistake. Such mistakes, like mistakes of law, will be described as government programs or policies that are not expressions of the popular sovereign.

An age of people's republics needs a law of war much more than did the age of premodern states. A state that understands itself as an expression of a divine or a natural order can look to meanings outside itself to limit its actions. A state based on family or class can subordinate the political to the continuing interests of those prepolitical elements of civil society. But the nation-state under law knows only itself—without end and without limit. A state that is the source of its own meaning creates and sustains belief in its own ultimate value. There are no implicit principles of restraint on self-defense for the state that understands itself as the expression of popular sovereignty under the rule of law. Its existence is the source and condition of all the value it is prepared to recognize.

The democratization of the state is linked to the increasing militarization of the state, not accidentally, but essentially. People's states produce people's armies, until the point at which the very distinction between combatant and noncombatant disappears. On the one side, the state has an ultimate value for its citizens; on the other, those outside the state can appear to have no value whatsoever. The autonomy of the political leaves no way in which to assign a measurable value to those outside the state, except by reference to the state itself. Those who are not allies are enemies or potential enemies.[33] Of course, they continue to have value from a moral point of view, but the moral does not register directly in the scale of political meanings. The modern nation-state defends itself, not human-

[32] *Hamdi v. Rumsfeld*, 124 S. Ct. 2633, 2648 (opinion of Justice O'Connor) (2004).

[33] President Bush invoked this theme in warning states that they must take sides in the "war on terrorism."

ity. The rise of humanitarian intervention, like recognition of the refugee, again suggests the beginnings of a postmodern political consciousness.

The turn toward international legal regulation of war at the beginning of the last century reflected an awareness of this lack of internal limits. As it became clear that the modern state was capable of waging war without limits, international law became an increasingly attractive resource. Politics, even the politics of modern nation-states, is not the only normative perspective that we occupy. Politics can always be judged by morality, and modern warfare passed the boundaries of reasonable moral limits sometime in the nineteenth century.

Nevertheless, this turn to an international law of war proved singularly ineffective. One of the great puzzles of the last century was the simultaneous growth of law and of war. Even as the legal regulation of the use of force spun an ever finer web, war itself continually slipped the boundaries of law. At the center of the legal effort were two principles that could gain little traction because they contradicted the fundamental self-conception of the modern nation-state: the principles of proportionality and of discrimination. If the final cause of the nation-state is its own continued existence, then proportionality could never mean more than "use no more force than necessary to achieve that objective." That might be a very great amount of force indeed, as the turn to weapons of mass destruction and the course of the European wars suggests. Similarly, the distinction of combatants from noncombatants fails to recognize the democratic project that is embodied in the modern nation-state: all of the state's resources—including all of its citizens—can be asked to sacrifice. A politics that is diffused through an entire population supports not only universal sacrifice but reciprocally broad attacks.

The autonomy of the political, characteristic of the modern nation-state, was carried to its logical end point with the development of nuclear weapons and the policy of deterrence based upon mutual assured destruction. This policy has been the background condition for several generations of Americans. The state expresses a willingness not only to destroy itself in its full material extension—all citizens—but to end history itself. If not this state as a particular political formation, then nothing at all. This is just the logic of the modern nation-state. If the American nation-state cannot continue, then there is no reason for history to continue. There is not some higher end: whether humanity or the planet. In every dimension—all four causes—the state can see only itself.

This has been the lived meaning of all within the modern, American nation-state. Citizenship as a willingness to respond to the demand for sacrifice for the continued existence of the state is not the privilege of an elite, nor even the male privilege of the battlefield. Law and war are not

antithetical forces but common expressions of the modern political culture of the sovereign nation-state. That state writes itself into existence
by drafting a constitution. It expresses the historical permanence of that
law by defending it at all costs. It demonstrates its own ultimate significance in the life of the individual citizen through the demand for sacrifice
that war entails. The sovereign people's state applies these principles without limit. All citizens become appropriate subjects of sacrifice, and all
history becomes coterminous with the continuation of the state. The dominance of war in the modern era has not been an unfortunate accident;
rather, it has been a measure of how seriously we take our politics.

Because we are not just political subjects but moral agents as well, we
will recoil from the totalizing claim—and threat—of the politics of the
modern nation-state. Humanitarian law identified the problems of the
modern nation-state quite accurately. But the expression of an international legal rule proved to be an altogether weak force in comparison to
the totalizing claim of an autonomous politics. The United States remains
committed to that conception of political autonomy.

National Politics, Liberal Legalism, and International Law

My account has deliberately blurred the distinction between the politics
of the modern nation-state and that of the United States. The broader
category defined an ideal of politics for two hundred years. The United
States remains deeply embedded in that ideal, while much of the rest of
the world is turning away from it. In Europe, that turn was occasioned
in substantial part by a kind of moral revulsion over the wars that
attached to that political form. In much of the rest of the world, the turn
has been occasioned by the repeated failures of democratic politics to
produce stable regimes under law and by a recognition of material necessity. The United States has often encouraged the development of transnational regimes as the appropriate response for just these problems of other
states. Their politics and their economies have indeed failed, and repair
is to come from a transnational order. There is no similar perception of
failure in the United States and, therefore, no sense of a need to participate
in the remedy.

The successful and continued achievement of the autonomy of the political grounds the claim for American exceptionalism. This political autonomy makes the state a normative order closed in upon itself in the same
way that a religious order does not rest on some higher end or justification. Not even the well-being of the individual serves as such an end.
Instrumental justifications of the political will always fail at the moment
of conscription. Yet without the potential for sacrifice, we are not speak-

ing of modern politics at all. What modern politics demanded of us has always been too much and too terrible to find its reason elsewhere. The internationalization of human rights law, however, represents just the opposite set of beliefs: politics is instrumentalized; it is a means to an end located in the well-being of the individual.

The point of contact between the American, domestic political order and the international law of human rights is their common appeal to the morality of liberalism. There is no substantial disagreement on fundamental norms that a legal order should protect: liberty, equality, and due process. There are, of course, interpretive disagreements on the particular content of these values and the extent to which their realization is properly the responsibility of public, as opposed to private, institutions. But such interpretive disagreements characterize domestic institutions as well.

This common moral content, however, is not a ground for a common political identity. It is a mistake to believe that the content of law can be stripped from its political context. The political matrix within which our liberalism operates is entirely different from the implicit political matrix of a global order of human rights law. Indeed, the contemporary advocates of a human rights perspective are often inclined to see the autonomy of the political, which expresses itself in a vibrant idea of state sovereignty, as a pathological condition from which a global order of law is to save us.

Our national politics has lived with the same conundrum that has characterized theological speculation in the West for thousands of years: Is the source of value of the commandments the fact that they were spoken by God, or were they spoken by God because they were right? If we think liberal legalism is spoken because it is right, then we may think we can do away with the sovereign voice, and even with the particularity of the state. Liberalism becomes a program seeking to transcend the political conditions of its own existence. This is the contemporary phenomenon of globalization of a liberal order of law. It is law without politics.

Yet we may find that we are no more able to adopt half of the synthetic proposition that defines our political order of law—the popular sovereign speaks a liberal order of law into existence—than the religious faithful could adopt half of the synthetic proposition of their belief. That God spoke was not a matter of indifference to the faithful. What God said was important, but never more important than that he said it. The question politics answers is not only "What should we do?" but "Who are we?" If we are not made in God's image, if we are not a part of the popular sovereign, we must be something else. In the United States, there is not a lot of interest in being something else.

Because it is a "made" order, the legal character of the nation-state appears as experimental, that is, open to endless debate and reform. But this openness to reform should not be mistaken for a lack of commitment to its substance. Politics is an unending project, but it simultaneously appears as an ultimate value to be defended at any cost. Only a politics of ultimate meanings could see reason in the practice of mutual assured destruction. This is no longer the morality of liberalism but the threat of a political sovereign that has become a vengeful God. If we believe in such a God, we cannot say that this is a vice of the system of belief. Rather, it is simply the way the world is. Our politics appears to us as simply the way the world is—not in the sense that we cannot reform its content, but in the sense that we find ourselves with a political identity.

Until the contemporary development of the legal doctrine of *jus cogens*, it had been part of the modern understanding of the nation-state that all international law gave way in the extreme instance of self-defense. The Germans called this *Kriegsraison*; the English spoke of a doctrine of military necessity.[34] No state had to accept application of a legal rule that would lead to its own demise. The emergence of *jus cogens* norms is the best signal of the beginning of a new era of international law and, thus, of a new perspective on the nation-state. Such norms necessarily displace the state from a position of ultimate value. A norm that cannot be violated even as a matter of the defense of the state must rest on a value greater than that of the continued existence of the state.[35]

Jus cogens norms depend on a transnational perspective not available within a system of sovereign nation-states. There were simply no resources in that system by which we could get beyond the state. To the classic international lawyer, who believes that state consent is the sole ground of all international legal norms, the idea of *jus cogens* makes little sense, just because it suggests a ground of law beyond the consenting agent.[36] That a state would agree to conditions of international law that would threaten its own survival is a possibility ruled out in advance.[37] It

---

[34] *See* C. Jochnick & R. Normand, *The Legitimation of Violence: A Critical History of the Laws of War*, 35 Har. Int'l. L. J. 49, 63 (1994); B. Carnahan, *Lincoln, Lieber and the Laws of War: The Origins and Limits of the Principle of Military Necessity*, 92 Am. J. Int'l. L. 213 (1998).

[35] *But see* P. Kahn, *Nuclear Weapons and the Rule of Law*, 31 N.Y.U. J. Int'l. Law & Pol. 349 (1999) (on the continued peremptory power of self-defense).

[36] The classic statement of this view is that of P. Weil, *Towards Relative Normativity in International Law*, 77 Am. J. Int'l. L. 413 (1983).

[37] Modern examples of this debate go back at least to the Kellog-Briand Pact; they surface again in the debate over the place of self-defense under Article 51 of the Charter. The traditionalists argue that a promise not to use force must be limited by a doctrine of necessity as measured by the state's own political perspective. The state alone can set the parameters of its vital interests. *See* P. Kahn, *From Nuremberg to the Hague: The United States Position in Nicaragua v. United States and the Development of International Law*, 12 Yale J. Int'l. L. 1 (1987).

is not just unlikely; it is conceptually impossible. A nation-state could not bind itself to its own demise without entering into a logical contradiction. This is what it means to say that the final cause of the state is nothing apart from its own continued existence.

The sources of contemporary *jus cogens* claims have been, first of all, an idea of the ultimate moral value of the prepolitical individual and, increasingly, an idea of an apolitical nature. A state has value, on this view, just to the degree that it furthers the norm of human dignity or preserves a natural environmental order. The state becomes a means to ends that are defined quite apart from politics.[38] The actual extent to which such transnational supernorms operate in contemporary international law, however, remains controversial—at least once we look beyond the self-serving statements of the contemporary proponents of international law.

A new generation of international lawyers, academics, and transnational activists have abandoned state sovereignty and its vision of the irreducible quality of the political. In its place, they would put human rights. International law has become part of a liberal project of creating a single global order subject to the rule of reason in which the individual is the source of substantive value. This cosmopolitanism of rights is the contemporary version of the traditional liberal misunderstanding of the political. The liberal sees the individual—through the social contract— as the efficient cause of the state; he fails to see the origin of the state in the transgenerational, collective actor that is the popular sovereign. He sees the final cause of the state as only individual well-being, the satisfactions individuals can obtain before their unique deaths. He does not see the endurance of the nation-state as an end in itself. He sees the material cause of the state in property—the liberal state is an organization of ownership, including the individual's ownership of his or her own body. He does not see the instantiation of the popular sovereign in the body of the citizen. The autonomy of the political for the liberal is reduced to the argument over formal causes. Here, he says that the rule of law should be guided by public reasons, which all "reasonable" citizens should—and therefore, as a matter of theory, do—accept. Because liberal politics has a determinate content only at the level of formal causes, it moves effortlessly to a cosmopolitan claim: universal rules of law for reasonable people everywhere.

But the argument over formal causes is not politics. Although not without deep relevance to politics, it is hardly the source of political identity.

---

[38] As is likely to become increasingly clear over the next generation, these norms are in substantial tension—one cannot celebrate equally the individual subject as agent and the order of nature. *See* P. Singer, *Animal Liberation* (1975), *Practical Ethics* (1997).

Formal causes alone are wholly inadequate to explain the core political phenomenon of distinguishing citizen from alien, and of imagining the possibility of sacrifice for the state. Not surprisingly, the development of a rights-based international law has made little contact with much of the world. This is the problem not just on the killing fields of the former Yugoslavia; it is the problem in the United States as well. Never in history has a whole population been so exposed to the threat of political sacrifice as we have been for the last half century. Even the end of the Cold War may not have substantially changed this, as we see the new threat of terrorist use of weapons of mass destruction. This is the essence of democratization of the experience of the political. It may also be completely immoral. This is just the point. Political meanings are not moral meanings. They are their own ultimate values.

The United States has greeted many of the recent international-law developments with a substantial degree of skepticism. It has declined to participate in many; it has halfheartedly acknowledged some. It is likely to believe that behind the articulation of international-law values is a political agenda: potential adversaries using law to gain a tactical advantage against the United States. These political perceptions are not going to be legislated out of existence at a global conference called by the United Nations. They have less to do with the actual existence of threats than with a political imagination that maintains the ultimate value of the nation-state and thus sees a world divided between self and other.

Of course, the United States does not oppose every move toward an international legal order. No less than any other state, it makes tactical judgments about how to advance its own self-interests. In particular, its economic interests can often be advanced through a global regime of law. Similarly, as a superpower, it has interests in maintaining conditions of political order around the globe; as a liberal state, it does want to advance the rights and well-being of others. A global order of law may usefully advance all of these interests. International law as a useful tool for creating order and securing rights abroad is hardly inconsistent with a self-understanding that sees little need for international law to limit and define its own politics of self-government. The United States will instinctively avoid application of that law to its own political order. To the rest of the world, this is bound to look hypocritical. In the United States, it will look like an insistence on democratic self-government.

Even in the United States, recent political life may have been less vibrant, less a source of identity and ultimate meanings, than it was in the past. Politics has appeared increasingly as the practice of lobbying by special interest groups. Political sacrifice has seemed removed from our ordinary understanding of ourselves. We no longer live with the draft. We have created specialists in military affairs, just as we create police and firemen. We did not imagine our armies defending ourselves so much as carrying out moral missions to help others. On September 11, we saw that was hardly the whole story. The country quickly and easily fell back into a political register of ultimate values made real in the bodies of citizens.

The moralists among us—and we are all moralists on occasion—will always be dismayed by the tenacity of politics. That tenacity can be explained only on its own terms. I have tried to explain this quality by developing the idea of political autonomy and ultimate values. That account does not offer a justification for our political beliefs. Indeed, it denies the possibility of such a justification. On that issue, all that could be said is that it is a part of the human condition to read the self as bearing a meaning, that the fear of death and the effort to find satisfactions before death are not an adequate imaginative field. We don't decide that it should be this way. We are already a product of the meanings we create.

Part III

EVALUATING EXCEPTIONALISM

Chapter 8

American Exceptionalism: The New Version

STANLEY HOFFMANN

I

Each nation tends to see itself as unique. Two, France and the United States, consider themselves as exceptional because—or so they claim—of the universality of their values. One only, the United States, has tried to develop foreign policies that reflect such exceptionalism. Whereas France and most of the European powers have tended, or been forced, to practice balance-of-power politics for their protection and for the creation of minimal order in the international jungle, the United States has had much leeway to be original. The main component of its exceptionalism has been, for more than a century after its independence, its geographically privileged position: far enough away from Europe and Asia to be able to be safe and uninvolved, yet capable of expanding into contiguous territories easily and without much of a contest. A second component was its institutions: it grew into being the greatest representative democracy, with greater participation of the public and of the legislative branch in foreign affairs than occurred anywhere else. Finally, American principles turned geography and institutions into guidelines for behavior: a distaste for the rule of force that characterized European diplomacy and colonialism, the repudiation of aristocracy and its wiles, enshrined in a sacred text, the Constitution, which served and still serves as the glue that amalgamates all the ingredients of the melting pot. (France, with its vast number of constitutions, could use only its language and culture as the glue of Frenchness.)[1]

The sense of special mission imparted by these components left ample room for contradictions and complexities. The lofty feeling of democratic superiority and universal relevance was perfectly compatible, in practice, with a pursuit of national interest and advantage that was just as fierce as elsewhere—indeed geographical position and political faith facilitated

[1] See S. Hoffmann, *Gulliver's Troubles* (New York: McGraw Hill, 1968), pt. 2.

and licensed quite ordinary crass behavior, as continental expansion was going to show; the usual behavior of states never became the policy makers' ideal, with a few exceptions such as Hamilton, but this was not the only domain in which the ideal and the real were allowed to diverge. The complexity was provided by the two very different forms that American exceptionalism took, which I called elsewhere the Wilsonian syndrome. One form, less and less relevant as U.S. might grew, was isolationism. As Wilson said when World War I began, the United States was "too proud to fight": it was a beacon of light, a model perhaps for others, but it wasn't going to get involved in others' fights. Hence the Founding Fathers' imperative of "no entangling alliances." The other face was more crusading and militant: making the world safe for democracy, which entailed working with others yet did not supersede distrust of European-style alliances, marinated in secret diplomacy and cynical deals. Rather it meant a willingness to build global institutions, good both for the promotion of U.S. interests and for the expansion of America's mission and ideals, yet designed such that the risks of unwelcome entanglements would be minimized (remember that article 10 of the League of Nations covenant, which Wilson's intransigence refused to water down, left it to each state to protect the political independence and territorial integrity of another state from aggression). One characteristic was common to the two versions of exceptionalism: the desire to protect (in both cases) and to project (in the second) what made the United States, in American eyes, unique—its values and institutions.

Indeed, Wilson had not given up isolationism for power politics: he joined the war as an associate, not an ally. The League, even with imprecise commitments, was too much for the public, and the design, especially in its preference for open diplomacy, anticolonialism, and self-determination, was unwelcome among Wilson's traditional foreign associates, and often unrealistic. The result was a return to isolationism, in the age of the totalitarian tyrants.

II

After Franklin D. Roosevelt's death, U.S. foreign policy had to be reconstructed. FDR's vision of the "four policemen" who would rule the world (through the UN Security Council), designed to be more effective than the League, was quickly crippled by the Cold War. The shapers of the new strategy of containment were all intensely aware of, and responsive to, the formidable new power of the United States. The rest of the West and much of Asia were down, and the sole challenger, Stalin's Soviet Union, could be dealt with in only one of two ways: preemption, at a time when the United States had a monopoly of nuclear power (but the Soviets had the means of invading Western Europe) or containment, which became the doctrine and entailed military alliances with the countries that had to be saved from Soviet domination. This was the Realist moment, whose chief theorist, Hans Morgenthau, excommunicated Wilsonian idealism and moralism. But the policy makers tried to mitigate the Realists' celebration of power with various kinds of appeals to idealism that Wilson could have applauded. The struggle against Communism was presented not as a power contest but as a crusade of the good (the democracies) against evil. The vast new network of international and regional organizations, Truman's four-point program for development, reflected the dimensions of the power struggle, but this development was also presentable as idealistic measures for peace and welfare. The realism of the dark side of the struggle (such as subversion) was sugarcoated by a genuine idealism: think of American cultural diplomacy in Western Europe, animated by the CIA. A synthesis of traditional power politics, in the prudent forms advocated by George Kennan, and of American idealistic and multilateralist exceptionalism seemed to be accomplished.

After more than forty years, the outcome was—of course—complex. On the one hand, the synthesis won great victories: the collapse of the Soviet Union (in a way close to "Mr. X" 's prediction in 1947), the rebirth of Western Europe and Japan as protégés of Washington, the subtle management of the Sino-Soviet split, the acrobatic success of having Israel as well as several Arab states as clients, the waning of colonialism. But on the debit side decolonization produced failed states with often miserable populations and violent ethnic conflicts; further, a permanent U.S. military presence was needed in Western Europe and Japan, both because of a potential for continuing external threats and because the United States was needed to preserve harmony in Western Europe and the Far East. The end of the Soviet Union deprived the U.S. network of often disparate alliances of its glue and created new headaches. Above all, there was the scar of Vietnam: a bitter lesson in the impotence of force in some situations, a demonstration of the limits of doctrines, as well as of America's appeal, a discovery of the fragility of America's domestic front—points that present-day policy makers should not forget.

III

After the Cold War, the United States talked about a new world order, but what they faced was a bewildering and disorderly new world. The end of the Soviet empire meant anything but a peaceful scene. The Arab-Israeli conflict continued; the Gulf War was for the military both good (because of the rise in military credits) and perplexing (were the stringent conditions of the Powell doctrine a tough road map for future conflicts, or a warning against most limited uses of force?). Once more, the unexpected struck: ethnic conflicts (some of horrendous scope) that raised each time the question of whether, where, and on which side to intervene, and provoked a debate between Realists resistant to foreign policy as "social work" and the idealists of humanitarian interference. In these new circumstances allies began to diverge. American diplomacy found itself pressured, both by a public eager to return to domestic affairs (as Clinton understood, in 1992), and by the military eager to avoid any new Vietnam—hence Powell's decision to end the Gulf War far indeed from Baghdad, and his reluctance concerning humanitarian expeditions.

The first indication of a new attempt by American strategic thinkers to define a doctrine for so complicated and elusive a world was provided by what has been called "Dick Cheney's masterwork,"[2] the Defense Planning Guidance draft of 1992, which was toned down before it was published, given the outcry it had produced. It was doubly important. In 1947, the containment rationale was written by a diplomat—one who wanted to deter, not to wage, war, and was particularly suspicious of a militarization of America's alliances, as well as of any resort to nuclear weapons. Forty-five years later, the tract that was the first draft of the Bush doctrine of 2002 was produced by a group of civilian and military officials of the Defense Department. Moreover, it launched a new form of exceptionalism and carried the American enthusiasm for power way beyond that of the late 1940s. There had been nothing exceptional then about the U.S. discovery of the need for and utility of power—a rebuke and corrective to the two alternative forms of American exceptionalism until then. But there is something wondrous about its new incarnation, for it is an exceptionalism based almost exclusively on military domination. The 1992 draft went not so much beyond the Powell doctrine (when using force, do it overwhelmingly enough to win and only if the chances of success are good), as in a different direction. The document introduces explicitly the idea of the possible necessity of unilateral action, of the preemptive use of force, and of a U.S. nuclear arsenal strong enough to deter the development of nuclear programs elsewhere. It was clearly aimed at reducing the challenges Russia and China might want to launch someday, as well as at the constraints imposed by America's allies. This still left one puzzle and one serious tension. The document proposes a strategy capable of deterring all challengers and of carrying out interventions anywhere, but it provided little guidance about where the more dangerous challenges

---

[2] See David Armstrong, "Dick Cheney's Song of America," *Harper's Magazine*, October 2002, 78–83.

and the more necessary interventions might occur. It soon became clear, for example, that Powell had no intention to intervene in Yugoslavia, prompting Mrs. Albright, then Clinton's UN representative, to ask him what he was keeping his forces for. The tension was between this implicit ideal of a liberation of U.S. force from restraints, and the agreements, based on reciprocity, reached with so many governments in the previous forty-plus years. It was not just a turn to a doctrine of the national interest pure and simple, now that the Cold War no longer required alliances and an idealistic stance, but something radically new that led away from the Wilsonian syndrome: it called on the United States neither (obviously!) to cultivate its own garden, nor to pursue a world mission by leading others in directions acceptable to them, through multilateral organizations defining and legitimizing the common goals. Exceptionalism now meant being, remaining, and acting as the only superpower, and its substance was capabilities, not ideals and missions.

Let us look more closely at this new exceptionalism. When George W. Bush came to power, the doctrine that seemed to be in favor was a return to Realism: a concentration on those conflicts that could impair the global, or important regional, balances of power, a retreat from involvement in conflicts devoid of such significance (as in Africa), or hopeless (such as the Palestinian issue). However, this is not what prevailed. Already before 9/11/2001, we find a remarkable mix of "sovereignism" (an avatar of the old isolationism's suspiciousness) and distrust of the opinion of others. The rejection of the Kyoto Protocol, the withdrawal from the ABM treaty, the scuttling of the land-mines treaty and of the comprehensive test ban treaty: most of these marks of defiance of the UN had appeared before George W. Bush came to power, when Congress was already in Republican hands. The extraordinary vendetta conducted—largely but not exclusively by John Bolton—against the International Criminal Court brought out not only the Bush administration's paranoia about how a malevolent UN and Court could indict innocent American soldiers and officers, but how punitive the United States could become against states (allies or not) unwilling to meet U.S. demands. As Michael Ignatieff has quipped, here exceptionalism meant exemptionism.

What are the new exceptionalists' main arguments? One—rather bizarre—insists on the idea that the U.S. Constitution is the law of the land, excluding any kind of superior law—such as international law—and any transfer, pooling, or delegation of sovereignty (a British judge commented that even Mrs. Thatcher had subscribed to such transfers to the European Union; so had General de Gaulle). Then, there is the theme of benevolent imperialism, developed in particular by Robert Kagan, who has called the United States "a Behemoth with a conscience." Kagan offers valid criticisms of the new "Kantian" Europe, arguing that it is toothless and preoccupied by "challenges" such as immigration and ethnic conflicts; whereas mighty America focuses on threats. But these criticisms are mixed, in the same article, with a great deal of condescending hubris: he explains that the new sense of "civilian" mission of the Europeans is made possible by the military power and presence of the United States and expresses only their own weakness.[3] A third argument, presented by Michael Reisman, states that the United States, being, by its might, responsible for world order, is justified in rejecting those parts of international law that would make order more difficult;[4] thus he gives to the United States the right to decide what parts contribute to world order and what parts do not—a strange position for a professor of law. Finally, there is the argument of brute force. The United States has it in abundance, while others do not; hence allies, when they do not bend to the will of the United States, are both nuisances and unnecessary. International law and organizations are constructs that can be discarded whenever they stand in the path of American power. This case has been made by John Bolton and Donald Rumsfeld; in their view U.S. might is at the service of a very narrowly defined national interest, which excludes humanitarian flings. It is clear that those arguments all agree on downgrading restraints and on preserving American preponderance, even though opinions on the nature of America's mission range from a responsibility for world order to pure self-interest.

Who are the proponents of these ideas? They are, on the whole, variants of familiar types, the stock figures of American exceptionalism. What is new is that they are extreme in their conviction that the United States is the only country that matters. There are the sheriffs, who see the world through the epic *High Noon* with the eyes of Carl Schmitt—a world in which politics is seen as a struggle for power between foes and friends. In this sense, they are the heirs of the Cold War, with whose ending they credit Reagan. They are suspicious of diplomacy: in the Cold War days, they distrusted arms control and found Kissinger, with his policy of détente, too soft. Now that the United States is the sole superpower, they deem allies less necessary and insist on a very selfish notion of the national interest. As Miss Rice has said, the role of the U.S. army is not to conduct children into the kindergarten of troubled countries. A second group is that of the imperialists with a good conscience, because the United States

---

[3] See Robert Kagan, "Power and Weakness," *Policy Review* 113 (June–July 2002): 3–28. Kagan also mocks France's "punching far above his weight class" (*Washington Post*, November 3, 2002, B 07). What would, in 1940–45, de Gaulle have obtained for France, if he hadn't "punched above its weight class"? Can the United States today, with all its power, really dominate the world?

[4] See W. Michael Reisman, "The United States and International Institutions," *Survival*, Winter 1999–2000, 62–80, at 63, 66–71, and 75 especially.

offers others the public good of order and pays the price of preserving it. They share with the previous group a desire for "moral clarity," for a world in black-and-white, divided between the good, represented by the United States, and the bad; by contrast, Reinhold Niebuhr, once so influential, saw a world of multiple moral ambiguities.

Both these groups were well represented in the Reagan administration and had populated the Committee on the Present Danger of the late 1970s. The sheriffs were disappointed by the turn of Reagan from his "evil empire" days to his embrace of Gorbachev, which softened the Soviet Empire's fall. The imperialists—men like Charles Krauthammer or William Kristol—had been frustrated by the (in their eyes truncated) ending of the Gulf War in 1991. These two groups react to the new challenges and troubles as displaced, partly triumphant but also partly scared, ex–Cold Warriors who behave a bit like Kafka's beast in the burrow: they see threats everywhere. A third group is less important in foreign affairs, except insofar as it shares the Manichaean vision: those for whom the world is a contest pitting America's traditional conservative and religious values against all those who attack them, be they modern secular and dissolute liberals or Islamic fundamentalists. These are the American fundamentalists.

To these clans, one has to add a group that could be called "friends of Israel," who believe in the identity of interests between the Jewish state and the United States: both are democracies; both are surrounded by foes; both need to rely on force to survive. Israel is seen as the one sturdy ally in a crucial area in which Israel's enemies are either also America's enemies or else very dubious and flawed allies and clients of Washington. These men and women look at foreign policy through the lenses of a dominant concern: is it good or bad for Israel? They are a potent force in American politics. Never in very good odor at the State Department— since 1947—they are now well ensconced in the civilian offices of the Pentagon, around such men as Paul Wolfowitz, Richard Perle, and Douglas Feith.

IV

A discerning reader might object that many of my new exceptionalists are no more than Realists drunk with America's new might as the only superpower. This is true, but whereas the lesson of past Realists (Niebuhr, Morgenthau, Kennan, even Kissinger) had been the kind of discerning prudence and moderation Thucydides had praised, the new voices are exceptional in their paean to American might; many of the more tradi-

tional Realists, in academia and in government, are worried by the excesses of the present ones, so much closer to Alcibiades than to Pericles.

Moreover, things changed after September 11. Before that traumatic
day, the new exceptionalism was a doctrine in search of a cause, or one
defining its cause as America's own national interest. After September 11,
it found its cause, just as the post–World War II United States had found
its in the Cold War. It was the war on global terrorism, on the terrorists
and on those states that protected them. This was going to be the rationale
of the Bush presidency, the great simplifier, the chief new foreign policy
doctrine. It had the advantage of providing a lever for domestic mobilization, diversion from controversial domestic issues, and increase in the
powers of the Executive, given the shocking discovery of palpable vulnerability. It flattered the exceptionalists of all tendencies by emphasizing the
indispensable role of the United States, and it appealed especially to the
more idealistic ones by stressing that the defense against terror, America's
cause, was also the world's cause: self-interest and morality, power and
values, the sheriff and the missionary, were back together.

But there were signal difficulties. Already during the Cold War, many
issues could not be squeezed into the corset of the Soviet-American conflict. Could all important issues now be fitted into the new straitjacket,
and could those issues be treated by primarily military means (two questions raised by then French foreign affairs minister Hubert Védrine)? The
phenomenon of terrorism is extraordinarily heterogeneous. If terrorism
means deliberate attacks on the innocent, one would have to amalgamate
the gangs of "private" terrorists with state terrorism (carpet bombings,
totalitarian terror, etc.), as well as conflating the multiplicity of reasons
for the resort to terror: the will to self-determination, as in the case of the
Palestinians or the Chechens; a fight over territory, as in Kashmir; a form
of domestic action against a repressive regime, as in the Sudan and in the
Algeria of the 1990s; a religious holy war, such as that of Al Qaeda, and
so forth. Obviously one size doesn't fit all, and concentrating on the acts
of terror at the expense of the causes could well contribute to the global
destabilization sought by the terrorists.

Another difficulty is the choice of a method to combat them. Should it
be through a coalition of states, or—given their own diversity of regimes
and situations—should it be primarily America's war? Both alternatives
seemed unpromising. Should the United States focus on the threats to
American lives and installations? This would have clashed with the new
verbal universalism of the doctrine. Being the sole superpower does not
help resolve such issues.

Moreover, there is the danger of a slippery slope, of a constant extension of the new "war." From September 11 on, the Bush administration
widened the war against transnational terrorists into a war against the

regimes that gave them shelter—but hasn't Al Qaeda found hiding places in a very large number of states, the United States included? A much more controversial extension has been that from terrorism to states with weapons of mass destruction, but only those hostile to the United States—not, for instance, Israel, Pakistan, or India. This makes world order even more shaky; it incites others to use the new American doctrine for their own very special ends: the Indians against Pakistan, the Russians against Chechen rebels and occasionally Georgia, the Sharon government against not only Palestinian terrorists but the Palestinian Authority. This blurs the distinctions a more discerning United States should be able to observe. The war on terrorism becomes a vast tent under which all kinds of settlements of accounts can fit—including our own quarrel with the bizarre "axis of evil." Within a year of Bush's invidious characterization of three very different states, he has been obliged to diversify American responses in order to limit the dangers to peace and the risk of American "imperial overstretch." At present, Iran is largely left to the UN and to a European triumvirate, and North Korea is being treated with diplomacy; only Iraq is under the American gun.

Bush, during the campaign of 2000, had spoken about the need for modesty in foreign affairs. How far from this we are now is shown both by the doctrinaires of the new exceptionalism and by the final avatar of the 1992 defense draft: the new "National Security Strategy of the United States of America," dated September 2002. It is something of a hodgepodge, speaking about primacy *and* balance of power, using also traditional Wilsonian language ("we will actively work to bring the hope of democracy, development, free markets, and free trade to every corner of the world"). It talks about organizing coalitions, but also about not hesitating to act alone for self-defense. Still, in the main, it codifies all the new aspects of exceptionalism: the doctrine of preemption, so as to destroy threats before they reach U.S. borders (while warning others not to use preemption as a pretext for aggression); the emphasis on the deadly threat of rogue states that try to acquire weapons of mass destruction, and that "reject basic human values and hate the U.S. and everything for which it stands"; the promise to maintain the capability needed to defeat any attempt by any state to impose its will on the United States and its allies, and to dissuade potential adversaries from building up their forces to equal or surpass the power of the United States; and last, but clearly not least, the determination to protect U.S. nationals from the International Criminal Court.

The promise of preemption, which the UN Charter rules out as a form of aggression, except when an aggression is obviously imminent, is a formula for chaos, if it becomes a frequent claim by others, and if disputes break out about how urgent the need for anticipatory self-defense really is. The document never refers to the UN as a body whose endorsement would be needed—clearly, it would be the United States that would judge on both the legitimacy of its own preventive acts of force, and on that of others. The exceptionalists are protected by their good conscience, which does antedate Bush: it was Mrs. Albright who described the United States as the indispensable nation that sees farther than the lesser breeds. The whole new doctrine is pervaded by the view that not only do we see farther, we can better distinguish what is good and bad, and others are not to be allowed to act like us.

This imperial conception risks plunging the United States into a morass of double standards. For this administration, Palestinian terror is bad, but Sharon's attacks on Palestinian civilians are, at worst, imprudent; proliferators are bad if they are anti-American tyrants, and thus candidates for American preemption, but not otherwise. It is fortunate that we did not practice this doctrine on the USSR in the 1940s or China in the 1960s. As Pierre Hassner has noted, the United States pressured Serbia into sending Milošević to the Hague tribunal but refuses to accept the jurisdiction of the International Criminal Court for itself.[5] The reduction of international politics to the fight against enemies of the United States raises in acute form the problem of unsavory allies: after all, many terrorists hate us not because of our democratic values and system, because of what we are, but because of what we *do*, or what they think we do: because of our policies that support antidemocratic regimes. To be sure, we vaguely promise democracy for all, but short of universal intervention we cannot reach that goal—and even with universal intervention we would have trouble maintaining democracy in countries that have no experience of it. Indeed, if our goal is really not just rhetorical but genuine, reaching for it would destroy many of our alliances and, by revolutionizing and depacifying world affairs, actually risk wounding the process of economic globalization for which the United States also stands.

In sum, the Bush doctrine means more than the emancipation of a colossus from constraints that are based on an ideal, and on the practical benefits, of reciprocity—constraints that the United States, for all its superiority, had restored and enshrined in networks of international and regional organizations after 1945. It amounts to a doctrine of global domination, inspired by the fact of U.S. might, founded on the assumption that America's values are universally cherished except by nasty tyrants and evil terrorists.

The design may be grandiose, but there is something breathtakingly unrealistic about this unilateralist power and grand exceptionalism

---

[5] See Pierre Hassner, *The United States: The Empire of Force or the Force of Empire*, Chaillot Papers No. 54 (September 2002): 41 ff.

coated in all too familiar moralism—what Hassner has called "Wilsonianism in boots."[6] There are two main obstacles. One is the world itself,
and the other the U.S. public. The world is not reducible to two cleavages—between terrorists and antiterrorists, between democratic and nondemocratic regimes; this is clearly demonstrated by U.S. alliances, and
occasional unilateral interventions—for instance, in Central America. We
have helped terrorists abroad, when we deemed them useful, even aiding
the Taliban against the Soviets; some of our allies, from Guatemala to
Pakistan, have practiced state terrorism on a grand scale. Charles Maier
reminds us that empires have always had troubles with those excluded
from their benefits, both inside and outside their borders.[7] Just as Cold
War "globalists" never paid enough attention to the regional and local
causes of conflicts, our exceptionalists, today, pay far too little attention
to such problems as development or the environment, whose relative
neglect (in the latter case) or dogmatic treatment (in the former) feed
hostility against the United States. Going way beyond the banalities of
the National Security Strategy document, they have, under the rubric of
"regime change," promised an energetic effort at replacing tyrannical regimes with democracies; this, if attempted, would not only topple friendly
tyrants but manifest a blind hubris: we don't have the skill or knowledge
to manipulate the domestic politics of a large number of other countries,
to tell others who their leaders should or should not be, or to "improve"
the world by projecting on them a model of democracy that has worked—
not without upheavals—in the rich and multicultural United States
but has little immediate relevance in much of the present world. "Regime
change" in Germany and Japan required a prolonged occupation
and came out of a total war. These are not the circumstances of today.
What we would see as a selfless or benevolent policy of democratization
would be received as a policy of satellitization and clientelism. Even
Palestinian reformers did not respond kindly to George W. Bush's
call for a displacement or replacement of Arafat, whose waning power
was bolstered by Bush's excommunication.

Here is where the other flaw lies: the misfit between this democratic
imperialism (a fine contradiction in terms, from the start) and the American polity. A strategy of frequent preemptive use of force and of domestic
restrictions on public liberties necessitated by the global wars against evil
is unlikely to get public support for very long, especially if the claims for
prosperity and well-being are pushed behind the necessity of winning
these wars; today's would-be imperialists cannot simply rely on exploiting

---

[6] Ibid., 43.

[7] Charles Maier, "An American Empire?" *Harvard Magazine*, November–December
2002, 20–31.

the resources of others. Sooner rather than later, the public will suffer from battle fatigue, especially if its officials continue to explain simultaneously that the United States is the most powerful nation in history, and that it is the most threatened. A world order based on American might, but whose imperial master has little enthusiasm for peacekeeping operations, and little patience with nation building, would be doomed. A world order, to have a chance of stability, and especially if it is threatened by pervasive terrorism, would require among its states a code of cooperation, rules of behavior and engagement (as during the Cold War), and restraints in order not to appear even more threatening than the enemies they hope to defeat by a mix of violence and incantations. But, alas, all the new exceptionalism offers is a mix of force and faith—a huge force that often is not usable or is counterproductive, and a grandiose faith in the appeal of an American model that is a cause of resentment as well as of admiration—and of envy, closer to the former than to the latter. Taming a tempestuous world, overcoming its uncertainties, by military power and a variety of bribes would be insufficiently effective abroad, and increasingly unacceptable at home.

V

Iraq was seen by the new exceptionalists as the best place to test the new doctrine: it had a horrid regime, a record of aggressions and of violations of UN demands, a patient and relentless quest for weapons of mass destruction. What better case could be found? If the United States should succeed, even alone (or with only Mr. Blair), in destroying Saddam and his arsenal, what a wonderful lever for transforming the whole Middle East, for furthering modernization in the Muslim world, for assuring the victory in that world of the reasonable over the rabid, and for a settlement of the Israeli-Palestinian issue on terms more favorable to Israel than those that Barak had appeared to offer Arafat, or those that Clinton had offered at Taba? What Mark Danner has called "a vision of great sweep and imagination: comprehensive, prophetic, evangelical— . . . wholly foreign to the modesty of 'containment' " (which was the "ideology of a status quo power") signals a determination "to remake the world" and to deal with the "evil of terror" by "making new the entire region from which it springs."[8] It may be this vision that inspired the new exceptionalists to focus on Iraq, whereas an attack on North Korea does not have the same potential for transforming a whole unstable and dangerous area. Nor

[8] Mark Danner, "The Struggles of Democracy and Empire," *New York Times*, Op-ed, October 9, 2002, A-31.

does it have oil, certainly a potent factor in the drive to oust Saddam at a time when the Saudi alliance is in trouble. But what if the risks exceed the expected gains?

That Saddam Hussein was an evil man and a threat to his neighbors and to U.S. interests is undeniable. But was it a threat that called for and justified preventive action? What were the risks of acting now? Were there alternatives worth trying?

Iraq's alleged arsenal of weapons of mass destruction and its quest for nuclear arms were worrisome but not unique. Saddam was not suicidal; under U.S. attack, he was much more likely to resort to deploying these against either U.S. forces or Israel. We hesitate to "preempt" against North Korea because that action could incinerate Seoul. Indeed, we hesitate to impose on it sanctions comparable to those we have applied to Iraq, because North Korea could respond by accelerating its nuclear program. Iraq, "as far as nuclear weapons are concerned, is much less of a threat now than it was in 1991."[9] If Saddam had still had weapons of mass destruction, our attempt to eliminate him and his weapons might well have provoked the disaster we were saying we wanted to prevent. We contained the Soviet Union, its huge army, and its enormous weapons for almost fifty years.

Indeed the risks of such an attempt were very high. The case against it was both political and moral. The burden of proof lay on those who told us that we'd win easily, that Saddam's regime would crumble, and that democracy would then prevail in a liberated nation. Even if official optimism was based on more than wishful thinking (remember Vietnam!), the aftermath of victory was likely to be chaos and violence—and so it proved to be. Moreover, the war was fought on false pretenses: the intelligence services' misinformation about weapons of terror, and the government's assertions about links between Saddam and Al Qaeda. The opposition to Saddam remains divided—not only the Kurdish one. It is untested and devoid of experience in democratic rule and traditions. A U.S. administration with deep doubts about nation building and very little help from other nations has been stuck with running a vast Muslim country, racked by internal ethnic and religious divisions and aspirations for revenge. This has fostered more anti-Americanism and terrorism in the Muslim world. Indeed, the unilateralism of the administration risked, if the United States acted alone, shaking many of our carefully built alliances—in Europe and in the Middle East. If we wanted them to last and to help, our interest required that we concentrate on the Israeli-Palestinian issue, and on the "war" on terrorism, *before* we turned on Iraq; indeed, for some of the

---

[9] Norman Dombey, "What Has He Got?" *London Review of Books* 24:20 (October 17, 2002).

hawks in the administration one of the attractions of an early war on Iraq was that it would postpone and render even more difficult an evenhanded solution of the Palestinian problem.

Our unilateralists tell us that a superpower does not need to have its hands tied by international agreements and the United Nations. What they forget is that, as in the war on terrorism, we cannot achieve any of our goals alone, and it was the United States—the dominant power after 1945—that had the wisdom to understand this. An order founded on force and American beliefs alone does not create legitimacy or guarantee effectiveness, and it instigates anti-Americanism.

It is said that critics of a U.S. attack on Iraq failed to understand "the moral clarity" the president wants to impose on world politics. It is argued that Hussein's regime gave us a moral foundation for action. In Bryan Hehir's words, which have inspired the paragraphs that follow, "The invocation of moral reasoning for any contemplated policy decisions is to be welcomed as long as the complexity of moral issues is given adequate attention. Moral reasoning can indeed support military action, at times obligate such action. It also, equally importantly, can restrain or deny legitimacy to the use of force. To invoke the moral factor is to submit to the full range of its discipline."

The proposed strategy had three characteristics pertinent to its moral character. It was proposed as a preemptive strike, an intervention, and a unilateral action. Each characteristic raises serious moral questions. Preemption is morally conceivable but only within the most stringent limits. The case against it lies in the need to legitimate the use of force only in the most extreme conditions. Self-defense is the most obvious case, but the arguments proposing that a preemptive attack on Iraq met the self-defense standard were thin. Eroding the restraints against preemption—especially in the policy of the world's most powerful state—is a dubious moral move. Deterrence is more complex today, as the president has argued. But maintaining deterrence rather than preemption as an international standard is of the highest moral and legal importance.

There is a solid case for expanding moral legitimation of military action in cases of humanitarian intervention (Somalia, Rwanda, Kosovo), but the abiding value of the principle of nonintervention must be recognized and protected. Its basic role is to preserve order among sovereign states that acknowledge no higher political authority. Action against Iraq was clearly not a case—after many years of Hussein's tyranny—of humanitarian intervention. It was not comparable to the overthrow of the Taliban: Saddam's links with Al Qaeda are unconvincing. It was classic Great Power intervention, the principal case that nonintervention was meant to restrain. Like deterrence, nonintervention is designed to produce a conservative pattern of world politics, giving primacy to order and restraint.

Preemptive military intervention, save in the most extreme cases, erodes basic principles of international order.

Finally, a unilateral intervention, undertaken without authorization and with little or no allied support, intensified the moral and legal problem. Authorization for the use of force, embodied in the UN Charter, is an extension of the moral principle that force should not be invoked quickly or easily. Unilateralism, however much lauded as the prerogative of a Great Power by supporters of a preemptive strike, in fact omits other meanings of Great Power responsibility. Great Powers set precedents in world politics; hence each choice they make must be measured by the consequences of the precedent they set. Eroding deterrence, nonintervention, and authorization in one stroke is at least morally reckless.

There was an alternative to America's acting as the self-appointed policeman and promoter of "regime change" (a daunting task in areas unfamiliar with democracy, and something of a potential boomerang for a country like the United States, many of whose allies are highly dubious regimes whose support Washington needs). It was a collective, UN-supported policy of containment, entailing a strong border-monitoring system and the return of weapons inspectors to Iraq. Indeed, instead of acting alone and justifying military action by the risk of future Iraqi aggression, the United States ought to have pleaded for collective enforcement of past UN resolutions and the fulfillment by Iraq of obligations it had accepted after the Gulf War—specifically, the dismantling of weapons of mass destruction, to be followed by a lifting of sanctions. The United States, in other words, should have presented itself not as the lone sheriff but as the trustee of the society of states. The greatest chance of success in the task of eliminating Iraq's arsenal lay not in attacking Saddam but in creating a coalition on behalf of the objectives most states had subscribed to—*not* in acting alone, entangled in difficulties with allies and encumbered by the Israeli-Palestinian issue. The administration, obviously divided, seemed to have begun to understand this by going to the Security Council in September 2002, but it still insisted on preserving the possibility of unilateral action either if the UN didn't meet American demands or if the Iraqis made the inspections impossible.

The zealots who celebrate America's might and its benevolent imperialism forget that world order requires more than force, that a modern "empire" needs a consensus of states, and that it undermines its leadership by acting as a bully or a spoiler. As for eliminating evil regimes and leaders, especially when their successors might turn out to be no better, that is a form of arrogance the wiser conservatives and liberals in our past (and today) have always warned us against.[10]

---

[10] For another critical evaluation of the Iraq policy of the administration, see John Lewis Gaddis, "A Grand Strategy," *Foreign Policy*, November–December 2002, 50–57.

VI

Empire, or the dream of empire, has invariably gone to the heads of the imperialists. The dream of Wilsonian missionaries, deeply suspicious of any force other than that of world public opinion, still inspires many international agencies and nongovernmental organizations. The dream of a benevolent empire sustained by an illusion of the world's gratitude, but resting in fact only on the opinion of its own Establishment, and on a determination to avoid clear obligations, shows how wide the gap has become between America's ever more flattering self-image and the nation's image abroad, even in countries as long staunchly pro-American as Germany and Britain. Given the fact of America's preponderance in many forms of power, hard and soft (to use Joseph Nye's useful distinction),[11] the United States is bound to remain the most important state actor in the world. But there is a major difference between a leader and an empire: "The choice is between authoritarian, if not tyrannical rule tempered by anarchic resistance, and hegemony tempered by law, by concert and by consent."[12] The Bush administration remains a puzzle, with grandiose ideas floating over many improvisations. It has a State Department that still believes that imperial power can be maintained only if accompanied by a measure of reciprocity, even if it is partially illusory or contrived, in its obligations and dealings with others. It has, in the Pentagon and the White House, the new exceptionalists whose vision is one of an American worldwide "mission civilisatrice" deploying Roman Imperial, or Prussian, methods. And it has a president who talks mainly like the latter but often acts more cautiously. Maybe, as Andrew J. Balevich has written, "no one is really in charge; ours is an Empire without an Emperor,"[13] given the domestic restraints on the presidency. Such an Empire, functioning not by direct rule over others but in a world of states of all kinds, faces a Sisyphean task. It is not reassuring, either for Americans with little desire to be the twenty-first-century Romans or Britons, or for the foreign tribes. It is time to remember Vietnam. Nevertheless, there is no reason to believe that the lessons of Iraq will be more potent than those of Vietnam. Even if the recent form of exceptionalism—unilateral and militaristic—recedes, traditional views of American uniqueness in power and in vision, in attractiveness and in "can-do-ism," are still well represented all over the political class. It is time to reread Thucydides.[14]

[11] See Joseph S. Nye, Jr., *The Paradox of American Power: Why the World's Only Superpower Can't Go It Alone* (Oxford: Oxford University Press, 2002).

[12] Pierre Hassner, "Definitions, Doctrines, Divergences," *National Interest* 69 (Fall 2002): 34.

[13] In "New Rome, New Jerusalem," *Wilson Quarterly*, Summer 2002, 56.

[14] For more on Iraq, see my *Gulliver Unbound* (Boulder, CO: Rowman and Littlefield, 2004).

Chapter 9

Integrity-Anxiety?

FRANK I. MICHELMAN

Introduction

Twenty years ago, talk of American exceptionalism in the field of human rights would doubtless have been tinged, at least, with congratulation; these days, maybe not. Spoken today, the term probably insinuates a degree, at least, of insularity and smugness.[1]

Consider the movement dubbed "judicial globalization" by one of its chroniclers.[2] Ever more widely and regularly, judiciaries in democracies abroad have been treating each other's judgments as required reading in the work of domestic or regional bill-of-rights adjudication. From this movement the American Supreme Court has stood noticeably aloof, thus earning itself a mildly pariah status, at least in globalist circles. In their daily work of applying the guarantees in our Constitution's Bill of Rights to contested cases, our judges, by and large, have proceeded with what has been called a "parochial" disregard for parallel human-rights interpretations occurrent elsewhere in the world.[3] "Parochial" is not a term of endearment. (One might, after all, have spoken, more colorlessly, of "legal particularism.")[4]

Assertions of various sorts of exceptionalist chiseling by the United States are in the air. Do Americans (Grenada? Iraq?) claim undeserved, special privileges to act unilaterally against human rights violations abroad? Do Americans (the International Criminal Court?) obnoxiously

[1] But see Harold Hongju Koh, "Foreword: On American Exceptionalism," *Stanford Law Review* 55 (2003): 1479–1527, at 1480 (speaking of "the negative and the overlooked positive faces of American exceptionalism").

[2] See Anne-Marie Slaughter, "Judicial Globalization," *Virginia Journal of International Law* 40 (2000): 1103–24; Anne-Marie Slaughter, "A Global Community of Courts," *Harvard Journal of International Law* 44 (2003) 191–219.

[3] Slaughter, "Globalization," *supra* note 2, at 1117–18; see Lorraine E. Weinrib, "Constitutional Conceptions and Constitutional Comparativism," in *Defining the Field of Comparative Constitutional Law*, ed. Vicki C. Jackson and Mark Tushnet (Westport, CT: Praeger, 2002), 3–34, at 4 ("The constitutional jurisprudence of the United States has remained remarkably untouched by the new comparative constitutionalism").

[4] See Sujit Choudhry, "Globalization in Search of Justification: Toward a Theory of Comparative Constitutional Interpretation," *Indiana Law Journal* 74 (1999): 819–92, at 830.

resist submission of the conduct of U.S. agents or citizens to international systems of human rights inspection or control? Do Americans (the Convention on the Rights of the Child?) unreasonably withhold adherence from widely accepted and appealing international instruments setting human-rights standards meant to govern domestic lawmaking?

Those who find some substance in such charges may be prone to view the behaviors they describe as all stemming from a single, underlying attitudinal or behavioral complex—"exceptionalism," to wit—for which a single, social-psychological explanation may reasonably be sought, say, in terms of U.S. geopolitical situation past and present, U.S. culture past and present, or some combination thereof. The papers in the surrounding collection certainly do not rule out that sort of interpretation. Nor will this one. They do, though—as this will—show a receptiveness to more particularized sorts of explanations, opening the possibility that the sundry forms of "exemptionalist" behavior named, for example, in Michael Ignatieff's typology[5] are severally explainable by an assortment of different motives and other causes. Focusing on the American judiciary's widely observed tendency—perhaps recently relaxed, as we'll soon be considering—to disdain comparative study when engaged in construing our legally operative, domestic commitments in the field of rights, this chapter considers a line of possible explanation that would have little application to the other items on Ignatieff's charge sheet.

Note that the precise question here is not about any reluctance by the U.S. judiciary to treat positive-legal norms launched or pronounced from abroad as "a part of our law."[6] It is not, that is, about our judiciary's responses to claims that one or another transnational norm has become a binding rule of decision for American courts by force of treaty, convention, or some positive rule of U.S. or state law that directs the incorporation of customary international legal norms into U.S. domestic law, as components of that law.[7] Our concern is with the American judiciary's transactions with legal norms understood by all to have a strictly local provenance in what we call American constitutional law. Granted, it's not a clearly settled matter what goes to make up American constitutional law, or where one looks to find its content, but the following rough ac-

---

[5] See Michael Ignatieff's introduction to this volume.

[6] *The Paquete Habana*, 175 U.S. 677, 700 (1900). See Harold Hongju Koh, "International Law as Part of Our Law," *American Journal of International Law* 98 (2004): 43–47.

[7] Regarding the relation between treaties and indigenous constitutional rights, see Peter J. Spiro, "Treaties, International Law, and Constitutional Rights," *Stanford Law Review* 55 (2003): 1999–2028. Regarding customary international law as "a part of" American law, see Koh, "International Law," *supra* note 6; T. Alexander Aleinikoff, "International Law, Sovereignty, and American Constitutionalism: Reflections on the Customary International Law Debate," *American Journal of International Law* 98 (2004): 91–108.

count will serve for present purposes. As commonly understood by American jurists, American constitutional law is a body of legal doctrine produced by the decisions of U.S. state and federal courts engaged in construing and applying some combination of (a) a historically particular compendium of norm statements identified as the Constitution of the United States and (b) the precedents left by prior U.S. judicial and other official dealings with this same, accumulating and evolving (or unfolding) body of legal-doctrinal material. American constitutional law, then, is root-and-branch domestic law.

Now, it appears to many that a body of legal doctrine can retain its domesticity in the sense described, even while exposing itself quite deliberately to influence and persuasion from abroad. Take, for example, a U.S. court faced with deciding whether a certain sort of affirmative action measure violates *our* Constitution's strictures against race-based discrimination. The court—or so it is claimed—may find it relevant to know of any gathering consensus on the point among courts abroad deciding parallel questions under their countries' respective constitutions.[8] It may so find for reasons quite aside from any belief that the foreign consensus forges a rule (say) of customary international law that is, as such, in the least degree binding here.[9] We consider below what these other reasons might be. Suppose, for now, that cogent ones exist.

---

[8] In oral argument in *Gratz v. Bollinger*, 123 S. Ct. 2411 (2003), Justice Ruth Ginsburg addressed counsel arguing the case as follows: "[W]e're part of a world, and this problem is a global problem. Other countries operating under the same equality norm have confronted it. Our neighbor to the north, Canada, has, the European Union, South Africa, and they have all approved this kind of, they call it positive discrimination. Do we—they have rejected what you recited as the ills that follow from this. Should we shut that from our view at all or should we consider what judges in other places have said on this subject?" 2003 Trans Lexis 27, *23, cited in Mark Tushnet, "Transnational/Domestic Constitutional Law," *Loyola of Los Angeles Law Review* 37 (2003): 239–69, at 260 n. 104.

[9] Harold Koh and others doubt that a sharp boundary exists any longer in practice, or deserves to exist, between "international" and "foreign" (or "comparative") law from the standpoint of domestic adjudicators in human rights cases. See Koh, "International Law," *supra* note 6, at 53 & n. 74, citing Harold Hongju Koh, "The Globalization of Freedom," *Yale Journal of International Law* 26 (2001): 305–12; Stephen Breyer, "The Supreme Court and the New International Law" (address to American Society of International Law, 97th Annual Meeting, Washington, DC, April 4, 2003), available at http://www.supremecourtus-.gov/publicinfo/speeches/sp_04-04-03.html (cited and quoted in Koh, "International Law," *supra* note 6). This essay takes no position regarding such claims. We simply adopt the standpoint of those trying to assess or explain the relevance of foreign adjudications for American adjudicators, when those adjudicators themselves take their task to be that of deciding the meaning or application of strictly American constitutional-legal norms to the case at hand.

The relevance question, thus posed, has been the topic of a great deal of recent academic and judicial debate. Some recent American judicial debate is recalled briefly just below. Contributions to the academic debate to which I am indebted include Slaughter, works cited

In that case, exceptional reluctance by the American judiciary to pay heed to foreign constitutional law may seem in one way both the toughest to explain and the most embarrassing of all the types of U.S. exceptionalism in the field of human rights noted by Ignatieff and others. Unlike the rest, this one is not explicable as a simple reflex of American power, as just another hardheaded refusal by Americans to give up control over events that concern us, when we don't have to. For the question here does not appear to be one about control. It's not about submitting final decisions of our Supreme Court to review and possible reversal by some tribunal sitting in Strasbourg. It's not even about importing into American domestic law the abstract terms of some treaty whose concrete meanings are to be suggested—although not dictated—by a UN committee of experts. It's "only," one might say, about joining a discussion. It's "only" about plugging American judicial debates about the basic rights of people here, under our practices and laws, into a parallel global conversation, or call it a network of "cross-fertilization."[10]

The impression nevertheless persists that resistance by American justices to the idea of paying some heed to constitutional-legal practice across the world does, in fact, reflect their wish to preserve their institution's tight control over the content of American constitutional law against encroachment by other actors on the legal scene at home or abroad.[11] We can take the case either way. If we assume that control is not, in fact, felt to be at risk, the question is what remains to explain the resistance save sheer moral vanity and smugness. If we assume the opposite, the question becomes why so—it being far from obvious why members of an institution as august and entrenched as the American Supreme Court would feel threatened with a loss of control, merely as a result of letting themselves be seen attending to practice and opinion elsewhere, in the course of reaching what manifestly would still be their own legal conclusions.

---

supra note 2; Koh, "International Law," supra note 6; Koh, "Foreword," supra note 1; Vicki C. Jackson, "Narratives of Federalism: Of Continuities and Comparative Constitutional Experience," Duke Law Journal 51 (2001): 223–87, at 245–71; Sanford Levinson, "Looking Abroad When Interpreting the U.S. Constitution: Some Reflections," Texas International Law Journal 39 (2004): 353–65; Gerald L. Neuman, "The Uses of International Law in Constitutional Interpretation," American Journal of International Law 98 (2004): 82–90; Weinrib, supra note 3. Aside from its brief concluding speculation, this essay takes no position on the substantive question of relevance. Its main aim is to display one possible motivation for denials of relevance.

[10] Slaughter, "Global Community," supra note 2, at 202. Gerald Neuman calls this the "minimal" form of possible accommodation by national constitutional systems to the international human rights system. See Gerald L. Neuman, "Human Rights and Constitutional Rights: Harmony and Dissonance," Stanford Law Review 55 (2003): 1863–1900, at 1890.

[11] See Jackson, supra note 9, at 245–46.

In search of answers to both questions, I have taken a cue from Charles Fried. Remarking on an American judge's affirmation of the relevance of foreign law to the work of American constitutional adjudicators, Fried has warned that the result would be to expand the "universe" or "canon" of "authoritative materials" upon which American lawyers and judges base their constitutional-legal arguments and decisions.[12] Eventually, we'll consider why such an expansion might be thought undesirable, and in exactly what sense control might be threatened by its onset. As a preliminary matter, though, it will be necessary to survey the current state of the American debate in the wake of the very prominent, widely noted reference to foreign legal materials in the Supreme Court's June 2003 decision in the case of *Lawrence v. Texas*.[13]

"Comparative Analysis" in U.S. Constitutional Adjudication: The Recent Intracurial Debate

A Selective, Brief History[14]

In the 1958 case of *Trop v. Dulles*,[15] the U.S. Supreme Court had to decide whether an Act of Congress prescribing involuntary loss of U.S. nationality, as a consequence of conviction of the crime of desertion of the military forces in time of war, is compatible with our Constitution's prohibition of cruel and unusual punishments.[16] Five justices answered "no," making up a majority of the Court. Chief Justice Earl Warren filed an opinion for four of them, construing the Eighth Amendment in terms that have since achieved a canonical status in American constitutional law.[17] Just as the amendment's words are not "precise," Warren wrote, its scope is not "static." The amendment must "draw its meaning," he reasoned, from "the evolving standards of decency that mark the progress of a maturing society."[18]

---

[12] Charles Fried, "Scholars and Judges: Reason and Power," *Harvard Journal of Law and Public Policy* 23 (2000): 807–32, at 819.

[13] 123 S. Ct. 2472.

[14] For an incisive account of the recent history, see Tushnet, *supra* note 8. For more inclusive catalogs than will be found here of "foreign" citations by current and recent members of the Supreme Court, and relevant extracurial statements by them, see Jackson, *supra* note 9, at 247–54; Koh, "Foreword," *supra* note 1, at 1514–16 & nn. 111, 113–14; Koh, "International Law," *supra* note 6. The latest round in this history, the Supreme Court's decision in *Roper v. Simmons*, March 1, 2005, came too late for inclusion here.

[15] 356 U.S. 86.

[16] See U.S. Const. amend. 8.

[17] Justice William Brennan added a fifth vote for unconstitutionality, but he did so in a separate, concurring opinion and cannot be counted a signatory to any of the specific argumentation in Warren's opinion. See 356 U.S. at 105 (Brennan, J., concurring).

[18] 356 U.S. at 100.

Standards of decency for punishments, the Warren plurality evidently thought, must have some reference to the consequences of a punishment for its bearer. In the course of describing the baleful consequences of loss of nationality, the chief justice's opinion remarked that statelessness is "a condition deplored in the international community of democracies," citing a UN document to prove the point.[19] "The civilized nations of the world," Warren continued, "are in virtual unanimity that statelessness is not to be imposed as punishment for crime."[20] Specifically, "the United Nations' survey of the nationality laws of 84 nations of the world reveals that only two countries, the Philippines and Turkey, impose denationalization as a penalty for desertion."[21] In the recent annals of the Supreme Court, Warren's *Trop* opinion appears to be an early gesture toward (I follow Anne-Marie Slaughter) globalization of domestic bill-of-rights adjudication.[22]

Warren devoted only four short pages of his opinion to the proposition that denationalization, considered as a form of punishment, is "cruel and unusual" in the applicable, legal sense.[23] In that brusque treatment, the appeal to opinion and practice in other countries—presumably as indicative of "evolving standards of decency"—plainly is load-bearing; in fact, little else in the way of substantive argument is to be found there. Given later developments, it is interesting that this key resort by the *Trop* plurality to foreign legal material raised no eyebrows elsewhere in the Court. Justice Felix Frankfurter's dissenting opinion (for four justices) not only made no objection to this method, it connived in the use of it.[24] With the same scholarly authorities before him that Warren invoked, Frankfurter found it apt to remark that "many civilized nations impose loss of citizenship for indulgence in designated prohibited activities,"[25] and that "some

[19] 356 U.S. at 102 & n. 35. Warren cited *Study on Statelessness*, U. N. Doc. No. E/1112, along with academic secondary material.

[20] 356 U.S. at 102. Granting that some countries prescribe denationalization in the event that their nationals engage in conduct that directly insinuates repudiation of home allegiance, that is different, Warren explained, from using it as "punishment for crime." Id. at 102–03 & n. 137.

[21] 356 U.S. at 103, citing *Laws Concerning Nationality*, U. N. Doc. No. ST/LEG/SER.B/ 4 379, 461 (1954).

[22] For recollection of much earlier engagements by American courts in this practice and that of looking to customary international law or the law of nations for some of the content of "our law," see Koh, "International Law," *supra* note 6.

[23] Much of the rest of Warren's opinion went to establishing that the act in question imposed expatriation as a "punishment" and not as a mere "regulation of citizenship."

[24] Frankfurter has been called "probably the twentieth century's foremost U.S. judicial practitioner of explicit comparative analysis as an aid to constitutional interpretation," largely because of his references to historic English rules and understandings in procedural due process cases. See Jackson, *supra* note 9, at 248–49.

[25] Id. at 126 (citing *Laws Concerning Nationality*, *supra* note 21).

countries have made wartime desertion result in loss of citizenship—native-born or naturalized."[26]

Fast-forward twenty years. In *Coker v. Florida* (1977),[27] another Eighth Amendment case, another plurality looked abroad for support of its conclusion that a criminal sentence—it was a death sentence for rape—would be so grossly "disproportionate" and "excessive" a punishment as to be cruel and unusual within the meaning of the amendment.[28] Citing the *Trop* plurality, Justice Byron White's opinion for the *Coker* plurality vouched—in a footnote—for the relevance of an international "climate of opinion" to a standards-of-decency appraisal in Eighth Amendment litigation.[29] No other justice objected to the extramunicipal reference.

In *Enmund v. Florida* (1982),[30] the question was whether the Eighth Amendment would permit execution of a "constructive aider and abettor" to a robbery/murder (i.e., the driver waiting in the getaway car, who was not shown to have planned or intended a killing). This time—for the first time—it was a clear majority of the Court who, through White's opinion (answering "no"), affirmed the relevance to U.S. Eighth Amendment analysis of the climate of international opinion. Again, a footnote was the vehicle, and it simply echoed the *Coker* plurality's footnote that in turn had fed off the plurality opinion in *Trop*.[31] Again, no objection to

[26] Id.

[27] 433 U.S. 584.

[28] Id. at 592. The four plurality justices (White, Stewart, Blackmun, and Stevens) were joined by two others (Brennan and Marshall) whose separate opinions said only that they regarded the death penalty as unconstitutional, period, and one other (Powell) who found the death penalty unconstitutional when imposed for a rape that was not attended by notable (additional) brutality or serious bodily injury to the victim, thus making a majority of seven for unconstitutionality. See id. at 600 (concurring opinions of Brennan and Marshall, JJ.); id. at 601 (Powell, J., concurring in part and dissenting in part).

[29] See id. at 596 n. 10: "In Trop v. Dulles . . . the plurality took pains to note the climate of international opinion concerning the acceptability of a particular punishment. It is thus not irrelevant here that out of 60 major nations in the world surveyed in 1965, only 3 retained the death penalty for rape where death did not ensue. United Nations, Department of Economic and Social Affairs, Capital Punishment 40, 86 (1968)."

[30] 458 U.S. 782.

[31] Id. at 796 n. 22: " '[The] climate of international opinion concerning the acceptability of a particular punishment' is an additional consideration which is 'not irrelevant.' Coker v. Georgia, 433 U.S. 584, 596, n. 10 (1977). It is thus worth noting that the doctrine of felony murder has been abolished in England and India, severely restricted in Canada and a number of other Commonwealth countries, and is unknown in continental Europe. ALI, Model Penal Code § 210.2, pp. 39–40 (Off. Draft and Revised Comments 1980) (hereafter Model Penal Code). It is also relevant that death sentences have not infrequently been commuted to terms of imprisonment on the grounds of the defendant's lack of premeditation and limited participation in the homicidal act. See Wolfgang, Kelly, & Nolde, Comparison of the Executed and Commuted Among Admissions to Death Row, 53 J. Crim. L. C. & P. S. 301, 310 (1962)."

looking outward in this way, in this context, came forth from any other justice. Subterraneously, as it were, a postwar vein of globalist sensibility was being leached, bit by bit, into American constitutional-legal scripture, a.k.a. *The United States Reports*. Drip, drip, drip.

The trail of footnotes lengthened in *Thompson v. Oklahoma* (1988).[32] An opinion by Justice John Stevens, for a four-justice plurality, found that a punishment of death for a fifteen-year-old murderer would contravene evolving standards of decency, hence was constitutionally prohibited.[33] Above the line, Stevens claimed support from "views that have been expressed by respected professional organizations, by other nations that share our Anglo-American heritage, and by the leading members of the Western European community" (detailing them).[34] As for the subtended footnote, you probably could write it yourself: "We have previously recognized the relevance of the views of the international community in determining whether a punishment is cruel and unusual. See Trop v. Dulles, . . . ; Coker v. Georgia, . . . ; Enmund v. Florida. . . ."[35] Drip, drip, drip, drip.

This time, though—for the first time—the globalist move (if that is what it was) met resistance. It came in a dissenting opinion by Justice Antonin Scalia, who had joined the Court in 1986. Scalia planted his own counterfootnote:

> The plurality's reliance upon Amnesty International's account of what it pronounces to be civilized standards of decency in other countries . . . is totally inappropriate as a means of establishing the fundamental beliefs of this Nation. That 40% of our States do not rule out capital punishment for 15-year-old felons is determinative of the question before us here, even if that position contradicts the uniform view of the rest of the world.[36]

"We must never forget," Scalia went on, "that it is a Constitution for the United States of America that we are expounding."[37] Moreover, "the views of other nations . . . cannot be imposed upon Americans through the Constitution."[38]

Scalia took pains, even so, to reserve a space in American constitutional analysis for a proper use of information concerning normative opinion elsewhere. "The practices of other nations, particularly other democra-

---

[32] 487 U.S. 815.

[33] Justice O'Connor supplied a fifth vote for reversal of the death sentence, on the basis of more complicated reasoning that made no reference to extramunicipal materials. See id. at 848 (O'Connor J., concurring in the judgment).

[34] Id. at 830.

[35] Id. at 830–31 n. 31.

[36] Id. at 869–70 n. 4.

[37] Id.

[38] Id.

cies," Scalia wrote, "can be relevant to determining whether a practice uniform among our people is not merely a historical accident, but rather so 'implicit in the concept of ordered liberty' that it occupies a place not merely in our mores but, text permitting, in our Constitution as well."[39] In other words, the work of applying the Constitution may sometimes oblige the Court to decide, as best it can, whether an ostensible regularity in American institutional and legal practice is merely accidental or random, or rather is normatively grounded, inspired by American "mores." A congruence of the ostensible, American, practice regularity with prevailing (or historic) practice across the democratic world would be some evidence that the pattern truly is a reflection of contemporary *values*— American, if also more widely "democratic"—and not just a product of mindless habit. Scalia's reservation thus, in some nontrivial degree, assimilates *our* mores to those of the world's democracies at large. It posits, however guardedly, American participation in a more encompassing community of normative opinion.

Scalia's antiglobalist side prevailed in *Stanford v. Kentucky* (1989).[40] The question, again, was whether the Eighth Amendment broadly precludes American governments from imposing and executing sentences of death upon murderous juveniles, for this occasion defined as persons younger than eighteen years of age. The answer was that it does not. Scalia, for the majority, agreed that the Court's precedents bound it to rule against the constitutional permissibility of any punishment it might find to be "contrary to the 'evolving standards of decency that mark the progress of a maturing society' " (even if that punishment would not have been considered out-of-bounds by Americans at the time the Eighth Amendment was ratified).[41] However, a survey of current American (state and federal) statutes, and of the recent sentencing requests and choices of American prosecutors and juries, revealed to the Court no contemporary "consensus" against execution of sixteen- and seventeen-year-olds; and that, for the Court, was the end of the matter.[42]

In dissent, Justice William Brennan presented materials to show that execution of juveniles is "overwhelmingly disapproved" around the world.[43] The "relevance" of such a fact had been recognized by "our

---

[39] Id. (citing *Palko v. Connecticut*, 302 U.S. 319, 325 (1937) (Cardozo, J.)). Scalia reissued this declaration in his opinion for the Court in *Stanford v. Kentucky*, 492 U.S. 361, 370 n. 1 (1989).

[40] 492 U.S. 361.

[41] Id. at 369 (quoting *Trop v. Dulles*, 356 U.S. 86, 101 (1958) (plurality opinion)). That aspect of the *Trop* plurality's opinion, it seems, had ripened into confirmed doctrine.

[42] Id. at 377, 380.

[43] Id. at 390 (Brennan, J., dissenting).

cases," Brennan added (citing *Thompson, Enmund, Coker,* and *Trop*).[44] Rejoining, Scalia bypassed the question of what "the cases" may or may not have recognized.[45] He simply framed a flat disavowal of the relevance proposition, on behalf of a current majority. "We emphasize," Scalia wrote for his majority, that "it is *American* conceptions of decency that are dispositive" for Eighth Amendment purposes, and accordingly "we . . . reject" the contention that other nations' sentencing practices are "relevant." That would seem to have settled the matter.[46]

Our story now moves to 1996 and the case of *Printz v. United States.*[47] For the first time in the postwar period, Supreme Court justices pointedly debated the relevance of extramunicipal materials to American constitutional adjudication outside the Eighth Amendment context. In fact, the *Printz* case involved not a personal (or "human") rights claim at all but rather an issue of American governmental arrangement on which foreign sources might have seemed relatively unlikely to shed a useful light. The question was whether Congress could impose duties of federal law enforcement on state and local officials, without transgressing a constitutional-legal limit on its power to compromise state-government autonomy. A Court majority, Scalia writing, said no, basing its conclusion not on any specifically decisive constitutional text (there being none), but rather on a survey and analysis of historical understanding and prac-

[44] Id. at 389.

[45] Had he chosen to do so, Scalia might have observed that, in three of the four cases cited by Brennan, no majority of the Supreme Court had said or done anything at all to the point.

[46] Justice Sandra Day O'Connor joined this portion of Scalia's opinion. See 492 U.S. at 382 (O'Connor, J., concurring in part and concurring in the judgment). O'Connor later became a noted advocate of receptivity by American lawyers and judges to possible learning from foreign law and practice. In one published speech, she predicted approvingly an increasing frequency of attention by Supreme Court justices engaged in judicial review of legislation to "the decisions of other constitutional courts," with a view to possibly "discover[ing] ways of improving our own system." Sandra Day O'Connor, "Broadening Our Horizons: Why American Lawyers Must Learn about Foreign Law," 45-Sep Fed. Law. 20, 21 (1998). See also "Justices See Joint Issues with the E.U.," *Washington Post,* July 9, 1998, at A24 (cited in Slaughter, "Global Community," *supra* note 2, at 199). In her own practice as a judicial opinion writer (and joiner), O'Connor has seemingly been circumspect about granting to foreign legal materials a visible influence on American constitutional adjudication. I am aware of no opinion by O'Connor that refers to foreign materials, much less relies on them. I know of one occasion when she joined an opinion that does so (*Atkins v. Virginia,* discussed *infra*), three when she (for whatever reason) refrained from joining an opinion that does so although she agreed with its bottom line (*Thompson, Lawrence v. Texas,* discussed *infra,* and *Grutter v. Bollinger,* discussed *infra*), and two—both of them prior to 1997—when she joined opinions expressing hostility to doing so (*Stanford* and *Printz v. United States,* discussed *infra*).

[47] 521 U.S. 898.

tice, general features of American constitutional structure, and the Court's precedents.[48]

Dissenting, Justice Stephen Breyer looked abroad for assistance. "Some countries," Breyer observed, "have found that local control [and individual liberty are] better maintained through application of a principle that is the direct opposite of the principle the majority derives from the silence of our Constitution," and he went on to detail the claim, citing numerous scholarly authorities as well as the European Council.[49] Breyer stopped well short of suggesting that foreign practice could in any way be authoritative for American constitutional interpretation. He urged only that the experiences of other countries could shed "an empirical light" on "the consequences of different solutions to a common legal problem."[50] Breyer's argument simply was that experience abroad confirmed the practical nonnecessity, and hence suggested the unwisdom, of a judicially constructed, absolute rule against occasional congressional impressment of local officials into the performance of congressionally prescribed tasks.[51]

In a footnote, Scalia repulsed Breyer's suggestion. "We think," Scalia wrote, that "such comparative analysis [is] inappropriate to the task of interpreting a constitution, though it was of course quite relevant to the task of writing one."[52] Scalia gave no reason in support of the "inappropriate" proposition; he must have thought its truth self-evident. But he soon thereafter joined without comment an opinion by Chief Justice Rehnquist that quite pointedly relied on exactly the kind of "comparative analysis"—of the consequences of legal choices—that Breyer had urged in *Printz*. The case was *Glucksberg v. Washington*.[53] The question was whether the state had a sufficient governmental interest to justify its criminal ban on assisting suicide, as applied to physicians treating terminally ill patients who seek such assistance. The state, surmised Rehnquist, "may fear that permitting assisted suicide will start it down the path to voluntary and perhaps even involuntary euthanasia"[54]—a concern, he said, that was "supported by evidence about the practice of euthanasia in the Netherlands" which he then went on to detail, citing documentary sources, in a lengthy paragraph.[55]

---

[48] See id. at 905.

[49] Id. at 976–77.

[50] Id. at 977–78 (the common problem in this instance being that of "reconciling central authority with the need to preserve the liberty-enhancing autonomy of a smaller constituent governmental entity").

[51] See id. at 977–78.

[52] Id. at 935 n. 11.

[53] 521 U.S. 702.

[54] Id. at 732.

[55] See id. at 734.

Breyer returned to the fray in 1999. *Knight v. Florida*[56] was another Eighth Amendment case. Lower courts had denied prisoners' claims that execution after prolonged incarceration on death row (twenty-five years, in one of the cases) is constitutionally prohibited cruel and unusual punishment. Dissenting from the Court's decision to deny review, Breyer offered a batch of material showing that a great many countries, although not all, do rule out such treatment as impermissibly "cruel," "inhuman," or "degrading."[57] Emphasizing, again, that nothing in this material could possibly be binding on a judge construing the U.S. Constitution, Breyer thought it could still be "relevant and informative," just as, he said (citing *Enmund* and, with a bit of license, Stevens's plurality opinion in *Thompson*), "this Court" had "long considered it" to be.[58]

This time, it was Justice Clarence Thomas who rose to squelch the globalist impulse. He did so smartly, if without explaining what the positive objection is to a U.S. judge's looking to experience abroad, as he tries to figure out the correct application of U.S. constitutional law to debatable cases. The petitioners, Thomas wrote—and, by implication, Breyer— would not have had to beg support from "the European Court of Human Rights, the Supreme Court of Zimbabwe, the Supreme Court of India, or the Privy Council," had they been able to produce any out of "the American constitutional tradition" or "this Court's precedent."[59] Essentially the same colloquy between Justices Thomas and Breyer was replayed in *Foster v. Florida*,[60] where the Court again denied review in a case raising a claim very similar to that in *Knight*. The Court, said Thomas, had no business imposing "foreign moods, fads, or fashions on Americans" under cover of "Eighth Amendment jurisprudence."[61]

The pendulum apparently swung back in *Atkins v. Virginia* (2002),[62] a case holding that the death penalty is unconstitutionally excessive when imposed for a crime committed by a mentally retarded person. Into a majority opinion devoted mainly to a survey of practice in the American states, Stevens tucked a single sentence observing that "within the world community, the imposition of the death penalty for crimes committed by mentally retarded offenders is overwhelmingly disapproved."[63] Stevens

---

[56] 528 U.S. 990 (1999).

[57] See id. at 995–96 (Breyer, J., dissenting from the denial or certiorari).

[58] Id. at 996–97. "Willingness to consider foreign judicial views in comparable cases," Breyer added, "is not surprising in a Nation that from its birth has given a 'decent respect to the opinions of mankind.' " Id.

[59] See id. at 990 (Thomas, J., concurring in denial of certiorari).

[60] 123 S. Ct. 470 (2002).

[61] Id. at 360 n. * (Thomas, J., concurring in denial of certiorari).

[62] 536 U.S. 304.

[63] Id. at 316 n. 21.

claimed for this fact only a limited kind of relevance, and a kind that would seem to have fit neatly into Scalia's own reservation in *Thompson*.[64] The fact went, Stevens said (along with a lot of material regarding professional and other opinion in the United States), to showing that the American state legislative data centrally under survey reflected a broad social and professional consensus.[65] Even that was too much for the antiglobalist contingent to take lying down. Both Scalia and Rehnquist protested, in dissenting opinions joined by each other and by Thomas.[66]

Echoing and citing Scalia's *Stanford* opinion, Rehnquist claimed that admission of foreign legal-practice information to the Court's deliberations runs against both principles of democratic self-government and the Court's precedents.[67] Yes, there had been some Eighth Amendment stuff purporting to connect the climate of international opinion to judicial ascertainment of "evolving standards of decency," but that idea, Rehnquist said, had been overtaken by *Stanford*'s clear stipulation that *American* conceptions of decency were the only ones that counted.[68] Scalia added the cheering thought that the "'world community's'" notions of justice "are (thankfully) not always those of our people."[69]

All of which brings us to 2003 and *Lawrence v. Texas*.[70] Justice Anthony Kennedy's opinion for the Court listed sundry foreign legal sources in support of a decision to uphold a claim to a textually nonspecified American constitutional right to conduct consensual, adult, sexual relations free of state regulation. Kennedy's opinion, however, no more squarely bottomed its reading of the U.S. Constitution on the pitch of world-community opinion and practice than Breyer had proposed to do in *Printz* or *Knight*, or Stevens had done in *Atkins*.

Kennedy's main task, of course, was to make a positive case for the proposition that the Fourteenth Amendment due process clause protects the dimension of liberty at issue in the case before him, and that he did without reliance on foreign materials. A state must have a "legitimate

[64] See *supra* text accompanying note 39.

[65] 536 U.S. at 316 n. 21.

[66] O'Connor joined Stevens's majority opinion. See id. at 305. I include Rehnquist in the antiglobalist contingent despite his comparativist move in *Glucksberg* and his extracurial expression of a comparativist sentiment. See The Hon. William H. Rehnquist, "Constitutional Courts—Comparative Remarks (1989)," in *Germany and Its Basic Law: Past, Present and Future—a German-American Symposium*, ed. Paul Kirchhof and Donald P. Kommers (Baden-Baden: Nomos, 1993), 411, 412 (cited in Koh, "International Law," *supra* note 6).

[67] See id. at 322–23 (Rehnquist, C.J., dissenting).

[68] See id. at 325. Rehnquist also pointed out that the series of climate-of-opinion endorsements had all stemmed from the opinion of a mere plurality in *Trop*.

[69] Id. at 347 (Scalia, J., dissenting).

[70] 123 S. Ct. 2472.

interest" at stake, he said, before it may permissibly intrude its criminal laws into people's "personal and private lives," and Texas in this case didn't have any.[71] Kennedy relied heavily on a passage from Stevens's dissenting opinion in *Bowers v. Hardwick*,[72] which in turn relied exclusively on prior American decisions.

Beyond presenting that positive case for unconstitutionality (made-in-U.S.A.), Kennedy had to discredit *Bowers v. Hardwick*,[73] the precedent that stood so glaringly against him. Obviously proceeding on the theory that a precedent is the more open to reconsideration the worse reasoned it is, Kennedy went to town to show that *Bowers* was a botched job. Among the gaffes Kennedy charged against the *Bowers* majority was reliance on a premise that a legally protected status for sodomy would be contrary to the established ways of "Western" or "Judeo-Christian" civilization. Such reliance appeared expressly only in Chief Justice Warren Burger's concurring opinion,[74] but Kennedy evidently thought—or found it convenient to suppose—that it might also have been doing some work in White's opinion for the Court. "To the extent *Bowers* relied on values we share with a wider civilization," Kennedy wrote, that prop for its holding had been swept away by subsequent legal developments abroad.[75] As for Burger's references to civilizational history and tradition, they were

---

[71] See id. at 2484.

[72] See id. at 2183 (quoting *Bowers v. Hardwick*, 478 U.S 186, 216 (1986) (Stevens J., dissenting)): "Our prior cases make two propositions abundantly clear. First, the fact that the governing majority in a State has traditionally viewed a particular practice as immoral is not a sufficient reason for upholding a law prohibiting the practice; neither history nor tradition could save a law prohibiting miscegenation from constitutional attack. Second, individual decisions by married persons, concerning the intimacies of their physical relationship, even when not intended to produce offspring, are a form of 'liberty' protected by the Due Process Clause of the Fourteenth Amendment. Moreover, this protection extends to intimate choices by unmarried as well as married persons. 478 U.S., at 216 (footnotes and citations omitted)."

[73] 478 U.S. 186 (1986).

[74] *Bowers*, 478 U.S. at 196 (Burger, C.J., concurring).

[75] Id. at 2483: "To the extent *Bowers* relied on values we share with a wider civilization, it should be noted that the reasoning and holding in *Bowers* have been rejected elsewhere. The European Court of Human Rights has followed not *Bowers* but its own decision in Dudgeon v. United Kingdom. See P. G. & J. H. v. United Kingdom, App. No. 00044787/98, P56 (Eur. Ct. H. R., Sept. 25, 2001); Modinos v. *Cyprus*, 259 Eur. Ct. H. R. (1993); Norris v. *Ireland*, 142 Eur. Ct. H. R. (1988). Other nations, too, have taken action consistent with an affirmation of the protected right of homosexual adults to engage in intimate, consensual conduct. See Brief for Mary Robinson et al. as *Amici Curiae* 11–12. The right the petitioners seek in this case has been accepted as an integral part of human freedom in many other countries. There has been no showing that in this country the governmental interest in circumscribing personal choice is somehow more legitimate or urgent."

fatally compromised when written, Kennedy said, by contemporaneous evidence that Burger ignored.[76]

Glucksberg aside, no citation by a Supreme Court justice to foreign law or legal practice has gone unreprimanded since Scalia joined the Court, and this one did not. Scalia's response, though, was oblique. It took the form of disputing Kennedy's accusation against White's *Bowers* opinion—"the *Bowers* majority opinion *never* relied on 'values' we share with a 'wider civilization,' . . . but rather rejected the claimed right to sodomy on the ground that such a right was not 'deeply rooted in *this Nation's* history and tradition' "[77]—and, accordingly, dismissing Kennedy's appeal to comparative materials as "meaningless dicta."[78] We do not know whether Scalia noticed that this use of foreign material by Kennedy, supposing the Bowers majority *had* deserved it, would have been a sort of use that he himself had precisely authorized. If, as Scalia had allowed in *Thompson*,[79] one may invoke evidence of opinion and practice elsewhere in the world to help show that an ostensible regularity in American legal-institutional practice is not accidental or mindless but rather is deeply, normatively grounded in values considerably held, then surely it must follow that one may use such materials *in rebuttal* of a claim that an

---

[76] Id. at 2481, 2483:

The sweeping references by Chief Justice Burger to the history of Western civilization and to Judeo-Christian moral and ethical standards did not take account of other authorities pointing in an opposite direction. A committee advising the British Parliament recommended in 1957 repeal of laws punishing homosexual conduct. The Wolfenden Report: Report of the Committee on Homosexual Offenses and Prostitution (1963). Parliament enacted the substance of those recommendations 10 years later. Sexual Offences Act 1967, § 1.

Of even more importance, almost five years before *Bowers* was decided the European Court of Human Rights considered a case with parallels to *Bowers* and to today's case. An adult male resident in Northern Ireland alleged he was a practicing homosexual who desired to engage in consensual homosexual conduct. The laws of Northern Ireland forbade him that right. He alleged that he had been questioned, his home had been searched, and he feared criminal prosecution. The court held that the laws proscribing the conduct were invalid under the European Convention on Human Rights. Dudgeon v. United Kingdom, 45 Eur. Ct. H. R. (1981) P52. Authoritative in all countries that are members of the Council of Europe (21 nations then, 45 nations now), the decision is at odds with the premise in *Bowers* that the claim put forward was insubstantial in our Western civilization.

[77] Id. at 2494 (Scalia, J., dissenting) (citations omitted).

[78] Id. at 2495. Scalia added that they were "dangerous dicta, however, since 'this Court . . . should not impose foreign moods, fads, or fashions on Americans' " (quoting from Thomas's *Foster* opinion, see *supra* text accompanying note 61).

[79] See *supra* text accompanying note 39.

ostensible pattern of American practice is deeply, normatively grounded
in values considerately held. That is what Kennedy did in *Lawrence*.

Why Not "Persuasive Authority?" (Search for a Principle)

Suppose we put the question this way: As a general matter, does the bare
fact that courts or lawmakers outside the United States predominantly—
or let us even say uniformly—act in a certain way, or hold a certain opinion, give American judges a reason to follow suit or to construe our Constitution or our laws to parallel effect? (I don't mean a preemptive or
decisive reason, but just a reason to be laid alongside other reasons.) In
our little historical survey, we have found not a single opinion filed by a
Supreme Court justice saying that it does.[80] Justices advancing claims for
the relevance of foreign (or international) legal experience and practice
to domestic constitutional adjudication have expressly urged nothing beyond what we may call an "empirical" relevance. Knowledge of foreign
experience and practice, they have claimed, can enlighten factual or state-
of-affairs assessments that American judges are called upon to make in
the daily course of deciding the proper application of strictly homegrown
constitutional norms to pending cases.[81]

The history we have sketched discloses three ways in which foreign
legal materials may be thought empirically relevant to indigenous, American, constitutional-legal judgments respecting rights (and there may be
any number of other ways waiting to be recognized). First: A particular
text of American constitutional law may be read to mean that a result
should in some measure depend on the state of parallel law elsewhere or
internationally, or that it should depend on the state of normative opinion
in some population not confined to the present-day United States. Sundry

---

[80] The opinion that perhaps comes the closest to implying it is one we have not noticed
yet. In *Grutter v. Bollinger*, 123 S. Ct. 2325 (2003), Justice Ruth Bader Ginsburg, joined
by Breyer (but not by O'Connor, the writer of the main opinion for the Court for which
Ginsburg was providing support), made a point of observing that the Court's plea that
race-conscious programs "must have a logical end point" accords with the "international
understanding" of the proper use of affirmative action. See id. at 2347 (Ginsburg, J., concurring). That is, she made a point of observing it, and then stopped right there. Ginsburg
said not a word about why or how she thought this observation was relevant to the
Court's task, which leaves us to infer that she thinks that a fact of international opinion
sometimes can, just as such, provide some modicum of support for a parallel reading of
U.S. constitutional law.

[81] In a recent speech, Justice Ginsburg spoke of "sharing with and learning from others."
Ruth Bader Ginsburg, "Remarks for the American Constitution Society, Looking beyond
Our Borders: The Value of a Comparative Perspective in Constitutional Adjudication" (August 2, 2003), available at http://www.americanconstitutionsociety.org/pdf/Ginsburg%20
transcript%20final.pdf (last visited November 30, 2003).

majority, plurality, and solo opinions by Supreme Court justices since *Trop* have read the Eighth Amendment's cruel-and-unusual clause that way—*Stanford contra*—and Burger clearly read the due process clause that way in *Bowers*.[82] Insofar as such a reading is accepted, a judge giving faithful application to that U.S. constitutional-legal norm *must* make an assessment of external law, or of a historical or current state of trans-American normative opinion, and that could cover what Kennedy did in *Lawrence*. Second: A standing American constitutional-legal norm might prescribe that a result is to turn on the state of *American* opinion, and examination of foreign legal materials may be deemed relevant to appraisal of evidence regarding American opinion. That is the use of such materials that Scalia endorsed in his *Thompson* dissent and that Stevens made in *Atkins*.

Third: When, as often happens, American constitutional-legal norms stand in need of further judicial specification before they can be applied to decide a pending case, a judicial assessment of the practical consequences of available doctrinal choices may be in order. A judge may feel obliged to consider which of two or more alternative doctrinal paths will lead to results that best satisfy some set of values and aims that the judge draws from the law to date. Granted, that is a contested approach to constitutional interpretation, but it does not lack for wide support.[83] In such an exercise of judicial practical wisdom, a consultation of foreign experience, it is said, can sometimes be of assistance. That is the use of foreign materials proposed by Breyer in *Printz* and made by Rehnquist in *Glucksberg*.

Is there any conceivable objection in principle to such empirical uses of foreign legal-practice information? You will look for it in vain in the his-

---

[82] *Bowers v. Hardwick*, *supra*, at 196–97 (Burger, C.J., concurring) ("Decisions of individuals relating to homosexual conduct have been subject to state intervention throughout the history of Western civilization. . . . To hold that the act of homosexual sodomy is somehow protected as a fundamental right would be to cast aside millennia of moral teaching. This is essentially not a question of personal 'preferences' but rather of the legislative authority of the State").

At least one twentieth-century, lower federal court has read the Fifth Amendment's due process clause, as applied to the case of an alien's claim of unconstitutionally arbitrary treatment by U.S. immigration authorities, to incorporate international law by reference. See *Rodriguez-Fernandez v. Wilkinson*, 654 F.2d 1382, 1388–89 (10th Cir. 1981), holding that attention to principles of customary international law was required of a U.S. court deciding whether certain statutes governing detention of aliens could be construed as the government proposed without raising serious questions of compatibility with our Constitution's due process guarantee. One can only speculate as to the extent to which the intrinsically international dimensions of the case's factual setting were an operative factor.

[83] See Mark Tushnet, "The Possibilities of Comparative Constitutional Law," *Yale Law Journal* 108 (1999): 1232–33, at 1225 (explaining the Breyer vs. Scalia disagreement in

tory I have recounted. But *something*, obviously, is worrying the objec-
tors—something they have seemed anxious to nip in the bud. Kennedy's
Lawrence "dicta" were "dangerous," Scalia said.[84] One thing leads to
another. Had Breyer's carefully bounded use of comparative materials in
Printz gone "unchallenged," Charles Fried has written, "it would have
been a step towards legitimizing their use as points of departure in constitutional litigation."[85] Cite comparative materials today for innocuous
purposes, normalize the use of them in our judicial discourse, and next
thing you know. . . . Well, *what*? What is the Greek in this horse?

The Greek would seem to be the gradual accretion to foreign legal materials of a kind of influential but not controlling force on American adjudication that Anne-Marie Slaughter, endorsing it, calls "persuasive authority."[86] Now, let us be clear. By "persuasive authority," Slaughter does not
mean merely that an American judge reads foreign or ECHR decisions
for whatever help or stimulation can luckily be found in their reasoning
and insight, as justices might read law reviews (but probably don't very
often). She means American judges accord those decisions *weight*, out of a
recognition of their authors' engagement, together with us, in "a common
enterprise of protecting human rights."[87]

As Slaughter sees the case, American judges, by granting persuasive
authority to comparative materials in domestic constitutional adjudication, would be joining in "a common global enterprise of judging."[88]
Slaughter thus envisions American judges acting on the premise of a substantive congruence between a certain, "suprapositive" component in
American law and its suprapositive counterpart in the constitutional adjudications of a family (as we may call it) of other countries.[89] She might be
looking, then, in something like a natural-law direction.[90] That is not,

---

Printz as a reflection of their disagreement over approaches to constitutional interpretation:
Breyer's functionalism vs. Scalia's originalism).

[84] See note 78, *supra*.

[85] Fried, "Scholars," *supra* note 12, at 820–21.

[86] Slaughter, "Community," *supra* note 2, at 199–202.

[87] Slaughter, "Globalization," *supra* note 2, at 1117.

[88] Id. at 1106.

[89] See Neuman, "Human Rights," *supra* note 10, at 1899: "[T]o the extent that constitutional adjudication in the United States has any suprapositive component, . . . the normative
arguments of international human rights tribunals are at least potentially relevant.'). By a
"suprapositive component," Neuman means that element in our response to a local, positive
legal norm by which we regard it as a reflection of principles that emanate from outside the
local system of formal, positive law.

[90] Vicki Jackson describes the approach as one "with affinities to natural law traditions" in which "something like universal meaning is plausible," so that "transnational
omnipresences" become "a measure of the correctness of a legal rule." Jackson, *supra*
note 9, at 257–58. It has also been said, conversely, that "if one understands a constitution
as the embodiment in higher law of . . . a concrete political practice, then the new compar-

however, a necessary inference, because Slaughter might rather be positing a contingent, concrete relation of ethical kinship among a set of historically situated political communities, including the United States and the other democracies in which the comparative materials are generated.[91] That concrete kinship would supply a reason—although never a preemptive or necessarily controlling one—why the very fact that foreign or international legal authorities respond more or less uniformly to a question regarding (say) the death penalty, hate speech, or special accommodation for religious practices should give pause to American judges about to reach a different result under our Constitution. As Slaughter puts it, our judges would do best to grant a modicum of "weight" to any "visible international consensus" respecting such matters.[92] In practical, operational terms, this must mean that if you—the American judge—on some occasion decline to construe or revise American law to follow the visible consensus, you owe a statement of a reason why not.[93]

On the other hand, "persuasive" authority would not be "formal" authority. It would not "bind" you. As a judge disinclined to follow it, you would be free to claim a very substantial margin of appreciation for national circumstantial, cultural, or institutional difference. (For example, Mark Tushnet has suggested that U.S. constitutional law may reasonably be leery of Canadian tolerance for hate speech regulation, just because the relatively centralized structure of justice institutions in Canada might make abusive prosecution less likely there than here.)[94] Even sheerly arbitrary, historical difference, or call it path-dependency, would suffice to explain a refusal to follow a foreign lead.

Consider, for example, *Raines v. Byrd*.[95] The question was the validity of a provision in an act of Congress conferring standing on members of Congress (who lacked individualized stakes in the matter) to litigate the constitutionality of the act. Rehnquist, for the Court, volunteered that it would be quite "rational" for a constitutional system to allow standing in this case, as indeed many European systems would have done, but he found—on the basis of American judicial precedent, which he cited— that such "obviously" is not "the regime that has obtained under our

---

ativism will challenge one's most basic constitutional presuppositions." Weinrib, *supra* note 3, at 5.

[91] Peter Spiro speaks of a partial "migration" of the rights-defining community to "a global level." Spiro, *supra* note 7, at 2021. It seems unlikely, though, that he means "global" to be taken literally.

[92] Slaughter, "Community," *supra* note 2, at 202.

[93] See Weinrib, *supra* note 3, at 5 ("At the very least, the Court would feel called upon to account for the divergence").

[94] See Tushnet, *supra* note 8, at 259–60.

[95] 521 U.S. 811 (1997).

Constitution to date."[96] In other words, we have, as it happens, chosen otherwise, and our law, in consequence, is different. Had Rehnquist been under strict obligation to treat the comparative material as persuasive authority, he would have satisfied it.[97]

Given the laxity of "persuasive authority" thus expounded, why should any American judge react so vehemently, so doggedly, against the idea as some of them have? Our inveterate resisters on the Supreme Court have not been very forthcoming about this. One has to search hard in their opinions for a single, cogent statement of a reason for resistance. It is as if they do not know how to name what is bothering them.

Dissenting in *Atkins*, Scalia remarked that the " 'world community's' " notions of justice are "not always those of our people."[98] So what? Might they be sometimes? Use of comparative materials as persuasive authority allows easily for "not always." Dissenting in *Thompson*, Scalia enjoined his colleagues not to forget that "it is a Constitution for the United States of America that we are expounding."[99] Yes, and what follows? Well, "the views of other nations cannot be imposed upon Americans through the Constitution."[100] But would it be an *imposition* if judges applying the Constitution sometimes considered and weighed such views, having first concluded that the Constitution as written means that they shall—exactly as a fraction of the Court has long maintained is true of the Eighth Amendment?[101] Why should comparative analysis conducted under constitutional direction be considered an illicit imposition on American self-government? Well, perhaps there is some manifest principle of juridical prudence or political morality that makes it wrong to find any such directive in the Constitution, absent the clearest textual compulsion. But if so, what is that principle? Scalia does not say, not in *Thompson*, anyway.

Does he in *Stanford*? "We think comparative analysis inappropriate to the task of interpreting a constitution" is not a reason, nor does it state a principle of political prudence or morality, nor does any such statement

---

[96] Id. at 828.

[97] The posture I am describing here is close, I believe, to that commended by Gerald Neuman. See Neuman, "Uses," *supra* note 9; Neuman, "Human Rights," *supra* note 10.

[98] 536 U.S. at 347 (Scalia, J., dissenting).

[99] 487 U.S. at 869–70 n. 4.

[100] Id. Compare Thomas's "foreign moods, fads, or fashions." See *supra* text accompanying note 61.

[101] See Neuman, "Human Rights," *supra* note 10, at 1875 ("[F]rom the national constitutional perspective, the degree of monism or dualism is subject to specification in the constitution. Popular sovereignty legitimates the choices that the constitution expresses, and assign international law its place in the legal hierarchy"); Tushnet, *supra* note 8 ("[W]henever a U.S. decision-maker invokes a non-U.S. rule of decision, the decision is as fully domestic as any other decision the decision-maker makes. . . . This point is so obvious that I find it hard to believe that the opponents of so-called global governance have overlooked it").

immediately ensue.[102] But perhaps one can be drawn from a later passage in the opinion, which Scalia addressed not to the use of foreign materials but rather to the use of *American* materials in the forms of opinion polls, interest-group manifestos, and professional association position statements. Constitutional law may not be left to rest on foundations so "uncertain," Scalia wrote. "A . . . national consensus so broad, so clear, and so enduring as to justify a permanent prohibition upon all units of democratic government must appear in the operative acts (laws and the application of laws) that the people have approved."[103] Granted, this looks like one of those "familiar . . . challenge[s] to so-called judicial activism," which Mark Tushnet aptly warns us not to mistake for an argument against abdication of national sovereignty to outsiders.[104] But Rehnquist did later deploy this passage in opposition to references to "foreign laws" by judges engaged in constitutional adjudication, so we may consider it in that light.[105]

Perhaps the passage seems, in that light, to state an antidelegation principle. So, perhaps, does Thomas's warning in *Foster*: "This Court's Eighth Amendment jurisprudence should not impose foreign moods, fads, or fashions on Americans."[106] Is that, then, the principle of political prudence or morality we are looking for, against reading the Constitution to mean that "the views of other nations" shall *ever* be considered and weighed by judges engaged in American constitutional interpretation? A truly self-governing people would never, in that way, permit their most basic political-normative choices to get out of their own hands?[107] It may

---

[102] The rest of that footnote is devoted to supporting the other branch of the aphorism, that comparative analysis *is* relevant to "writing" a constitution. Scalia maintains that the framers, while they did indeed engage in comparative analysis, also self-consciously contrived a new federalist model, which they regarded as different from any other then known in the world or to history. "Persuasive authority" can make full allowance for that historical fact, if it be one.

[103] *Stanford*, 492 U.S. at 377 (Scalia, J., dissenting). This portion of Scalia's opinion was joined by only a plurality, not including O'Connor.

[104] See Tushnet, *supra* note 8, at 264.

[105] See *Atkins*, 536 U.S. at 322–23 (Rehnquist, C.J., dissenting).

[106] *Foster*, 123 S. Ct. 470 n. * (Thomas, J., concurring in denial of certiorari).

[107] I must be candid here. I do not really think that's the most natural construction of what Scalia and Thomas are saying. Scalia laid down a demand that norms to be given a countermajoritarian effect must "appear" in "operative acts" approved by the people. That looks like a manifestation of Scalia's textualist, anti-"moral reading" stance toward constitutional interpretation. In other words, it could well be that Scalia and Thomas are inveighing here (as usual) against usurpation of American constitution-making authority by *judges*, not against delegation of it to foreigners. See Tushnet, *supra* note 8. I have offered the "delegation" reading just as a way of finding *something* said by them that conceivably could count as a reason for their entrenched and diligent opposition to "comparative analysis" or citation of foreign materials.

seem rigid. It may seem "parochial."[108] It may seem to contradict Scalia's own presupposition, in *Thompson*, of a partial congruence of American mores with those of the world's democracies.[109] It is, however, all that the resisters have given us to work with. Soon, we shall consider a possible way to give it legs.

"Sources" and Ideological Stakes

Well, maybe not *it*, exactly, but a precept closely enough related. The antidelegation idea does not, after all, respond to what any sensible person can regard as a real threat. No one today is close to proposing any relinquishment of American legal-normative authority to global consensuses.[110] Somewhere in this bank of forensic fog is lurking, I shall suggest, not an antidelegation principle but a half-baked anti*conversation* principle—or anti-"cross fertilization" principle—and one that could perhaps have some punch if sincerely held and adequately presented and defended.

Charles Fried is on to it, I believe, when he writes of Breyer's "foray" in *Printz* that it was a move toward expanding the "universe" or "canon" of "authoritative materials" upon which lawyers and judges base their constitutional-legal arguments and decisions. Had Breyer's proposal not been met at the pass, says Fried, "it would have introduced a whole new range of materials to the texts, precedents and doctrines from which the Herculean task of constructing judgments in particular cases proceeds."[111] All that is missing from Fried's observation is an explanation of why such a future course of legal-discursive development should be a cause of concern to anyone involved in, or responsible for, the practice of American

---

[108] See *supra* text accompanying note 3.

[109] See *supra* text accompanying note 39.

[110] Of course, just as one might fear that a merely empirical use of comparative materials could ripen into their use as persuasive authority, so one might fear that their use as persuasive authority could ripen into a claim for their recognition as formal or binding authority. For example, the view of Justice L'Heureux-Dubé, discussed in Slaughter, "Community," *supra* note 2, at 196, could be regarded as having traveled some distance along the path from persuasive to formal authority. See Claire L'Heureux-Dubé, "The Importance of Dialogue: Globalization and the International Impact of the Rehnquist Court," *Tulsa Law Review* 34 (1998): 15–40, at 17. Likewise, Harold Koh's challenge to the "international law"/"foreign law" distinction, see *supra* note 9, may be read to look in that direction. I say no more about this possibility, because my aim in this essay is to flush the motives for resistance to granting even persuasive, let alone formal, authority to comparative materials in domestic, American constitutional adjudication.

[111] Fried, "Scholars," *supra* note 12, at 818–19. Fried's "Herculean" alludes to Ronald Dworkin's account of adjudication—including constitutional adjudication—in Ronald Dworkin, "Hard Cases," *Harvard Law Review* 88 (1975): 1057–1110; see Fried, *supra* note 12, at 810–11.

constitutionalism. (Fried probably isn't worried about the extra reading load for the participants.)

The issue, Fried says, is whether the opinions and decisions of other national courts and international tribunals are now (as never before) to be treated as proper legal sources for American courts—a standard, expected dimension of their "frame of reference"[112]—when the latter are engaged in deciding controversial questions of American constitutional law respecting rights. This means the nondomestic materials would be properly and routinely citable by lawyers, and our judges would be obliged to respond in their opinions to arguments reared on such citations. Even though no judge (in domestic constitutional adjudication) would be required to follow foreign sources slavishly or even, in the end, to follow them at all, such a switch in the sources rules would represent a distinct break in American constitutional-legal practice, and some American jurists seem to sense or perceive that something of great moment would be placed at risk by it.[113]

What, then? The plainest, and not wild, speculation is that the stakes are first-order ideological. Is it nonpartisan, in the United States today, to declare oneself or one's adversary an "internationalist"? Mark Tushnet detects a concern on the antiglobalists' part about the "cosmopolitan" sympathies of globally involved American judges.[114] Bricker has heirs who feel deeply, as he did, that the UN-bred declaration and covenants on human rights are un-American *in substance*.[115] And of course that is a feeling that could easily extend to bodies of constitutional-legal doctrine that have since taken shape, or are now taking shape—plainly under the influence of the UN-bred instruments—in Canada, Germany, Hungary, India, South Africa, and "Europe" (to name some of the chief suspects in cross-fertilization). If those become part of the lingua franca of American constitutional-legal argument, will not the hand of the litigating "liberal interest groups" be strengthened?[116]

By and large, these bodies of "postwar model" doctrine[117] (it would play them false to call them a single body) seem less committed to strict

---

[112] Kent Greenawalt, *Private Conscience and Public Reasons* (New York: Oxford University Press, 1995), 149.

[113] To take this view is, admittedly, to enter a jurisprudential debate. See, e.g., Frederick Schauer and Virginia Wise, "Legal Positivism as Legal Information," *Cornell Law Review* 82 (1997): 1080–1109, at 1082 (defending the view that what differentiates legal decision making, supposed to be respect-worthy as such, from other sorts of public-policy determinations is the confinement of legal argumentation to an "information set" that is "structurally differentiated and extensionally divergent from" the sets used by other public decision makers).

[114] See Tushnet, *supra* note 8, at 265–66.

[115] See, e.g., Spiro, *supra* note 7, at 2012–14.

[116] Tushnet, *supra* note 8, at 265.

[117] Weinrib, *supra* note 3, at 19.

constitutional-legal protection of property rights than American conservatives are. In varying ways and degrees, some of them make socialism—active state provision for people's basic material needs—a constitutional-legal requirement. By comparison with us, they tend as a group to be receptive to political campaign regulation, soft on censorship of "hate speech," committed to affirmative action, and prepared to hold governments accountable for racial and other disparate impacts of formally neutral regimes of law. I don't mean the ideological tilt is strictly one-sided by American measures. The American liberal Left divides over hate speech and campaign regulation, and it would doubtless prefer the American constitutional-legal stances toward law enforcement and criminal procedure (pre-9/11), abortion, and church-state separation to those more typical abroad. But when all is said and done, it is not beyond imagining that both the "conservative" resisters to comparative analysis (Rehnquist, Scalia, Thomas) and the "liberal" promoters (Breyer, Ginsburg, Stevens) believe that letting foreign sources in can only tend to tip American constitutional-legal discourse toward "liberal" outcomes. Scalia's "thankfully"[118] and Thomas's "foreign moods, fads, and fashions"[119] ring in our ears.

But perhaps we can do better by them; and if they don't care, then at least by Charles Fried, who I don't believe was voicing a substantive, ideological preference when he lodged his worry about a switch in the sources rules. Fried did not say further what might be bothering him. I wonder whether it could be a perceived threat to the integrity, in a certain sense, of the historic discourse of American constitutional law respecting rights.

What Is Integrity-Anxiety?

Integrity and Why It Matters

To view American constitutional law as a *discourse* is to see it as something beyond a raw deposit of substantive rules, doctrines, results, and precedents. It's to see the law as composed of an entire broad-sense "vocabulary" or dialect—including paradigmatic concepts, categorizations, value-orientations, and argumentative tropes—in which American constitutional lawyers and judges frame, convey, and comprehend their forensic exchanges.[120] To speak of the *integrity* of this discourse is to speak of its

---

[118] See *supra* text accompanying note 69.

[119] See *supra* text accompanying note 61.

[120] See, e.g., Owen Fiss, "Conventionalism," *Southern California Law Review* 58 (1985): 177–97; Owen Fiss, "Objectivity and Interpretation," *Stanford Law Review* 34 (1982): 739–63 (1982).

unbroken identity through time as a distinctly cognizable, self-contained discursive object—a kind of discursive domain unto itself, visibly separate and freestanding from other normative discourses.[121]

Why might this integrity be felt to be important? For one reason, perhaps, because of fear that the loss of it might strip our constitutional law of its ability to perform a vital political function we've assigned to it, that function being nothing less than the defense of the legitimacy of government in this country. Defense against what? Against corrosion by acidulous moral disagreement when it comes to defining and delineating people's rights. It has seemed to many that the fact of American pluralism, as John Rawls would have called it, poses a standing menace to political legitimacy here, for defense against which Americans have come to rely, in large part—for better or for worse—on the perceived integrity of our judicially patrolled discourse of constitutional law.

Let me offer a case in point. A symposium in the periodical called *First Things* attracted some notoriety around the end of 1996.[122] In a series of short essays, noted social conservatives raised the alarms about recent American court decisions in the fields of abortion and abortion protest, rights to refuse medical treatment or to assist suicide, gay rights, gender rights, distribution of sexually explicit media materials, and public religious observances. The alarms going up were not just moral, they were political. The essays expressly heralded an American "crisis of legitimacy."[123] The authors pointedly raised the question whether, if things went on in this way much further—or indeed no further but without a rollback—morally serious inhabitants of this land could any longer retain an undiluted allegiance to the extant American political order. A mini-uproar ensued. Some of the notables constituting the *First Things* editorial

---

[121] See, e.g., Owen Fiss, "The Autonomy of Law," *Yale Journal of International Law* 26 (2001): 517–26, 519.

[122] See "Symposium: The End of Democracy? The Judicial Usurpation of Politics?" *First Things* 67 (November 1996), http://www.firstthings.com/ftissues/ft9611/articles/sympintro.html; "The End of Democracy, A Discussion Continued," *First Things* 69 (January 1997), http://www.firstthings.com/ftissues/ft9701/articles/theend.html.

Individual essays in the symposium include Richard John Neuhaus, "Introduction"; Russell Hittinger, "A Crisis of Legitimacy"; Hadley Arkes, "A Culture Corrupted"; Charles W. Colson, "Kingdoms in Conflict"; and Robert P. George, "The Tyrant State." A follow-up compendium under the title "The End of Democracy? A Discussion Continued," includes untitled contributions, critical in various ways and degrees of the first series of essays, from William J. Bennett, Midge Decter, James C. Dobson, Mary Ann Glendon, and John Leo.

My account of the symposium here is taken from Frank I. Michelman, "Living with Judicial Supremacy," *Wake Forest Law Review* 38 (2003): 579–611, at 580–83, where more detailed quotations, and citations to individual articles, may be found.

[123] "A Crisis of Legitimacy" is the title of Russell Hittinger's contribution to the symposium. See also Neuhaus, *supra* note 122 ("What is happening now is a growing alienation of millions of Americans from a government they do not recognize as theirs; what is happening now is an erosion of moral adherence to this political system").

board resigned in protest against the essays' endorsement by the journal's main editor.[124]

Now, maybe the *First Things* outburst was unusual or extreme. Maybe, in some eyes, it was hyperventilation. It drew rebuke. It seems to have died down. Yet two points about it seem clear:[125] First, this sort of thing can be worrisome to officials who feel themselves responsible for upholding political unity, loyalty, and stability in this country—a group that doubtless includes justices of the Supreme Court.[126] Second, this sort of thing can seem a constantly looming threat when constitutional law is asked to meet the country's need for a shared basis for public appraisals of government's performance of the political contract respecting protection of people's rights, there being no felt moral consensus to serve this basic political need.

Rights-Talk, Disagreement, and Constitutional Law

To speak of rights is to deal in ideas about how persons are and are not to be treated by others. Meaning what, exactly? Meaning that a consequence of an agent's failure to comply is for that agent to incur a justified judgment of having acted wrongly—not just inefficiently or imprudently but *wrongly* toward some person entitled, as a person, to better treatment.[127] On that level of discussion, using the rights idea in that way, it seems we don't need law in order to have or to discuss rights. All we need is morality, the idea of right and wrong treatment of persons.

On the ground, though, the situation has been more complicated. Some rights talk is what we may call political or public rights talk, meaning talk by which people consider how well their governments are upholding the civic contract or the civic trust. In public rights talk, not only are people discussing the moral rights and wrongs of how persons get treated by others, they are discussing these questions in a politically loaded way,

---

[124] See David Glenn, "The Schism," *Lingua Franca*, February 1997, at 24, and Jacon Heilbrun, "Neocon v. Theocon," *New Republic*, November 1996, at 20, both cited in Suzanna Sherry, "Religion and the Public Square: Making Democracy Safe for Religious Minorities," *De Paul Law Review* 47 (1998): 499–517, at 517.

[125] I discuss them in Michelman, "Judicial Supremacy," *supra* note 122, at 606–11.

[126] See, e.g., *Bush v. Gore*, 531 U.S. 98 (2000); Richard A. Posner, *Breaking the Deadlock: The 2000 Election, the Constitution, and the Courts* (Princeton: Princeton University Press, 2001); Frank I. Michelman, "Machiavelli in Robes? The Court in the Election," in *The Longest Night: Polemics and Perspectives on Election 2000*, ed. Arthur J. Jacobson and Michel Rosenfeld (Berkeley and Los Angeles: University of California Press, 2002), 256–75.

[127] See, e.g., Ronald Dworkin, *Taking Rights Seriously* (Cambridge: Harvard University Press, 1977), 169–71.

with a view to assessing the government's performance of the public trust and its deservingness of continued, full confidence and loyalty. Perhaps not every national culture is geared to taking rights so seriously as to make governmental performance regarding people's rights a pivotal political concern, but American culture is and has been so geared, it seems, since the founding and before. Judgments of governmental performance with regard to people's rights have always been very much a part of our civic discourse, very much a part of our politics, and sometimes a very dangerous part at that. (Never mind *First Things*. Consider the Revolution[128] and the Civil War.)

In theory, as I have said, it seems people shouldn't need any reference to law to frame their public rights talk. In practice, it seems Americans do. In this country, one rarely hears public rights talk conducted without immediate reference to law and particularly constitutional law, and that, too, has been our habit since the very beginning.[129] Public rights talk in this country is overwhelmingly legal rights talk, and it is mostly bill-of-rights talk.

No doubt there are some sheerly accidental reasons of history for this tendency on our part to juridify our public rights talk. There is also at least one practical reason for it, maybe not present at the creation but surely central now: our vaunted pluralism.[130] Things could be different if Americans had all along felt themselves mainly of a single mind regarding morally apt interpretations of human-rights ideals as applied, say (in the mid-Republic), to slavery and race, women's "place," or rights of free labor,[131] and (in our own day) to the death penalty, affirmative action, racist speech, state aid to religious institutions, the state's duty to "accommodate" minority religious practices, its duty to protect gays and lesbians from civic discrimination, a doctor's freedom to assist abortion, or to assist suicide, and so on. If Americans felt a unity of the moral sense regarding such matters, we could perfectly well bottom our public rights-talk directly on moral grounds. However, we don't, and so we can't. In order to maintain a *public* discourse on governmental performance re-

[128] See, e.g., Bernard Bailyn, *The Ideological Origins of the American Revolution* (Cambridge: Harvard University Press, 1992).

[129] See Larry D. Kramer, *The People Themselves: Popular Constitutionalism and Judicial Review* (Oxford: Oxford University Press, 2004). Kramer maintains that constitutional law was not, at that early stage, a professionally specialized province of lawyers, but he is equally emphatic that it was *law*, a body of conventional norms, intended to be binding on officials whether they liked or agreed with it or not, distinct from both "politics" and natural reason.

[130] See id.

[131] See William E. Forbath, "The Ambiguities of Free Labor: Labor and Law in the Gilded Age," *Wisconsin Law Review* 1985 (1985): 767–817.

garding people's rights, Americans apparently need some point of normative reference more publicly objective than it feels as though morality can be for us. Enter constitutional law.

The definition of people's rights is often, among us, a matter of disagreement so intractable as to seem beyond all hope of consensual resolution in real political time.[132] Yet our felt need to have these issues resolved for official purposes, on some publicly shared basis, is very great. A given affirmative action law or abortion law either is permissible and valid on our system or is not. There is no middle ground; a law cannot be a little bit valid.[133] Institutions need answers, and every answer is fraught with divisive potential. For reasons you can read in Hobbes (and in Kant, too),[134] we don't want our people's judgments of what does and does not derogate from continued full confidence in our system of government—people's judgments, at the limit, regarding continued political obligation to this political society—falling prey to their fiercely felt divisions of ethical outlook and sensibility. We want a more publicly objective basis for public, political judgments of governmental probity, including judgments of governmental performance regarding people's rights, and it seems Americans have come, for better or for worse, to depend heavily on their system of constitutional law to provide that basis.

Legalism as Objectivity

Now, this may seem something of a mystery, because American constitutional law on its face does not appear to be all that publicly objective. To be sure, it is all-round inoffensive on the level of its abstract canonical propositions—no cruel and unusual punishments allowed, no slavery, no groundless or arbitrary deprivations of life or liberty or property, no abridgments or prohibitions of the freedoms of speech and religious exercise, no denials of the equal protection of the laws. What American could possibly disagree?

---

[132] See, e.g., Jeremy Waldron, *Law and Disagreement* (Oxford: Oxford University Press, 1999).

[133] Maybe once upon a time in our history one could be (see Kramer, *supra* note 129), but not in the prevailingly positivist mode of late American legal culture. Even here, constitution writers or judicial interpreters can try to draw the line between valid and not valid in a way that splits some difference, but—to repeat—no law once laid down can be a little bit valid.

[134] See Jeremy Waldron, *The Dignity of Legislation* (Cambridge: Cambridge University Press, 1999), 36–62; Immanuel Kant, *The Metaphysical Elements of Justice* (1797), trans. John Ladd (Indianapolis: Hackett Publishing Company, 1999), § 42; Thomas Hobbes, *Leviathan* (1651), ed. Richard Tuck (Cambridge: Cambridge University Press, 1991), chaps. 13–17.

But most (maybe all) of those no doubt universally accepted canons, as they stand, are merely nominal. In order to resolve rights controversies of the sorts I mentioned above—death penalty, abortion, defamation, gay rights, etc.—the textual canons require not just specifications at their margins but decodings at their cores.[135] It hardly needs saying that Americans often find they have deeply held, we may assume well-considered, but nevertheless sharply differing convictions about the correct decodings. To some indefinite but nonnegligible extent, our interpretive disagreements—so to name them—will inevitably be felt to reflect directly the first-order ethical divisions among us that prompt us in the first place to look to the law to supply our need for an objective basis for public rights-talk. Interpretive disagreements are the joint product of our ethical pluralism and what John Rawls called "burdens of judgment."[136] Accordingly, it has seemed to many that our resort to law to supply a measure of objectivity to public rights-talk must come to naught—*unless*. Unless, first, we concentrate authority in some single body to pronounce the decodings that finally are to bind everyone in the land and that thus finally are to count for purposes of public rights-talk.[137] Unless, second, that body can contrive to make those interpretations in a way that carries an aura of objectivity, of nonpartisanship, sufficient to allow everyone to feel they can accept the results and live with them, without a stinging sense of insult to one's full and respected membership in the American polity.

Suppose you are one whose thoughts are grooved along the lines I have just been sketching. You think American political legitimacy rides in that way on people's confidence in the objectivity of the processes of official decision making respecting the government's dispositions over people's rights. You think legitimacy here rides on people's sense of assurance that the decisions emanating from those processes are dependably impartial enough that they, as morally responsible persons but also as loyal Ameri-

---

[135] I owe the useful notion of "decoding" to Michael J. Perry, *We the People: The Fourteenth Amendment and the Supreme Court* (New York: Oxford University Press, 1999).

[136] "Burdens of judgment" encompass sundry causes of obdurate disagreement about justice among persons who, as reasonable, all observe and report honestly, argue cogently, and share "a desire to honor fair terms of cooperation." John Rawls, *Political Liberalism* (New York: Columbia University Press, 1996), 55. Among these causes Rawls lists the likelihood that "the way we assess evidence and weigh moral and political values is shaped by our total experience, our whole course of life up to now; and our total experiences must always differ. Thus, in a modern society with its numerous offices and positions, its various divisions of labor, its many social groups and their ethnic variety, citizens' total experiences are disparate enough for their judgments to diverge, at least to some degree, on many if not most cases of significant complexity." Id. at 57. See also Thomas Nagel, "Moral Conflict and Political Legitimacy," *Philosophy and Public Affairs* 16 (1987): 215–40, at 234–35.

[137] Kramer, *supra* note 129, recounts the emergence of this conviction in American constitutional culture.

cans, can and ought to live with them. Unless you are extremely dense, you cannot think this will work if any sizable group is going to insist that its members cannot and ought not live with decisions that *they* are convinced are morally wrong. Grave moral wrongness was what the *First Things* writers charged against the judicial rulings that fired them up, but they must have known—even if they were not (alas) much disposed to say anything about it—that opposite rulings would similarly have fired up a no doubt equally numerous, equally sincere, and equally intense fraction of our population.

In a deeply pluralized political society, there will inevitably be strains of political commitment on all sides.[138] The polity cannot survive if commitment cannot withstand the strains of one side's or another's heartfelt moral revulsion from one or another legal decision respecting rights. Political legitimacy, it may therefore seem, must be allowed to depend, in part, on something procedural—must be allowed, that is, to depend on belief in the sincerity and objectivity, or say the nonpartisanship, of the judges' rulings on constitutional meanings that finally control applications of governmental force in the country. Granted, preserving this sense of interpretive nonpartisanship could not ever be a *sufficient* condition of legitimacy. There must also be the sense of an effective, outermost constraint on human rights interpretations that gives everyone assurance that they won't be awful unto the Tenth Circle of Hell (or maybe not beyond the Seventh or so). The point for now is that the sense of interpretive nonpartisanship, or objectivity, is felt to be a *necessary* condition of legitimacy.

The Supreme Court cannot pretend to objectivity in this business, without having some *object* to point to as the basis for its pronouncements and their justification. For reasons we have mentioned, the object cannot, in this case, be morality alone, or reason alone. In American conditions, for judges frankly to decide rights questions by the light of morality or reason alone simply cannot register as nonpartisan. To the contrary, that seemingly would be maximally divisive, for the judicial act then becomes a direct pronouncement on which of the contending parties is morally in the right and which (all the others) are moral dropouts.[139]

Enter constitutional law. Enter legalism. What the judges feel they need is a *conventional* discourse—one that is freestanding from morality (to adopt that useful notion from John Rawls)—in which to debate, hammer out, and convey their decisions. That is what they look for law to give them: a set of argumentative premises, resources, and moves, laid down

---

[138] See Rawls, *supra* note 136, at 17–18 (on "strains of commitment" in ideal theory).

[139] See Frank I. Michelman, "Dilemmas of Belonging: Moral Truth, Human Rights, and Why We Might Not Want a Representative Judiciary," *U.C.L.A. Law Review* 47 (2000): 1221–52, at 1248–52.

by history and professional practice, if also (as one may still hope) by reason, the trouble with reason alone being our sensed inability to agree as a nation on what it advises. In the result, the judicial nonpartisanship on which political legitimacy seems to ride becomes, in effect, the credible fidelity of the judges to a historically evolving but nevertheless distinctly bounded body of American constitutional-legal discourse in the sweeping sense of "discourse" I have already defined.

But Why Not, Then, a Global Legal Discourse of Rights?

"But suppose we grant all that," you well may ask. "It still begs the question. Right there, before our eyes, we see taking place a contemporary, transnational *legal* conversation on rights. This conversation involves not only international tribunals and UN expert committees but the constitutional courts of innumerable nation-states and regional formations, working on issues ostensibly similar to ours with comparably indecisive texts. This conversation has all the earmarks of a freestanding, professionalized legal discourse of the very kind you mean, Professor. It assiduously differentiates legal authorities and 'sources' from reason, nature, and other normative materials; restricts its gaze to the former; cites, parses, and distinguishes them; and so forth. So why couldn't *it* serve the United States as exactly what you have said the United States feels it needs? Unless you can answer that one, Professor, you won't have explained why the American Supreme Court's rights interpretations for America should have become and remained exceptionally and remarkably closed off to the global discourse."

The question is well posed. If there be an answer, history must supply it, along roughly the following lines. A centralized, professionalized, process of judicial decoding of American constitutional rights guarantees did not begin in full earnest until after the Civil War. We need not here go into the reasons for the delayed takeoff.[140] The fact simply is that our indigenous constitutional-legal discourse of rights ripened to its maturity over a period running from then through the mid–twentieth century. That was a time of

---

[140] A part of the explanation may be found in Kramer's review of a history of contestation, lasting until the Civil War (and recurrent even beyond), over the professionalization and centralization (in the Supreme Court) of authority to interpret the Constitution. See Kramer, *supra* note 129. Some other factors are probably significant, too: that state laws, by and large, were not considered subject to federal constitutional rights guarantees until after the Civil War, and that the prewar Constitution contained no guarantee respecting equality needing to be decoded. Antebellum Americans certainly were aware of the risks of dangerously divisive ruptures of opinions regarding the applied meanings of the guarantees in the original Bill of Rights. Divisions over national governmental powers to create corporations and fund internal improvements may not have risen to quite that level, but divisions over the Constitution's applications to slavery and sedition certainly did.

relative absence, at least from U.S. legal consciousness, of a vibrant, seriously taken, transnational-legal conversation on rights.[141] By the time of the blossoming of the transnational human-rights discussion in the period following World War II (led in large part by Americans), the American centralized judicial decoding process had compiled what felt like a critical mass of normative, conceptual, and dialectical resources, sufficient without more to ground an indefinite future course of American constitutional-legal doctrinal development. The process had aged into the freestanding discourse known as "American constitutional law," which there was no possibility of getting confused with the new, internationalist human rights palaver, the "postwar model."[142] There was no pressing reason to bridge the two and no professional instinct to do so.

Early American, professional legal consciousness had been noninsular. From Commonwealth models and antecedents, it imbibed a transnational sensibility.[143] Office-educated lawyers of the early Republic cited Grotius, Pufendorf, and Vattel in utterly local cases.[144] They knew an ongoing transnational, post-Enlightenment discourse of natural right and the *jus gentium*—a sibling, conventionalized, customary international law of human rights. At least as late as 1825, one could see an American Supreme Court opinion taking both of those easily on board.[145] So why didn't this early American judicial conversance with transnational, legal human-rights opinion enter naturally, over the ensuing decades, into the American Supreme Court's production of a centralized, autonomous, professional legal discourse of constitutional rights? Because, it seems, the former had died off before the latter gathered steam. The conversion of American constitutional-rights law into an autonomous body of professional discourse—one that might make some credible pretense to serving as a bulkhead sealing off institutionally binding decision from partisan, ideological strife—occurred mainly over a period of relative dearth, at least to American ears, of any salient transnational, lawyers' conversation on human rights.

As we already have noted, justices of our Supreme Court believe themselves responsible for safeguarding political legitimacy here. To many of

[141] As our present chief justice has said, "For nearly a century and a half, courts in the United States exercising the power of judicial review had no precedents to look to save their own, because our courts alone exercised this sort of authority." Rehnquist, *supra* note 66.

[142] Weinrib, *supra* note 3, at 19.

[143] See Slaughter, "Community," *supra* note 2, at 195–96.

[144] See, e.g., *Pierson v. Post*, 3 Cai. R. 175 (N.Y. Sup. Ct. 1805) (the first legal case ever read by many law students of my generation).

[145] See the opinion of Marshall, C.J. in *The Antelope*, 23 U.S. 66 (1825), which takes shape as a debate between the two. John Adams, who appointed Marshall to the chief justiceship, had sized him up as a man "learned in the law of nations." Charles Francis Adams, ed., *The Works of John Adams* (Boston: Little, Brown, 1856), 8:549, cited in David McCullough, *John Adams* (New York: Simon & Schuster, 2001), 486.

them, for reasons we have reviewed, that may mean safeguarding the integrity of the American discourse of constitutional law. Would judges risk failing in that duty if they were just now to take it upon themselves to fold our hitherto indigenous constitutional-legal discursive object into another widely viewed as having its own, distinct ideological flavor and momentum?[146] Might such a move reasonably strike conscientious American judges as an irresponsible deviation from fidelity to the Constitution, one that could dangerously compromise the perceived integrity of the discourse? Those are my questions. I put them in full awareness of how naive they may seem, in a setting where the resistance to the folding-in comes only from "conservative" judges and the push comes mainly from "liberals."

Is Any Anxiety Warranted?

I forbear from trying to answer the questions directly, or to defend them further against suspicion of naïveté. I merely suggest that integrity-anxiety may not finally be a well-considered reason for excluding comparative sources from American constitutional adjudication, even accepting, if only *arguendo*, that it is a reason both respectable and plausibly attributed to the players. First, it seems that an opening to comparative analysis could almost certainly be managed by a Supreme Court jointly bent on doing so without jeopardizing legal-discursive integrity. Second, such an opening, if it could be judiciously accomplished, might actually help to alleviate whatever threat American pluralism may pose to American political legitimacy.

Discourses undergo "paradigm shifts"—as they are called by historians of science—yet retain their identities, their integrities. Science remains science across Newton, Darwin, and Einstein. In its short life, American constitutional law has undergone major shifts without losing its discursive identity. Once upon a time, its central cases of government malfeasance in the field of rights were interferences with contract and property. More recently, the central cases have been interferences with free speech and discrimination on the basis of race. Also undergoing profound shifts have been allocations of authority to decode and specify constitutional rights, as among the people,[147] the state governments, the Congress, and the Supreme Court. No special reason appears why judges motivated to

---

[146] Weinrib, *supra* note 3, writes at length on a "postwar conception of the constitution" that, "by design, transcends the history, cultural heritage, and social mores of any particular nation state." Id. at 15.

[147] See Kramer, *supra* note 129.

do so could not see Americans safely through another constitutional-legal discursive conversion—say, a conversion of our hitherto relatively isolated constitutional-rights jurisprudence into one locked in sustained engagement with the transnational discourse of human rights.

There are grounds, furthermore, for thinking that not only might our judges, by doing this, not aggravate strains of commitment here, they actually might ease them. Integrity-anxiety itself, after all, is the reflection of a hope that will not die: the hope, that is, that political legitimacy here can find support in general belief—this is how I put it before—"in the sincerity and objectivity, or say the nonpartisanship, of the judges' rulings on constitutional meanings that finally control applications of governmental force in the country." But it is unclear, at best, how convincing a veneer of objectivity anyone can really provide these days for the American judiciary's renditions of people's rights, just by calling them applications of the American Constitution, or of American constitutional law. Think of *Bush v. Gore* (decided, remember, on the basis of a finding of arbitrary deprivation of the individual right to vote). Think of the *First Things* symposium and its authors' claim that the American Bill of Rights has been corrupted, falsified, by judges' becoming participants in a process in which contenders on all sides press to make it yield responses to questions that—the critics say—it was never meant to answer at all, either way.

The case today could be that by referring morally freighted controversies over rights to the American discourse of constitutional law for official resolution, Americans do not any longer provide much of a cover of objectivity and impartiality for the resolutions. We may rather be stripping the legal discourse—we may already have stripped it—of whatever semblance of objectivity, of distance and insulation from our raging moral disagreements over rights issues, it may ever have possessed. To the extent that morally motivated citizens these days simply cannot bring themselves to believe that judicial rulings on the application of constitutional law to rights controversies are independent of the judges' own moral orientations and moral certainties,[148] placing the entire weight of justification, of legitimation, on the historic American discourse of constitutional law could be taking us in the wrong direction—spreading our culture wars to the law, rather than cooling them down through appeals to the law.

That, in fact, is what Scalia says is true. His solution is to stop the Court—could he but do so—from pronouncing on rights claims that are both socially controversial and legally debatable.[149] Since that would be

---

[148] See, e.g., Duncan Kennedy, *A Critique of Adjudication: Fin de Siècle* (Cambridge: Harvard University Press, 1997), 8, 304, 311–14, 361 (on "loss of faith" in rights adjudication).

[149] See, e.g., *Cruzan v. Dep't of Health*, 497 U.S. 261, 300–01 (Scalia, J., concurring): "This Court .<ht>. . has no authority to inject itself into every field of human activity where

to shrink the project of legal pacification of divisive social controversies over rights to a point of virtual abandonment, perhaps a different solution is worth considering. Maybe our local legal discourse of *constitutional* rights could gain some protection from the danger of divisiveness by entering full-scale into open, visible, robust colloquy with the transnational discourse of *human* rights. The world, even that fraction of it falling within what John Rawls calls the historical public culture of constitutional democracy, is bigger than America, and Americans presumably know it. If Americans could see their judges grappling, openly and apparently honestly, with emergent world legal opinion—world *legal* opinion, not world moral opinion—regarding the human-rights matters that divide us, maybe that could help them rebuild confidence in the objectivity— the *objectivity*, not the precise rightness; often we will remain obdurately divided over the precise rightness—of the resulting adjudications.[150]

It is in that way, perhaps, that "narrowing the gap between the interpretation of a national constitutional right and the interpretation of the corresponding international human right may serve rather than disserve" the institutional goals of a national judiciary,[151] and that "evidence of likeminded foreign decisions could enhance the legitimacy" of one or another judicial ruling on a hot-button issue.[152] The sight of American judges visibly engaged with a more encompassing network of legal discourse might be reassuring with regard to the objectivity of whatever is decided. Or it might not. It would depend entirely on the extent to which Americans really do feel a valued sense of membership in a political-moral community transcending the boundaries of the United States, and really could find satisfaction in seeing that membership manifested in judicial interpretations of their own constitutional Bill of Rights.[153]

The speculation that they might is Habermasian,[154] and maybe utopian.[155] But it is worth trying, at least, to imagine what it might mean for

---

irrationality and oppression may theoretically occur, and if it tries to do so it will destroy itself."

[150] See Neuman, "Uses," *supra* note 9, at 90 ("Widespread recognition of the right to homosexual intimacy in other liberal democracies . . . added to the objective character of the Court's decision" in *Lawrence v. Texas*).

[151] Neuman, "Human Rights," *supra* note 10, at 1879.

[152] Slaughter, "Community," *supra* note 2, at 201.

[153] As Vicki Jackson has noted, it is "uncertain," an "empirical question" that probably has no "universal answer," whether "it is necessary, for law to perform its coercive and legitimating functions to speak as if it were *indigenously* autonomous." Jackson, *supra* note 9, at 262 (emphasis supplied).

[154] See Jürgen Habermas, *The Inclusion of the Other: Studies in Political Theory* (Cambridge: MIT Press, 1998), 155–61.

[155] Consider Frederick Schauer's speculation that post-"pariah" states are the ones most likely to want to demonstrate membership in the family of democracies, and whose courts thus will most likely be motivated to engage demonstratively in "borrowing." See Frederick

Americans, encouraged by their judges, to come to understand themselves as participants in a transnational legal culture of rights or, if you prefer this phrase, of constitutional democracy. The gains for us could be immense in the event that it did occur, or reoccur, to Americans how profoundly we hold things in common with a family of constitutional democratic societies—moral things, things that are basic, things that are dear. The experience could help to revive among us a sense of internal moral commonality and ethical fellowship that our current, insular fights over American constitutional meanings can only tend to damage. This would not, to be sure, be an exclusively American fellowship but would be, nonetheless, an inclusive fellowship of Americans.

Schauer, "The Politics and Incentives of Legal Transplantation," in *Governance in a Globalizing World*, ed. Joseph S. Nye and John J. Donahue (Washington, DC: Brookings Institution Press, 2000), 253, 259.

Chapter 10 _____

A Brave New Judicial World

ANNE-MARIE SLAUGHTER

AMERICAN EXCEPTIONALISM in the judicial context is not exceptional so much as temporal. One of the three elements of Michael Ignatieff's definition of American exceptionalism is judicial isolation. "American judges," he writes, "are exceptionally resistant to using foreign human rights precedents to guide them in their domestic opinions." This attitude, he adds, "is anchored in a broad popular sentiment that the land of Jefferson and Lincoln has nothing to learn about rights from any other country."[1] Several other contributions to this volume, most notably those by Frank Michelman and Harold Koh, directly address the extent to which American judges defiantly define themselves outside the mainstream of global judicial conversation. I have also written repeatedly in this vein.[2] In fact, however, when American judicial behavior is examined over a decade, what is most striking is the extent to which U.S. judges have come to understand and accept that they are deciding cases in a global as well as a national context.[3] In this longer view, what we are witnessing is more likely a clumsy and contested process of judicial globalization than an enduring and exceptional isolationism.

Increased American judicial globalization is most evident in private commercial cases in which, owing to economic globalization, U.S.

I am indebted, as I am so often, to William Burke-White and Terry Murphy for research and editing assistance. I also thank two anonymous reviewers and Ian Malcolm of Princeton University Press.

[1] *See* Michael Ignatieff's introduction to this volume.

[2] *See* Anne-Marie Slaughter, "Judicial Globalization," *Virginia Journal of International Law* 40 (2000): 1103–24; Anne-Marie Slaughter, "A Global Community of Courts," *Harvard Journal of International Law* 44 (2003): 191–219; Anne-Marie Slaughter, "A Typology of Transjudicial Communication," *University of Richmond Law Review* 29 (1994): 99–137.

[3] I first started chronicling "transjudicial communication" in 1994. In 1995 Thomas Franck held a seminal conference at New York University that was chaired by Justice O'Connor and included Justices Breyer and Ginsberg and an astonishing assembly of top supreme court judges and judges from international tribunals from all over the world. The American participants were noticeably impressed by their global colleagues. In the intervening decade, the frequency of citations to foreign law and of face-to-face meeting of judges

judges are required more and more often to apply either foreign law or a treaty to resolve the issue before them. These cases also bring them into increased contact with their foreign counterparts, who are often hearing some version of the same dispute: in parallel litigation where the plaintiff sues the defendant in one country and the defendant turns around and sues the plaintiff in another; in a *forum non conveniens* case where the defendant to a suit brought in one country tries to convince the judge that it should be transferred to another; or in cases with tentacles in many lands, such as global bankruptcies. In all these situations U.S. judges have proven themselves quite up to the task of finding, interpreting, and applying foreign or international law. Further, a number of judicial leaders, on both the Supreme Court and lower courts, have supported measures and taken steps directly to educate their colleagues about international law issues.[4]

Where U.S. judges are proving to be much more parochial, at least in comparison with the judges from many other nations, is their willingness to participate publicly in an ongoing global judicial conversation conducted primarily among constitutional judges. Indeed, the chief justice of the Supreme Court of Canada has openly chided the U.S. Supreme Court for its failure to engage in what she describes as a global judicial human rights dialogue. The roots of this reluctance may indeed be a form of judicial isolationism. Yet before we brand and condemn such behavior as American exceptionalism, it is worth pausing for a moment to contemplate the extent to which the conversation itself is exceptional. For these judges are not only communicating across borders because the applicable law to a case before them directs them there. They are reaching out to one another in a form of collective deliberation, clearly mindful of the differences of national legal systems and traditions and their own resulting obligations to uphold national laws, yet nevertheless recognizing how often they confront similar issues and how much they are engaged in a common professional enterprise.

In this context, American judicial foot-dragging becomes easier to understand, if not to approve. What is the precise boundary between a judge's obligations as a national public servant, sworn to uphold and

---

across borders, as well as other evidence of judicial globalization, has increased at a remarkable rate.

[4] For example, the American Society of International Law has undertaken a wide variety of judicial outreach activities over the past eight years, including regular panels on international law topics at circuit conferences and the publication of an *International Law Handbook* that has been distributed to every member of the federal bench. These activities are guided by a Judicial Advisory Board chaired by Justice O'Connor and comprising a number of distinguished federal judges who have actively encouraged their colleagues to take the opportunity to educate themselves further on international law issues.

indeed to safeguard national law, and his or her membership in a global judicial community? Those U.S. judges and justices who are actively engaged in talking to and learning from their foreign counterparts argue that such interaction simply makes them better judges—better at their craft by virtue of having better tools. Their opponents rail against the imposition of "foreign fads and fashions" on U.S. citizens, insisting that "it is the constitution of the United States we are expounding." This debate, while often politically charged, is neither surprising nor unreasonable in a proud and pluralist constitutional democracy.

Indeed, Frank Michelman, in an admirably Dworkinian spirit, has developed a potential justification for rejecting comparative judicial analysis that is thoughtful, carefully reasoned, and congruent with the deepest traditions of American constitutionalism. Michelman accepts the proposition that many U.S. judges, beginning with a number of Supreme Court justices, feel actively threatened by the citation of foreign judicial decisions, even though it is clear that those decisions are being cited for purposes of the information they convey and the persuasiveness of their reasoning, rather than any kind of precedent or evidence of some emerging global consensus that the United States should join. What, he asks, could the judges of the most powerful country in the world and the oldest constitutional democracy in the world possibly have to fear? His answer is "integrity-anxiety." In a republic as pluralist as ours, he argues, vehement moral disagreements will constantly threaten to tear the society and even the polity apart. For a combination of theoretical and historical reasons, Americans look to the Supreme Court to keep those disagreements in check by finding a way through that all sides accept—not because they agree but because it is "the law." That presumed objectivity, however, depends on the integrity of a larger constitutional "discourse," in which lawyers and judges and commentators and litigants all draw from a limited and agreed set of sources.

If U.S. judges reaching out to and drawing on the experience of their counterparts abroad do not have at least a degree of integrity-anxiety, they should. It is precisely the kind of concern that should guide principles concerning how and when comparative analysis is used in U.S. opinions. Nevertheless, Michelman concludes, and I agree, that it should be possible for U.S. judges to engage in a global judicial human rights dialogue without in fact undermining the integrity of U.S. constitutional discourse as a political bulwark of our democracy. Indeed, the most immediate outcome of such engagement will be a greater appreciation of the distinctiveness of U.S. law and hence a search for its roots in a distinctive historical, cultural, geographic, and political experience.

Equally important, as an empirical matter, I predict that U.S. judges will increasingly participate in global judicial conversations on paper and

in practice. The reasoning behind such a prediction goes beyond the concrete evidence found in judicial opinions and speeches and the remarkable
changes that have occurred over the past decade, led by what is now a
solid majority of Supreme Court Justices. Judicial globalization changes
not only what our judges know and need to know, as a practical matter,
but also how they think about who they are and what they do. The boundaries of their professional identity expand beyond national borders. This
change will come about whether or not justices and judges *cite* foreign
opinions; it is enough for them simply to know of their existence, and,
equally crucial, to know the individual judges who authored them. Globalization—for all individuals—operates most fundamentally at this very
basic, human level.

An interesting indicator of this psychological shift is growing support,
among judges, for global judicial education. The International Organization for Judicial Training (IOJT) was created in March 2002 at a conference of judges from twenty-four countries who came together "to establish a global organization dedicated to providing training and continuing
education for judges" and to create a network of institutions already providing judicial education in these various countries.[5] American judge Clifford Wallace, a former chief judge of the Ninth Circuit Court of Appeals,
is one of the founding members of the IOJT. In a recent article entitled
"Globalization of Judicial Education," he argues, based on his own experience, that principles of judicial education are far more generic than national legal establishments typically assume.[6] He offers various functional
reasons as to why globalizing judicial education would be a good idea,
such as keeping up with a "globalizing legal community" and improving
the quality of national and local judicial training through information
sharing and collective experimentation to supplement national judicial
training with more global offerings.[7] But he also defines globalization in
more elemental terms, as "attracting worldwide participation," "widening the horizons" of judges from different nations.[8] He has come to see
that the "rule of law and the concept of justice are worldwide and fundamental principles."[9] Judges should thus come together to work for "the
global establishment of the rule of law."[10]

---

[5] Conference brochure for the Second International Conference on the Training of the
Judiciary, "Judicial Education in a World of Challenge and Change," October 31–November 3, 2004, Fairmont Château Laurier Hotel, Ottawa, Ontario, Canada.

[6] J. Clifford Wallace, "Globalization of Judicial Education," *Yale Journal of International Law* 28 (2003): 355–64.

[7] *Id.* at 356.

[8] *Id.*

[9] *Id.* at 364.

[10] *Id.*

If American judicial parochialism is more temporal than exceptional, we need not look for more fundamental explanations of the differences between American and foreign judges. Ignatieff, however, takes a different tack. Building on the work of Paul Kahn, who argues that Americans' suspicion of human rights law is linked to their suspicion of anything not directly authorized by American representatives and institutions, Ignatieff ponders whether what appears to outsiders as judicial narcissism might not instead be a commitment to defending the "democratic legitimacy of its distinctive rights culture."[11] He hypothesizes further that "these rights, authored in the name of 'we the people,' are anchored in the historical project of the American revolution: a free people establishing a republic based in popular sovereignty." The suggestion is that advocates of human rights face more obstacles in the United States than elsewhere because majority prejudice in the country is more likely to trump the rights claims of minorities.

This claim is certainly jarring to an American lawyer weaned on *Brown v. Board of Education* and footnote 4 of *Carolene Products*, which John Ely relied on to develop an entire theory of American constitutionalism based on the courts' role as the indispensable protectors of "discrete and insular minorities."[12] And lest that seem ancient history, in 2004, the year of *Brown*'s fiftieth anniversary, it was the Massachusetts Supreme Judicial Court that took the lead in protecting the right of homosexuals and lesbians to marry—hardly a national majority position.[13] It may be true that Americans are more reflexively nationalist than citizens of other countries (although more so than the French? the Mexicans? the Poles?), and that they cover this reflex with a comforting myth about being more attached to "democracy" than other nations, but American judges have a profound commitment to minority rights as a fundamental pillar of American liberal democracy.

These disagreements notwithstanding, however, I deeply applaud the overall spirit and message of this volume. Americans, even the most internationalist and multilateralist among us, must confront the phenomenon of American exceptionalism and try to sift myth from fact. We far too often confuse our normative commitments with our empirical assessments about what America does and is. As Ignatieff wrote powerfully in the summer of 2004, even those Americans who were the most vocal and most outraged in denouncing the abuses of Abu Ghraib saw it as a horri-

---

[11] *See* Ignatieff's introduction to this volume.

[12] *United States v. Carolene Prods. Co.*, 304 U.S. 144, 152 n.4 (1938). *See, generally,* John Hart Ely, *Democracy and Distrust: A Theory of Judicial Review* (Cambridge: Harvard University Press, 1980).

[13] *See, e.g., Hillary Goodridge & others vs. Department Of Public Health & another.* SJC-08860, November 18, 2003, Supreme Judicial Court of Massachusetts.

ble stain on what America stands for in the world, incapable of relating it back to other dark moments in our history.[14] This inability to absorb and indeed internalize unpleasant facts, to see ourselves as others—even our close friends and allies—see us, may help explain our celebrated optimism. Yet Ignatieff's point, offered in the spirit of friendship, is that as a national trait, this blindness is better characterized as national narcissism than as exceptionalism.

The first part of this essay reviews a number of different factors contributing to judicial globalization and distinguishes the current global judicial conversation among constitutional judges as a particularly novel and unusual phenomenon. It differs from more functional forms of judicial globalization, as well as from the classic "reception" of foreign law by newer courts. Understanding these differences is important to understanding the deeper psychological effects of participation in this conversation. The second part turns to Michelman's argument and my embellishment of his conclusion. I look to the reasons actually given by many judges regarding the benefits of engaging in regular exchange, both written and face-to-face, with their foreign colleagues. I also analyze the experience itself to support the claim that once judges have become aware that they are part of a wider judicial world they cannot go back to a more bounded existence, on the bench or off. The final section turns from the phenomenon of judicial globalization to part of Ignatieff's explanation for American judicial isolationism in the face of it. I reject the proposition that American rights are expressions of majority will rather than blocks against majority prejudice, although without trying to meet the argument in any proper depth. Given the limitations of this brief essay, I simply sketch a number of counterarguments that I suggest would at least have to be addressed if the point is to be carried.

A Novel and Remarkable Global Judicial Conversation

Judicial globalization takes many forms and is driven by many causes.[15] To begin with, as the economic and social transactions that give rise to disputes become increasingly globalized, courts in countries around the world find themselves facing cases with tentacles stretching across borders, linking them to foreign courts or at least raising questions of foreign

[14] Michael Ignatieff, "The Unbearable Burden of Destiny: America, the Good and the Ugly," *International Herald Tribune*, June 30, 2004, at 6.

[15] For a much more comprehensive description of the many ways that judges are currently interacting around the world, *see* "Judges: Constructing a Global Legal System," in Anne-Marie Slaughter, *A New World Order* (Princeton: Princeton University Press, 2004), 65–103.

and international law. Justice Sandra Day O'Connor has been out in front exhorting U.S. judges to realize and respond to these changes. She asks: "[W]hy does information about international law matter so much? Why should judges and lawyers who are concerned about the intricacies of ERISA, the Americans with Disabilities Act, and the Bankruptcy Code care about issues of foreign law and international law?" She answers: "The reason, of course, is globalization. No institution of government can afford now to ignore the rest of the world."[16]

Justice O'Connor's argument is functional. Judges who must decide more and more cases involving issues governed by international or foreign law must familiarize themselves with those bodies of law, just as they must know the general dimensions of different areas of American law. She is joined, perhaps surprisingly to some, by Justice Scalia, who is equally insistent that U.S. judges should be prepared to apply international treaties and look to the national decisions of other treaty parties in interpreting those treaties. Thus in a 2004 decision involving the application of the Warsaw Convention (a treaty governing airline liability) to a claim against Olympic Airways for the death of an asthmatic passenger—the result of secondhand smoke from the smoking section—Scalia dissented on the grounds that his colleagues in the majority had ignored decisions by Australian and British appellate courts that interpreted the relevant provision of the Warsaw Convention very differently.[17] In his words, "Today's decision stands out for its failure to give any serious consideration to how the courts of our treaty partners have resolved the legal issues before us."[18]

In still other cases judges negotiate their own treaties. Global bankruptcies, for instance, require judges to communicate directly with one another with or without an international treaty or guidelines to ensure a cooperative and efficient distribution of assets. Governments have left these matters up to courts; courts have responded by creating their own regimes. Two commentators describe these court-to-court agreements, which have come to be known as "Cross-Border Insolvency Cooperation Protocols," as "essentially case-specific, private international insolvency treaties."[19] Global bankruptcies could not occur absent the larger driving

[16] Sandra Day O'Connor, "Keynote Address," *American Society of International Law Proceedings* 96 (2002): 348.

[17] *Olympic Airways v. Husain*, 124 S. Ct. 1221 (2004).

[18] *Id.* at 1230. Justice Scalia similarly emphasized the importance of looking to decisions by the courts of treaty partners in any case raising an issue of treaty law in his address to the 2004 Annual Meeting of the American Society of International Law, forthcoming in the *2004 Proceedings of the American Society of International Law*.

[19] Evan D. Flaschen and Ronald J. Silverman, "Cross-Border Insolvency Cooperation Protocols," *Texas International Law Journal* 33 (1998): 587–612, at 589. For a discussion

economic forces of globalization, bringing elites everywhere, including judges, closer together.

A second set of factors behind judicial globalization are more explicitly political. The European Commission for Democracy through Law (the Venice Commission) operates a Web site called CODICES, in addition to a paper *Bulletin on Constitutional Case-Law,* which regularly collects and digests the decisions of constitutional courts and courts of equivalent jurisdiction around the world. CODICES has liaisons in more than fifty countries; it not only offers a précis of each case in the database but also makes it possible to search the entire database by keyword or phrase to allow researchers to find out quickly what courts in many different countries have said on a particular issue.[20]

The expressed purpose of CODICES is instructive. It is "to allow judges and constitutional law specialists in the academic world to be informed quickly about the most important judgments" in constitutional law.[21] But the underlying reason is explicitly political: to build democracy through law. According to the CODICES Web site, "The exchange of information and ideas among old and new democracies in the field of judge-made law is of vital importance. Such an exchange and such cooperation, it is hoped, will not only be of benefit to the newly established constitutional jurisdictions of Central and Eastern Europe, but will also enrich the case-law of the existing courts in Western Europe and North America."[22] The aim is to strengthen the new constitutional courts in the fledgling democracies and facilitate convergence of constitutional law across Europe.

Across the Pacific, LawAsia is a form of regional bar association, composed of different kinds of legal associations across the region as well as individual lawyers, law firms, and corporations. It publishes law bulletins and offers many different venues for its members to come together and exchange information and ideas. Its primary goal as a professional association has been to offer networking opportunities for its members, but a secondary goal, made quite explicit, includes promoting the rule of law through "disseminating knowledge of the law of members' countries,"

---

of how practitioner input, through the Insolvency and Creditors' Rights Committee of the International Bar Association, has influenced these proceedings by developing a "Concordat" ready to be adopted as a cross-border Protocol in these cases, *see* Bruce Leonard, "Managing Default by a Multinational Venture: Cooperation in Cross-Border Insolvencies," *Texas International Law Journal* 33 (1998): 543–56.

[20] In the CODICES homepage [cited June 1, 2004]; available from http://www.codices .coe.int3.

[21] In the CODICES homepage [cited June 1, 2004]; available from http://codices.coe .int/cgi-bin/om_isapi.dll?clientID=380820158&infobase=codices.nfo&softpage=Browse_ Frame_Pg42.

[22] *Id.*

"promoting the efficient working of the legal systems of members' countries," and "promoting development of the law and uniformity where appropriate."[23] Other goals refer to the promotion of human rights and the administration of justice throughout the region.

Third, increased technological supply is facilitating if not encouraging functional demand. The extraordinary increase in information availability through the Internet has made it almost as easy to research foreign and international case law as to find domestic decisions in many countries. The two principal electronic legal databases, LexisNexis and Westlaw, now include legislation and decisions from the EU, the UK, Australia, Hong Kong, Russia, Mexico, Ireland, New Zealand, Singapore, and Canada.[24] Access to these foreign sources has expanded primarily in the last decade.

If judicial globalization were driven only by functional need and technological supply, however, it would be less remarkable and certainly less controversial. Yet in the same Olympic Airways case discussed above, Justice Scalia could not resist an extra dig at his colleagues.

> This sudden insularity is striking, since the Court in recent years has canvassed the prevailing law in other nations (at least Western European nations) to determine the meaning of an American Constitution that those nations had no part in framing and that those nations' courts have no role in enforcing. See *Atkins v. Virginia* (whether the Eighth Amendment prohibits execution of the mentally retarded); *Lawrence v. Texas* (whether the Fourteenth Amendment prohibits the criminalization of homosexual conduct). One would have thought that foreign courts' interpretations of a treaty that their governments adopted jointly with ours, and that they have an actual role in applying, would be (to put it mildly) all the more relevant.[25]

This is the Scalia of *Thompson v. Oklahoma*, the 1988 death penalty case in which the plaintiffs cited international and foreign decisions barring the death penalty. Rejecting such evidence, Scalia expostulated, "We must not forget that it is the Constitution for the United States that we are expounding."[26]

Contrast the following statement by the chief justice of the Norwegian Supreme Court: "The Supreme Court has to an increasing degree taken part in international collaboration among the highest courts. It is a natu-

---

[23] "About Lawasia." In The Law Association for Asia and the Pacific homepage [cited June 1, 2004]; available from http://www.lawasia.asn.au.

[24] In the LexisNexis homepage [cited June 16, 2003]; available from http://www.lexis-nexis.com; in the Westlaw homepage [cited June 16, 2003]; available from http://web2.westlaw.com/signon/default.wl?newdoor=true.

[25] *Olympic Airways v. Husain, supra* note 17, at 1230–31.

[26] 487 U.S. 815, 869 (1988).

ral obligation that, in so far as we have the capacity, we should take part in European and international debate and mutual interaction. We should especially contribute to the ongoing debate on the courts' position on international human rights."[27] More generally, he notes, "It is the duty of national courts—and especially of the highest court in a small country—to introduce new legal ideas from the outside world into national judicial decisions."[28]

Here is the strand of judicial globalization that has created the most controversy in the United States and the greatest division between the United States and much of the rest of the world. Justice Smith is not talking about cases involving international treaties or transnational disputes. He is referring to a process of constitutional cross-fertilization for its own sake, in which high court judges—judges with constitutional jurisdiction, whether or not they serve on courts limited to constitutional cases—are engaging in a growing dialogue with their counterparts around the world on the issues that arise before them. They conduct this dialogue through mutual citation and increasingly direct interactions, often electronically. In the process, as Justice Smith suggests, they both contribute to a nascent global jurisprudence on particular issues and improve the quality of their particular national decisions, sometimes by importing ideas from abroad and sometimes by resisting them, insisting on an idiosyncratic national approach for specific cultural, historical, or political reasons. Further, they are remarkably self-conscious about what they are doing, engaging in open debates about the uses and abuses of "persuasive authority" from fellow courts in other countries.

In the words of Justice Claire L'Heureux-Dubé of the Canadian Supreme Court, "More and more courts, particularly within the common law world, are looking to the judgments of other jurisdictions, particularly when making decisions on human rights issues. Deciding on applicable legal principles and solutions increasingly involves a consideration of the approaches that have been adopted with regard to similar legal problems elsewhere."[29] From England comes confirmation from Lord Brown-Wilkinson, citing comments by "several senior members of the British judiciary" on their increased willingness "to accord persuasive authority to the constitutional values of other democratic nations when dealing with ambiguous statutory or common law provisions that impact upon

---

[27] Carsten Smith, "The Supreme Court in Present-Day Society," in *The Supreme Court of Norway*, ed. Stephan Tschudi-Madsen (Oslo: H. Aschenhoug & Co., 1998), 134–35.

[28] *Id.* at 135.

[29] Claire L'Heureux-Dubé, "The Importance of Dialogue: Globalization and the International Impact of the Rehnquist Court," *Tulsa Law Journal* 34 (1998): 15, at 16.

civil liberties issues."[30] The new South African Constitution requires the South African Constitutional Court to "consider international law" and permits it to consult foreign law in its human rights' decisions;[31] in a landmark opinion holding the death penalty unconstitutional, the Court cited decisions of the U.S. Supreme Court, the Canadian Constitutional Court, the German Constitutional Court, the Indian Supreme Court, the Hungarian Constitutional Court, and the Tanzanian Court of Appeal.[32] More systematically, scholars have documented the use of comparative material by constitutional courts in Israel, Australia, South Africa, Canada, India, New Zealand, Zimbabwe, and Ireland.[33]

Is such cross-fertilization really new? It is a well-recognized phenomenon among imperial powers and their colonies.[34] It is well established in the Commonwealth.[35] Plenty of evidence of borrowing from English law can also be found in the nineteenth-century U.S. and federal reports. In this century, the traffic has largely flowed in the other direction; since 1945 recent constitutional courts around the world, frequently established either by the United States or on the model of the U.S. Supreme Court, have borrowed heavily from U.S. Supreme Court jurisprudence.[36]

[30] Ian Loveland, "The Criminalization of Racist Violence," in *A Special Relationship? American Influences on Public Law in the UK*, ed. Ian Loveland (Oxford: Clarendon Press, 1995), 253, at 257 (citing comments by Lord Browne-Wilkinson).

[31] Constitution of South Africa, Sect. 39.

[32] *The State v. T Makwanyane and M Mchunu*, Case No. CCT/3/94 (South Africa June 6, 1995).

[33] Christopher McCrudden, "A Common Law of Human Rights? Transnational Judicial Conversations on Constitutional Rights," *Oxford Journal of Legal Studies* 20 (2000): 499–532, 506.

[34] To take the most obvious example, the architects of the U.S. Constitution were steeped in the principles of the common law and in the political theories of the Age of Enlightenment. The legal ideas expounded in the Constitution in turn influenced the framing of the French Declaration of the Rights of Man and of the Citizen, and in turn spread to other continents through imperial rule. Anthony Lester, "The Overseas Trade in the American Bill of Rights," *Columbia Law Review* 88 (1988): 537–61, at 541. On the reception and internalization of foreign law generally, *see* H. Patrick Glenn, "Persuasive Authority," *McGill Law Journal* 32 (1987): 261, at 296.

[35] David McClean, "A Common Inheritance? An Examination of the Private International Law Tradition of the Commonwealth," in *Recueil des Cours 1996: Collected Courses of The Hague Academy of International Law* (The Hague: Académie de Droit International ed., 1997), 9–98.

[36] This phenomenon is well documented. *See* Lester, *supra* note 34, at 541; Helmut Coing, "Europaisierung der Rechtswissenschaft," *Neue Juristische Wochenschrift* 15 (1990): 937–41; Andrzej Rapaczynski, "Bibliographical Essay: The Influence of U.S. Constitutionalism Abroad," in *Constitutionalism and Rights: The Influence of the United States Constitution Abroad*, ed. Louis Henkin and Albert J. Rosenthal (New York: Columbia University Press, 1990); Bruce Ackerman, "The Rise of World Constitutionalism," *Virginia Law Review* 83 (1997): 771–97; Mary Ann Glendon, *Rights Talk: The Impoverishment of Political Discourse* (New York: Free Press, 1991), 158.

Thus it is difficult to show from existing data that the use of comparative materials in constitutional adjudication has in fact increased.[37]

On the other hand, many participating judges and a number of observers think today's constitutional cross-fertilization is new in important ways.[38] They point to a number of distinctive features: the identity of the participants, the interactive dimension of the process, the motives for transnational borrowings, and the self-conscious construction of a global judicial community. On the demand side, many commentators note the impact of the end of the Cold War and the resulting emergence of many fledgling democracies with new constitutional courts seeking to emulate their more established counterparts. A flood of foundation and government funding for judicial seminars, training programs, and educational materials under the banner of "rule of law" programs helped provide personal contacts and intellectual opportunities for these new judges.[39] However, Frederick Schauer points out that in countries seeking to cast off an imperialist past, be it colonial or communist, it is likely to be particularly important to establish an indigenous constitution, including a set of human rights protections.[40] Borrowing constitutional ideas is thus likely to be politically more problematic than borrowing a bankruptcy code.[41]

Individual courts are thus often quite particular about when they borrow and from whom. Schauer argues that governments that want to demonstrate their membership in a particular political, legal, and cultural community are likely to encourage borrowing from members of that community.[42] In this regard, consider again the provision in the new South African Constitution requiring the constitutional court to look abroad. The clear message, from a state emerging from pariah status during the years of apartheid, is a desire to be part of a global legal community and to make explicit the consistency of South African constitutional law with

---

[37] *See, generally*, Alan Watson, *Legal Transplants* (Edinburgh: Scottish Academic Press, 1974); Alan Watson, "Legal Change: Sources of Law and Legal Culture," *University of Pennsylvania Law Review* 131 (1983): 1121–46; T. B. Smith, "Legal Imperialism and Legal Parochialism," *Juridical Review*, n.s., 10 (1965): 39–54.

[38] In addition to L'Heureux-Dubé, *supra* note 29, at 16, Sujit Choudhry, "Globalization in Search of Justification: Toward a Theory of Comparative Constitutional Interpretation," *Indiana Law Journal* 74 (1999): 819–91. Note that this most recent burst of scholarship contrasts with scholarship at the end of the 1980s that focused more on "one-way" traffic from the United States outward. *See supra* note 34.

[39] *See, generally*, Choudhry, *supra* note 38.

[40] Frederick Schauer, "The Politics and Incentives of Legal Transplantation," in *Governance in a Globalizing World*, ed. Joseph S. Nye and John D. Donahue (Washington, DC: Brookings Institution Press, 2000), 253–54, at 256.

[41] *Id.* at 257.

[42] Schauer, *supra* note 40, at 258.

the law of other leading liberal democratic legal systems. For the South African court itself, becoming part of a global judicial conversation has become a badge of legitimacy.

The identity of the most influential "lender" or "donor" courts in recent years is equally striking. The South African and Canadian constitutional courts have both been highly influential, apparently more so than the U.S. Supreme Court and other older and more established constitutional courts.[43] In part, their influence may spring from the simple fact that they are *not* American, which renders their reasoning more politically palatable to domestic audiences in an era of extraordinary U.S. military, political, economic, and cultural power and accompanying resentments.[44] But equally if not more important is the ability of these courts themselves to capture and crystallize the work of their fellow constitutional judges around the world. Schauer argues that the "ideas and constitutionalists of Canada have been disproportionately influential" in part because "Canada, unlike the United States, is seen as reflecting an emerging international consensus rather than existing as an outlier."[45]

Canada and South Africa—one old democracy and one new—with two new constitutional courts (the Canadian Supreme Court has existed since the mid–nineteenth century, but the new Canadian Constitution was enacted only in 1982; the South African Constitutional Court was created in 1994): each is looking around the world and canvassing the opinions of their fellow constitutional courts, and each is disproportionately influential as a result. Here is the most dramatic difference from past patterns of legal transplantation or cross-fertilization. According to Canadian justice L'Heureux-Dubé, the most important break with the past is that "the process of international influences has changed from *reception* to *dialogue*. Judges no longer simply *receive* the cases of other jurisdictions and then apply them or modify them for their own jurisdiction."[46] Instead, appellate judges around the world are engaging in self-conscious conversation.[47]

This *awareness* of constitutional cross-fertilization on a global scale—an awareness of who is citing whom among the judges themselves and a concomitant pride in a cosmopolitan judicial outlook—creates an incentive to be both lender and borrower. Indeed, the Taiwanese Constitu-

---

[43] *Id.*; These patterns of influence operate not just among Commonwealth countries, but far more broadly as well. Schauer observes that "the phenomenon appears to be strong not only in countries with a British Commonwealth background but also in countries as culturally removed from the British Commonwealth as Vietnam." *Id.*

[44] Compare Schauer, *supra* note 40, at 258.

[45] *Id.*

[46] L'Heureux-Dubé, *supra* note 29, at 17 (emphasis in original).

[47] *Id.*

tional Court has translated large portions of its case law into English and made them available on its Web site to ensure that it is part of this global dialogue.[48] Further, constitutional judges in many different countries, including the United States, are actively and openly discussing the legitimacy of this phenomenon. It is one thing to borrow to fill a gap or even build a foundation, as courts in fledgling states or newly decolonized countries have long had to do. It is another to have a domestic legal system developed enough to be able to decide the case in question, but nevertheless to search out how foreign judges have responded to a comparable case. The point is less to borrow than to benefit from comparative deliberation.

Here is the larger context within which U.S. judicial parochialism must be placed and evaluated. Justice L'Heureux-Dubé chides her colleagues on the U.S. Supreme Court for lagging behind, warning that they risk loss of influence in an increasingly self-conscious and self-constituted global community of judges. Ignatieff labels this behavior "judicial isolationism" and treats it as an established facet of the larger phenomenon of American exceptionalism. Yet suppose that it is in fact more of a lag? An inevitably slow turning of the gigantic ocean liner of U.S. constitutional jurisprudence and judicial practice? After all, even Chief Justice Rehnquist now urges all U.S. judges to participate in international judicial exchanges, on the ground that it is "important for judges and legal communities of different nations to exchange views, share information and learn to better understand one another and our legal systems."[49] And as discussed below, the debate among Supreme Court justices—with Breyer, Ginsberg, and apparently Stevens firmly on one side; Scalia, Thomas, and Rehnquist on the other; and O'Connor and Kennedy apparently in the middle with regard to canvassing and citing foreign decisions even when they are not a necessary ingredient in reaching a decision—seems less evidence of a culture of exceptionalism than of contentiousness.

Michelman's contribution to this volume focuses precisely on this debate. His is an admirable effort to develop the best possible argument in favor of a self-contained national jurisprudence, but one that in the end he and I reject. I accept his arguments, but suggest that it is likely to be overborne by the psychology and epistemology of judicial globalization—forces that strongly favor increased forms of collective global judicial deliberation. At the same time, whether such decisions are actually cited or

[48] In The Republic of China Constitutional Court Grand Justices Council Reporter [cited June 1, 2004]; available from http://www.judicial.gov.tw/j4e/.

[49] William Rehnquist, Remarks of the Chief Justice Court of Appeals for the Federal Circuit 20th Anniversary Judicial Conference April 8, 2002. In the Supreme Court of the United States homepage [cited June 14, 2003]; available from http://www.supremecourtus.gov/publicinfo/speeches/sp_04-08-02a.html.

not, as opposed to being part of the world of material available to judges in reaching a particular decision, will become increasingly less important.

Persuasive Authority, Integrity-Anxiety, and Judicial Identity

Michelman challenges himself to develop a justification for judicial nationalism among U.S. judges that is rooted in something other than parochialism, elitism, or political partisanship. After carefully chronicling the recent debates among U.S. Supreme Court justices on the question of whether and how it is permissible to cite foreign law, Michelman notes that "[o]ne has to search hard in [the opinions of the resisters] for a single, cogent statement of a reason for resistance. It is as if they do not know how to name what is bothering them."[50] He helpfully supplies such a reason, constructing an ideal account of the resisters' position that is rooted in "integrity-anxiety": "a perceived threat to the integrity, in a certain sense, of the historic discourse of American constitutional law respecting rights."[51]

The core of Michelman's argument is best captured in his own words:

> To view American constitutional law as a *discourse* is to see it as something beyond a raw deposit of substantive rules, doctrines, results, and precedents. It's to see the law as composed of an entire broad-sense "vocabulary" or dialect—including paradigmatic concepts, categorizations, value-orientations, and argumentative tropes—in which American constitutional lawyers and judges frame, convey, and comprehend their forensic exchanges. To speak of the *integrity* of this discourse is to speak of its unbroken identity through time as a distinctly cognizable, self-contained discursive object—a kind of discursive domain unto itself, visibly separate and freestanding from other normative discourses.[52]

The importance of this integrity is "nothing less than the defense of the legitimacy of government in this country . . . [against] corrosion by acidulous moral disagreement when it comes to defining and delineating people's rights."[53] Americans, in all their pluralist splendor, look to the Supreme Court to rescue them from their inevitable quarrels, some of which run very deep indeed. Whether or not the Court is actually as objective as it should or could be, its revered place in American political life derives from its supposed ability to hand down objective legal decisions that cut through moral disagreements. Theoretically at least, opening American

---

[50] *See* Frank Michelman's essay in this volume.
[51] *Id.*
[52] *Id.* (Emphases in the original.)
[53] *Id.*

constitutional discourse to a plethora of foreign sources could adulterate it to the point that it could undermine the Court's vital legitimacy.

Michelman's is an elegant, spare argument, compelling in its invocation of something that the vast majority of American constitutional lawyers—I would go further and say all lawyers—feel in their bones. This is precisely the integrity that John Paul Stevens sought to defend so passionately in his dissent in *Bush v. Gore*, when he wrote: "Although we may never know with complete certainty the identity of the winner of this year's Presidential election, the identity of the loser is perfectly clear. It is the Nation's confidence in the judge as an impartial guardian of the rule of law."[54] For my own part, I am convinced. If the members of the Supreme Court who resist the citation of foreign decisions did so out of integrity-anxiety, and if their anxiety seemed likely to be justified, then I would regard this as good and even sufficient reason to question the practice by U.S. judges in U.S. decisions.

Note the "ifs." As Michelman points out, "an opening to comparative analysis could almost certainly be managed by a Supreme Court jointly bent on doing so without jeopardizing legal-discursive integrity."[55] Moreover, such an opening could actually strengthen the Court's legitimacy.[56] Thus in the end he makes the best possible argument for resisting public acknowledgment of judicial cross-fertilization in American judicial opinions but then knocks it down.

Michelman's rejection of his own argument is strengthened by the actual reasons given by a number of judges and justices in favor of judicial cross-fertilization, reasons that make it harder to avoid the conclusion that the resistance of a three-person minority is politically motivated. In addition, the arguments in favor of judicial cross-fertilization advert to deep processes of personal growth, of a changed awareness of the actual parameters of the world they inhabit that is almost impossible either to change back or to compartmentalize. Third, these same processes mean that whether or not U.S. judges actually *cite* the foreign law they learn about as the result of transnational cross-fertilization, their view of their own law and hence their decisions will be inalterably changed. In this context it is far better to be able to trace the evolution of their views through citations than to guess at it through their itineraries. Moreover, their personal and professional growth as members of a larger judicial world will simply mirror the evolution, willy-nilly, of vast numbers of

[54] *George W. Bush and Richard Cheney v. Albert Gore, Jr.*, 531 U.S. 98, 128–129 (Stevens, dissenting) (2000).

[55] Michelman, *supra* note 50.

[56] *Id.*

American citizens who are having to relocate their lives and their country on a larger map.

Foreign decisions can be persuasive because they offer new information and perspectives that may cast an issue in a different and more tractable light. Canadian Supreme Court Justice G. V. La Forest writes: "The greater use of foreign material affords another source, another tool for the construction of better judgments. . . . The greater use of foreign materials by courts and counsel in all countries can, I think, only enhance their effectiveness and sophistication."[57] Compare Justice Ruth Bader Ginsberg, writing about the motives behind and deficiencies in U.S. affirmative action programs. She noted India's experience with affirmative action, including a decision by the Indian Supreme Court imposing a ceiling on the number of positions that can be reserved for disadvantaged citizens. "In the area of human rights," she observes, "experience in one nation or region may inspire or inform other nations or regions."[58]

Justice Stephen Breyer agrees. After citing foreign legal decisions on the death penalty in his dissent in *Knight v. Florida*, he wrote: "In these cases, the foreign courts I have mentioned have considered roughly comparable questions under roughly comparable legal standards. Each court has held or assumed that those standards permit application of the death penalty itself. Consequently, I believe their view[s] [*sic*] are useful even though not binding."[59] Compare Justice Albie Sachs of the South African Constitutional Court, who writes: "If I draw on statements by certain United States Supreme Court Justices, I do so not because I treat their decisions as precedents to be applied in our Courts, but because their *dicta* articulate in an elegant and helpful manner problems which face any modern court dealing with what has loosely been called church/State relations. Thus, though drawn from another legal culture, they express values and dilemmas in a way which I find most helpful in elucidating the meaning of our own constitutional text."[60]

Justice Shirley Abrahamson, chief justice of the Wisconsin Supreme Court and an intellectual leader among state judges, observes, "[W]hen courts from around the world have written well-reasoned and provocative opinions in support of a position at odds with our familiar American views, we would do well to read carefully and take notes."[61] She points

---

[57] Gerard V. La Forest, "The Use of American Precedents in Canadian Courts," *Maine Law Review* 46 (2994): 211–20, at 216 (1994).

[58] Ruth Bader Ginsburg, "Affirmative Action as an International Human Rights Dialogue," *Brookings Review* 18 (2000): 2, at 3.

[59] *Knight v. Florida*, 528 US 990, 120 S. Ct. 459, 464 (U.S. 1999) (Breyer, dissenting from denial of cert.).

[60] *S. v Lawrence; S. v Negal; S. v Solberg*, (4) SA 1176, 1223 (South Africa 1997).

[61] *Id.* at 284.

out that U.S. state court judges automatically canvass the case law of sister states for ideas and perspectives on the issues before them, yet shrink automatically from looking at case law even from so near a geographic and cultural neighbor as Canada.[62] "We are already comparatists," she writes. "We just don't think of ourselves that way."[63]

Still another argument in favor of persuasive authority is that it can help American judges come up with new approaches that they might not otherwise have thought of. Judge Calabrese of the Second Circuit, for instance, argued in a 1995 case that U.S. courts should follow the lead of the German and the Italian constitutional courts in finding ways to signal the legislature that a particular statute is "heading toward unconstitutionality," rather than striking it down immediately or declaring it constitutional.[64] Or recall Justice O'Connor's functionalist rationale described above, urging U.S. lawyers and judges to look abroad to prepare themselves to decide cases in a globalized world. As Michelman points out, Justice O'Connor has not yet cited a foreign decision in one of her opinions, but in her 2002 address to the American Society of International Law she said, "Although international law and the law of other nations are rarely binding upon our decisions in U.S. courts, conclusions reached by other countries and by the international community should at times constitute persuasive authority in American courts."[65]

Justice Kennedy, for his part, is evidently comfortable with looking abroad when the nature of the issue before the Court makes the experience of other countries directly relevant, as when claims about the nature of U.S. rights are grounded in the larger traditions and values of Western civilization.[66] Here he tacitly acknowledged the centuries-old reciprocal relationship between U.S. courts and their foreign colleagues, in which U.S. courts borrowed heavily from Britain. After 1945 it was the United States that was doing the lending. U.S. judges and apparently the U.S. public have never questioned the propriety or legitimacy of courts in countries around the world citing the U.S. Supreme Court on issues ranging from free speech to federalism. And indeed, U.S. judges continue actively counseling their foreign fellow jurists in setting up new courts; Jus-

---

[62] Shirley S. Abrahamson and Michael J. Fischer, "All the World's a Courtroom: Judging in the New Millennium," *Hofstra Law Review* 26 (1997): 276–92.

[63] *Id.* at 285.

[64] *United States v. Then*, 56 F.3d 464, 468–69 (1995).

[65] O'Connor, *supra* note 16, at 350.

[66] *Lawrence v. Texas*, 539 U.S. 558 (U.S., 2003) (observing that "to the extent *Bowers* relied on values shared with a wider civilization, the case's reasoning and holding have been rejected by the European Court of Human Rights, and that other nations have taken action consistent with an affirmation of the protected right of homosexual adults to engage in intimate, consensual conduct").

tices Sandra Day O'Connor and Anthony Kennedy met with newly appointed Iraqi judges two months before the planned transfer of sovereignty in Iraq.[67] Why should it be any different when information flows the other way?

The judges looking abroad are talking about better-reasoned and better-informed decisions, about being open to new ideas, about recognizing that the United States can learn as well as teach. Indeed, they embrace comparative analysis in part because of the ways in which it helps them appreciate the distinctiveness of U.S. law, culture, and history, an appreciation that is as likely to result in informed divergence as in convergence. Suppose, for instance, that in a conference of constitutional judges from around the world U.S. judges become aware of just how far out of line they are with prevailing doctrine in other countries. They might discover that their fellow constitutional judges from different countries, having consulted one another's decisions, virtually all agree that hate speech should not be permitted, that it should be an exception to a liberal constitutional right of freedom of speech.

Suppose further that the next First Amendment case before the U.S. Supreme Court involves hate speech. In the Court's opinion, the justices openly discuss the prevailing trends in global constitutional jurisprudence and announce that under U.S. constitutional precedents, they have decided to continue to permit hate speech as a necessary concomitant, however deplorable, of freedom of speech. They might justify their decision on the grounds that they are U.S. judges bound by a distinct legal and political tradition. Alternatively, they might declare that the U.S. historical and cultural trajectory has been sufficiently distinct from that of other nations as to warrant a different understanding of what freedom of speech must mean. Or they might invoke the specific text of the U.S. Constitution as opposed to the texts of other constitutions.

Any of these options would be informed divergence, a deliberate decision to pursue an explicitly idiosyncratic path in the face of global trends in the other direction.[68] It is equally possible to imagine legislators or regulators being made aware of the divergence between their laws or rules and those of a substantial number of other countries and nevertheless concluding to prize and preserve their differences on historical, cultural, political, economic, social, religious, or any other distinctive national grounds. What is critical is that the same forces pushing *toward* convergence—the forces of regulatory export, technical assistance, distilled information, and soft law—can also result in informed

---

[67] "Iraq Gets Court Aid from 2 U.S. Justices," *New York Times*, May 5, 2004, at A20.

[68] *See* Lawrence R. Helfer and Anne-Marie Slaughter, "Toward a Theory of Effective Supranational Adjudication," *Yale Law Journal* 107 (1997): 273–391, at 281.

divergence. They permit any subset of national officials, or indeed all three branches of a national government, to decide deliberately to affirm their difference.

In this context, the self-imposed insularity championed by Justices Scalia, Thomas, and Rehnquist looks increasingly suspect. As long as any sources other than precedent are admitted as aids to judicial reasoning, can we really justify excluding ideas of foreign provenance, even if they serve only to confirm our own uniqueness? Would the three self-proclaimed judicial "sovereigntists" bar the judicial reading of law review articles authored by foreign legal scholars? Of articles published in American law reviews by non-American law students that discuss American law in comparative perspective? Or even that purport to discuss only American law but that are inevitably influenced by the author's foreign background? Justices Scalia, Breyer, and Ginsberg were all law professors before becoming judges. Should they try to block out whatever knowledge of foreign legal systems they may have acquired in the classroom?

Or is the problem rather the *citation* of foreign legal decisions, the piling up of foreign precedents on a particular side of a U.S. argument? That is the nub of the fracas between Justices Breyer and Thomas in *Knight v. Florida*, in which Thomas accuses Breyer of looking to foreign decisions because he can't find any U.S. law on point.[69] And certainly the views of many courts around the world on the death penalty are closer to Breyer's position than to Thomas's. To decide that twenty-seven years on death row is cruel and unusual punishment because that is the view of a majority of other nations, or even of a majority of other nations that the United States might consider its "peer group," might look like "imposing a foreign fad or fashion" on the United States. But are the contemporary views of nations such as England and Canada, Germany and Japan (where we, after all, drafted their current constitutions) really more "foreign" than the views of a group of white men who lived over two centuries ago, owned slaves, and denied women the vote?

At the 2004 meeting of the American Society of International Law, Justice Scalia denounced the citation of foreign law or judicial decisions on the grounds that it was antioriginalist.[70] Yet adhering dogmatically to the view of the framers is as likely to distort judicial decision making in unhealthy ways as is reflexively bowing to some kind of global consensus on a particular issue. The right answer in both cases is to eschew any notion that a set of sources other than direct precedent can "dictate" a

---

[69] *Knight v. Florida*, 528 U.S. 990, 990 (U.S. 1999).

[70] Antonin Scalia, Keynote Address, Annual Meeting of the American Society of International Law, April 2, 2004.

decision, but to allow and indeed encourage judges to draw inspiration and influence where they will.

As long as they tell us about it. The worst of all worlds would be for judges to be deeply but secretly influenced by any set of sources. Yet that is the far more likely alternative to citing foreign decisions. Judges who travel abroad, learn about foreign legal systems, and interact regularly with their foreign counterparts will change in ways that cannot be compartmentalized. They will understand that they inhabit a wider and richer world, that they write for a wider audience, that they compete for the laurels of professional respect in a wider global arena. That understanding becomes gradually internalized in ways that shape the most basic conceptions of identity: the relation of oneself to others.

Two anecdotes may help to make the point. The first is related by Rita Hauser, a distinguished international lawyer who worked for Dean Roscoe Pound while she was a student at Harvard Law School. She recalls translating French legal documents for Dean Pound in the majestic reading room of the Harvard Law School library, with the names of great American judges and legal scholars engraved on a marble frieze around the ceiling. After she read him a particular passage, he paused in thought for a moment and then said, in a faintly surprised tone, "They have a better idea than we do." Hard as it may be for Americans steeped in what is indeed a great national legal tradition to imagine, foreign legal systems may indeed have better ideas than we do on some thorny legal issues, just as they may have in industrial organization, environmental protection, or scientific discovery—and just as we may also have better ideas than they do.

The second anecdote involves a young Princeton alumnus who has taken a defunct charter school in southwest Washington, DC, and transformed it into the nation's first urban public boarding school. He recounts that even among the students enrolled at the school—students who enter in the seventh grade and have chosen to try a more academically rigorous school that is specifically designed for college prep—when he asked at a school meeting how many expected to go on to college, only a few raised their hands. When he asked why, the most frequent explanation was "I'm not a good enough athlete." In the experience of these youngsters, *in their world*, the chief attribute necessary for college admission was athletic prowess. Bringing them into contact with peers who have different experiences and expectations is above all a matter of widening their world. Once they are part of that wider world, their points of reference and their standards of comparison will change forever.

Once judges have been introduced to a wider world of peers, it is impossible for them to recabin their intellectual and professional world. And trying to insulate them in the first place from foreign contacts and foreign opinions is like trying to block the Internet. Judges, like the rest of us, indeed like the litigants before them, live in a globalized world. They have access to more information; they have friends and colleagues across borders; they know irrevocably that even the full richness of American federal jurisprudence, which itself draws on the cumulative and ongoing experience of fifty state courts as well as almost 250 years of federal precedents, is only one way among many.

In this context, consider again Justice Rehnquist's exhortation to American judges to participate in international judicial exchanges, encouraging them precisely to "share information and learn to better understand one another and our legal systems."[71] I am arguing that if they heed his advice they will not be able to turn back. They will grow in sophistication and appreciation for both other legal systems and our own. Consider the following excerpt from Judge Wallace's discussion of judicial education:

> Up to this point, judicial education (and training) has largely been considered to be local and insular. The assumption has been that each country's judicial system is unique and therefore requires a unique type of judicial education. After consulting with judiciaries and judicial education institutions around the world, I have come to doubt that assumption.[72]

This reaction to exposure to foreign systems is predictable and praiseworthy. Yet even if American judges reject some or all of what they find abroad, it will change who they are and how they think—if not in every case, then surely in some. Should they then cover their tracks and deny these influences the minute they put pen to paper or fingers to keyboard to write an opinion? Are they not supposed to track their reasoning accurately and fully to allow the litigants and the wider public who receive their opinions to have the maximum prospect of developing counterarguments the next time round? Or to allow their future colleagues a chance to understand the precise nature of the precedents established?

Judges are allowed to take judicial notice of the world around them. The parameters of that notice can be debated as a matter of identifying the precise sources of the facts relied on in an opinion. But the larger point is that judges are men and women living in the same world as the rest of us, subject to the same forces that are making that world smaller. They do not need the exhortations of scholars to feel bonds with their fellow judges in other countries, the bonds of pride in craft and devotion to the enterprise of judging as fairly and faithfully as possible. That pride and discipline should ensure that judges divulge the sources of their reasoning and accept the strictures of precedent or code as their legal system demands. But where they must make difficult judgments based on a compound of philosophy,

---

[71] Rehnquist, *supra* note 49.
[72] Wallace, *supra* note 6, at 355.

values, and experience—judgments that in the end we appoint them to make—they cannot artificially restrict their knowledge and deny their identity. On the contrary, American judges should draw on comparative analysis to further enrich American law and to reach decisions and write opinions that will in turn be cited and grappled with by judges in other countries who have long looked to us.

Majority Will or Minority Rights?

In this final section I turn from the existence and longevity of the phenomenon of judicial exceptionalism to Michael Ignatieff's particular explanation for it. He suggests that American judges may define American rights in ways that are more connected to the will of the majority of the American people than to the desire or indeed the compulsion to protect the rights of American minorities. He begins by accepting Paul Kahn's identification of the deep connection between American national identity and popular sovereignty.[73] The point here is that Americans purportedly cannot accept international human rights even when they are codified in treaties ratified in accordance with the U.S. Constitution because they are still "foreign," not homegrown products of American constitutional soil.

As evidence for this proposition, Ignatieff refers to the death penalty, arguing that that if capital punishment "gives public expression to the values that ought to hold Texas society together—as repeated polls indicate that they do—it is hardly surprising that such settled domestic political preferences should trump international human rights."[74] He appears to assume that because European courts have apparently defied popular support for capital punishment there to let the elite imposition of no death penalty stand—as opposed to American courts, which have pulled back from their position in the 1970s finding that virtually all forms of the death penalty constituted cruel and unusual punishment—American courts see rights more as expressions of majority interest than as instruments for the protection of minorities.

To an American lawyer educated in the 1980s by law professors who were steeped in the Supreme Court decisions of the 1950s, 1960s, and 1970s, or indeed to any American engaged even distantly with the politics of desegregation, criminal procedure, feminism, prison reform, deinstitutionalization of the mentally ill, handicapped rights, Native American rights, and gay and lesbian rights, Ignatieff's claim is almost unintelligible. This reaction may simply confirm that I and others in my cohort are too

---

[73] See Ignatieff's introduction to this volume.
[74] See Ignatieff's introduction to this volume.

deeply steeped in the conventional wisdom, or worse yet, conventional wisdom compounded by sentimental and uncritical idealism. Nevertheless, four counterarguments come to mind.

First, American courts have certainly not always gotten it right: *Brown v. Board of Education* was preceded by *Plessey v. Ferguson*, after all. But an impressive number of the opinions that are most celebrated in American law are those that have stood up for oppressed minorities.[75] *Lawrence v. Texas*, overturning *Bowers v. Hardwick*'s upholding of the constitutionality of antisodomy laws is just the latest in a long list of civil rights for minorities vindicated through the courts. Conversely, those decisions that are regarded as "stains on the Court's honor," most notably *Korematsu v. United States*, the World War II decision to uphold the internment of Japanese American citizens, are those that acquiesce in the oppression of minorities.[76] *Korematsu*, and the behavior it legitimated, stood as such a black mark on the nation's honor that President Bush was very careful to warn against similar discrimination against Arab Americans in the days after September 11.

Second, much of the evidence cited by Ignatieff and others who purport to distinguish between the rights traditions of the United States and Europe is of very recent vintage and largely reflects a backlash against what many American voters perceived to be *excessive* interference with majority will. No court can afford to get too far out of step with its populace, as the very logic of courts requires, whether at the village or the national level.[77] Just as the European Court of Justice pulled back after several decades of groundbreaking constitutional decisions establishing and extending a European legal order, so too did the Burger Court and then, with a vengeance, the Rehnquist Court, go about redressing the "judicial activism" of the Warren Court—often with activism of its own. Reinstating the death penalty, restricting abortion rights, cutting back on the rights of criminal defendants, limiting the power of the federal government itself over the states—all these decisions must be understood not as expressions of American rights culture in and of themselves, but rather as part of a lively dynamic with a far more minority-rights-protective court of a previous era. That back-and-forth across decades between justices appointed by different political parties and with different understandings of both the text of the Constitution and the ideal

---

[75] *See, e.g., Shelley v. Kraemer*, 334 U.S. 1 (1948) (barring enforcement of restrictive covenants limiting occupancy of land to Caucasians on equal protection grounds); *Goldberg v. Kelley*, 397 US 254 (1970) (requiring an evidentiary hearing to satisfy equal protection requirements before the termination of welfare benefits).

[76] *Korematsu v. United States*, 323 U.S. 214, 89 L. Ed. 194, 65 S. Ct. 193 (1944).

[77] *See* Martin Shapiro, *Courts: A Comparative and Political Analysis* (Chicago: University of Chicago Press, 1981).

role of judges is a fundamental element of the American constitutional tradition, but one that moderates rather than detracts from a fundamental judicial commitment to the protection of minority rights.

Third, America's greatest judicial exports all revolve around the protection of minority rights. The institution of judicial review itself is designed to prevent the will of the majority from ever overriding the rights guaranteed in a democratically approved constitution. The United States directly ensured that the high courts of Germany and Japan would exercise judicial review; the chief architects of the European Court of Justice's assertion of the equivalent of judicial review were European judges educated in the United States; the younger courts of Canada and South Africa directly borrowed from the *Marbury v. Madison* tradition.[78] Further, the fruit of judicial review is the U.S. version of "rights talk." As chronicled memorably by Louis Henkin, Anthony Lester, and Mary Ann Glendon,[79] constitutional courts around the world looked to the U.S. Supreme Court for inspiration in protecting the rights of their own minorities and women against majority interference.

Finally, beyond the institution of judicial review and judicial decisions themselves, America's other great contribution to global legal culture is the institution of public interest litigation, in which public interest groups (in American parlance; the British call them "pressure groups"; other countries may simply call them pests) turn to the courts to protect minorities and other oppressed groups, from the Roma to indigenous peoples to endangered species. Harold Koh began his work on his theory of transnational legal process with a chronicling of the phenomenon of transnational public interest litigation; a number of scholars have documented the rise of such litigation on behalf of women and minorities in Europe, drawing on national, EU, and European human rights law.[80] The whole point and purpose of such litigation is social and political change through law—specifically through courts' willingness to stand up to legislatures.

It is impossible, in this short compass, to do more than to debate Ignatieff's claim with argument and hypothesis. Indeed, it is difficult to know what proof would look like. Thus I can close only with a competing hypothesis of my own. On balance, I find it far more likely that what is exceptional about American rights culture is the substance of the rights

---

[78] *See* Ackerman, *supra* note 36.

[79] *See* Henkin and Rosenthal, supra note 36; Glendon, *supra* note 36, at 158; Lester, *supra* note 34.

[80] *See* Harold Hongju Koh, "Transnational Legal Process," *Nebraska Law Review* 75 (1996): 181–207; Carol Harlow, *Pressure through Law* (London: Routledge, 1992); Karen Alter and Sophie Meunier, "Judicial Politics in the European Community: European Integration and the Pathbreaking Cassis de Dijon Decision," *Comparative Political Studies* 26 (1994): 535–61.

themselves—the peculiar twist that American courts have given them over two centuries of interpreting the U.S. Constitution in light of American history and culture. Such exceptionalism is hardly exceptional to the United States; it is the exceptionalism of virtually any proud and insular nation, great or small.

—————

Globalization is associated worldwide with Americanization; conversely, antiglobalization often fuses murkily but readily with anti-Americanism. Ironically, however, at least in the judicial realm, Americans have been slow to globalize. American corporations eagerly reach across borders to absorb and assimilate; American courts have been content to send their decisions out across the world but quite reluctant to reach out themselves. The result has been a substantial lag behind the constitutional courts of most other mature democracies, which are engaging in what participants themselves describe as a global human rights dialogue or simply transjudicial conversation.

Slow or not, the justices of the U.S. Supreme Court are now hotly disputing the propriety and the value of looking to and citing foreign judicial decisions in their own opinions, with a majority apparently in favor of the practice. Given that all nine, or at least eight, justices favor foreign travel and meetings with foreign fellow jurists to exchange information about each other's legal systems and specific opinions, they will become globalized whether they wish to or not. At that point, a refusal to cite sources that have influenced them, even if only to highlight the distinctiveness or superiority of American law in a particular case, becomes a matter more of deception than of disinclination. Moreover, judges of the quality of the majority of U.S. federal judges will naturally respond to their own desire and the pressure of their peers to rise to the bar of global competition for precision of reasoning, range of arguments considered, and empirical investigation.

Many of these changes are already happening. They mirror the experience and the composition of American society and the American polity. In a decade, perhaps two, judicial references to the decisions of their foreign counterparts will be no more surprising than the introduction of myriad foreign elements into American cuisine, which has moved in the space of several decades from "purely American fare" such as hamburgers, hot dogs, and French fries (note the irony) to fusion everything—yet that fusion is known as "the new American cuisine."

In short, I predict that American judicial narcissism, understood as a desire to be the best on any playing field, is likely to lead American judges *toward* participation in global judicial dialogues. If American judges can travel abroad to help train their counterparts in fledgling or transitional democracies, as so many have, then they can also travel to participate in colloquies with their peers in countries such as England, Germany, South Africa, Canada, India, Argentina, and Japan, not to mention the EU. They are likely strongly to defend American jurisprudence and legal traditions in these meetings and to recall its profound impact on many of the other courts that are now active participants in a global human rights dialogue. But they are also likely to learn and to grow. As Judge Guido Calabrese, former dean of the Yale Law School, put it, in exhorting several of his panel members to follow the lead of the Italian and German constitutional courts, "Wise parents learn from their children."[81]

In the end, judges participating in the processes of judicial globalization, willingly or not, are likely to regard themselves as better judges as a result, and so they will be. But they will still be American judges, interpreting, implementing, and creating American law, for American citizens living in an increasingly globalized economy, society, and polity. While we hope and expect that they will be exceptionally good at their craft, and thus serve as an example for many of their colleagues around the world, they are less likely to think that they are exceptional because they are American.

[81] *United States v. Then*, 56 F.3d 464, 468–69 (1995).

Chapter 11

American Exceptionalism, Exemptionalism, and Global Governance

MORE THAN ANY other country, the United States was responsible for creating the post–World War II system of global governance. But from the start, that historic mission exhibited the conflicting effects of two very different forms of American exceptionalism. For Franklin Roosevelt, the key challenge was to overcome the isolationist legacy of the 1930s and to ensure sustained U.S. engagement in achieving and maintaining a stable international order. Old-world balance-of-power reasoning in support of that mission held little allure for the American people—protected by two oceans, with friendly and weaker neighbors to the north and south, and pulled unwillingly into two costly world wars by that system's break-down. So Roosevelt framed his plans for winning the peace in a broader vision that tapped into America's sense of self as a nation: the promise of an international order based on rules and institutions promoting human betterment through free trade and American-led collective security, human rights and decolonization, as well as active international involvement by the private and voluntary sectors. For Roosevelt's successors, countering the Soviet threat reinforced the mission and in many respects made it easier to achieve. This first form of American exceptionalism—pursuing an international order that resonated with values the American people saw as their own—became the basis for a global transformational agenda whose effects are unfolding still.[1]

Earlier versions of this chapter were presented at the Bucerius University Program on Global Governance in Hamburg, Germany; the Kennedy School's Carr Center for Human Rights Policy seminar on American Exceptionalism; a conference on American Unilateralism at the Woodrow Wilson School, Princeton University; the Yale Law School Globalization Seminar; and the University of Toronto Law School Workshop on Law, Globalization and Justice. I am indebted to Cary Coglianese, Michael Ignatieff, Kal Raustiala, Frederick Schauer, and Anne-Marie Slaughter for their helpful comments; to Jason Scott for bibliographical assistance; and to the Kennedy School Initiative on Corporate Social Responsibility for research support.

[1] I have discussed Roosevelt's strategy of engagement and its legacy at length in John Gerard Ruggie, *Winning the Peace: America and World Order in the New Era* (New York:

Yet from the outset the United States also sought to insulate itself from the domestic blowback of certain of these developments. This, too, has been justified on the grounds of American exceptionalism: a perceived need to safeguard the special features and protections of the U.S. Constitution from external interference. And it also taps into a core element of American identity: ours is a civic nationalism, defined by the institutions and practices that bind us, not by blood and soil, and none is more foundational than the Constitution itself. While the executive branch traditionally drove the international transformational agenda, the "exemptionalist" resistance has been anchored in Congress. It has been most pronounced and consequential in the area of human rights and related social issues, where it has typically been framed in terms of protecting states' rights against federal treaty-based incursions. In drafting the United Nations Charter, for example, the U.S. delegation introduced language "reaffirming faith" in fundamental human rights. But because the support of southern Democrats was critical to the Charter's ratification by the Senate, keeping Jim Crow laws beyond international scrutiny obliged the United States to balance that reaffirmation by adding what became Article 2.7: that "nothing contained in the present Charter shall authorize the United Nations to intervene in matters which are essentially within the domestic jurisdiction of any state."[2] Reacting sharply against U.S.-initiated negotiations of several UN human rights instruments, beginning with the Genocide Convention, the Senate nearly adopted a constitutional amendment in 1954—the Bricker amendment—which, in effect, would have eviscerated the president's formal treaty-making powers.[3] That same political constituency historically has resisted all forms of international jurisdiction and has led congressional opposition to the UN.

During the Cold War, presidents from Harry Truman to Ronald Reagan sought to minimize the international embarrassment resulting from the

---

Columbia University Press, 1996). The vision drew on Woodrow Wilson but was tempered by a pragmatic understanding of both domestic and international politics.

[2] Carol Anderson, *Eyes off the Prize: The United Nations and the African American Struggle for Human Rights, 1944–1955* (New York: Cambridge University Press, 2003), chap. 1; and Ruth B. Russell, *A History of the United Nations Charter* (Washington, DC: Brookings, 1958), chap. 39. The Soviets and many others were happy to have the provision included.

[3] It was so called for the Ohio Republican who first introduced it in 1951. In addition to the existing ratification requirement of a two-thirds Senate supermajority, the amendment would have required subsequent implementing legislation by both houses of Congress and approval by *all* state legislatures. A weakened substitute fell one vote short of the required two-thirds. Natalie Hevener Kaufman, *Human Rights Treaties and the Senate: A History of Opposition* (Chapel Hill: University of North Carolina Press, 1990), chap. 4. The amendment would not have affected executive agreements or congressional-executive agreements.

exemptionalist impulse, especially in relation to civil rights, often acting through executive agreements or other such means.[4] Starting in the 1990s, however, the escalating wave of globalization and the international "soft law" it has generated, coupled with the end of the external disciplining effects imposed by the Cold War, have produced a broader and more unrestrained exemptionalist opposition to global governance. Scholarship on the role of international law in domestic courts has been consumed by what Harold Koh calls the transnationalist-vs.-nationalist debate, in which the latter appears to have seized the intellectual offensive.[5] A "new sovereigntist" movement has shaped corresponding Beltway policy debates.[6] The Senate rejected the Comprehensive Test Ban Treaty and made it clear that it would not ratify the international inspections provisions of the biological weapons convention—in the latter case raising the constitutional specter of unreasonable searches. A straw poll in that chamber made it clear that the Kyoto Protocol would face a similar fate, even before President George W. Bush rejected it altogether. President Bill Clinton did not dare submit the statute of the International Criminal Court (ICC) for ratification, knowing that it stood accused of giving away Americans' constitutional due process protections and, therefore, was dead on arrival. But what may be the politically most significant shift, the Bush administration has been far more hospitable to the exemptionalist agenda than any of its predecessors. Indeed, in its vigorous opposition to the ICC it may end up sabotaging what most American allies consider the crowning achievement of the postwar move toward global governance.[7]

---

[4] Mary L. Dudziak, *Cold War Civil Rights: Race and the Image of American Democracy* (Princeton: Princeton University Press, 2000).

[5] Harold Hongju Koh, "On American Exceptionalism," *Stanford Law Review* 55 (May 2003). The most influential statement setting out the nationalist position is Curtis A. Bradley and Jack L. Goldsmith, "Customary International Law as Federal Common Law: A Critique of the Modern Position," *Harvard Law Review* 110 (February 1997).

[6] See, for example, Jeremy Rabkin, *Why Sovereignty Matters* (Washington, DC: American Enterprise Institute, 1998).

[7] Under the threat of cutting off military and economic assistance the United States has negotiated bilateral "non-surrender agreements" (pledges not to turn U.S. citizens over to the ICC) with more than seventy countries, mostly in the developing world and Eastern Europe. And under the threat of blocking UN peacekeeping missions, the United States has also demanded that the Security Council grant it permanent exemption from the ICC; the council twice agreed to one-year exemptions, but in 2004 the United States failed to get the necessary nine votes and withdrew its request. Congress initiated the "American Service-Members' Protection Act," which among other things authorizes the president "to use all necessary and appropriate means" to free any member of the U.S. armed services detained by or in connection with the International Criminal Court—and which critics promptly called "The Hague invasion act" because, in principle, it includes that possibility. For the administration's case in support of these policies, see John R. Bolton, Under Secretary for Arms Control and International Security, United States Department of State, "American

What does this augur for the future? Are America and global governance on a collision course? And if so, with what consequences? I make
two arguments in this chapter. First, unlike the situation in 1945, when
the United States truly was the world's political Archimedean point,
global governance in the twenty-first century is being stitched together by
a multiplicity of actors and interests—in considerable measure reflecting
the success of America's own postwar transformational agenda. Indeed,
the very system of states is becoming embedded within an increasingly
mobilized and institutionalized global public domain that includes not
only states but also nonstate actors involved in the promotion and production of global public goods. While the American state remains by far
the most powerful force among them, platforms and channels for transnational action that it does not directly control have proliferated—and are
deeply entwined with American society itself. Therefore, enacting a strict
exemptionalism posture, I contend, has become much harder than it
seems. Second, although some of the issues raised by the recent upsurge
of U.S. resistance to global governance involve highly technical questions
of constitutional law, I argue that the exemptionalist position also reflects
a distinctive set of doctrinal preferences and feeds into a specific ideological agenda. Indeed, by privileging doctrine over practical considerations,
not only do many of the solutions proposed by the exemptionalists turn
out to be unnecessary in policy terms, but they would also impose a
greater burden on us than the problems they purport to solve. In the conclusion I spell out some implications for the future relationship between
U.S. power and global governance of the continuing dialectic, if you will,
between the two forms of American exceptionalism, acknowledging that
the path ahead does not promise to be smooth, but noting that neither
has it been so in getting to where we are today.

A New Global Public Domain

Global governance has been defined as govern*ance* in the absence of formal govern*ment*.[8] And governance, at whatever level of social organization it may take place, refers to conducting the public's business: to the
constellation of authoritative rules, institutions, and practices by means
of which any collectivity manages its affairs.

Justice and the International Criminal Court," Remarks at the American Enterprise Institute, Washington, DC, November 3, 2003, available online at http://www.state.gov/t/us/rm/
25818.htm.

[8] James N. Rosenau and Ernst-Otto Czempiel, eds., *Governance without Government:
Order and Change in World Politics* (New York: Cambridge University Press, 1992).

Once upon a time, governance at the global level was entirely a statist affair. It was a system made by and for states, and it concerned relations among them. States constituted the international "public"—as in public international law and public international unions, the name given to nine-teenth-century international organizations. Whether the instruments of governance were alliances, regimes, law, or organizations, states monopolized its conduct, and they were the subjects of their joint decisions and actions. Rules, institutions, and practices were authoritative to the extent they were so recognized by states. In key respects, this traditional system of global governance still characterized the international institutional order constructed after World War II.

Over the course of the past generation, the traditional system has evolved in significant ways, not by replacing states but by having its boundaries stretched in two directions. Today, the global governance agenda includes a host of issues that go well beyond the traditional subjects of interstate relations, and many reach deeply into what had been exclusively domestic spheres. Moreover, the "public" involved in the business of global governance now routinely includes not only states but also social actors for which territoriality is not the cardinal organizing principle or national interests the core driver. These developments, in short, are producing what I have elsewhere called a reconstituted global public domain.[9]

The new global public domain is intertwined with and exists alongside the traditional interstate and domestic public domains. It does not itself determine global governance outcomes any more than its domestic counterpart does at the national level, but it introduces opportunities for and constraints upon global governance that did not exist in the past. Although the new global public domain is hardly uncontested, its emergence, like globalization, to which it is closely linked, is part and parcel of a gradually broadening and deepening sociality at the global level.

Below, I present a stylized overview of these changes, emphasizing the emergence of new issues that have been placed on the global agenda, the new actors that now play a significant role alongside states and interstate organizations, and the workings of global political processes that these changes entail.

New Agendas

The number and diversity of issues on the global governance agenda continue to grow. The traditional system was concerned mainly with inter-

---

[9] I elaborate on this concept in John Gerard Ruggie, "Reconstituting the Global Public Domain: Issues, Actors and Practices," *European Journal of International Relations* 10 (December 2004).

state diplomacy, war, and commerce, and, from the mid–nineteenth century on, also technical rules of the road to facilitate the flow of international transactions. Contrast this with the subject matter of the UN global conferences convened since the 1970s, each of which generated new action plans and means of implementation: the environment, population, human rights, women, children, social development, human settlements, food security, racism, and HIV/AIDS.[10]

In addition, traditional issues have been expanded in scope to encompass entirely new elements. In the area of trade, for example, services had not generally been regarded as being "traded" before 1972, when they were first so construed in an Organization for Economic Cooperation and Development (OECD) experts' report;[11] by the 1990s a General Agreement on Trade in Services was in place. Intellectual property rights had never been viewed as falling within the purview of the international trade regime; the Uruguay Round of negotiations (1986–94) made them so. The current Doha Round is divided over the inclusion of rules protecting investment, among other matters. A similar expansion has occurred in many other issue areas on the global governance agenda.

But the number and diversity of issues tell only part of the story. More significant is a shift in the locus of some of these issues along a set of axes depicting the "external," "internal," and "universal" dimensions of policy space. Providing collective assistance to a state that has fallen victim to military aggression deals with matters that are "external" to the states involved: reconfiguring the military balance of power or imposing other sanctions on the offending party. Human rights provisions, in contrast, concern the most intimate of "internal" political relations: that between a state and its citizens. And the ICC may prosecute individuals, if their own state fails to act despite good cause, who are accused of genocide, crimes against humanity, and war crimes—not only individuals who are nationals of signatory states, but also those of nonsignatory states if the alleged crime is committed in the territory of a state that has ratified the ICC statute. Thus it represents a step toward universal jurisdiction.[12]

---

[10] See full listing at http://www.un.org/events/conferences.htm.

[11] William Drake and Kalypso Nicolaidis, "Ideas, Interests, and Institutionalization: 'Trade in Services' and the Uruguay Round," *International Organization* 46 (Winter 1992): 42.

[12] Actual universal jurisdiction requires no territorial connection whatever between the entity exercising it and either the victim or the accused. Belgium adopted such a law for certain crimes against humanity in 1993, giving Belgian courts the power to try suspects regardless of their nationality or where the alleged acts were committed. Under U.S. pressure, including threats by defense secretary Donald Rumsfeld to move NATO headquarters elsewhere, the law was recently amended to cover only cases in which either the victim or the suspect is Belgian. "Belgium Scales Back Its War Crimes Law under U.S. Pressure," *New York Times*, August 2, 2003. For a careful discussion of the theory and practice of universal jurisdiction, see M. Cherif Bassiouni, "The History of Universal Jurisdiction and Its Place

Shifts in the locus of issues on the global governance agenda away from the traditional "external" realm have occurred in a variety of other issue areas as well, not only in human rights. In the global trade regime, Richard Blackhurst, then a highly regarded GATT economist, noted more than twenty years ago that international trade negotiations had begun to migrate away from concern with border measures, toward *any* policy, no matter what the instrument or where it was applied, that had an "important" impact on international trade flows.[13] Indeed, the United States fought low-intensity trade wars with Japan during the latter's economic boom in the 1980s and into the 1990s precisely on the grounds that Japan's internal economic structures and even cultural practices gave it "unfair" trade advantages.[14] The reason for this migration—apart from protectionist pressures by adversely affected industries or workers—is simple: as point-of-entry barriers were progressively dismantled, and as trade continued to intensify, the significance of "internal" factors inevitably increased.

There has been a corresponding shift in the area of international peace and security, resulting from the steady decline of interstate wars relative to various types of "internal" armed conflicts, which became particularly pronounced in the 1990s. According to one standard source, "over one-third of the world's countries (54 of 158) were directly affected by serious societal warfare at some time during the 1990s and, of these states, nearly two-thirds (34) experienced armed conflicts for seven or more years during the decade."[15] It is hardly surprising, therefore, that the United Nations and its member states have been drawn into trying to come to grips with these internal conflicts—or to rationalize their avoiding getting involved—especially when they impose egregious violations of human rights or acts of genocide. The results on the ground have been mixed at best.[16] But it is noteworthy that Article 2.7 objections to such involvement have played a progressively diminishing role.

---

in International Law," in *Universal Jurisdiction: National Courts and the Prosecution of Serious Crimes under International Law*, ed. Stephen Macedo (Philadelphia: University of Pennsylvania Press, 2004).

[13] Richard Blackhurst, "The Twilight of Domestic Economies," *The World Economy* 4 (December 1981).

[14] John Gerard Ruggie, "Unraveling Trade: Global Institutional Change and the Pacific Economy," in *Pacific Economic Relations in the 1990s: Cooperation or Conflict*, ed. Richard Higott, Richard Leaver, and John Ravenhill (Boulder, CO: Lynne Rienner, 1993).

[15] Monty G. Marshall and Ted Robert Gurr, *Peace and Conflict 2003: A Global Survey of Armed Conflicts, Self-Determination Movements, and Democracy* (College Park: University of Maryland, Center for International Development & Conflict Management, 2003), 13–14.

[16] Good discussions may be found in J. L. Holzgrefe and Robert O. Keohane, eds., *Humanitarian Intervention: Ethical, Legal, and Political Dilemmas* (New York: Cambridge University Press, 2003).

Turning to the environment, such issues as transborder pollution have been on the global agenda for decades. They are classic cases of externalities and have triggered an array of responses including international monitoring and regulatory regimes, lawsuits, as well as side payments to get offenders to change their ways.[17] But a new type of global environmental problem has emerged in the past generation wherein the offending activity has "universal" impact from which no state can exclude itself, no matter where it is located or how powerful it may be. Unlike traditional global commons issues, including fisheries and marine pollution on the high seas, they are indivisibly part of the "internal" space of states. Ozone depletion in the upper atmosphere was one such instance. It was dealt with relatively expeditiously because one of its main causes was the emission of chlorofluorocarbons, used in refrigeration among other things, for which a substitute could readily be developed. The Montreal Protocol was adopted to regulate their phaseout.[18] In the case of climate change, the sources of greenhouse gas emissions are far more diffuse, more deeply woven into the production and transportation systems of modern economies, and also far more costly to change in the short-to-medium term. Although the Kyoto Protocol is now in force, the United States continues to reject it.[19]

In sum, not only has the global governance agenda become more crowded and diverse, but it also projects more deeply into the domestic policy sphere of states, while some issues on it pull in the direction of greater universality of impact and even jurisdiction. Several of these developments are closely related to the emergence of new actors, to which I now turn.

New Actors

Surely the most consequential institutional development in governance beyond the confines of the territorial state has been the creation and evolution of the European Union. Formal institutional innovation has been more limited at the global level, as one would expect given the vastly larger numbers, greater heterogeneity, and comparatively fewer common

[17] Lynton Keith Caldwell and Paul Stanley Weiland, *International Environmental Policy*, 3rd ed. (Durham: Duke University Press, 1997), provides a useful overview of the main issues and arrangements.

[18] Edward Parson, "Protecting the Ozone Layer," in *Institutions for the Earth*, ed. Peter M. Haas, Marc A. Levy, and Robert O. Keohane (Cambridge: MIT Press, 1993).

[19] The Bush administration is also impeding UN discussions on follow-up steps. See Larry Rohter, "U.S. Waters Down Global Commitment to Curb Greenhouse Gases," *New York Times*, December 19, 2004.

interests among states there. Nevertheless, the present web of global treaties and intergovernmental organizations is without historical parallel. The United States led or actively facilitated many of these developments.[20]

In recent decades, actors other than territorial states and intergovernmental organizations have also steadily expanded their role in global politics. They may be driven by universal values or factional greed, by profit and efficiency considerations or the search for salvation. They include transnational corporations (TNCs), civil society organizations, private military contractors that are beginning to resemble the mercenaries of yore, and such illicit entities as transnational terrorist and criminal networks. While the mere existence and proliferation of nonstate actors is no longer news, below I describe briefly how two of the most prominent such actors—civil society organizations and transnational corporations, both with deep roots in American society—affect the evolution in global governance sketched out in the previous section.

National governments and international agencies have come to recognize the involvement of civil society organizations (CSOs) in several areas related to global governance today—where by "recognize" I mean that they regard CSOs' participation to be more or less legitimate, and in varying degrees actually count on them to play those roles.[21] In other words, their roles have become institutionalized—much as, for example, the environmental movement did within the industrialized countries a generation ago.[22]

[20] For its global role, see Ruggie, *Winning the Peace*. The United States not only supported European economic integration from the Marshall Plan on, but in the early 1950s it was well out in front of the Europeans themselves in promoting defense integration—to the point where secretary of state John Foster Dulles told the North Atlantic Council in 1953 that if Europe failed to ratify the European Defense Community, "grave doubts" would arise in the United States concerning the future of European security, and America would be obliged to undertake an "agonizing reappraisal" of its European role. Brian Duchin, "The 'Agonizing Reappraisal': Eisenhower, Dulles, and the European Defense Community," *Diplomatic History* 16 (Spring 1992).

[21] I use the term CSO here rather than NGO because it also includes transnational social movements, coalitions, and activist campaigns as well as nongovernmental organizations. For useful introductions, see Sanjeev Khagram, James V. Riker, and Kathryn Sikkink, eds., *Restructuring World Politics: Transnational Social Movements, Networks, and Norms* (Minneapolis: University of Minnesota Press, 2002), and Ann M. Florini, ed., *The Third Force: The Rise of Transnational Civil Society* (Washington, DC: Carnegie Endowment for International Peace, 2000). In writing this section, I also draw on personal experience in establishing the UN Global Compact, which was carefully positioned in relation to the universe of different CSOs, transnational corporations, and business associations; see Georg Kell and John Gerard Ruggie, "Global Markets and Social Legitimacy: The Case of the 'Global Compact,' " in *The Market or the Public Domain?*, ed. Daniel Drache (London: Routledge, 2001).

[22] See Kal Raustiala, "States, NGOs, and International Environmental Institutions," *International Studies Quarterly* 41 (December 1997). A good comparable discussion of the

To begin with, civil society organizations have become the main international dispensers of direct assistance to people in developing countries, through foreign aid, humanitarian relief, and a variety of other internationally supported services. We might call this social outsourcing.[23] Governmental entities, such as the United States Agency for International Development, have largely become contractors while CSOs deliver the goods. The rationale is that assistance is delivered more effectively through nongovernmental channels, bypassing top-heavy (and sometimes corrupt) bureaucracies, better targeting the intended recipients, and leveraging community-based skills and experience that might not otherwise be tapped.

The role of CSOs is even more consequential in certain areas of norm creation and implementation. The global agenda in human rights, the environment and anticorruption, for example, would not be nearly as advanced were it not for their influence. CSOs exercise that influence through their own global campaigns, and also by direct involvement in official forums like periodic UN conferences or the ongoing UN human rights machinery, where the documentation provided by an Amnesty International, for example, carries weight precisely because it is detached from national interests.[24]

Coalitions of domestic and transnational civil society actors play significant roles in promoting human and labor rights, environmental standards, and other social concerns within countries where political institutions limit or repress activities in support of those aims. Human Rights Watch, for example, originated in the effort to monitor the implementation of the human rights provisions of the 1975 Helsinki Accords within the Soviet bloc.[25] Daniel Thomas traces the impact of those norms, through the people and groups they inspired, to the subsequent collapse of communist rule itself.[26] Margaret Keck and Kathryn Sikkink have doc-

---

U.S. domestic level may be found in Cary Coglianese, "Social Movements, Law, and Society: The Institutionalization of the Environmental Movement," *University of Pennsylvania Law Review* 150 (November 2001).

[23] Obviously this trend does not encompass IMF stabilization loans, but virtually any World Bank loan these days requires extensive consultations with civil society groups even when they are not the main implementers.

[24] On human rights, see Thomas Risse, "The Power of Norms versus the Norms of Power," in Florini, *The Third Force*; on the environment, Daniel C. Esty and Maria H. Ivanova, eds., *Global Environmental Governance* (New Haven: Yale School of Forestry and Environmental Studies, 2003); and on anticorruption, Fredrik Galtung, "A Global Network to Curb Corruption: The Experience of Transparency International," in Florini, *The Third Force*.

[25] Aryeh Neier, *Taking Liberties: Four Decades in the Struggle for Rights* (New York: Public Affairs, 2003).

[26] Daniel C. Thomas, *The Helsinki Effect: International Norms, Human Rights, and the Demise of Communism* (Princeton: Princeton University Press, 2001).

umented the impact of transnational human rights and environmental activist networks on several authoritarian or corrupt regimes in developing countries, through these networks' formation of alliances with similar groups elsewhere as well as with supportive states and international agencies.[27] In the United States and Western Europe the courts have featured prominently in these strategies—in the United States through the practice of what is called "transnational public law litigation," typically initiated by human rights organizations and often supported by law school clinics, under the U.S. Alien Tort Claims Act or the Torture Victims Protection Act.[28]

CSO coalitions have also become a significant if episodic force in blocking and promoting international agreements. Two exemplars have acquired iconic status. The most celebrated blockage was of the Multilateral Agreement on Investment, negotiated at the OECD, which would have been the high-water mark of global neoliberalism in the 1990s. A coalition of more than six hundred organizations in seventy countries sprang into "virtual existence" on the World Wide Web almost overnight to oppose it. They made the case that certain of the MAI's provisions on investment protection would enable TNCs to challenge domestic environmental and labor standards on the grounds that they had an effect equivalent to expropriation, as a result of which companies adversely affected by them could claim compensation.[29] The world press did the rest.

The most dramatic instance of civil society organizations' successfully promoting a new agreement—and even participating in its negotiation and drafting—is the land-mines ban, which was begun, literally, by two people with a fax machine and ended up helping to produce an international treaty over the opposition of the most powerful bureaucracy in

---

[27] Margaret E. Keck and Kathryn Sikkink, *Activists beyond Borders* (Ithaca: Cornell University Press, 1998).

[28] Harold Hongju Koh, "Transnational Public Law Litigation," *Yale Law Journal* 100 (June 1991). President Bush's Justice Department urged the Supreme Court to restrict, if not gut, the Alien Tort Claims Act in *Sosa v. Alvarez-Machain*. In an extremely complicated but unanimous decision, the Court seems to have upheld the first wave of ATCA cases without signaling how it might rule on its more expansive interpretations in the future. Supreme Court of the United States, *Sosa v. Alvarez-Machain et al.*, No. 03–339, Decided June 29, 2004.

[29] Supporting that fear was a 1996 case involving the Ethyl Corporation, which successfully sued the Canadian government under a similar provision of the North American Free Trade Agreement when Canada banned a gasoline additive Ethyl produced, with Canada agreeing to an out-of-court settlement of $13 million. Andrew Walter, "NGOs, Business, and International Investment: The Multilateral Agreement on Investment, Seattle, and Beyond," *Global Governance* 7 (January–March 2001); and Stephen J. Kobrin, "The MAI and the Clash of Globalizations," *Foreign Policy* 112 (Fall 1998). Both authors stress that factors other than activist pressure also contributed to the MAI's demise.

the world's most powerful state: the U.S. Pentagon.[30] Nongovernmental groups of legal experts assisted in the drafting of the ICC statute, and the pioneering work of Transparency International (TI)—started by a former World Bank official with his personal retirement savings—paved the way for the anticorruption convention recently adopted by the UN.[31]

Lastly, CSOs are a major source of pressure for the reform of other international entities, including the WTO, World Bank, and IMF,[32] as well as the global corporate sector. From the vantage point of the present discussion, the most significant point of intersection between CSOs and transnational corporations is the domain of corporate social responsibility.

The rights enjoyed by transnational corporations have increased manifold over the past two decades, as a result of multilateral trade agreements, bilateral investment pacts, and domestic liberalization—often urged by external actors, including the leading states and the international financial institutions. Moreover, corporate influence on global rule making is well documented, including such instances as the pharmaceutical and entertainment industries pushing the WTO intellectual property rights agenda, or Motorola managing to write many of its own patents into International Telecommunication Union standards.[33]

Along with expanded rights, however, have come demands, led by civil society actors, that corporations accept commensurate obligations. To oversimplify only slightly, while governments and intergovernmental agencies were creating the space for TNCs to operate globally, other social actors have attempted to infuse that space with greater corporate social responsibilities.[34]

The imbalance between global corporate rights and obligations remains a key source of CSO pressure. But two more proximate factors also drive their desire to engage the global corporate sector. The first is that individual companies make themselves and in some instances their entire indus-

[30] Motoko Mekata, "Building Partnerships toward a Common Goal: Experiences of the International Campaign to Ban Landmines," in Florini, *The Third Force*; and Ramesh Thakur and William Malley, "The Ottawa Convention on Landmines: A Landmark Humanitarian Treaty in Arms Control?" *Global Governance* 5 (July–September 1999).

[31] On TI, see Galtung, "A Global Network to Curb Corruption," in Florini, *The Third Force*.

[32] Robert O'Brien, Jan Aart Scholte, Marc Williams, and Anne Marie Goetz, *Contesting Global Governance* (New York: Cambridge University Press, 2000).

[33] See, respectively, John Braithwaite and Peter Drahos, *Global Business Regulation* (Cambridge: Cambridge University Press, 2000); and William J. Drake, "Communications," in *Managing Global Issues*, ed. P. J. Simmons and Chantal de Jonge Oudraat (Washington, DC: Carnegie Endowment for International Peace, 2001).

[34] This section in part draws on John Gerard Ruggie, "Taking Embedded Liberalism Global: The Corporate Connection," in *Taming Globalization: Frontiers of Governance*, ed. David Held and Mathias Koenig-Archibugi (Cambridge, UK: Polity Press, 2003).

tries targets by doing bad things: think of Shell in Nigeria, Nike in Indonesia, the *Exxon Valdez* spill and others like it, unsafe practices in the chemical industry as symbolized by Union Carbide's Bhopal disaster, upscale apparel retailers' purchasing from sweatshop suppliers, unsustainable forestry practices by the timber industry, and so on. Even where companies are breaking no local laws, they may stand in violation of their own self-proclaimed standards, or be accused of breaching international community norms in such areas as human rights, labor practices, and environmental sustainability.

CSOs have pushed for companies and industries to adopt verifiable measures to help reduce the incidence of such behavior. Firms not directly involved have taken steps to avoid similar problems, or to turn their own good behavior into a brand advantage. A voluntary reporting industry is emerging as a result. It consists of corporate statements of principles and codes of conduct (company-based or sectoral; unilateral or multistakeholder); social and environmental performance reports by companies; the growing interest of nonprofits and commercial firms in auditing company codes or certifying reports; a Global Reporting Initiative, established as a Dutch NGO, which provides standardized social and environmental reporting systems; and so-called certification institutions, which verify that an entire production and distribution cycle—be it of forest products, coffee beans, or diamonds—meets prescribed conditions.[35]

The number of these arrangements has grown rapidly, though their reach remains limited and thus far they involve mainly large and brand-sensitive firms.[36] At the same time, they are becoming mainstreamed within firms, no longer dependent entirely on CSO pressure. Moreover, governments are slowly entering the fray. Several OECD countries—the UK, France, the Netherlands, Sweden, and Belgium among them—have begun to encourage or require companies to engage in one form or another of social reporting. A new British company statute may be the most far-reaching of these measures, both in stipulating heightened social expectations about the public role of private enterprise, and in the requirement that companies issue an annual directors' report of social and environmental information relevant to an understanding of the entire business.[37]

---

[35] The most comprehensive survey of company codes is *Corporate Responsibility: Private Initiatives and Public Goals* (Paris: OECD, 2001). On the GRI, consult www.globalreporting.org; and for certification institutions, see Gary Gereffi, Ronie Garcia-Johnson, and Erika Sasser, "The NGO-Industrial Complex," *Foreign Policy* 125 (July/August 2001).

[36] On this social potential of corporate branding, see Simon Anholt, *Brand New Justice: The Upside of Global Branding* (Oxford: Butterworth-Heinemann, 2003).

[37] United Kingdom, Department of Trade and Industry, "Company Law: Draft Regulations on the Operating and Financial Review and Directors' Report—A Consultative Document" (May 2004), available online at http://www.dti.gov.uk/cld/condocs.htm.

In the past few years, a very different rationale for engaging the corporate sector has emerged: the sheer fact that it has global reach and capacity, and that it is capable of making and implementing decisions at a rapid pace—whereas the traditional international governance system tends to operate on the basis of the lowest and slowest common denominator. The universe of transnational corporations consists of roughly 65,000 firms, with more than 800,000 subsidiaries and millions of suppliers and distributors connected through global value chains.[38] Other social actors are increasingly looking for ways to leverage this global platform in order to advance broader social objectives within and among countries—in other words, to help fill governance gaps and compensate for governance failures. Many CSOs that had mastered the art of running campaigns against transnationals are now also having to learn how to forge partnerships with them. Few major issue areas have been left entirely untouched.

AIDS activists picked Coca-Cola for special embarrassment at the 2002 Barcelona AIDS conference, not because Coke causes HIV/AIDS, but because the company has a universally recognized brand and one of the largest distribution networks in Africa.[39] "If we can get cold Coca-Cola and beer to every remote corner of Africa," Dr. Joep Lange, president of the International AIDS Society, told reporters, "it should not be impossible to do the same with drugs."[40] Coke subsequently committed to providing antiretroviral treatment, in partnership with PharmAccess, the Dutch NGO led by Dr. Lange, not only to its own immediate staff, but also to its independent bottlers throughout Africa.[41] The motivations of other firms differ. The transnational mining company, Anglo American, offers the most comprehensive workplace coverage in southern Africa.[42] The fact that more than 25 percent of its labor force—heavily male, migrant,

[38] The number of multinationals and their subsidiaries are reported in the *World Investment Report* (Geneva: United Nations Conference on Trade and Development, 2001). It is impossible to calculate the actual number of suppliers; Nike, for example, has approximately twelve hundred (personal communication from Nike executive).

[39] "AIDS Activists Protest Coke's Deadly Neglect of Workers with AIDS in Developing Countries" (press release, dated July 10, 2002), which was widely distributed along with a twenty-five-foot inflatable Coke bottle bearing the slogan "Coke's Neglect = Death for Workers in Africa." Available online at www.actupny.org/reports/bcn?BCNcoke.html.

[40] Quoted in Lawrence T. Altman, "Former Presidents Urge Leadership on AIDS," *New York Times*, July 13, 2002, 5.

[41] Robert Ahomka Lindsay, "The Coca-Cola Africa Foundation/Coca-Cola Bottlers in Africa HIV/AIDS Program," Workshop on HIV/AIDS and Business in Africa and Asia: Building Sustainable Partnerships (Center for Business and Government, Kennedy School of Government, Harvard University, February 20–21, 2003), available online at www.ksg.harvard.edu/cbg/hiv-aids/workshop_ksg.htm/.

[42] Anglo American, "Anglo American plc Supporting HIV and AIDS Awareness," available online at http://www.angloamerican.co.uk/hivaids/ourresponse/policy.asp.

and living in dormitories separated from their families—are HIV positive makes its active involvement an economic necessity and also posed a moral dilemma for the company. Merck, the giant pharmaceutical company, faced a public relations debacle over AIDS drugs pricing but also had a long-standing reputation for medical philanthropy to protect; they have partnered with the Gates Foundation and the government of Botswana to provide a comprehensive national HIV/AIDS program in that country.[43]

None of these factors, however, played a role in the decisions of Heineken, the Dutch brewery, or DaimlerChrysler, the automotive firm, both of which were also early movers in providing workplace treatment in Africa. Indeed, a net-present-value analysis commissioned by Heineken showed that the costs at the margin would exceed direct and immediate monetary benefits, yet the board proceeded to adopt the policy as a longer-term business proposition, in light of the inability or unwillingness of governments to act.[44] Illustrating yet another driver, Novartis, the Swiss pharmaceutical firm, became the first company to provide antiretroviral treatment for its employees in China—on the grounds that, as a global company, it made the strategic determination to move toward greater uniformity in its global human resources policy.[45]

At a more macro level, the UN Global Compact engages the corporate sector to help implement principles drawn from the Universal Declaration on Human Rights, the International Labor Organization's Fundamental Principles on Rights at Work, the Rio Principles on Environment and Development, and the recently adopted UN convention against corruption.[46]

[43] Linda Distlerath, "African Comprehensive HIV/AIDS Partnership," available online at www.ksg.harvard.edu/cbg/hiv-aids/ksg/Distlerath_presentation.pdf.

[44] Diana Barrett and Daniella Ballou, "Heineken International: Workplace HIV/AIDS Programs in Africa," Harvard Business School Case # 9–303–063, 2003. Other brief cases, including DaimlerChrysler, are available online at World Economic Forum, http://www.weforum.org/site/homepublic.nsf/Content/Global+Health+Initiative%5CGHI+Business+Tools%5CGHI+Case+Studies+and+Supporting+Documents.

[45] This policy was announced at a Workshop on HIV/AIDS as a Business Challenge, convened in Beijing by the Center for Business and Government, Harvard University, together with the World Economic Forum and UNAIDS (see Center for Business and Government, 2003).

[46] The ten principles are as follows: support and respect for the protection of internationally proclaimed human rights; noncomplicity in human rights abuses; freedom of association and the effective recognition of the right to collective bargaining; the elimination of all forms of forced and compulsory labor; the effective abolition of child labor; the elimination of discrimination in respect of employment and occupation; a precautionary approach to environmental challenges; greater environmental responsibility; encouragement of the development and diffusion of environmentally friendly technologies; and working against all forms of corruption, including extortion and bribery. For full texts and other relevant information see http://www.unglobalcompact.org. The first book-length study is Malcolm McIn-

Nearly two thousand firms worldwide participate, up from a mere fifty in 2000 when the initiative began, along with two dozen transnational NGOs and international labor federations representing 150 million workers. Going beyond the Compact's minimum commitments, the International Federation of Chemical, Energy, Mine and General Workers' Unions negotiated an agreement with Statoil of Norway to extend the same labor rights as well as health and safety standards that it applies in Norway to its overseas operations—including Vietnam, Angola, Venezuela, and Azerbaijan. This type of agreement is being replicated in other industries, including mining.[47]

The role of companies in third world conflict zones has drawn increased attention. At issue is not only how to reduce the (inadvertent or deliberate) contribution that firms make to fueling internal conflicts, which are often related to factional competition for the control of natural resource extraction, but also their potential role in conflict prevention.[48] An activist campaign against diamond giant DeBeers led to the adoption of a company-based UN certification scheme prohibiting trade in so-called blood diamonds; President Bush has signed an executive order bringing the United States into compliance.[49] The Chad-Cameroon Pipeline may be the most ambitious partnership yet in this context, involving several oil companies (including ExxonMobil), the World Bank, numerous NGOs, and the respective governments. Its aim is to maximize the funds devoted directly to poverty reduction under international safeguards.[50]

These examples show how the reluctance or inability of governments to act collectively at the global level, or individually within their own societies, can get firms pulled into assuming roles that were traditionally more strictly confined to the sphere of public governance. Civil society

---

tosh, Sandra Waddock, and Georg Kell, eds., *Learning to Talk: Corporate Citizenship and the Development of the UN Global Compact* (Sheffield, UK: Greenleaf Publishing, 2004).

[47] "Statoil Signs Agreement with ICEM," *Europe Energy*, March 30, 2001; and "Historic First for Mining in Africa—Anglo Gold Signs Global Labour Agreement," available online at http://www.icem.org/update/upd2002/upd02–36.html.

[48] Jane Nelson, *The Business of Peace: The Private Sector as a Partner in Conflict Prevention and Resolution* (London: Prince of Wales International Business Leaders Forum, 2000). Even large and highly visible companies continue to pay no attention to these issues, but some of those have been sued in U.S. courts under the Alien Tort Claims Act. Others, like Canadian oil company Talisman, which had a major concession in Sudan, withdrew its operations after activist campaigns caused its stock prices to plunge.

[49] The text is available online at http://www.whitehouse.gov/news/releases/2003/07/20030729–20.html.

[50] http://www.worldbank.org/afr/ccproj, and David White, "Chad Starts Scheme to Track Oil Cash," *Financial Times*, October 6, 2003. Revenues from royalties and dividends will go into an escrow account in London. After loan service payments, 10 percent is earmarked for a "future generations fund," 5 percent for the producing region, and the remainder dedicated to priority spending in social sectors, vetted by an oversight group.

organizations typically do the initial pulling. This phenomenon is not limited to the developing countries, however, as the contested issue of climate change in the United States strikingly illustrates.

After President Bush rejected the Kyoto Protocol, several major oil companies lobbied the U.S. Congress for some form of greenhouse gas limits. They included Shell and BP, both of which, in collaboration with civil society organizations, have carefully cultivated "green" images, instituted companywide emissions reductions programs, and feared suffering a competitive disadvantage.[51] European activist groups organized a boycott of Esso, whose parent company, ExxonMobil, has been one of Kyoto's most determined opponents.[52] The number of shareholder resolutions demanding that firms adopt climate change risk management policies doubled in just one year, while lawsuits have been filed against the federal government and firms.[53] Swiss Re, one of the world's largest insurers, began to request information from energy-intensive companies for which it provides directors and officers liability coverage concerning whether those companies have a carbon accounting or reporting system in place, and how they intend to meet their obligations under Kyoto or any similar such instrument—the clear implication being that future rates and possibly coverage itself could be affected by the response.[54] Even Wall Street bankers and analysts are increasingly concerned.[55]

Meanwhile, in the U.S. governmental arena, a group of state and municipal treasurers, as fiduciaries of public sector pension funds worth

[51] "These companies have concluded that limits on carbon dioxide and other greenhouse, or heat-trapping, gases are inevitable. . . . And to plan long-term investments, they want the predictability that comes from quick adoption of clear rules." Andrew C. Revkin and Neela Banerjee, "Energy Executives Urge Voluntary Greenhouse-Gas Limits," *New York Times*, August 1, 2001.

[52] Information available online at http://www.stopesso.com.

[53] Amy Cortese, "As the Earth Warms, Will Companies Pay," *New York Times*, August 18, 2002; Jeffrey Ball, "Global Warming Threatens Health of Companies," *Wall Street Journal*, April 16, 2003; Vanessa Houlder, "Climate Change Could Be Next Legal Battlefield," *Financial Times*, July 14, 2003; Danny Hakim, "States Plan Suit to Prod U.S. on Global Warming," *New York Times*, October 4, 2003; and "A Novel Tactic on Warming" (editorial), *New York Times*, July 28, 2004, A18.

[54] Mark Nicholls, "Executives Could Lose Climate Change Insurance Coverage," *Environmental Finance* 4 (November 2002): 8.

[55] Demetrios Sevastopulo and Vanessa Houlder, " 'Greening' of Financial Sector Gaining Speed," *Financial Times*, June 4, 2004, 6. American auto manufacturers are deemed particularly vulnerable; see Danny Hakim, "Catching Up to the Cost of Global Warming," *New York Times*, July 25, 2004, sec. 3, p. 5. At the June 2004 Global Compact Leaders Summit, Goldman Sachs, on behalf of twenty major investment firms, presented a report entitled "Who Cares Wins," endorsing the idea that social and environmental performance should become a core element in the assessment of investment risks. The report is available online at http://www.unglobalcompact.org.

nearly $1 trillion, held an Institutional Investors Summit in November 2003. Its aim was to devise a strategy for promoting the adoption of climate change policies by firms in their funds' portfolios. As if to demonstrate the blurring of roles between different social sectors, the event was organized by an NGO, coconvened by a Harvard University research center, and held in the chamber of the UN Economic and Social Council.[56] Also in 2003, fully half of all U.S. states introduced so-called son-of-Kyoto bills, aiming to build frameworks for regulating carbon dioxide emissions—with the support of environmental groups hoping that these initiatives at the state level will generate industry demands for uniform federal standards.[57]

No central mechanism coordinates these actions; they are interconnected only by a common concern with climate change. With U.S. federal policy changes effectively blocked for the moment, other social actors have found different channels to advance their aims. None substitutes for a viable treaty, but they do change the political equation. Moreover, disclosure often leads to benchmarking and codification of best practices. And now that Kyoto has entered into force, a global market in emissions trading will emerge from which U.S. firms will be excluded until the United States comes into compliance, giving them yet additional incentives to support a different policy. Sooner or later, therefore, any U.S. administration will have to come to grips with climate change.

Needless to say, this dynamic has generated pushback by firms, and many manage to resist being drawn into it. Enough others are engaged, however, for it to have become an institutionalized fixture on the global governance stage. Once engaged, however, corporate leaders at the frontier of corporate social responsibility issues have begun to realize that the concept is quite elastic: the more they do, the more they will be asked to do. As a result, they have begun to ask, "*Where* is the public sector?" Companies providing AIDS treatment programs in southern Africa, for example, are beginning to work with governments to help build broader social capacity to respond to the pandemic.[58] At the global level, the World

---

[56] The NGO in question is the Coalition for Environmentally Responsible Economies (Ceres), whichalso created the Global Reporting Initiative. Harvard's Center for Business and Government, which I direct, was a coconvener. The Better World Fund, an offshoot of Ted Turner's United Nations Foundation, financed the event.

[57] Jennifer Lee, "The Warming Is Global but the Legislating, in the U.S., Is All Local," *New York Times*, October 29, 2003.

[58] This observation is based on interaction with some forty companies active in Africa, at a series of workshops under the rubric HIV/AIDS and Business in Africa and Asia: Building Sustainable Partnerships (Center for Business and Government, Kennedy School of Government, Harvard University); presentations are available online at http://www.ksg .harvard.edu/cbg/hiv-aids/home.htm.

Economic Forum, the single most influential global gathering of business leaders, recently launched a global governance initiative, seeking not to *curtail* the public sector but to help clarify where private sector responsibility ends and public responsibility must begin.[59]

Finally, national governmental agencies themselves, especially in the European and transatlantic context, increasingly manage day-to-day routine issues that affect them all through networks of peers across states. By now, such transgovernmental networks exist in virtually all areas of national policy that have any international dimension, including banking, defense, environment, health, and even the courts. In several areas of policy, UN conference diplomacy has extended such networks to the rest of the world.[60]

Let us bring this discussion to a close. In the previous section, we saw how some of the issues on the global governance agenda have migrated away from traditional transborder concerns toward more inclusive global issue spaces. The present section has shown that the existence of these issue spaces has pulled into the global governance arena new actors, above all civil society organizations and the transnational firms. By intent or by default, they have become involved in the promotion and production of global public goods. And they constitute platforms and channels for transnational action that are increasingly institutionalized and capable of operating in real time. Thus the traditional interstate system of global governance is becoming embedded in a broader global public domain: an arena of discourse, contestation, and action organized around global rule making, and affecting the capacity to make and enact global rules.[61] It is akin to the situation domestically where the state is similarly embedded, though the global variant, of course, is much thinner and considerably more fragile, and it remains far from being universal.

These developments must not be romanticized. The world of global governance is not necessarily more "democratic" as a result, though it has become more pluralistic.[62] Moreover, vast asymmetries of power re-

---

[59] The World Economic Forum publishes an annual Global Governance Report, which assesses the respective contributions that various sectors of society are making to solving global problems; http://www.weforum.org/site/homepublic.nsf/Content/Global+Governance +Task+Force.

[60] Anne-Marie Slaughter, "The Real New World Order," *Foreign Affairs* 76 (September/ October 1997); also, Slaughter, "Judicial Globalization," *Virginia Journal of International Law* 40 (Summer 2000). On the UN conference role, see Peter M. Haas, "UN Conferences and Constructivist Governance of the Environment," *Global Governance* 8 (March 2002).

[61] Ruggie, "Reconstituting the Global Public Domain."

[62] The major work in the cosmopolitan democracy genre is David Held, *Democracy and the Global Order: From the Modern State to Cosmopolitan Governance* (Stanford: Stanford University Press, 1995); and, more recently, David Held, "Law of States, Law of Peoples: Three Models of Sovereignty," *Legal Theory* 8:1 (2002).

main in place—among states, between states and the new actors, and between the corporate sector and civil society. But equally, this new global public domain should not be viewed as existing only somewhere "out there," an adversary of or substitute for states. With respect specifically to the United States, its own social and political institutions—not only civil society and the corporate sector, but also the courts and governmental agencies—are intimately involved in its propagation and everyday functioning. That is why the pursuit of American exemptionalism—easy enough to conjure up as an ideological desire—is increasingly difficult to achieve in practice.

The New Exemptionalism

Advocates of the Bricker amendment framed their arguments entirely in constitutional terms, consistently asserting that the UN human rights conventions then being negotiated would violate states' rights, undermine the separation of powers, and diminish the basic rights of Americans by lowering them to international standards. Moreover, it was claimed, they would infringe on domestic jurisdiction, subject U.S. citizens to trials abroad, and promote world government. These constitutional objections, Natalie Kaufman observes, obscured "the highly political nature of the opposition and the essential congruence between the treaties and the United States Constitution."[63]

The actual cause of that opposition, as already noted, was race. During debates on the UN human rights covenant, Eleanor Roosevelt, the Godmother of the Universal Declaration, was sent to reassure southern Senators that it would not interfere in "murder cases"—that is, states' lynch laws—or the "right to education"—at the time still governed by the *Plessy* ruling of "separate but equal."[64] During debates on the Genocide Convention, Raphael Lemkin, who invented the very term and was the intellectual force behind the convention, found himself in the unenviable position of testifying that genocide occurred only when intent existed to exterminate an entire group, whereas "those who committed lynchings lacked this requisite motivation."[65]

President Eisenhower just barely defeated the Bricker amendment. But in return, his administration was obliged to withdraw from further negotiations on the Genocide Convention and the UN covenants, and subsequent administrations have had to agree to an ever-escalating series of

[63] Kaufman, *Human Rights Treaties and the Senate*, 2.
[64] Anderson, *Eyes off the Prize*, p. 4.
[65] Ibid., p. 228.

reservations and non-self-executing declarations limiting such treaties' domestic legal effects.[66] Even so, the United States ratified the Genocide Convention only in 1988, the International Covenant on Civil and Political Rights in 1992, and the Convention Against Torture as well as the Convention on the Elimination of All Forms of Racial Discrimination in 1994. Similarly, it took the Senate thirty-four years to adopt a 1957 ILO convention banning forced labor, codifying an issue that one would have thought had been settled by the Civil War.[67] Needless to say, non- or late ratification did not equate with noncompliance. U.S. authorities did not commit genocide or torture in the interval, and the Supreme Court declared Jim Crow laws unconstitutional while related political practices were redressed by the civil rights legislation of the 1960s.

A half century after the Bricker amendment, race is no longer the political driver of the exemptionalist quest that it once was. Its constituency base today is animated by a more diffuse set of social issues including capital punishment, abortion, gun control, unfettered property rights, and the role of religion in politics and policy—coupled with distrust of government and, therefore, even greater distrust of international entities. But the form of the exemptionalist arguments, as Kaufman observes, has remained remarkably similar over time.[68]

A main source of the recent resurgence of exemptionalism in the policy arena is the growing influence of neoconservative think tanks from the 1980s on, in particular the American Enterprise Institute (AEI) and the Heritage Foundation. As John Bolton wrote not long before he left AEI to join the Bush administration as a senior State Department official, "the harm and costs to the United States of [globalists'] belittling our popular sovereignty and constitutionalism, and restricting both our domestic and our international policy flexibility and power are finally receiving attention."[69] The UN has been a leading target of this attention, for pronouncing on such questions as when the use of force may or may not be legitimate, and nongovernmental organizations are criticized for being too influential and lacking democratic accountability. The EU is also seen to pose a danger, not only because it has, according to Jeremy Rabkin,

---

[66] Louis Henkin, "U.S. Ratification of Human Rights Conventions: The Ghost of Senator Bricker," *American Journal of International Law* 89 (April 1995).

[67] Edward C. Lorenz, *Defining Global Justice: The History of U.S. International Labor Standards Policy* (Notre Dame, IN: University of Notre Dame Press, 2001), 206.

[68] Kaufman notes of Senate debates in the 1980s "that the arguments against human rights treaties developed in the early 1950s have survived the decades with little modification." *Human Rights Treaties and the Senate*, 194.

[69] John R. Bolton, "Should We Take Global Governance Seriously?" *Chicago Journal of International Law* 1 (Fall 2000): 206. In March 2005 Bolton was nominated by President Bush to become U.S. permanent representative to the UN.

"many practical ramifications for U.S. policy. But it also presents a clear ideological alternative"—above all, by its members' agreeing to pool aspects of their sovereignty to achieve everyday policy aims.[70] In response to these perceived threats, neoconservatives have constructed a "new sovereigntist" defense around American institutions against international encroachment.[71] Writes Rabkin, in a somewhat circular fashion: "Because the United States is fully sovereign, it can determine for itself what its Constitution will require. And the Constitution necessarily requires that sovereignty be safeguarded so that the Constitution itself can be secure."[72] Put simply, the new sovereigntists propose to defend America against the world of global governance that the United States itself helped to create.

But the resurgence of exemptionalism is not limited to neoconservative activists and political commentators. What Koh describes as the "nationalist" school is flourishing in legal scholarship on the role of international law in domestic courts, best represented by Curtis Bradley and Jack Goldsmith.[73] Among many other issues, they raise the concern that judges might "make law" by incorporating rules and norms of customary international law into the domestic sphere through the courts, and that this practice could have adverse consequences for core features of the U.S. Constitution. Moreover, even though customary international law has traditionally been considered binding on states, the nationalists argue that in recent years large areas of it lack legitimacy for two reasons: they deal with subjects, like human rights, that are not "international" but fall within domestic domains; and they are not "customary" because in many instances they fail to reflect actual state practice but are the products of various forms of international agreements. As we have seen, these developments are part and parcel of the recent evolution of global governance,

[70] Jeremy Rabkin, "Is EU Policy Eroding the Sovereignty of Non-Member States?" *Chicago Journal of International Law* 1 (Fall 2000): 273. Bolton adds, presumably referring to the ICC, "Not content alone with transferring their own national sovereignty to Brussels, [the EU has] also decided, in effect, to transfer some of ours to worldwide institutions and norms" ("Should We Take Global Governance Seriously?" 221).

[71] Peter J. Spiro seems to have coined the term in his critique "The New Sovereigntists: American Exceptionalism and Its False Prophets," *Foreign Affairs* 79 (November/December 2000).

[72] Rabkin, *Why Sovereignty Matters*, 9.

[73] See Bradley and Goldsmith, "Customary International Law as Federal Common Law"; Bradley and Goldsmith, "U.N. Human Rights Standards and U.S. Law: The Current Illegitimacy of International Human Rights Litigation," *Fordham Law Review* 66 (November 1997); Goldsmith, "Should International Human Rights Law Trump U.S. Domestic Law?" *Chicago Journal of International Law* 1 (Fall 2000); and Bradley, "International Delegations, the Structural Constitution, and Non-Self-Execution," *Stanford Law Review* 55 (May 2003).

and Bradley and Goldsmith propose a number of new constitutional rules intended to insulate the United States from them.

But are the "new sovereigntist" and "nationalist" defenses really necessary? And what costs would they entail? I begin my assessment with some of the more technical constitutional questions and then take up their more overtly political dimensions.

Bradley and Goldsmith direct most of their attention to debates among legal scholars themselves. But the ascendancy of their own position demonstrates that these debates tend to be self-correcting. The nationalist position itself was a reaction against previous overreaching by liberal internationalists. A major case in point is the *Restatement (Third) of the Foreign Relations Law of the United States*, a semiauthoritative source used not only by academics but also by practitioners, including judges, which exaggerated how widely U.S. courts had accepted the principle that international law is part of federal law. In due course the nationalists successfully challenged those claims.[74] They have similarly challenged internationalist claims that countries are bound by customary international law even though they might have expressly rejected the same norms when these were contained in treaties and conventions; that attaching reservations, understandings, and declarations (RUDs) to treaties—a routine U.S. practice—does not entirely exempt countries from those obligations; and that the legality of RUDs themselves is in doubt.[75] Lastly, it is apparent that the category of *jus cogens*—peremptory norms originally limited to fundamental crimes against humanity, such as slavery, genocide, and torture—has seemed to expand inexorably in liberal internationalist writings, without solid legal bases.[76] But none of those claims any longer enjoys the authority it once did, so the core of the alleged problem cannot lie here—even if courts and political actors hung on every legal scholar's last word in these debates.

Nor can the problem reside in any failure of the existing ratification process to limit U.S. commitments. Recall that the Bricker debacle was followed by near-total nonratification of human rights treaties until 1988.

[74] Louis Henkin, Andreas F. Lowenfeld, Louis B. Sohn, and Detlev F. Vagts, eds., *Restatement (Third) of the Foreign Relations Law of the United States* (Philadelphia: American Law Institute, 1987).

[75] There are complex legal arguments, pro and con, on each of these, and I can pass no independent judgment on them. But on policy grounds Bradley and Goldsmith's contention seems compelling: "When the political branches cannot plausibly be viewed as having authorized the incorporation of CIL [customary international law], and especially when they have explicitly precluded incorporation, federal courts cannot legitimately federalize CIL." Curtis A. Bradley and Jack L. Goldsmith, "Federal Courts and the Incorporation of International Law," *Harvard Law Review* 111 (June 1998): 2270.

[76] Anthony D'Amato, "It's a Bird, It's a Plane, It's Jus Cogens!" *Connecticut Journal of International Law* 6 (Fall 1990).

From 1993 to 2000, according to David Sloss's calculation, the president transmitted to the Senate a total of 184 treaties on all subjects combined.[77] Of those, 40 were global. As of the end of 2002, the Senate had approved 31 of them, rejecting nearly one-fourth outright. Furthermore, the Senate attached conditions to 24 of the 31 that it approved, ratifying a mere 7 without conditions. In addition, the Senate has declared that human rights treaties are not self-executing in any event. Sloss also notes that the United States is party to only 12 of 27 treaties the UN secretary-general has identified as "most central to the spirit and goals of the Charter," every one of them subject to conditions.[78] Equally striking, as of June 2003 the ILO had concluded 7,147 legal conventions on labor practices, of which 1,205 are deemed "fundamental." The Senate had ratified a mere 14, of which just *two* fell into the "fundamental" category.[79] In short, the U.S. Senate can hardly be accused of inundating the domestic legal system with large numbers of unconditionally ratified or self-executing international treaty instruments.

How much of a problem, then, are the courts? A systematic response would require a more detailed analysis of court decisions than is possible here. But I am struck by several impressions. First, there is no consensus in this literature that any *actual* case has ever adversely skewed constitutional arrangements or practices as a result of a bad call by a court involving the domestic incorporation of international norms. The alleged dangers appear to be entirely hypothetical—and have been so for the past half century.[80] Problems might yet emerge, of course.[81] But is an under-

[77] David Sloss, "International Agreements and the Political Safeguards of Federalism," *Stanford Law Review* 55 (May 2003): 1984–85.

[78] Ibid., 1986.

[79] Available online at http://webfusion.ilo.org/public/db/standards/normes/index.cfm?lang=EN.

[80] In 1950, Frank Holman, a former president of the American Bar Association and an intellectual force behind the Bricker amendment, wrote: "By and through treaty law-making the federal government can be transformed into a completely socialistic and centralized state. It only requires that the present provisions of the Declaration on Human Rights be incorporated into a treaty . . . to change the relationship between the states and the federal government and to change even our Constitution and our form of government. . . . It is not an overstatement to say that the republic is threatened to its very foundations." Cited in Kaufman, *Human Rights Treaties and the Senate*, 9.

[81] One case the nationalists have their eyes on and would like to see overturned because they fear its potential as a precedent is *Missouri v. Holland* (252 U.S. 416 (1920)). It concerned a 1918 treaty with the United Kingdom (Canada) protecting endangered migratory birds, with the state of Missouri claiming its unconstitutionality because it infringed on states' rights (Holland being a U.S. game warden). Justice Holmes delivered the opinion of the Supreme Court, finding that "the subject matter is only transitorily within the State and has no permanent habitat therein," and that "but for the treaty and the statute there soon might be no birds for any powers to deal with." The Court ruled that the treaty represented a proper exercise of constitutional authority and did not violate the Tenth Amendment.

specified and indeterminate future risk adequate warrant for introducing new constitutional rules today? Next, one constant hypothetical refrain has been that judges might further stretch previously novel rulings. Often cited in this context is the *Filartiga* decision, permitting U.S. as well as foreign individuals and corporations to be tried in U.S. courts under the Alien Tort Claims Act for certain human rights crimes committed abroad. It is of great interest, therefore, that the Second U.S. Circuit Court of Appeals, which broke new ground in deciding the original case in 1980, recently ruled in *Flores v. Southern Peru Copper* that the act did not extend to environmental claims even when they involved loss of life—suggesting that at least this pioneering court is quite capable of drawing lines.[82] Lastly, as Frank Michelman documents in his chapter, the current Supreme Court is an unlikely perpetrator of expansive views in this direction. A mere reference to a 1981 ruling by the European Court of Human Rights in the recent decision declaring Texas's antisodomy law unconstitutional drew this stinging rebuke from Justice Antonin Scalia: "The Court's discussion of . . . foreign views is meaningless [and] dangerous dicta."[83]

Whatever the legal doctrinal merits of the nationalists' position, then, it is not at all clear what compelling public policy problem they would have us solve. From a policy perspective, therefore, its proposed solutions seem unnecessary. What is worse, however, acting on them would impose significant policy-related costs. Take just one of several new constitutional rules advocated by Bradley and Goldsmith. They recommend that customary international law be incorporated into the domestic legal system only upon case-by-case political branch approval. That would have the effect of reducing the constitutional status of this body of law and has been criticized on those grounds.[84] But it is also highly problematic on

[82] The plaintiffs, residents of Ilo, Peru, and representatives of deceased residents, asserted that the company's "shockingly egregious" acts of pollution violated an internationally recognized "right to life" and "right to health," but the court said that these are "insufficiently definite" to constitute customary international law. Mark Hamblett, *New York Law Journal*, September 9, 2003. The use of American courts to try international human rights violations has become increasingly controversial, thanks to various strands of conservative/nationalist criticism, but recently found a strong supporter in Republican Senator Arlen Specter, "The Court of Last Resort," *New York Times*, August 7, 2003; also see n. 28 above.

[83] Supreme Court of the United States, *Lawrence v. Texas*, Decided June 26, 2003, Scalia, J., dissenting (Preliminary print of the United States reports), 14. On the other hand, Justice Sandra Day O'Connor, a frequent swing vote on the Court, recently said in a speech, "I suspect that over time, we will rely increasingly—or take notice at least increasingly—on international and foreign law in resolving domestic issues." Quoted in Jonathan Ringel, "O'Connor Speech Puts Foreign Law Center Stage," *Fulton Country Daily Report*, October 31, 2003.

[84] Harold Hongju Koh, "Is International Law Really State Law?" *Harvard Law Review* 111 (May 1998). In *Sosa v. Alvarez-Machain* (see n. 28 above), the Supreme Court stipulated

policy grounds. As Lawrence Lessig notes, "In their strictly positivistic view, the only law is domestic law, and the only domestic law is statute or constitution based."[85] This narrow and formalistic position would require us to sacrifice the value of justice to a particular normative preference as to how law should be made—one for which there is no basis in the Constitution itself.

Much the same can be said about the nationalists' critique of the "delegation" of authority to international agencies and officials, which is also a core plank in the new sovereigntist campaign against global governance. It concerns the fact that, as the agenda of global governance has expanded, international actors are doing more things than they did in the past. And some are quite sensitive, whether resolving international trade disputes through the WTO or exercising operational command and control over UN peacekeeping missions. This task expansion raises many practical challenges of accountability, which require creative thinking and innovative practices.[86] But the nationalists/sovereigntists are not interested in devising effective practical solutions. Their response, as David Golove observes, is simply to argue that it is unconstitutional for the federal government to delegate *any* governmental authority affecting U.S. citizens to officials who are not accountable, directly or indirectly, "*exclusively* to the American electorate."[87] Golove finds no such provision in the Constitution, or in the views of the founders. But even leaving that aside, think of the monumental policy implications of adopting this stricture: apart from the United States, the United Nations has an additional 190 member states, and each one could make a perfectly legitimate claim that any delegation of authority would *also* need to be held exclusively accountable to *their* electorates. Obviously, it is humanly impossible to design such a governance structure, so that the only alternative would be

---

that U.S. law recognizes the law of nations, though it also acknowledged deference to the aims and statements of the political branches. This would appear to reject any categorical position that international law must first be domesticated by legislative action to become part of the law of the United States. I am grateful to Kal Raustiala for pointing this out to me.

[85] Lawrence Lessig, "Erie Effects: An Essay on Context in Interpretive Theory," *Harvard Law Review* 110 (June 1997): 1810.

[86] For an excellent discussion, see Robert O. Keohane and Joseph S. Nye, Jr., "Redefining Accountability for Global Governance," in *Governance in a Global Economy: Political Authority in Transition*, ed. Miles Kahler and David A. Lake (Princeton: Princeton University Press, 2003).

[87] David Golove, "The New Confederalism: Treaty Delegations of Legislative, Executive, and Judicial Authority," *Stanford Law Review* 55 (May 2003). For Bradley on this point, see "International Delegations, the Structural Constitution, and Non-Self-Execution"; and for the new sovereigntist argument, see Bolton, "Should We Take Global Governance Seriously?" as well as Rabkin, *Why Sovereignty Matters*.

to roll back the system of global governance—which may well be the point of the nationalist/sovereigntist exercise.

Furthermore, their argument misconstrues the nature of international authority in the first place. It externalizes and objectifies the very concept, as though this authority were embodied in some*one* or some*thing* other than states. With rare exceptions, authority in global governance involves no formal relations of super- and subordination, but remains largely horizontal in character. And enforcement is not a specialized function performed by specialized actors, akin to a branch or division of domestic government.[88] Thus the WTO dispute resolution procedure cannot force any state to comply even if it is found to be in the wrong; only states have troops that they may—or may not—make available for UN peacekeeping operations; and even the much stigmatized ICC requires the cooperation of states to function. International officials or entities may be endowed with normative authority that comes from legitimacy, persuasion, expertise, or simple utility; but they lack the basis and means to compel.

Finally, it is worth noting that leading nationalist scholars contributed to developing the Bush administration's categorization and treatment of detainees in "the war on terrorism"—including foreign nationals held in Guantánamo and Iraq as well as American citizens in this country—"exempting" the United States from certain provisions of the Geneva Conventions and even domestic law, and imputing highly expansive "commander in chief" powers to the president. These legal opinions, on their face, seemed anything but concerned with preserving constitutional guarantees and balances, while they gravely damaged America's reputation; indeed, several have been rejected by the Supreme Court.[89]

In sum, there are good reasons to challenge the nationalist school, and to be deeply troubled by the adverse impact its proposals would have on

---

[88] Golove addresses these issues in the context of self-executing treaties; strictly speaking, he notes, there is no such thing (ibid., 1734–41). For a broader discussion of international authority, see John Gerard Ruggie, *Constructing the World Polity* (London: Routledge, 1998), especially 59–61.

[89] On June 28, 2004, the Court ruled on two cases involving American citizens who were detained in the United States (*Hamdi et al. v. Rumsfeld, Secretary of Defense, et al.*, No. 03–6696; and *Rumsfeld, Secretary of Defense v. Padilla et al.*, No. 03–1027), and a third case involving some six hundred Guantánamo prisoners of various nationalities (*Rasul et al. v. Bush, President of the United States, et al.*, No. 03–334). Broadly speaking, all three decisions affirmed the detainees' right to challenge their detentions in American courts, which Bush administration rules had prohibited. However, when fourteen detainees who were involved in the *Rasul* case sought to file petitions challenging their detentions, the Justice Department maintained that they were not entitled to access to their lawyers to do so: "As aliens detained by the military outside the sovereign territory of the United States and lacking a sufficient connection to the country," its brief said, "petitioners have no cognizable constitutional rights." Neil A. Lewis, "New Fight on Guantánamo Rights," *New York Times*, July 31, 2004, A28.

key aspects of policy making, domestic as well as international. Needless to say, however, its doctrinal positions do have their political uses.

For the more overtly political new sovereigntists, the nationalists—Bolton calls them the "Americanists"—provide legal cover for a direct assault on the institutions and practices of global governance. But unlike Bradley and Goldsmith, who acknowledge that they are dealing largely with issues of doctrine, for Bolton and Rabkin the danger to the Republic is clear and present. Writes Bolton: "In substantive field after field—human rights, labor, health, the environment, political-military affairs, and international organizations—the Globalists have been advancing while Americanists have slept. Recent clashes in and around the United States Senate indicate that the Americanist party has awakened."[90] Rabkin seems gloomy rather than feisty, decrying "the demise of our constitutional traditions" at the hands of global civil society and international bureaucrats.[91]

Yet despite the alarmist language, examples of actual threats are few and feeble. For example, Bolton on several occasions has excoriated remarks by UN secretary-general Kofi Annan that "only the UN Charter provides a universally legal basis for the use of force"—calling this "the Annan doctrine," describing it as "unlimited in its purported reach" and "greatly inhibit[ing] America's ability . . . to use force to protect and advance its vital national interests."[92] But Annan's claim seems beyond dispute. Apart from the Charter—which includes and reaffirms the preexisting right of self-defense (Article 51), a fact that Bolton conveniently ignores—what *universally* legal bases are there for the use of force?

The U.S. invasion of Iraq in March 2003, without Security Council approval, starkly posed the related question of how far the justification of self-defense can be stretched, and it pitted the United States against much of the international community, including some of its closest allies. The right of *preemption* is well established in customary international law: it permits the potential target of an unprovoked attack to strike first in self-defense—as Israel did in the 1967 Six-Day War. The threat must be imminent and the response proportionate. The Bush administration, however, signaled a new *preventive* use-of-force policy in its 2002 National Security Strategy.[93] But preventive strikes have no such legal pedi-

[90] Bolton, "Should We Take Global Governance Seriously?" 206.

[91] Jeremy Rabkin, "International Law vs. the American Constitution—Something's Got to Give," *The National Interest* 55 (Spring 1999).

[92] John Bolton, "Kofi Annan's Power Grab," *Weekly Standard*, October 4, 1999, 13; Bolton, "Should We Take Global Governance Seriously?" Also, Bolton, "The UN Secretary General versus the United States," *Human Events*, November 5, 1999.

[93] For excellent discussions of its international political and legal implications, see François Heisbourg, "A Work in Progress: The Bush Doctrine and Its Consequences," *Washing-*

gree or standing. In 1981 Israel claimed that it was acting in self-defense when it bombed Iraq's Osirak nuclear reactors. The Security Council, including Ambassador Jeane Kirkpatrick representing the Reagan administration, criticized Israel on the grounds that it faced no imminent threat. In other words, preventing a potential future threat from ever materializing has not, historically, qualified as self-defense. And Henry Kissinger made it clear why when he expressed concern that the Bush strategy not become "a universal principle available to every nation."[94] After the Iraq war, the administration shifted its rhetoric onto the normatively safer preemptive grounds—but it continued to have a difficult time establishing that the threat the United States faced from Iraq was imminent.[95] Finally, there simply is no legal doctrine to justify the policy of "democratic imperialism" advocated by some neoconservatives—transforming political systems abroad by means of U.S. force. But this is not a problem created by Kofi Annan, or by the UN Charter.

Rabkin has a special interest in property rights and the environment. But he is similarly challenged to come up with concrete instances where the U.S. Constitution needs new sovereigntist protections from the instruments of global governance. In several publications he has cited the case of UNESCO's threatening to delist an Australian national park from its World Heritage registry because the government permitted a uranium mine to open nearby. Activist groups protested the potential environmental and health effects, and for some reason the European Parliament pronounced itself on the subject. As trivial as this case is, for Rabkin it has all the makings of a globalist incursion into sovereign property rights: an international agency, civil society actors, a European Union entity, and environmentalism. If this case is left to stand as precedent, he contends, "then it is reasonable to say that what the U.S. Park Service does in Yellowstone National Park [is also] properly subject to international inspection."[96]

---

ton Quarterly 26 (Spring 2003), and Anthony Clark Arend, "International Law and the Preemptive Use of Military Force," Washington Quarterly 26 (Spring 2003).

[94] Henry Kissinger, "The War Option," San Diego Union-Tribune, August 11, 2002.

[95] The Bush administration also used the auxiliary argument that it was enforcing previous UN Security Council resolutions, but presumably the council has the right to determine for itself when its resolutions should be enforced, and by whom. Quite apart from a threatened French veto, the United States failed to line up the necessary nine votes in support of military action and withdrew its last draft resolution before going to war. Nor was Kosovo a persuasive precedent. In that case, there was strong majority support for the United States and the sole impediment to council authorization was a threatened Russian veto. Moreover, Russia introduced a resolution condemning NATO air strikes after the fact that the council rejected by a vote of 12–3, which could be construed as a retroactive authorization.

[96] Rabkin, "International Law vs. the American Constitution," 39.

Andrew Moravcsik has studied the new sovereigntists' political agenda closely, and he concludes that it isn't global governance per se they oppose, "just multilateral cooperation around certain emerging policies."[97] They include, as we saw in Bolton's list, such issues as the environment, human rights, and labor standards. Trade treaties arouse no concern as long as they don't touch on these "social" issues. And the global power of transnational corporations is never mentioned, while NGOs get a drubbing. But the political agenda, in fact, reaches deeper still. Rabkin doesn't so much want to defend the *current* American constitutional order as to *restore* an earlier one. He writes, nostalgically, "Before the political upheavals wrought by the New Deal in the 1930s, established constitutional doctrine sought to limit the reach of federal power to matters of *genuinely* national concern"[98]—and what he considers to be "genuinely" national does not reach far beyond protecting private property rights and providing national security. Thus Rabkin desires a rollback of not only certain forms of global governance but also central elements of the entire post–New Deal domestic political order—the "upheavals" that he believes overturned some earlier idyllic state of affairs, and the legitimacy of which he rejects. Nothing in recent electoral results or public opinion polls, however, suggests that the American public shares this radical agenda.

Where the new sovereigntists have had their greatest success is in utterly delegitimizing the International Criminal Court in the American mainstream.[99] Bolton "unsigned" the ICC statute on behalf of the Bush administration—an act for which the UN legal counsel could find no precedent. And the American public never learned that the ICC is a court of last resort, not first; that most U.S. allies, including the United Kingdom, are satisfied with the built-in safeguards for their troops and officials; and that the only realistic alternative to some version of an ICC in the long run is a decentralized system of universal jurisdiction, uncoordinated if not chaotic, because the idea of ending impunity for the most heinous crimes against humanity has taken root in too many places for it to be eradicated.[100]

---

[97] Andrew Moravcsik, "Conservative Idealism and International Institutions," *Chicago Journal of International Law* 1 (Fall 2000): 298.

[98] Rabkin, *Why Sovereignty Matters*, 7, emphasis added.

[99] For an excellent analysis of the rhetorical strategies that have been employed in this effort, see Mariano-Florentino Cuellar, "The International Criminal Court and the Political Economy of Antitreaty Discourse," *Stanford Law Review* 55 (May 2003).

[100] A central institution, of course, is not required for the practice of universal jurisdiction. For a glimpse of the decentralized system at work, see the profile of Spanish Justice Baltasar Garzon, who indicted Chile's former military dictator, Augusto Pinochet—and more recently Osama bin Laden—by Craig Smith, "Aiming at Judicial Targets All over the

In the heat of the Bricker amendment battle the *Washington Post* accused Senator John Bricker of trying to erect "a sort of voodoo wall" around the United States on the basis of "fear" and an "aura of illusions."[101] The "new sovereigntists" have tried to do much the same in recent years, with some success. It would be folly to underestimate their influence: they are ensconced in well-funded conservative think tanks, effective inside the Beltway, and present at senior levels in the Bush administration.[102] But neither should one exaggerate their significance. For one thing, neoconservative influence as a whole may have reached its apogee with the war against Iraq. If so, its subsidiary doctrines, including those on global governance, may also suffer a loss of credibility. For another, the evolution of global governance is shaped not only by state power but also, as we have seen, by social power. And that fact, in turn, has certain countervailing effects on U.S. policy in the long run, which I briefly address in concluding this chapter.

Conclusion

Harold Koh wisely cautions against overinterpreting American exemptionalism in human rights, for three reasons.[103] First, the United States does have a distinctive rights culture—most notably in First Amendment protections, as discussed by Frederick Schauer in his chapter—which differs from but is hardly incompatible with universal human rights values. Second, in many cases the United States uses different terms to describe similar realities—"police brutality" or "cruel and unusual punishment" instead of "torture," for example. But different labels, Koh stresses, do not necessarily mean different rules, and while the unwillingness to change labels may be quirky, it is not fatal to the rights in question. Third, despite its embarrassing record of late and partial ratifications in the human rights area, the United States has a strong record of compliance with the underlying norms even of nonratified treaties: "Many countries

---

World," *New York Times*, October 18, 2003. Most observers believe that the proliferation of individual country claims to the exercise of universal jurisdiction would impose high transaction costs and would potentially result in a chaotic system. The nationalists, of course, oppose the decentralized model as well. But Jack Goldsmith and Stephen D. Krasner, for example, fail to address any need to make trade-offs between the two on practical grounds in their dismissal of the ICC as representing but the latest wave of woolly-headed idealism; see Goldsmith and Krasner, "The Limits of Idealism," *Daedalus* 132 (Winter 2003).

[101] Quoted in Anderson, *Eyes off the Prize*, 232.

[102] According to the *Economist*, some twenty self-identified neoconservatives occupy senior foreign policy and defense positions: "The Shadow Men," April 26, 2003, 21.

[103] "On American Exceptionalism," especially 1483–87.

adopt a strategy of ratification without compliance; in contrast, the United States has adopted the perverse practice of human rights *compliance without ratification*."[104]

So the truly problematic challenges arise, Koh concludes, when "the United States actually uses its exceptional power and wealth to promote a double standard"[105]—one for itself, and another for the rest of the world.

The power asymmetries between the United States and the rest of the world, especially in the military sphere, will in some measure inevitably produce divergent approaches to global governance.[106] But how pronounced these differences turn out to be surely also reflects other factors. For example, relative power cannot explain the substantial shifts in America's posture toward international treaties and institutions between the Clinton and Bush presidencies, for the simple reason that it did not change appreciably. Already in the 1990s, the American neoconservative commentator Charles Krauthammer heralded the advent of "the unipolar moment."[107] Secretary of State Madeleine Albright ceaselessly hectored the allies and the UN to the effect that the United States was "the world's indispensable nation."[108] And Hubert Védrine, French foreign minister at the time, coined the term *hyper-puissance* to express the unique extent of American hegemony.[109] Yet transatlantic grumbling was not appreciably worse than it had been in earlier times. And President Clinton successfully brought everyone on board for the U.S.-led Kosovo intervention—including the German Red-Green coalition government—even though it arguably had less legal justification going for it than did the war against Iraq.[110]

---

[104] Ibid., 1484, emphasis in original.

[105] Ibid., 1485.

[106] Or, in the often-repeated phrase of Robert Kagan, Europe is from Venus, America from Mars. See Kagan, "Power and Weakness," *Policy Review* 113 (2002).

[107] Charles Krauthammer, "The Unipolar Moment," *Foreign Affairs* 70 (1990/1991): 23–32.

[108] As the *Toronto Star* put it shortly after her appointment as secretary of state: "It so happens that the phrase 'indispensable nation,' first minted by the new U.S. Secretary of State Madeleine Albright, is now used constantly by American officials and commentators to describe the overarching role of the United States in the contemporary world. [It] is triumphalist and irritating—which doesn't mean that it isn't apt. From Bosnia to Haiti, only the U.S. has the will and means to address major global problems." Richard Gwyn, "Annan Shows He's Much More Than 'the U.S. Choice,' " *Toronto Star*, December 27, 1996, A31.

[109] Hubert Védrine, *Face à l'hyper-puissance* (Paris: Fayard, 2003); the original essay by that title was published in 1995.

[110] Post-9/11 security threats are also often cited to explain these differences, although there is no logical reason why they should have led in one direction or another. It is interesting to recall that the Clinton administration took its Defense Counterproliferation Initiative to NATO, which adopted it as alliance policy and established a Defense Group on Proliferation cochaired by the United States—and France. I thank my colleague Ashton Carter for this point.

Not raw power itself but the ends and means of its deployment account for the difference.

Domestic politics in the United States also plays a role. Moravcsik argues in his chapter that the poor prospects for U.S. ratification of pending international human rights treaties are a function of cleavages over various "social" issues as well as the strong tradition of states' rights, coupled with a two-thirds Senate supermajority requirement that makes it relatively easy to generate veto groups. Certainly, the differences in the Clinton and Bush administrations' policy postures toward international treaties and institutions also reflect their respective domestic political constituencies and electoral calculations.

But to spell out clearly the implications of our argument in this chapter, let us hold these other factors constant. How might various expressions of global governance themselves bring about countervailing pressures on the United States? Consider a few current cases in point.

The use of force may be the hardest test because it is so closely related to American military predominance. But, despite strong resistance, the Bush administration found it impossible to avoid seeking a UN Security Council resolution in the buildup to its campaign against Iraq, once senior Republican foreign policy leaders urged that course of action and domestic public opinion swung behind it; and then to propose a second resolution that would have been construed as authorizing the use of military force because public opinion in Great Britain, America's only major ally in the campaign, demanded it. Of course, in the end the United States proceeded to fight an "elective" war without UN approval. But the consequences of doing so imposed significant direct costs on the United States, while also causing a major rift within the international community.[111] Just four months into the postwar occupation, the Bush administration was back at the UN and in NATO asking for assistance with an increasingly unsustainable burden—assistance of which it has received little.[112] Thus

[111] Among the former senior foreign policy officials urging the administration to seek a UN resolution were Brent Scowcroft, James A. Baker, and Lawrence Eagleburger—respectively, national security adviser and secretaries of state in the first Bush administration, with direct experience at successfully organizing the 1991 anti-Saddam coalition. Thanks to financial contributions from its allies, that war is reported to have yielded the United States a net profit. For the second Gulf War, Lael Brainard and Michael O'Hanlon have estimated the cost differential to the United States of proceeding without a UN authorization, for the war and the occupation, at roughly $100 billion as of mid-2003: "The Heavy Price of America's Going It Alone," *Financial Times*, August 6, 2003.

[112] Christopher Marquis, "Bush Faces New Obstacles in Keeping Allies' Support," *New York Times*, July 31, 2004, A6. NATO has agreed to send fewer than forty officers to conduct some training of the Iraqi military; that could become the nucleus of a larger future involvement if the allies so chose.

Iraq may yet demonstrate not only the norm of power but also the power of norms, to adapt Thomas Risse's clever phrase.[113]

The more general point here is that as the number of democracies in the world continues to rise, so, too, does the demand for not only internal but also external accountability of states. American neoconservatives, who are among the most vigorous advocates of democracy promotion abroad, at the same time are also utterly disdainful of international public opinion. Their position entails an unsustainable contradiction. In the run-up to the Iraq war the United States had most "trouble" with other democracies, not authoritarian states or kleptocracies; and not only in "old Europe" France and Germany, but also Canada, Chile, Mexico, and Turkey. Neoconservative "democratic imperialists" or unilateralist members of Congress may not care what people elsewhere think of the United States. But leaders of other democracies do have to care what their own people think about them if they are to survive politically. Very few such leaders will risk siding with the United States when two-thirds or more voters in their countries oppose U.S. policy. Thus America's success at promoting democracy abroad will have the effect of constraining the United States from deviating too far from the norm if it desires or needs the help of others—or of imposing significant costs on the United States if it chooses to go it alone.[114]

In other areas, various forms of social power have come to overshadow U.S. state power. In the 1990s, direct foreign investment in emerging markets exceeded official development assistance (ODA) by a factor of six to one, though the ratio has since declined somewhat. In 2000, U.S. noncommercial private transfers to developing countries were more than twice ODA, even after private remittances are excluded.[115] The relevant names here are Gates, Soros, Turner, hundreds of NGOs, numerous foundations and religious organizations—not USAID. These actors have their own policy priorities, which are often more closely aligned with the broader global governance agenda than is the case with official U.S. policy or overseas spending.

Furthermore, significant divergence by the U.S. government from widely shared international norms also imposes costs on America's global corporate sector, costs which that sector can be expected at some point

---

[113] Risse, "The Power of Norms versus the Norms of Power."

[114] Robert Kagan, a leading neoconservative foreign policy analyst, of Mars and Venus fame, has come to realize, albeit grudgingly, that legitimacy matters; see his essay "America's Crisis of Legitimacy," *Foreign Affairs* 83 (March/April 2004).

[115] Carol A. Adelman, "The Privatization of Foreign Aid," *Foreign Affairs* 82 (November/December 2003). The Bush administration's Millennium Challenge Account and HIV/AIDS initiative will alter this picture only somewhat, and neither is yet funded at significant levels.

to resist. During the Iraq war, the *Financial Times* reported that "big American consumer brands such as Coca-Cola, McDonald's and Marlboro are paying a price as boycotts spread from the Middle East to the rest of the world, especially Europe."[116] More recently, Control Risks Group, a leading British business risk consultancy, described U.S. foreign policy as "the most important single factor driving the development of global risk. By using US power unilaterally and aggressively in pursuit of global stability, the Bush administration is in fact creating precisely the opposite effect."[117] Finally, the ever-expanding web of corporate social responsibility, as described earlier in this chapter, is bound to produce increased corporate demands for more conventional governance solutions, including those at the global level, if only to get the private sector off a steadily ascending corporate responsibility escalator.

In sum, I would venture the following concluding proposition: the drive toward globalization, the spread of democratic governance, and the international rule of law, coupled with increasingly dense transnational networks—public and private—involved in the promotion and production of global public goods, embody a historical momentum that only a major calamity could reverse. In this respect, then, the consequences of American exceptionalism continue to hold their own vis-á-vis its exemptionalist counterpart.

[116] Richard Tomkins, "Anti-war Sentiment Is Likely to Give Fresh Impetus to the Waning Supremacy of US Brands," *Financial Times*, March 27, 2003.

[117] Quoted and summarized in Stephen Fidler and Mark Husband, "Bush Foreign Policy 'Is Creating Risks for US Companies,' " *Financial Times*, November 11, 2003, 11.

Contributors

STANLEY HOFFMANN is the Paul and Catherine Buttenwieser University Professor at Harvard, where he has taught since 1955. He is the author of *Gulliver Unbound* (Rowman and Littlefield, 2004) and is currently working on a book on ethics and international affairs.

MICHAEL IGNATIEFF is Carr Professor of Human Rights Practice and the Director of the Carr Center of Human Rights Policy at the John F. Kennedy School of Government, Harvard University. His books include *Isaiah Berlin: A Life, Blood and Belonging* (Chatto & Windus, 1998), *The Needs of Strangers* (St. Martin's, 2001), and *The Lesser Evil* (Princeton, 2004).

PAUL W. KAHN is Robert W. Winner Professor of Law and Humanities at Yale Law School, where he is also Director of the Orville H. Schell, Jr. Center for International Human Rights. He is the author of *Legitimacy and History* (Yale, 1992), *The Reign of Law* (Yale, 1997), *The Cultural Study of Law* (Chicago, 1999), *Law and Love* (Yale, 2000), and *Putting Liberalism in Its Place* (Princeton, 2004).

HAROLD HONGJU KOH is Dean and Gerard C. and Bernice Latrobe Smith Professor of International Law at Yale Law School. He is the author most recently of *Foundations of International Law and Relations* (with O. Hathaway, 2004).

FRANK I. MICHELMAN is Robert Walmsley University Professor at Harvard University. He is the author of *Brennan and Democracy* (Princeton, 1999) and a contributor to "Rawls on Constitutionalism and Constitutional Law" in the *Cambridge Companion to Rawls* (ed. Samuel Freeman, Cambridge, 2003).

ANDREW MORAVCSIK is Professor of Politics and Director of the European Union Program at Princeton University. He is author of *The Choice for Europe: Social Purpose and State Power from Messina to Maastricht* (Cornell, 1998.)

JOHN GERARD RUGGIE is the Evron and Jeane Kirkpatrick Professor of International Affairs and Director of the Center for Business and Government at the John F. Kennedy School of Government, Harvard University. From 1997 to 2001 he was Assistant Secretary-General and chief adviser for strategic planning to United Nations Secretary-General Kofi Annan.

FREDERICK SCHAUER is the Frank Stanton Professor of the First Amendment and former Academic Dean at the John F. Kennedy School of Government at Harvard University. His books include *Profiles, Probabilities, and Stereotypes* (Harvard, 2003), *Free Speech: A Philosophical Enquiry* (Cambridge, 1982), and *Playing by the Rules: A Philosophical Examination of Rule-Based Decision-Making in Law and in Life* (Oxford, 1993).

ANNE-MARIE SLAUGHTER is Dean of the Woodrow Wilson School of Public and International Affairs at Princeton University. She is the author of *A New World Order* (Princeton, 2004).

CAROL S. STEIKER is Professor of Law at Harvard Law School. She is the author of numerous scholarly articles on the legal regulation of capital punishment and on American criminal justice more generally.

CASS R. SUNSTEIN is Karl N. Llewellyn Distinguished Service Professor of Jurisprudence, at The Law School and Department of Political Science, University of Chicago. His most recent publication is *The Second Bill of Rights: Franklin Delano Roosevelt's Constitutional Vision and Why We Need It More Than Ever* (Basic Books, July 2004), and *The Laws of Fear: Beyond the Precautionary Principle* is forthcoming with Cambridge, 2005).

Index

ABA. *See* American Bar Association
Abrams v. United States, 31n.4
Ackerman, Bruce A., 197
Adams, John, 272n.145
Afghanistan, 120–21
Agency for International Development, United States (USAID), 313, 337
AIDS. *See* HIV/AIDS relief
Albright, Madeleine: and indispensable nation, the United States as, 335; Middle East diplomacy, her engagement in, 121n.34; National Democratic Institute, as chair of, 126n.46; new American exceptionalism, her contribution to, 234; North Korea, her visit to, 122; Yugoslavia, as advocate of military intervention in, 229
Alien Tort Claims Act, United States, 314, 319n.48, 328
Alston, Philip, 194
American Bar Association (ABA), 22, 156–58, 178n.100, 182, 191–92
American Booksellers Association, 47
American Civil Liberties Union, 47, 149, 164, 180
American Convention on Human Rights (1969), 33n.11, 148
American culture. *See* culture, American
American Enterprise Institute (AEI), 324
American exceptionalism. *See* exceptionalism, American
American Society of International Law, 278n.4
Amnesty International, 182, 313
Annan, Kofi, 133, 331–32
Anti-Defamation League, 48n.68
Arafat, Yasir, 122
Aristotle, 202–3
Ashcroft, John, 71
Atkins v. Virginia, 89, 252–53, 257, 260, 285
Australia: capital punishment in, 59; comparative constitutional analysis in, 287; defamation law in, 40; and hate speech, control of, 34

Avena v. Other Mexican Nationals, 117n.24

Badinter, Robert, 85
Baker, James A., 336n.111
Bennett, William J., 265n.122
Bentham, Jeremy, 94
Berger, Samuel R. "Sandy," 121n.34
Better World Fund, 321n.56
Bird, Rose, 71
Black, Hugo, 44
Blackhurst, Richard, 310
Blackmun, Harry, 107, 110, 247n.28
Bolton, John: and Americanists vs. globalists, 324, 331; European Union, his objection to action by, 325n.70; International Criminal Court, his opposition to, 133n.65, 137n.74, 229; international standards, his rejection of, 22; power in the pursuit of national interest, his advocacy of using, 230
Botswana, 318
Bowers v. Hardwick, 254–55, 257, 300
Bradley, Curtis, 325–26, 328, 331
Brainard, Lael, 336n.111
Brandenburg, Clarence, 36
Brandenburg v. Ohio, 36
Brazil, 65
Brennan, William, 88, 245n.17, 247n.28, 249–50
Breyer, Stephen: comparative constitutional analysis, his support for, 9n.24, 290, 296; comparative constitutional analysis by, 251–53, 256n.80, 257–58, 262, 293; as moderate at time of appointment, 109; transjudicial communication, his conference participation regarding, 277n.3
Bricker, John, 184n.118, 191n.136, 263, 334
Bricker Amendment, 157, 170n.78, 179–81, 191n.136, 305, 323
Bright, Stephen, 58
Britain. *See* United Kingdom
British Petroleum (BP), 320

Brown v. Board of Education, 281, 300
Brown-Wilkinson, Lord, 286
Buergenthal, Thomas, 8
Bulgarian Constitution, 91
Burger, Warren, 107, 110, 254–55, 257
Bush, George H. W., 123, 127, 181, 186n.121
Bush, George W.: Alien Tort Claims Act, his opposition to, 314n.28; Arafat, his call for replacement of, 235; blood diamonds, his support for UN effort prohibiting trade in, 319; the Bush doctrine (*see* Bush doctrine); conservative nationalists, his support for, 22; discrimination against Arab Americans, his warning against, 300; foreign affairs, his campaign of 2000 remarks regarding, 233; and human rights exceptionalism, implications of, 195; and Hussein, prosecution of, 134; Iraq, his justification of invasion of, 331–32; and Iraq, necessity of going to the United Nations for approval and assistance, 336–37; Kyoto Protocol, his rejection of, 306, 320; national security and human rights, his rhetoric linking, 24–25; North Korea identified by him as part of "axis of evil," 123; rhetoric of exceptionalism, his use of, 112; torture, his rejection of as policy instrument, 114–15n.15; war on terrorism, his insistence on taking sides in, 215n.33
Bush doctrine: as exceptionalist strategy, 124–29; the Iraq war, 236–39, 331–32, 336–37; obstacles to realization of, 235–36; origins and proponents of, 228–31; September 11 and the operationalization of, 231–34
Bush v. Gore, 208, 274, 292

Calabrese, Guido, 294, 303
Canada: capital punishment in, 59, 68; constitutional cross-fertilization by courts in, 286–87, 289; defamation law in, 40; and freedom of expression, adjudication of cases regarding, 54–55; and hate speech, control of, 32n.8, 34, 37, 259; homicide rate in, 61; judicial authority and freedom of expression in, 50; and Multilateral Agreement on Investment, litigation based on, 314n.29; socialist movement and rights in, 104
Canadian Bar Association, 157

Canadian Charter of Rights and Freedoms, 44
capital punishment: abolitionist consensus and American exemptionalism regarding, 6; American exceptionalism regarding, 14–15, 57–61, 89, 116–17; children and, 116–18; constitutionality of, 247n.28; culture of violence and, 85–86; deterrent effect of, 64–65n.26; European exceptionalism and, 83–84; federalism and, 79–80; historical contingency thesis regarding, 86–89; homicide rates thesis and, 61–66; majority will and, 15, 72–76, 299; political institutions and, 188–90; politics and, 70–72; populism in the criminal justice system and, 76–78; populism theory regarding, 72–76; public opinion thesis and, 66–70; southern exceptionalism and, 80–83
Cardozo, Benjamin, 57
Carolene Products Co., United States v., 281
Chad-Cameroon Pipeline, 319
Chang Myon, 119–20
Children's Defense Fund, 182–83
China, People's Republic of, 57
Christian Coalition, 182
Civil Rights Act of 1964, 109
civil society organizations (CSOs), 312–17, 319–23. *See also* nongovernmental organizations
Clinton, Bill: Bush foreign policy, his criticism of, 127n.47; capital punishment, his validation of as governor, 71; Convention on the Rights of the Child, his signing of, 181; International Criminal Court, his action regarding, 116n.21, 132–33, 306; and Kosovo intervention, international support for, 335; and Middle East peace process, shuttle diplomacy in, 121n.34; Religious Freedom Restoration Act, his signing of, 180n.110
Coalition for Environmentally Responsible Economies, 321n.56
Coker v. Florida, 247
communication, freedom of. *See* freedom of expression
community values, American exceptionalism and, 45–46
comparative constitutional analysis: advantages of, 273–76, 292–99; exceptionalism and, 241–45, 290; and global judi-

cial human rights dialogue, 278, 285–90; history of, 245–56; ideological stakes regarding, 262–64; integrity-anxiety and, 271–73, 279, 291–92 (*see also* integrity-anxiety); and legal/judicial isolationism, 8–11, 277–78, 290; principle precluding, seeking a, 256–62. *See also* global justice system; transnational legal process

Comprehensive Test Ban Treaty, 306

Concerned Women for America, 182

Congo, Democratic Republic of, 58

conservatism: comparative constitutional analysis and, 263–66 (*see also* integrity-anxiety); exceptionalism in human rights and, 17–20, 150–51, 155–66 (*see also* human rights); and *First Things* controversy, 265–66, 270, 274; and international human rights, opposition to, 176–86

constitutional law: American, defined, 242–43; as conventional discourse providing legitimacy, 270–71; as a discourse, 264–66; foreign, American aloofness from considering (*see* comparative constitutional analysis); integrity-anxiety regarding (*see* integrity-anxiety); public rights talk and, 267–68

constitutions: as formal cause of the state, 205–11; national (*see* names of specific countries)

Convention Against Torture and Other Cruel, Inhuman or Degrading Treatment or Punishment, 2, 22, 114n.15, 184n.120, 324

Convention on the Elimination of All Forms of Discrimination against Women, 2, 7, 188

Convention on the Elimination of All Forms of Racial Discrimination. *See* International Convention on the Elimination of All Forms of Racial Discrimination

Convention on the Prevention and Punishment of the Crime of Genocide: American Bar Association opposition to, 22; delayed ratification of, 7, 148, 324; majority support for, 156; prosecution of U.S. soldiers under, fears of, 170; race as underlying factor in opposition to, 179, 188n.129, 323

Convention on the Rights of the Child (CRC), 2, 7, 116, 148, 181–83

Council of Europe Cybercrime Convention (2001), 35

CRC. *See* Convention on the Rights of the Child

crime: homicide rates, 61–66; political salience of, 70–72; populism in the criminal justice system, 76–78. *See also* capital punishment

Cross-Border Insolvency Cooperation Protocols, 283

Cruzan v. Dep't of Health, 274–75n.149

CSOs. *See* civil society organizations

Cuba, detainees at Guantánamo Bay, 138–40, 330n.89

cultural relativism, 152–53

culture, American: constitutional patriotism, 154–59; constitutions as pragmatic instruments in, 101–3; legal/constitutional, exceptionalism of, 51–53; libertarian preference for negative rights, 45–47, 162–65; political and the politics of crime, 74–75; popular sovereignty and local government, commitment to, 159–61; of rights, exceptionalism and, 10–11, 13–16, 113–14, 149–54, 165–66, 195–96, 299–302; social/economic rights, exceptionalism and, 103–5; unilateralism/parochialism of, 130; of violence, 85–86. *See also* national identity

Dandridge v. Williams, 108

Danner, Allison, 136

Danner, Mark, 236

Dawkins, Richard, 214n.31

death penalty. *See* capital punishment

DeBeers, 319

Debs, United States v., 31n.4

defamation law, 38–41

Defense Planning Guidance draft of 1992, 228–29

democracy: and biases in American institutions, 186–92; and CODICES Web site, 284; global governance and, 322–23; politics of crime and, 73–76; popular sovereignty and local government, American commitment to, 159–61; promotion of, change in U.S. policy regarding, 126–28; stable, human rights and, 171–76. *See also* popular sovereignty

Derian, Patricia, 192, 194

double standards: the Bush doctrine and, 128–29, 234; challenges posed by, 335; costs of, 130; as feature of American exceptionalism, 7–8, 113, 116–18; human rights enforcement and, 148; national security threatened by, 24; post–September 11 detainees and, 138

Douglas, William O., 44, 88

Douglas v. California, 106

Dukakis, Michael, 70–71

Dulles, John Foster, 312n.20

Dworkin, Ronald, 262n.111

Eagleburger, Lawrence, 336n.111

economic rights. *See* social and economic rights

Eisenhower, Dwight D., 19, 186n.121, 323

Eisentrager, Johnson v., 139–40

Ely, John Hart, 281

England. *See* United Kingdom

Enmund v. Florida, 247–48

equality: American opposition to promotion of, 162–66 (*see also* social and economic rights); liberty and, 45

Equal Rights Amendment (ERA), 98

ethnocentrism, 152–53. *See also* culture, American

European Commission for Democracy through Law, 284

European Convention on Human Rights, 17, 44, 84, 153n.20, 173–74

European Court of Human Rights, 11, 136, 180, 255n.76, 328

European Court of Justice, 177n.97, 300–301

European exceptionalism, 83–84

European Human Rights Convention, 10–11

European Union, 311, 324–25

exceptionalism: American (*see* exceptionalism, American); European, 83–84; French, 208–9, 225; of judicial globalization, 278; substantive and methodological distinguished, 30–32; unilateralism, distinguished from, 3, 5

exceptionalism, American: costs of, 24–26; cultural explanations of, 10–11, 13–16, 113–14, 149–66, 299–302 (*see also* culture, American); different labels explanation of, 113–14; double standards (*see* double standards); evaluating, 20–25; exemptionalism (*see* exemptionalism); fly-

ing buttress mentality, 115–16; global leadership and, 119–20; institutional explanations of, 16–17, 186–92; isolationism, distinguished from, 5; legal isolationism, 8–11, 277–78, 290 (*see also* comparative constitutional analysis; global justice system; transnational legal process); legal self-sufficiency, 113; and national and international rights, implications for relationship of, 26; paradox of, 1–3, 147–52; political explanations of, 17–20, 150–52, 154; positive and negative faces of, 120–24, 142; realist explanations of, 11–13, 167n.67, 169, 227–29; responses to, 129–32; southern, 80–83; types of, 3–11, 111–18; unilateralism, distinguished from, 5

exemptionalism: the Bricker Amendment, 157, 170n.78, 179–81, 191n.136, 305, 323; as form of exceptionalism, 4–7, 113, 242; global governance and, 305–7, 323–38; human rights enforcement and, 148; the new exceptionalism and, 229–30

expression, freedom of. *See* freedom of expression

Family Research Council, 182

federalism, capital punishment and, 79–80

Feith, Douglas, 231

Finland, 59, 62

First Amendment: absoluteness and scope of, 44–45; and advocacy vs. incitement, test distinguishing, 36–37; age of and judicial enforcement, 31; commercial advertising and, 42; defamation law and, 39–41; distrust of government and, 46–47; freedom of expression, exceptionalism in protecting, 30, 41–43, 113; judicial interpretation of, 105; methodological exceptionalism and, 53–56; political culture of, 47–49; viewpoint discrimination and, 35–38

First Things, 265–66, 270, 274

Flores v. Southern Peru Copper, 327n.81

foreign policy: American exceptionalism in, 112, 225–26; and the "axis of evil," 233; the Bush doctrine (*see* Bush doctrine); containment policy and the Cold War, 226–27; culture of, change in, 165–66n.62; Defense Planning Guidance draft of 1992, 228–29; and democracy promotion, 126–28; ideational liberal perspective on, 176; imperialism of the new exceptionalism, 240; implications of American exceptionalism for, 194–95; internationalism, questions regarding, 142–43; isolationism, 226; liberal internationalism, 21–23, 25, 326; messianism in, 13–16; the new world order, 227–28; the Powell doctrine, 228; realist approach to, 22–23, 167n.67, 169, 227–29; strategic unilateralism, 128–29; and Swiss cheese ratification, 115n.16; and the Wilsonian syndrome, 226. *See also* international politics; war

Forsythe, David, 153, 184

Foster v. Florida, 252, 261

France: and American hostile environment restrictions, beliefs regarding, 33n.10; capital punishment in, 59, 68; exceptionalism of, 208–9, 225; and hate speech, control of, 34, 36–37; homicide rate in, 61; messianism of, 15–16; political culture in, 74; and social reporting, encouragement of, 316

Franck, Thomas, 8, 21, 277n.3

Frankfurter, Felix, 246–47

freedom of expression, 29–30, 56; American exceptionalism regarding, explanation of, 42–49; American exceptionalism regarding, extent of, 41–42; criminal proceedings and, 41; defamation law and, 38–41; hate speech regulation and, 32–38; interest group support for, 47–49; international politics/transnational legal influence and exceptionalism regarding, 51–53; judicial review/supremacy and, 49–50; methodological exceptionalism and, 53–56; substantive vs. methodological exceptionalism and, 30–32

Fried, Charles, 245, 258, 262–64

Frohwerk v. United States, 31n.4

Furman v. Georgia, 63–64, 67, 86–87, 89

Garza, Juan Raul, 189

Gates Foundation, 318

gender, freedom of expression and discrimination based on, 33–34

Geneva Conventions: Bush administration position regarding, 22, 24; exceptionalism and, 2; Guantánamo Bay detainees and, 5, 138–39

Genocide Convention. *See* Convention on the Prevention and Punishment of the Crime of Genocide

German Basic Law, 44

Germany: capital punishment in, 68; and hate speech, control of, 34; homicide rate in, 61; violent crime and punishment in, 62

Ginsburg, Ruth Bader: comparative constitutional analysis, her support for, 243n.8, 290, 293; comparative constitutional analysis by, 256nn.80–81; as moderate at time of appointment, 109; transjudicial communication, her conference participation regarding, 277n.3

Glendon, Mary Ann, 265n.122, 301

Global Compact, 318–19

global governance: American exceptionalism and, 304–7, 334–38; civil society organizations and, 312–17, 319–23; definition of, 307; and exemptionalism, reality of and countervailing pressures against, 334–38; and exemptionalism, resurgence of in response to, 323–34; and new actors, 311–23; and new agendas, 308–11; and new global public domain, emergence of, 308; transgovernmental networks and, 322; transnational corporations and, 314–22

globalization: economic, 277–78, 283–84; judicial (*see* global governance; judicial globalization)

global justice system: American attitudes regarding, 117–18; American exceptionalism and, 132–38, 241–45 (*see also* comparative constitutional analysis); new sovereigntist opposition to, 325–34. *See also* judicial globalization; legal/constitutional/judicial systems; transnational legal process

Global Reporting Initiative, 316

Glucksberg v. Washington, 251, 257

Goldberg v. Kelley, 300n.75

Goldsmith, Jack: International Convention on Civil and Political Rights, his opposition to, 193; International Criminal Court, his opposition to, 334n.100; international standards for American rights, his rejection of, 22; and nationalist school arguments, 325–26, 328, 331

Golove, David, 154–55, 329

Gratz v. Bollinger, 243n.8

Greece, 59
Gregg v. Georgia, 58, 86–87
Griffin v. Illinois, 106
Grutter v. Bollinger, 256n.80
Guantánamo Bay, detainees at, 138–40, 330n.89

Habermas, Jürgen, 275
Habre, Hissene, 132
Haitian Ctrs. Council v. McNary, 139n.79
Haitian Ctrs. Council v. Sale, 139n.79
Hamdi, Yasser, 140–42
Hamdi v. Rumsfeld, 140–41, 215, 330n.89
Hamilton, Alexander, 202, 226
Harkin, Tom, 174
Harvard University: Carr Center for Human Rights Policy, 3
Hassner, Pierre, 234–35
hate speech, 32–38
Hathaway, Oona, 115
Hauser, Rita, 297
Hehir, Bryan, 238
Helms, Jesse: American Servicemen's Protection Act, his sponsorship of, 20n.42; Convention to Eliminate Discrimination against Women, his opposition to, 188; and exceptionalism distinct from isolationism, 184n.118; his institutional position and promotion of exceptionalism, 130; International Criminal Court, his opposition to, 20; international law, his opposition to, 19; United Nations, his skepticism regarding, 181n.113
Henkin, Louis, 8, 21, 115, 301
Heritage Foundation, 324
HIV/AIDS relief, 5, 317–18, 321
Holland, Missouri v., 327n.81
Holman, Frank, 162–63, 327n.80
Holocaust denial, 32, 34, 36–37
homicide rates, 61–66
human rights: American political institutions and, 186–92; American rhetoric regarding, 129–30; American rights culture and, 13–16, 149–66, 195–96; the Bush doctrine and, 125–26; conservative opposition to international, 176–86; constitutional patriotism and, 154–59; global governance and (*see* global governance); global judicial dialogue regarding (*see* judicial globalization); implications for of American exceptionalism, 192–95; libertarianism and, 162–65; lo-

calism and, 160–61; majority will and, 299–302; and national and international standards, relationship of, 25–26; national security interests and, 24–25; paradox of American exceptionalism regarding, 1–3, 147–52; pluralist explanations of American exceptionalism regarding, 150–52, 154, 165–92, 196–97; popular sovereignty and, 159–60, 281; post–September 11 detainees and, 138–42; stable democratic governance and, 171–76; state sovereignty, as alternative to, 218–21; superpower status of the United States and, 167–71
Human Rights Campaign, 48n.68
Human Rights Watch, 149, 180, 182, 313
Humphrey, Hubert, 108
Hungarian Constitution, 91
Huntington, Samuel, 155, 158n.36
Hussein, Saddam, 1, 24, 134, 136, 236–39

ICC. *See* International Criminal Court
ICCPR. *See* International Covenant on Civil and Political Rights
ILO. *See* International Labor Organization
IMF. *See* International Monetary Fund
India: Bush doctrine, use of, 233; comparative material used by constitutional courts in, 287; Constitution of, 92
individualism, American exceptionalism and, 45–47
institutions, American exceptionalism and, 16–17, 186–92
integrity-anxiety: discourse of constitutional law and, 264–66; global legal discourse and, 271–73, 279; limited need for, 273–76; objectivity through legalism, need for, and, 9, 268–71, 279, 291–92; public discourse on rights and, 266–68
Inter-American Human Rights Commission, 139–40
interests. *See* politics and pluralism
International Convention on the Elimination of All Forms of Racial Discrimination, 33–35, 324
International Court of Justice (ICJ), 117
International Covenant on Civil and Political Rights (ICCPR): and exemptionalism in ratification, criticism of, 149; exemptionalism of the United States regarding, 5, 10; limited United States participation

prior to ratification of, 194; and race as basis for hate speech, proscription of, 33–34; ratification of, 101, 324; rights covered by, limits of, 163; withdrawal of the United States from drafting of, 19

International Covenant on Social, Economic, and Cultural Rights, 91, 101, 104, 162–63

International Criminal Court (ICC): American exemptionalism and, 4, 113, 130, 306; the Bush doctrine and, 233; new sovereigntist attacks on, 333; opposition to, 20, 133, 136–38, 164n.57, 170, 192, 229; responding to exceptionalism, role in, 135–38; Rome Treaty, signing of, 4, 116n.21, 132–33; Rome Treaty, unsigning of, 4, 116n.21, 137–38; as step toward universal jurisdiction, 309

International Criminal Tribunal for the former Yugoslavia, 132–34

International Federation of Chemical, Energy, Mine and General Workers' Unions, 319

International Labor Organization (ILO), 163, 327

international law: compliance with, 131; development of despite exceptionalism, 23–24; as liberal project of unified global order, 220–21; and popular sovereignty, problem posed by, 200; post–September 11 detainees and, 138–42; of war, 215–17. See also comparative constitutional analysis; global justice system; judicial globalization; transnational legal process

International Monetary Fund (IMF), 313n.23, 315

International Organization for Judicial Training (IOJT), 280

international politics: American exemptionalism in, 113; American global leadership, exceptionalism of, 119–20; the Bush doctrine and, 124–29 (see also Bush doctrine); double standards and, 116–18; flying buttress mentality in, 115–16; popular sovereignty and, 159–61; positive and negative faces of American exceptionalism in, 120–24; republican liberal theories of, 172–73; superpower status of the United States in, 167–71; transnational legal influence and, 51–53. See also foreign policy; United Nations; war

IOJT. See International Organization for Judicial Training

Iran, 57–58

Iraq: costs of war, 336n.111, 337–38; double standards and historical support of Hussein, 24; post–September 11 detainees and war in, 138–42; and United Nations, seeking approval and assistance for war from, 331–32, 336–37; war in, the global justice system and, 134–35; war in as test case for new exceptionalism, 236–39

Ireland, 59, 287

isolationism: in American foreign policy, 226; judicial/legal, 8–11, 277–78, 290

Israel: and Bush doctrine, use of, 233; comparative constitutional analysis in, 8, 287; "friends of" in American foreign policy, 231; and hate speech, control of, 34; Iraq war and, 128; and preemptive and preventive military strikes, 331–32; quasi-constitutional protection of rights in, 30n.3; socialist movement and rights in, 104

Italy, 59

Japan, 65

Jefferson, Thomas, 24, 26, 96

John Birch Society, 182

Johnson, Lyndon Baines, 18, 97, 109

Johnson v. Eisentrager, 139–40

judicial globalization, 241, 277–82; the American debate regarding, 291–99 (see also comparative constitutional analysis); and constitutional cross-fertilization, 285–90; functional form of, 282–85; future of American participation in, 302–3; majority will and, 299–301. See also global justice system; transnational legal process

judicial review: freedom of expression, protection of, 50; human rights in stable democracies and, 174–75; majority will and, 301; strength of in American government, 16

jus cogens, legal doctrine of, 219–20, 326

Kagan, Robert, 229–30

Karadžić, Radovan, 134

Karzai, Hamid, 120

Kaufman, Natalie, 153, 323–24
Keck, Margaret, 313
Keegstra, James, 37
Keegstra, R. v. (Canada), 32n.8
Kennan, George, 227
Kennedy, Anthony, 140, 253–58, 290, 294–95
Kim Dae Jung, 122–23
Kim Jong Il, 122–23
King, Martin Luther, Jr., 26
Kirkpatrick, Jeanne, 332
Kissinger, Henry, 184n.118, 230, 332
Knight v. Florida, 252, 293, 296
Koh, Kwang Lim, 119–20
Korea, People's Republic of, 122–23, 237
Korea, Republic of, 119–20, 122–23
Korematsu v. United States, 300
Krauthammer, Charles, 231, 335
Kristol, William, 231
Kyoto Protocol, 2, 4, 306, 320–21

La Forest, Gerard V., 293
land-mines ban, 314–15
Lange, Joep, 317
LawAsia, 284–85
Lawrence v. Texas, 245, 253–58, 285, 294n.66, 300, 328
Lawyer's Committee on Human Rights, 149
League of Nations, 187, 226
legal/constitutional/judicial systems: American (*see* Supreme Court, United States; United States, Constitution of); comparative constitutional analysis (*see* comparative constitutional analysis); freedom of expression and (*see* freedom of expression); globalization of the judiciary (*see* judicial globalization); global justice system (*see* global justice system); governmental support required for, 94; international human rights and, 190–92; judicial education and globalization, 281; judicial review and support for human rights in stable democracies, 174–75; methodological exceptionalism in, 53–56; social/economic rights and, 101–3; transnational influence within, 51–53 (*see also* transnational legal process)
legal/judicial isolationism, 8–11, 277–78, 290. *See also* comparative constitutional analysis; judicial globalization

legal realism, 106
Lemkin, Raphael, 323
Leo, John, 265n.122
Le Pen, Jean, 36
Lessig, Lawrence, 329
Lester, Anthony, 301
L'Heureux-Dubé, Claire, 262n.110, 286, 289–90
libel, 38–41
liberal internationalism, 22–23, 25, 326
libertarian values, American exceptionalism and, 45–47, 162–65
Lincoln, Abraham, 26, 112
Lindsay v. Normet, 108
Locke, John, 97
Luxembourg, 59

Madison, James, 96, 110
Magge, Hema, 183
MAI. *See* Multilateral Agreement on Investment
Maier, Charles, 235
Marbury v. Madison, 301
Marshall, John, 206
Martinez, Bob, 71
Mattox, Jim, 71
McVeigh, Timothy, 189
Merck, 318
messianism, 13–16
methodological exceptionalism: freedom of expression and, 53–56; substantive exceptionalism, distinguished from, 30–32
Mexico, 65
Middle East peace process, 121–22
Millikin, Eugene, 178
Milošević, Slobodan, 1, 23, 132, 134, 138, 234
Missouri v. Holland, 327n.81
Mladić, Ratko, 134
Montesquieu, Charles-Louis de Secondat, 90, 96–97
Morgenthau, Hans, 227
Motorola, 315
Multilateral Agreement on Investment (MAI), 314
multinational corporations. *See* transnational corporations

National Association for the Advancement of Colored People (NAACP), 48n.68, 82
National Center for Home Education, 182

national identity: the citizenry and, 211–14; civic nationalism, 305; the Constitution and, 205–11; globalization of law and American, 198–99; the modern nation-state and, 199–203; political autonomy and American exceptionalism, 217–22; popular sovereignty and revolution in the, 203–5; war and the rule of law in the, 214–17. *See also* culture, American
nationalism, exceptionalism and, 152–59. *See also* culture, American
nationalist school of legal scholarship, 325–34
National Organization for Women, 48n.68
nation-state, the, 201–3. *See also* state, the
natural law, 200
Netherlands, the, 34, 59, 316
Neuman, Gerald L., 244n.10, 258n.89, 260n.101, 275n.150
New Deal, social and economic rights, support for, 90, 93, 97, 99–101, 105, 110
new sovereigntists, 325–34
New York Times Co. v. Sullivan, 39–41
New Zealand: comparative material used by constitutional courts in, 287; defamation law in, 40; and hate speech, control of, 34; quasi-constitutional protection of rights in, 30n.3
NGOs. *See* nongovernmental organizations
Niebuhr, Reinhold, 231
Nigeria, 58
Nixon, Richard, 70, 86–87, 106–10, 179
nongovernmental organizations (NGOs): global activism by American, 1; Global Compact, participation in, 319. *See also* civil society organizations
North Atlantic Treaty Organization (NATO), 336
North Korea. *See* Korea, People's Republic of
Norway: capital punishment in, 59; Constitution of, 91
Novartis, 318
Nye, Joseph, Jr., 12, 240

Ocampo, Luis Moreno, 136
O'Connor, Sandra Day: capital punishment, her opinions regarding, 248n.33, 253n.66; comparative constitutional analysis, her position regarding, 250n.46, 290, 294–95, 328n.83; Ginsburg point regarding international authority, her response to, 256n.80; and *Hamdi* case, plurality opinion regarding, 141; judicial globalization, her support for, 277–78nn.3–4, 283
Olympic Airways v. Husain, 283, 285
originalism, 158, 180, 296

Padilla, Rumsfeld v., 140–41, 330n.89
Paine, Thomas, 76
Pakistan, 58
PCIJ. *See* Permanent Court of International Justice
PEN, 47
People for the American Way, 47
Perle, Richard, 231
Permanent Court of International Justice (PCIJ), 135–36
Peru, Constitution of, 91
Pinochet, Augusto, 2, 132, 333n.100
Plessy v. Ferguson, 300
politics and pluralism: autonomy of the political and American exceptionalism, 217–22; comparative constitutional analysis and, 263–64; conservative opposition to international human rights, 17–20, 176–86; democratic governance, stability of and human rights, 171–76; domestic factors supporting exceptionalism, 150–52; exceptionalist human rights policy and, 150–52, 154, 165–92, 196–97; institutional biases, 186–92; legitimacy through legalism, 268–71; national identity and the rule of law (*see* national identity); public rights talk and, 267–71; superpower status of the United States in world affairs and, 167–71; winners and losers from American exceptionalism, 193–94
popular sovereignty: American exceptionalism and, 299–302; the American nation-state as the product of, 203–5; capital punishment and, 15, 72–78, 299; the citizenry and, 211–14; constitutions and, 205–11; human rights and, 159–60, 281; law, defense of through war and, 214–17; local government, American commitment to, 159–61; the modern nation-state and, 199–203; the rule of law and exceptionalism, 198–99. *See also* democracy
Portugal, 59
Pound, Roscoe, 297

Powell, Colin, 133, 229
Powell, Lewis, 107–8, 110, 247n.28
press, the: freedom of (*see* freedom of expression); as interest group in the United States, 47–48
Printz v. United States, 8, 9n.24, 250–51, 257–58, 262
property, right to private, 94
"Protocol on the Criminalization of Acts of a Racist or Xenophobic Nature," 35

Rabkin, Jeremy, 22, 324–25, 331–33
race: capital punishment in the South and, 80–83; exemptionalism regarding international human rights and, 323–24; freedom of expression and hatred/violence based on, 33–38; international human rights and, 19, 178–80, 188n.129, 191–92
Race Relations Act of 1965 (United Kingdom), 33
Raines v. Byrd, 259–60
Rasul v. Bush, 138–40, 330n.89
R.A.V. v. City of St. Paul, 35nn.17–19
Rawls, John, 265, 269–70, 275
Reagan, Ronald: and democracy promotion as foreign policy goal, 126; exceptionalism of, 112; and exemptionalism, effort to minimize, 305; and Genocide Convention, ratification of, 170n.77; new exceptionalists, his relationship to, 230–31; social safety net, his commitment to, 102
Rehnquist, William H.: appointment of, 107, 110; comparative constitutional analysis, his opposition to, 253, 260–61; comparative constitutional analysis, his position regarding, 290, 296; comparative constitutional analysis by, 251, 257; international judicial exchanges, his support for, 290, 298; on judicial review, 272n.141; and persuasive authority, foreign references as, 259
Reisman, Michael, 230
religion: capital punishment in the South and, 81–82; international human rights and, 178n.98, 180n.110
reservations, understandings, and declarations (RUDs) to treaties, 326
revolution: as efficient cause of the modern state, 203–5; popular sovereignty and, 200

Rice, Condoleezza, 230
Richards, Ann, 71
rights: discourse regarding, requirements of, 266–71; freedom of expression (*see* freedom of expression); human (*see* human rights); majority will and, 15, 299–302; negative and positive, 93–95, 162–65; quasi-constitutional protection of, 30n.3; social and economic (*see* social and economic rights)
Risse, Thomas, 337
Rodriguez, San Antonio School District v., 108
Rodriguez-Fernandez v. Wilkinson, 257n.82
Romanian Constitution, 91
Roosevelt, Eleanor, 1, 126, 323
Roosevelt, Franklin Delano: and economic rights, congressional but not constitutional protection for, 105; economic rights in a Second Bill of Rights, his support for, 18, 90, 93, 99–100, 110; foreign policy vision of, 226, 304; four freedoms, his crusade for, 13, 125–26; human rights, his promotion of, 1; liberal internationalism and, 25
Rostow, Walt W., 119
Rousseau, Jean-Jacques, 208
Rumsfeld, Donald, 130, 134, 230, 309n.12
Rumsfeld v. Padilla, 140–41, 330n.89
Russia, 233

Sachs, Albie, 293
San Antonio School District v. Rodriguez, 108
Sarat, Austin, 75–76
Saudi Arabia, 5, 57–58
Scalia, Antonin: comparative constitutional analysis, his opposition to, 8, 113, 248–51, 253, 255, 257–58, 260–62, 264, 290, 296, 328; exceptionalism, his advantageous position from which to promote, 130; and foreign and international decisions, need for familiarity with, 283, 285; rights claims, his desire to limit adjudication of, 274
Schenck v. United States, 31n.4, 44n.60
Schmitt, Carl, 230
Scowcroft, Brent, 336n.111
Senate, United States, 187–88
September 11, exceptionalist response to, 124–29, 232

sex discrimination, 98, 105
Shapiro v. Thompson, 107
Sharon, Ariel, 40, 122
Shell, 316
Shelley v. Kraemer, 300n.75
Sikkink, Kathryn, 313
Skokie, Illinois, American Nazi Party march in, 37–38
slander, 38–41
Sloss, David, 327
Smith, Carsten, 285–86
social and economic rights: American exceptionalism regarding, 10, 91–93, 109–10, 162–65; chronological account of American exceptionalism regarding, 95–98; and constitutional amendment, difficulties of and American exceptionalism, 98–101; cultural explanation of American exceptionalism regarding, 103–5; distinctiveness of compared to negative rights, 93–95; institutional explanation of American exceptionalism regarding, 101–3; New Deal era and, 90, 93, 97, 99–101, 105; partisan conflict regarding, 183–84; realist explanation of American exceptionalism regarding, 105–9
socialism, weakness of in the United States, 103–4, 183n.116
Somalia, 7, 116, 148, 181
Sosa v. Alvarez-Machain, 314n.28
Souter, David, 142
South Africa: capital punishment in, 65–66; comparative constitutional analysis in, 8, 287–89; Constitution of, 44, 92, 287–88; and hate speech, control of, 34; judicial authority and freedom of expression in, 50; judicial authority and social and economic rights in, 102–3
southern exceptionalism, 80–83
South Korea. *See* Korea, Republic of
Soviet Union, 15–16
Spain, 59
speech, freedom of. *See* freedom of expression
Stanford v. Kentucky, 113, 116n.20, 249–50, 260–61
state, the: the citizenry as material cause of, 211–14; constitution as formal cause of, 205–11; global governance and, 308–11; modern conception of, 199–203; perpetuation of its existence as final cause of, 214–17; political autonomy and, 217–22; revolution through popular sovereignty as efficient cause of the modern, 203–5
states' rights, 188–90
Stevens, John Paul: *Bowers v. Hardwick*, his dissenting opinion in, 254; and capital punishment, decisions regarding, 247n.28; comparative constitutional analysis, his position regarding, 252–53, 290; comparative constitutional analysis by, 248, 257; on integrity and the *Bush v. Gore* decision, 292
substantive exceptionalism: defamation law as case of, 38–41; hate speech regulation as case of, 32–38; methodological exceptionalism, distinguished from, 30–32
Suharto, 2
Sukarno, 24
Sullivan, New York Times Co. v., 39–41
Supreme Court, United States: and Alien Tort Claims Act, rulings regarding, 314n.28; and capital punishment, decisions regarding, 58, 63–64, 67, 86–89, 189–90, 192n.138, 247–50, 252–53; and comparative constitutional analysis (*see* comparative constitutional analysis); and defamation, regulation of and the First Amendment, 39–40, 46; foreign court borrowing from jurisprudence of, 287; and freedom of expression, decisions regarding, 48nn.69–70; and hate speech, regulation of and the First Amendment, 36–38; and judicial globalization, aloofness from, 241; popular sovereignty and, 208; popular trust enjoyed by, 160; and post–September 11 detainees, decisions regarding, 138–42, 214–15, 330n.89; and social and economic rights, decisions regarding, 106–10
Sweden, 59, 316
Swiss Re, 320
Switzerland: capital punishment in, 59; Constitution of, 92

Taiwanese Constitutional Court, 289–90
Talbott, Strobe, 127
terrorism: Bush doctrine and war against, 232–33; and post–September 11 detainees, 138–42

Thomas, Clarence, 252–53, 261, 264, 290, 296
Thomas, Daniel, 313
Thompson v. Oklahoma, 248, 255, 257, 260, 262, 285
TNCs. *See* transnational corporations
Tocqueville, Alexis de, 58, 112, 155
Tonry, Michael, 62
torture, 114
Torture Convention. *See* Convention Against Torture and Other Cruel, Inhuman or Degrading Treatment or Punishment
transnational corporations (TNCs), 312, 314–22, 337–38
transnational legal process: freedom of expression exceptionalism within, 51–53; the global justice system and American exceptionalism, 132–38, 241–45, 271–73 (*see also* comparative constitutional analysis); post–September 11 detainees and American exceptionalism, 138–42; as response to American exceptionalism, 130–32. *See also* global justice system; judicial globalization; legal/constitutional/ judicial systems
transnational public law litigation, 314
Transparency International, 315
triumphalism, 129
Trop v. Dulles, 245–48, 249n.41
Trudeau, Pierre, 157
Truman, Harry, 227, 305
Truth, Sojourner, 26
Turkey, 128
Tushnet, Mark, 259, 260n.101, 261, 263

UN. *See* United Nations
Union Carbide, 316
United Kingdom: capital punishment in, 59, 68; comparative material used by constitutional courts in, 286; defamation law in, 40; and European Human Rights Convention, incorporation into domestic law, 11; and hate speech, control of, 34; homicide rate in, 61–62; messianism of, 15–16; political culture in, 74; quasi-constitutional protection of rights in, 30n.3; socialist movement and rights in, 104; and social reporting, encouragement of, 316
United Nations (UN): Bush administration invasion of Iraq and, 331–32, 336; Bush administration opposition to, 229; the Bush doctrine and, 233–34; Convention Against Torture and Other Cruel, Inhuman or Degrading Treatment or Punishment, 2, 22, 114n.15, 184n.120, 324; Convention on the Elimination of All Forms of Discrimination against Women, 2, 7, 188; Convention on the Prevention and Punishment of the Crime of Genocide (*see* Convention on the Prevention and Punishment of the Crime of Genocide); Convention on the Rights of the Child (CRC), 2, 7, 116, 148, 181–83; Global Compact, 318–19; Human Rights Commission, 194–95; internal armed conflicts and, 310; International Convention on the Elimination of All Forms of Racial Discrimination, 33–35, 324; International Covenant on Civil and Political Rights (*see* International Covenant on Civil and Political Rights); International Covenant on Social, Economic, and Cultural Rights, 91, 101, 104, 162–63; new exemptionalism, as target of, 324; the United States and, 1–2, 6; Universal Declaration of Human Rights (*see* Universal Declaration of Human Rights)
United States, Constitution of: and amendment, difficulties of, and social and economic rights, 98–101; American politics and content of, 103–5; the Bill of Rights, 93–94; chronology of and social and economic rights, 95–98; comparative constitutional analysis and (*see* comparative constitutional analysis); distrust of government and, 46; Eighth Amendment, 245–53, 257; First Amendment (*see* First Amendment); Fourteenth Amendment, 44, 105–6, 212, 253–54; interpretation of and legal realism, 105–9; originalism, 158, 180, 296; popular sovereignty and national identity, constituting of, 205–11; pragmatic instrument, perception as and social and economic rights, 101–3; sanctity of as basis for exceptionalism, 154–59; and sex discrimination, ban on, 98, 105; Sixth Amendment, 44; and social and economic rights, absence of, 10, 92–93, 109–10
United States Agency for International Development (USAID), 313, 337

United States v. Carolene Products Co., 281

United States v. Debs, 31n.4

Universal Declaration of Human Rights: attachment to universal ideals of, question regarding, 25; drafting of, United States role in, 1; enforcement powers, its lack of, 101–2; postwar human rights construct in, 126; race as basis of opposition to, 323; and social and economic rights, protection of, 91, 103; socioeconomic rights combined with civil and political rights in, 163

Van de Kamp, John K., 71

van der Vyer, J. D., 153

Védrine, Hubert, 232, 335

Vienna Treaty on Consular Obligations, 6

viewpoint discrimination, 35–38

violence, culture of, 85–86

Virginia v. Black, 35n.17

Wallace, Clifford, 280, 298

war: citizen sacrifice through, 212–13; as defense of rule of law, 214–17; and international peace and security, shift in the focus of, 310

Warren, Earl, 245–46

Washington, George, 112

Weinrib, Lorraine E., 258–59n.90, 259n.93, 273n.146

Westmoreland, William, 40

White, Byron, 247, 254

White, Ronnie, 71

Wills, Garry, 74–75

Wilson, Woodrow, 13, 187, 201, 226–27, 305n.1

Wilsonian syndrome, 226

Winston Foundation, 3

Winthrop, John, 13

Wolfowitz, Paul, 231

World Bank, 313n.23, 315

World Economic Forum, 321–22

World Trade Organization (WTO), 315, 330

WTO. *See* World Trade Organization

Yahoo!, Inc. v. La Ligue Contre le Racisme et L'Antisemitism, 34n.14

Yates, Andrea, 78

Yemen, 58

Zimbabwe, 287

Zundel, Ernst, 37